SAILING DIRECTIONS
SOUTH AND WEST
COASTS OF IRELAND

The Irish Cruising Club also publishes a companion volume "Sailing Directions for East and North Coasts of Ireland." Both volumes obtainable from booksellers and chandlers or direct from Mrs. Barbara Fox-Mills, The Tansey, Baily, Co. Dublin.

ISBN 0 9501717 5 1

Printed by The Universities Press (Belfast) Ltd.
Alanbrooke Road, Belfast BT6 9HF

IRISH CRUISING CLUB

SAILING DIRECTIONS

for the

SOUTH AND WEST COASTS OF IRELAND

Compiled by Members of the Club
With a foreword by Geoffrey Nockolds,
Commodore, Royal Cruising Club

*"What joy to sail the crested sea and watch the waves beat white
upon the Irish shore."*
– St. Columba, A.D. 563.

Foreword

When anybody plans to cruise the coasts of Ireland the first and most important thing to do is to acquire a copy of the Irish Cruising Club Sailing Directions. They not only give you lots of ideas where to go but how to get there.

This is a most varied cruising ground with anchorages for all tastes, and a thorough study of these sailing directions well repays the time spent. Ashore there is always a warm welcome and plenty of attractions, be it history, architecture, views or the pub!

This new edition of the south and west coasts has taken a quantum leap forward, not only in content but in presentation.

The chartlets are now in colour, which makes it easier to assimilate the salient points quickly - there are also over sixty aerial colour photographs, these often give a perspective to a place which nothing else can. I wish we had had a photograph of Derrynane when we were trying to sort the entrance out in the gathering darkness and a rising gale some years ago.

There are now tidal stream chartlets for the west coast, waypoints for those who indulge in electronic pilotage, and, most imaginatively, information on restaurants and where to find them. But, above all it is the gathering of local knowledge by the members of the ICC that is the continuing and dominant factor in the success of these sailing directions. The rest of us in the cruising community should be grateful of them for sharing their knowledge of these beautiful coasts.

The eighth edition eclipses previous editions and I think is essential for anybody cruising these waters.

GEOFFREY NOCKOLDS
Commodore
Royal Cruising Club

January 1993

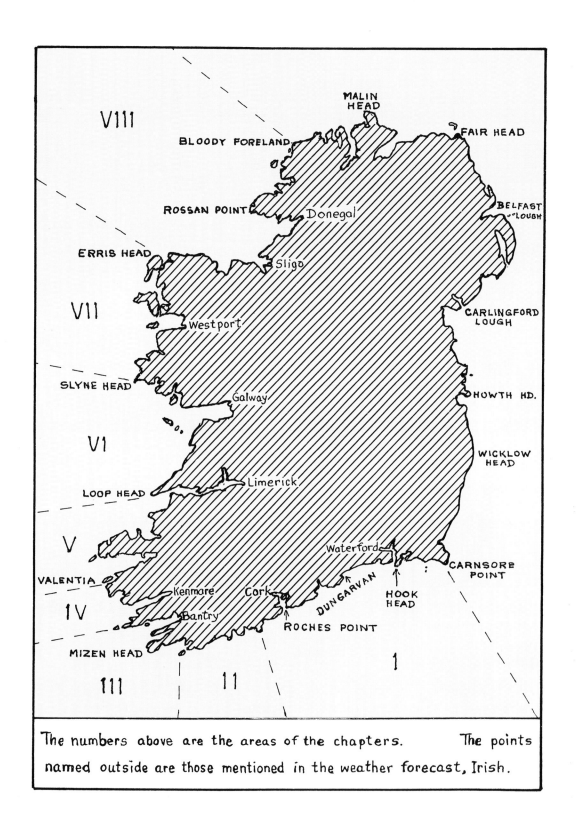

The numbers above are the areas of the chapters.   The points
named outside are those mentioned in the weather forecast, Irish.

CONTENTS

Additions and Corrections

Any new information or corrections to these Sailing Directions are welcomed. These should be sent to the Hon. Secretary, Cormac McHenry, 8 Heidelberg, Ardilea, Dublin 14, or The Hon. Compiler, Arthur Orr, Evergreen, 11 Old Holywood Road, Belfast, Northern Ireland BT4 2HJ.

Additions and corrections are published annually in the Spring and may be had for a small fee from Mrs. Barbara Fox-Hills, The Tansey, Baily, Co. Dublin. Please send a large self-addressed envelope.

These Directions are not included in corrections by Admiralty Notices to Mariners and are therefore offered for sale for reference purposes only.

Introduction

These sailing directions dealing with the South West Coast of Ireland are the seventh edition of the Clubs sailing directions covering this area. From humble beginnings in 1930 the Club first published the directions compiled by H. P. F. Donegan. These directions were later revised by his son H. E. Donegan and the original directions dealt only with the South and South West coasts of Ireland. Wallace Clark with the late Bob Berridge extended the sailing directions further Northwards and their task was ably assisted by Roger Bourke and by Paul Campbell. In the intervening years information has been fed to us by members of the Club and by non members who rely on the Clubs sailing directions.

For many years the West coast of Ireland was considered to be an inhospitable and dangerous place, open to swell and to unpredictable gales. As the years have progressed part 2 of the club's sailing directions have introduced members and non members alike to many new places of refuge and the West coast has gained a new and well deserved reputation as one of the least known but most rewarding cruising grounds in the world. It is hoped that this book will allow you to enjoy the many fine ports which can be found between Carnsore Point and Valentia. It is hoped that you will then consider proceeding with the adventure, to explore the whole coastline between Dingle Bay and Bloody Foreland. The eighth edition of the South and West Cruising Directions incorporates all of the annual corrections issued between 1990 and today's date which was the life span of seventh edition. Much of this work has been undertaken by members and by other users of the sailing directions but the entire organization and revision which allows this edition to go to press has been the responsibility of Arthur Orr; members and users alike are indebted to him for the many hours of midnight oil which he has burned in bringing this edition to you.

There is a distinction between the two parts of this book. Part 1 gives a fairly detailed description, with plans, of the coast as well as of all the anchorages of interest to yachtsmen. Part 2 is presented somewhat differently. On the west coast, especially north of Galway, the large-scale charts depicted most anchorages more clearly than can be done in this book and they are in any case indispensable for pilotage in the approaches. In our 1962 edition plans were included in part 2 only (a) where additional information could be shown (b) where large scale charts have been withdrawn and (c) where hitherto unpublished surveys of inlets and other features were available. As a result there were no plans for many of the best west coast anchorages. These have been added to the last three editions in order to make preparatory perusal of the book easier, but for pilotage, the large scale charts are still required except for the Shannon Estuary. Part 2 must be used in conjunction with the pilot, the detailed description of many coastal and offshore features not having been repeated here.

In late 1992 the Committee decided that the time had come to update our Sailing Directions. Consequently, they authorised that the 1993 edition should change in size and contain many new colour photographs to be depicted throughout the text; furthermore, the plans should have a colour to show them more clearly. As far as was possible, the photographs show the various anchorages taken from the angle of approach, which is also shown in the sketch plans.

With the help of Wallace Clark a new section in the appendices shows the expected tidal streams for each of the flood and ebb on the West coast. Further help with the accuracy of this work would be much appreciated.

Acknowledgements

Most of the plans in this book are based on British Admiralty Charts and Surveys and are Crown Copyright. Tidal information is based on the Admiralty Tide Tables, and other information is based on the Irish Coast Pilot. It is published with the permission of Her Majesty's Stationery Office. The remaining plans, individually acknowledged, are taken from the Irish Ordnance Survey by permission of the Minister of Finance from the Department of Marine, and a few are based on the contractors' plans for the building of harbours or marinas.

Other sources supplying information include – The Cruising Association, Harbour Masters and Authorities, Secretaries of various yacht clubs, and many of our own members, to all of whom we are very grateful.

Finally, Irish Cruising Club Publications Ltd. wish to record its gratitude for, and indebtedness to Kevin Dwyer for his photographs, and commend the professionalism and artistry of his valuable contribution.

HUGH P. KENNEDY
Commodore
Irish Cruising Club

January 1993

Photography

Kevin Dwyer (joined 1966) took all the aerial photographs, with three exceptions, involving a total of 10 hours flying, with Batt Coleman from Kinsale, on two separate trips: Crosshaven to Dingle on 6-7-92 and Shannon to Donegal on 22-9-92.

The photographs were taken to assist mariners - some help to illustrate the chartlets, some help to give a 'birds eye' view of certain harbour entrances. The cover shot was taken of Derrynane during an ICC week-end rally.

Kevin Dwyer's (ICC) photographs appear on pages: 19, 24, 27, 31, 32, 34, 36, 39, 45, 46, 48 (U), 50, 54, 56, 64, 68, 69 (U), 78, 80, 83, 86 (U), 87, 90 (U), 90 (L), 97, 98, 102, 104, 106, 109, 111, 112, 124, 140, 156, 159, 160, 161, 164, 173, 174 (U), 174 (L), 182, 186, 190, 192, 194 (U), 202, 205, 208, 209, 210, 214, 215, 218, 224, 225, 230, 232, 233, 243, 244, 246, 248, 250.

The following is a list of other photographic credits, practically all of which were taken by members of the Club:

Ronan Beirne, ICC, pages: 63 (L), 65, 67, 69 (L).
Michael Diggin, page: 132
Susan Grey, ICC, page: 150
W. M. Nixon, ICC, pages: 11 (U), 11 (L), 48 (L), 51, 58 (U), 63 (U), 71, 77, 86 (L), 96, 125, 127 (U), 127 (L), 153, 176, 194 (L), 195, 244 (L), 252.
Rex Roberts, ABIPP, ICC, pages: 10, 58 (L)
Joe Rooney, page 196
Shannon Maritime Developments Ltd, page 138
Donal Walsh, ICC, page 20
Neill Warner, page 152

Important information

Please read these three pages before using this book as an aid to navigation. The information which follows is essential to proper understanding of the book and for the safety of your yacht and crew.

Breakers. On the charts many rocky patches and shoals with depths up to 20 to 30 m are marked "Breaker" or "Breaks in Gales". This means that in bad weather a whole sea may break and, of course, if a yacht were caught in one she would be knocked down, certainly be damaged and possibly be sunk; it would be lucky if no one were injured or drowned.

In winter when the sea in the offing is often running high for long periods a storm or gale will quickly bring it into the coast where it may persist for days or weeks. The conditions on the coast can then become awesome and the strictest regard must be paid to these breaker warnings.

In summer the conditions are naturally far less severe, the seas rarely as big and big seas last for much shorter times. A yachtsman must judge from his own experience in what depths a sea is likely to break. There are no hard and fast rules and every case must be judged on its merits. Every few years in summer winds of strong gale force 9 or storm force 10 will be met with inshore on the coast and a yacht caught out in these conditions will experience very steep and breaking seas on any shoal waters and in wind against tide conditions in the open sea.

In general in normal fine to moderate summer weather and in semi-sheltered waters, such as for example Galway Bay North Sound, anything with 4 m on it is unlikely to break except possibly at LW or a big swell. In the open sea the critical depths in moderate weather are somewhat greater, say 4 to 6 m or where there is any strong tide such as off the big headlands, 6 to 8 m. At all times, tide races or rips marked on the charts should be treated with caution, though in fine weather it is frequently possible to sail anywhere, such as in the Blaskets or close in to the Mizen Head. Note that a rock may suddenly begin to break as the tide falls, the current changes direction or a larger sea than usual comes along. It may break intermittently, say every 5 or 10 minutes.

When a rock is on the point of breaking it will often form "blind" breakers, the sea building up into a steep pinnacle and then subsiding. These are very clear from leeward but almost impossible to see from windward.

In general it is best to err on the side of caution until much experience has been gained. It is very rare that a yacht gets caught in a breaker, normal commonsense and prudent seamanship keep them clear of trouble. However, even the very experienced sometimes get a surprise.

Drift Nets. In recent years there has been a huge increase in drift netting for salmon on the S and W coasts of Ireland, the principal months being from May to the end of July. These nets are set off headlands, along straight lengths of coasts and in and off the bays and estuaries of salmon rivers. On the S and SW coasts they are usually tended, the fishing boat lying at one end or the other of the net. They are mostly set in daylight hours but this cannot be guaranteed.

Further N they may be left unattended and in Donegal are frequently set by night and even unlit. Unusually long nets may be met off the mouth of the Shannon, sometimes 2 miles or more long.

The common marking is by an orange float at each end and nothing in between except for the small floats which support the net. This means that in any sea they may not be seen until too late. Watch should be kept for 2 orange buoys ½ mile or more apart, usually extending out at right angles to the shore with the inner buoy very close in to the land and the tending boat also at the inner end. This boat will, if it sees a yacht approaching its net, frequently get underway and steam fast along the line of the net waving to which side the yacht should go. It is often possible to make contact on VHF channels 16, 6 or 8 and get full details of the nearby nets.

If the worst happens it is considered safer to cross the net at right angles with engine and propeller stopped rather than turn away at the last moment and risk tangling with the net broadside on. A yacht with a traditional profile and propeller in an aperture will usually slide across safely. On a yacht with a separate rudder it would be worth carrying a "Y" end fitting which could attach to a spinnaker pole or long boathook or a hay fork with a long handle and possibly a sharp bread knife which could be firmly fixed to a pole. Watch should always be kept for a pair of coloured buoys ½ mile or so apart.

This menace has made it chancy to cruise close in to the coast at night. Scant regard is paid to the law or dates for salmon fishing, generally, so keep a good look out.

In various places along this coast there are now many fish farms. They are often very badly lit and can be quite a long way offshore. Furthermore, some of the anchorages can be fouled by abandoned fish farm gear. Mention has been made in the text as far as information has been received, but it is not always accurate and up to date.

Lobster pots are numerous in suitable localities all along the coast. The inconspicuous corks of recent times are rapidly giving way to coloured plastic buoys, but floating plastic ropes are also used so it is safer to pass down-tide of a buoy. The same type of buoy is used for both pots and salmon nets so intense vigilance is necessary when one is sighted. A single buoy may be a pot or the end of a net. A number of buoys are usually pots. Two buoys up to a cable apart are probably a string of pots. Pots are most commonly set close inshore and in passages between outlying rocks.

Radar. The small buoys marking nets and pots together with the very low configuration of fish farms very seldom show up on a yachts radar, even on short range. Great care must be taken when entering many of the anchorages at dusk and thereafter when visibility is poor and fishing operations have been mentioned in the text. As these operations change frequently, no responsibility is accepted by Irish Cruising Club Publications Ltd. for any mishaps.

Corrections. The Club proposes to issue an annual supplement to this book in April or May each year, bringing it up to date. Members will receive this automatically. Other users should apply to Mrs. Barbara Fox-Mills, The Tansey, Baily, Co. Dublin, enclosing a large self addressed envelope. The latest supplement will be found inside the back cover in books purchased after 1994. Each supplement will include still current amendments from previous supplements so that only the latest need be carried. A subscription of £2.00 is now charged for these.

Should any member or reader discover any incorrect statement or important omission in the book please write to the Hon Secretary, Cormac McHenry, 8 Heidelberg, Ardilea, Dublin 14, with the facts. It is through this cooperation that we hope to keep the book up to date.

Tidal information. All heights and depths are in metres. Details of tidal streams appear in the text as required. A general statement precedes Part 1 and each of the chapters of Part 2. Appendix 2 gives tidal constants for selected ports. Appendix 7 gives hourly directions of tidal streams. Heights of tides have been adjusted to LAT for the whole coast as well as all depths given in the text and on the plans.

Lights and Buoys. The IALA System A is used on the coast and the changeover to this has now been completed and is included in this book. Buoys and lights are described in the text except for the upper reaches of commercial ports. Appendix 8 list the principal lights. In the text the visibility of lights given is the luminous range as stated on the charts. The luminous range is given in Appendix 8. A number of minor lights are maintained by local authorities, they are mostly in the approaches to small fishing quays, and are only switched on when it is known that local fishing boats are at sea, in these circumstances they are unreliable and should be checked with local harbour masters before sailing off the coast at night. Abbreviations for the type of buoy are as follows: Cardinal – Card, Conical – Cone, Can – Can.

Quite a number of lighthouses are being automated, as these become so amendments are made to their ranges and also their sound signals. A current edition of the Admiralty Light of Lights should be carried at all times.

The Commissioners of Irish Lights request mariners navigating around the coast of Ireland to exercise the greatest care to avoid damage to floating aids to navigation. The body of a "Lanby" (Large Automatic Navigational Buoy) is 40 feet in diameter and of low profile. This is not apparent either from the charted symbol or when seen at night and, because the direction of the tide flowing past them may not be as readily estimated as when approaching a light-float, mariners should take special care to give them a wide berth so as to avoid risk of collision.

However, should a collision take place with a Lanby, light-float or buoy (or damage to, or malfunction of any of these marks be observed) it is imperative that in the interest of safety of other shipping the fact be reported immediately to the nearest Coast Radio Station.

Mariners are also reminded that under section 666 of the Merchant Shipping Act 1894, a fine can be imposed on any person who wilfully or negligently runs foul of, or makes fast to, any light-float, buoy or beacon, in addition to the expense of making good any damage so occasioned.

Radar Beacons: Marines are advised that there may be occasions when a response is not received from a radar beacon. On these occasions Mariners should check that the appropriate radar set is in use. "X" band radar beacons can only be received on 3cm radar sets, and "S" band radar beacons on 10cm sets. Details are published in Admiralty List of Radio Signals, Vol. 2.

In addition, depending on range, the lack of response may be due to a fall off in the performance of the ship's radar or to a malfunction of the radar beacon itself.

Radar beacons should therefore be used with caution.

Depths. Both in the text and in plans the depths are given in metres and decimetres on shallow places. (Otherwise to the nearest metre.) They refer to LAT which is chart datum. They are based on information of varying age and reliability (one third of the Admiralty charts of these coasts are based on 19th century editions). In general depths on bars and in small harbours or alongside are believed to be accurate. Two and five metre lines (represented by dots and double dots respectively) are nearly all copied from the charts. There is a table for converting depths to fathoms in Appendix 20 at back of book.

Abbreviations. These are those commonly used on Admiralty charts. Those unfamiliar with them are highly recommended to obtain chart 5011, now in booklet form. Also see Appendix 19.

Names. In the new metric charts many of the names differ from those on the old fathom charts. Where this difference is not immediately recognisable the new name is given in the text and when it appears for the first time the old fathom name is given after it in brackets.

Appendices. Considerable further information is contained at the back of the book under various headings viz. Communications, Weather forecasts, Repairs, Sailmakers, List of Charts, Navigational Information, Distances, etc., etc.

Magnetic Variation is westerly and decreasing about 5' annually. From 1992 it may be assumed to be as follows:

Tuskar to Courtmacsherry	..	..	..	8°W
Courtmacsherry to Aran Islands		..	..	9°W
Aran Island to Bloody Foreland		..	..	10°W

BEARINGS THROUGHOUT ARE TRUE FROM SEAWARD.

Caution. These Sailing Directions are not intended for large craft but are written for yachts of moderate draft. Every effort has been made to avoid inaccuracy, but no responsibility will be accepted for damage or loss arising from any mistake or omission herein, or in correction sheets subsequently issued.

Part 1

SOUTH AND SOUTH-WEST COASTS

CARNSORE POINT
to
VALENTIA

Introduction
to Part 1

CARNSORE POINT TO VALENTIA

Although the best harbours on the South Coast may be west of Kinsale, those cruising to the West should not overlook the estuary of Waterford Harbour, Dungarvan, Youghal, Ballycotton and Cork Harbour.

Cruise planning

As the prevailing winds are westerly yachtsmen are advised to take advantage of any free wind to get as far W as intended and to cruise back towards Cork at their leisure. Those coming from the English Channel should aim to make their landfall on the Fastnet, a passage only 30 miles longer than to the Hook. If headed it is easy to find a harbour further E. By night landfall can be made on one of the principal lights listed in Appendix 8 and by day there should be little difficulty in identifying the many prominent features of the coastline. In addition there are radiobeacons on Mizen Head, Old Head of Kinsale, Ballycotton and Tuskar, see Appendix 6. The courses and distances from a position 2 miles W of the Longships are as follows:

Tuskar Rock	353°	.. 130 miles
Hook Head	340°	.. 133 miles
Roches Point (Cork harbour)	317°	.. 139 miles
Kinsale Harbour	312°	.. 140 miles
Two miles SW of Galley Head	305°	.. 148 miles
Baltimore Harbour	302°	.. 159 miles
Fastnet Rock	300°	.. 164 miles

In westerly weather with a considerable sea running there is a set to the east which may easily amount to 10 miles in 24 hours.

Tidal Streams

Except off Carnsore Point, off the main headlands, in the entrances to some harbours and in the narrow channels, the offshore tidal streams nowhere exceed $1\frac{1}{2}$ kn at springs. The main tidal wave reaches the SW coast and divides off the Bull Rock, W of Dursey Island. One branch runs N to the Blaskets and on up the W coast, the other runs S and SE to the Fastnet Rock and thence ENE to Carnsore Point; known as the E-going stream. The opposite, or W-going stream, runs WSW from Carnsore Point to the Fastnet and thence NW and N to the Bull where it unites with the S-going stream from the Blaskets.

From the Bull Rock to Cork Harbour the stream changes simultaneously, the E-going stream making at -0420 Cobh (+0215 Dover) and the W-going at +0150 Cobh (-0400 Dover).

Between Cork Harbour and Carnsore Point the time at which the stream begins becomes gradually later. From -0035 to +0150 Cobh (+0600 to -0400 Dover) the E-going stream makes the whole way from the Bull to Carnsore Point, while from +0550 to -0420 Cobh (HW to +0215 Dover) the W-going stream makes the whole way from Carnsore Point to the Bull.

A more detailed description of the tidal streams in harbours and sounds and off the headlands is given in the text. Off the main headlands, where the stream runs strongly against fresh winds, tide races and overfalls may occur; in general they must always be treated with respect.

Strong and continuous winds from SW to NW result in an increase of up to $\frac{1}{2}$ kn in the rate and up to 1 hour ($\frac{1}{2}$ hr at each end) in the duration of the E-going stream, with corresponding reductions in the W-going stream. Similarly, winds from between NE and SE decrease the rate of the E-going stream by $\frac{1}{2}$ kn and its duration by $\frac{1}{2}$ hour at each end, with corresponding increases in the W-going stream. With winds between SE and SW the duration and rates of the streams are not affected though their direction may become more northerly.

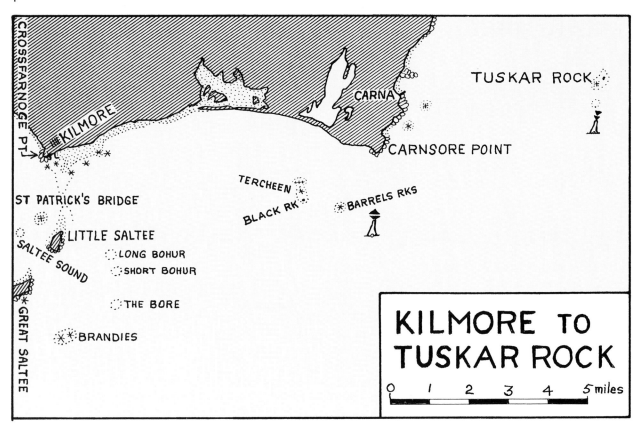

CROSSFARNOGE PT

KILMORE

ST PATRICK'S BRIDGE

LITTLE SALTEE

SALTEE SOUND

LONG BOHUR

SHORT BOHUR

THE BORE

GREAT SALTEE

BRANDIES

TERCHEEN

BLACK RK

BARRELS RKS

CARNA

CARNSORE POINT

TUSKAR ROCK

KILMORE TO TUSKAR ROCK

0 1 2 3 4 5 miles

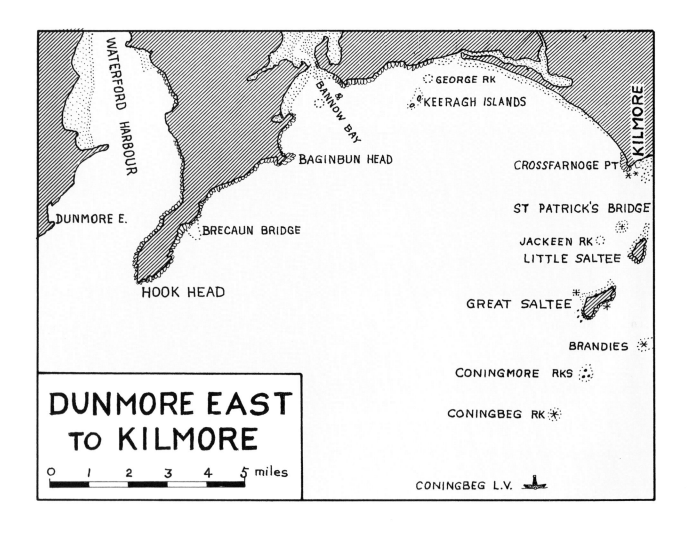

WATERFORD HARBOUR

DUNMORE E.

HOOK HEAD

BRECAUN BRIDGE

BAGINBUN HEAD

BANNOW BAY

GEORGE RK

KEERAGH ISLANDS

KILMORE

CROSSFARNOGE PT

ST PATRICK'S BRIDGE

JACKEEN RK
LITTLE SALTEE

GREAT SALTEE

BRANDIES

CONINGMORE RKS

CONINGBEG RK

CONINGBEG L.V.

DUNMORE EAST TO KILMORE

0 1 2 3 4 5 miles

Chapter 1

TUSKAR ROCK TO
OLD HEAD OF KINSALE

A yacht coming from the Irish Sea to cruise on the coast described in this chapter will either pass outside Tuskar Rock or round Carnsore Point fairly close. The approach to these from the N is described in the Irish Cruising Club's companion volume for the East and North coasts of Ireland, which describes the coast as far as Dunmore East.

Warning
The sea area off the SE corner of Ireland is one to be avoided in bad weather. The tide runs strong right across the entrance to St. George's Channel, 2½kn at springs, so it can be very rough even right out to sea. Between the Coningbeg and the Tuskar there are many rocks, shoals and irregular soundings up to 7 miles offshore. In gale conditions with wind against tide there may be heavy overfalls which could prove fatal for a small yacht. In recent years yachts have been lost in this area.

Tuskar Rock
is 5 m high and lies 6 miles E by N of Carnsore Point, the SE extremity of Ireland. A tall white lighthouse and a radio mast stand on the island. It is clean on the E side but foul for a cable N and W. 2 cables NNW is Gypsy Rock with 2 m over it, 2½ cables SW is a rock awash and 6½ cables SSW is South Rock with 2.4 m over it.

Yachts should give the Tuskar a good berth, especially in light weather for as well as the tide setting onto the rock there is probably an eddy running back towards it on the other side.

Light
A light is shown from a lighthouse on the rock, Q (2) 7·5 s, 35 m, 28 M. Fog signal Horn. (4) 45 s. Radiobeacon see Appendix 6.

Buoy
A light buoy, S Card Q (6) + LF 15 s, is moored almost a mile S of South Rock.

Shipping Lanes
There are shipping lanes off the Tuskar Rock whose position is shown on chart 2049. The SW lane passes 2 to 5 miles outside the rock, the NE lane passes 7 to 10 miles outside the rock. The inshore zone is between the rock and the SW lane.

OFFSHORE PASSAGE
A yacht passing E of the Tuskar should continue S to the South Rock light buoy before altering course for the Coningbeg LV, on which line she should leave the Barrels buoy (see below) ½ to 1 mile to starboard. This is a straightforward trouble-free route and is obligatory in darkness, bad visibility or heavy weather from the S or SE. A yacht rounding Carnsore Point in the evening or with deteriorating visibility should also make for the Barrels buoy and the Coningbeg LV. Greenore Point, some 5 miles N of Carnsore Point, seen 022° of Carnsore Point leads ½ mile E of the Barrels and rather less W of the buoy.

INSHORE PASSAGE
It is shorter, especially if bound for Waterford Harbour, to pass between the Saltees or N of them. It is only possible by day and in clear weather but it is more interesting and also often less rough, particularly with a head wind, than it would be out at the Coningbeg.

The many dangers surrounding this route are described below. The large scale chart, 2740, is almost essential for this passage. A yacht rounding the Tuskar and wishing to continue inshore should first round South Rock buoy and then make good a course to clear S of the Bailies Bank and then come in to, say, ¼ mile S of Carnsore Point. From Carnsore Point make for the N Saltee or for the gap between it and the mainland leaving Tercheen (N of Black Rock) and the wreck N of Tercheen and later the Bohurs to port; e.g. pass 8 cables N of Black Rock, 2 m high.

CARNSORE POINT
is a low clay cliff (16 m) with rocky shelves below it. There are several rocks to the NE of it but on the S side it is fairly clear with a depth of 18 m 3 cables off. In rough weather with wind against tide there is quite a bad race off it around the times of high and low water; the stream is slack at about half tide. Approaching from S or E in clear weather the position of the point may be judged by Forth Mountain (224 m) just SW of Wexford town which may be sighted from 20 miles offshore, but yachts from the S should not plan to make a landfall on this dangerous corner of the Irish coast.

DANGERS BETWEEN CARNSORE POINT AND THE SALTEES

Inshore of the course there are some shoal patches which should be avoided if there is a big sea running. There is a 3 m patch ³/₄ mile W of Carnsore Point. Kilturk Bank with 5 m lies ³/₄ mile offshore 5 miles W of the point. A 6 m rock lies halfway between Kilturk Bank and the point.

Nether Rock

with 5 m over it lies 1¹/₂ miles SW of Carnsore Point; it is clear of a yacht's direct course but should be avoided if beating.

The Barrels

a dangerous group of rocks which dry 1·5 m, lie 1¹/₂ miles SW by S of Carnsore Point. **Light buoy.** An E Card Q (3)10 s, Horn (2)10 s, is moored 1 mile SE of the rock.

Black Rock

is a conspicuous rock 2 m high and ¹/₄ cable long and lies 2 miles SW by S of Carnsore Point. **Tercheen Rock** lies 2 cables N of it and dries at LW. The latter rock will be ¹/₄ mile to port on a direct course from Carnsore Point to Saltee Sound.

The Bohurs

are 3 separate rocks. Long Bohur, the furthest N and shallowest of them, lies 1¹/₄ miles E of the S end of North Saltee and has 4 m over it; it is on the direct course from Carnsore Point to Saltee Sound. SSE of it is Short Bohur with 7·3 m and ³/₄ mile S of this is The Bore with 5·5 m. There are tide races and broken water over these three rocks with wind against tide.

Rocks southward of the Saltees

About 1¹/₂ miles SE of South Saltee are **The Brandies,** two dangerous rocks 2¹/₂ cables apart; the W rock dries 2·5 m and the E rock dries 0·9 m.

Coningmore

consists of 3 rocks within 1¹/₂ cables of each other, the largest 4 m high; they are steep-to and lie 1¹/₄ miles S of the South Saltee; they are a most useful mark by day to a yacht which has been unable to avoid this dangerous area.

Coningbeg Rock

which dries 2·8 m lies 1¹/₄ miles SW of Coningmore and 2¹/₂ miles from the South Saltee. When covered its position can often be seen by its breaker but a yacht should keep well away from it.

Lightship

Coningbeg LV moored nearly 2 miles seaward of the rock is painted red and shows Fl. (3) 30 s, 12 m, 24 M. Fog Signal Horn (3) 60 s. Now automatic

Red Bank

with least water 7·9 m, lies 1¹/₂ miles W of Coningmore. It extends ¹/₄ mile N and S and there is a tide rip over it.

Tidal streams

Between Carnsore Point and the Saltees the stream starts running ENE at -0110 Cobh (+0525 Dover), spring rate 2·4 kn. The WSW-going stream begins at +0510 Cobh (-0040 Dover), spring rate 2.6 kn. S of the Saltees the streams arc rotary - clockwise . The E-going stream begins N at -0100 Cobh (+0535 Dover), is at its greatest rate of 1·7 kn (springs) to the ENE at +0200 Cobh and ends SE. The W-going stream begins Sat +0530 Cobh (-0020 Dover) reaches l.9kn (springs) W by S at -0355 Cobh and ends NW. Slack water lasts about 1 hour. There are ripples near and over all the shoals.

SOUTH SALTEE ISLAND

is about 1 mile in length, ¹/₃ mile in breadth and is 57 m high at its S end. It is fringed by outlying rocks. The NW side of the shore has a boulder beach and these boulders continue out into a spit to the N of the island for ¹/₄ mile called Sebber Bridge. Least water 4 m at its N end and 0·6 m at its S. Power's Rock lies 3 cables NW of centre of island and has 0·3 m over it while Whitty Rock, which is awash at LW lies 3 cables W of the centre of the island. 2¹/₂ cables S of the S point of the island lies Shoal Rock with 0·9 m over it, but its position is usually indicated by a tide ripple. Panstown Rock, close to the SW side of the S point of the island, shows above HW and Molly Hoy lies a little over 1 cable to NW of Panstown and shows. There is a group of drying rocks close to the E side of the S tip of the island called the Seven Heads. Makestone Rock shows and is close to the shore on the E side of the island.

NORTH SALTEE ISLAND

is 35 m high and 1³/₄ miles off the shore. The beacon shown on the chart at its SE end is a cairn of loose stones. There are a number of rocks off the island. There is a ledge extending N which almost joins Kilmore Spit, a ledge running S from the shore, which together are called St. Patrick's Bridge, described below. Murroch's Rock, awash at LW, lies over ¹/₂ mile NW of the North Saltee and there is a rock with only 0·2 m over it ¹/₄ mile W of the centre of the island. Jackeen Rock lies a mile to the WNW of the S of the North Saltee and has 1·5 m over it. Galgee Rock, awash at LW, lies ³/₄ cable to the SW of the S point of the island. Goose Rock which dries 2·5 m is ¹/₄ mile NW of Galgee Rock and ³/₄ cable offshore.

Interest

There are reputed to be over 300 different species of birds to be found at various times during the year on the Saltee Islands.

SALTEE SOUND *(see plan)*

must be approached with caution owing to the numerous outlying rocks. Making the sound from the E steer for the N tip of S Saltee until you are nearly midway between the two islands and then steer 330° through the sound so as to avoid Sebber Bridge and the shoal soundings running N from S Saltee. Do not carry on too far on this course as it leads up near Jackeen Rock so alter course for the Hook when the cairn of stones on SE corner of N Saltee is in line with the SW point of that island, bearing 104°. Generally keep closer to the N Saltee when going through but not within 2 cables of it. Tidal streams in the sound are strong, reaching 3½ kn at springs, but do not set fairly through.

ST PATRICK'S BRIDGE

is the shortest and simplest route from Carnsore Point to Hook Head and is constantly used by fishing boats but unfortunately there is no mark to guide the stranger. The deepest water is only 2·4 m and is about half-way between Kilmore Quay and N Saltee, a little nearer the latter. It can only be recommended to a W bound yacht with a fair and therefore rising tide or to an E-bound yacht above ½ tide, otherwise Saltee Sound is to be preferred.

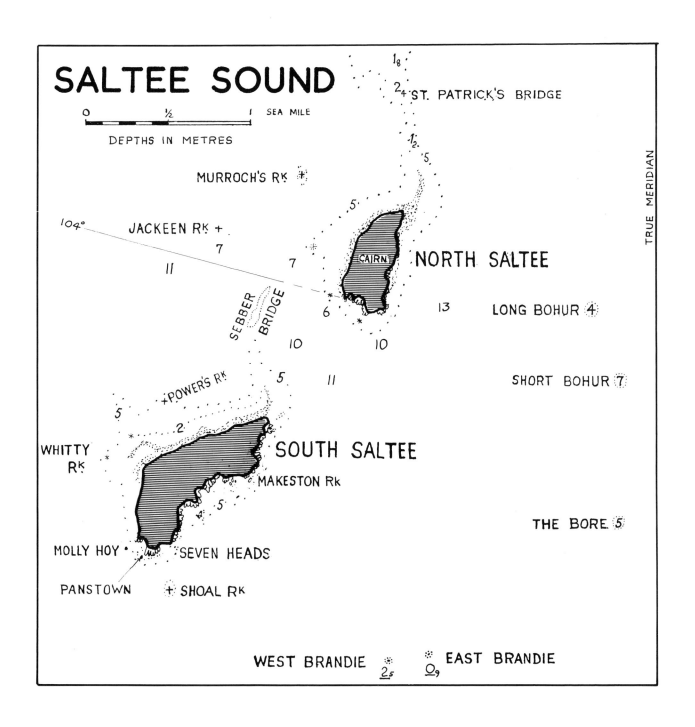

KILMORE QUAY (*see plan*)
is just E of Crossfarnoge (or Forlorn) Point and just W of St. Patrick's Bridge. The harbour consists of a pier with 0·3 m alongside protected by a breakwater. It is in active use by locally owned fishing boats. Because of its lack of depth, indifferent shelter and the rocks and shoal water in the approach it is not recommended to yachts but in some circumstances it might suit to put in there. Reported that there has been considerable storm damage to the quay. It should not be approached until repairs have been effected.

Directions
Do not approach without sufficient rise to berth in 0·4 m. Coming from the W take care to pass at least ¹/₂ mile S of Crossfarnoge Point so as to avoid Forlorn Rock with 1·5 m over it which is ¹/₂ mile SSW of the point. When the E end of the breakwater (with light beacon) comes in line with Ballyteige Castle bearing true N steer in on this line. Coming from the E this line will be picked up almost immediately after crossing St. Patrick's Bridge. It leads in safely between the rocks called Lings on chart 2740 (but known as the Blackberries locally) which never dry but have very little water over them. A light, QRG 6 m, 5 M. is shown from the end of the breakwater, visible between 269° through N to 077°. The G sector which leads safely in being from 354° to 003°. The fishermen use the village church instead of Ballyteigue Castle as the day mark for entering. This gives a line of about 354° coinciding with the E edge of the green sector. This line leads over a charted depth of 1·3 m on Kilmore Spit. Berth at the pier or alongside a trawler. There is one berth on the breakwater side of the pier. A yacht should not be left unattended. If wishing to dry out consult a fisherman.

Facilities
Water and diesel on quay. Petrol, PO and groceries in village, also chandlery at fishermans' co-op. A RNLI lifeboat is stationed here.

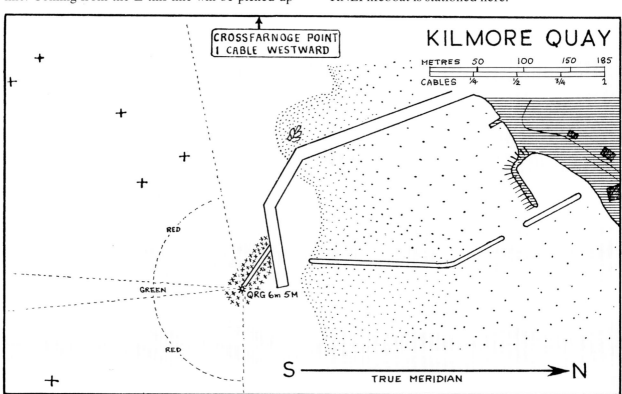

SALTEES TO HOOK
The rocks W of the islands have already been described. Ballyteige Bay lies W of Crossfarnoge Point, and while its E end is clear, there are rocks and shoals in its NW end. The Keeragh's are two islets 6 m high and are 1 mile offshore with a reef extending from them in to the mainland. George Rock over ¹/₂ mile NE of the Keeragh's has only 1·2 m over it and is ¹/₂ mile offshore. Bannow Inlet W of the Keeragh's is very shoal and has a bar with only 0·3 m of water over it. Selskar Shoal is in the centre of the entrance and has 0·3 m over it while Selskar Rock dries 2 m and lies ¹/₄ mile off Bannow Point on the E side of Bannow Bay. Baginbun Head is conspicuous with its Martello Tower and is SW of Bannow Bay. If beating down for the Hook the tides are slack inshore. Do not go too close in between Baginbun Head and the Hook as the shore here is foul for a few cables off and Brecaun Bridge 2 miles from Hook Head extends 3 cables off the shore and has a depth of only 1·4 m at its outer extremity. Forth Mountain, the only high point in SE Wexford, open to Baginbun Point 048° clears Brecaun Bridge.

Offshore anchorage

Baginbun and Bannow Bays are completely exposed to the SE but give good shelter in fresh W wind, so in these conditions, when the Hook Race is a formidable obstacle to any small yacht, they might provide a welcome overnight stopping place. The recommended anchorage is at the SW end of Bannow Bay just N of Ingard Point off the small drying dock there in 3 m sand, good holding. Ingard Point, 1 mile N of Baginbun Point, is foul for $1\frac{1}{2}$ cables offshore; the mark to clear this is the largest house in Fethard village open N of the dock. Selskar Shoal, mentioned above, is $\frac{3}{4}$ mile ENE of Ingard Point so if beating in do not go too far in that direction. The dock has been dredged, exposing the rock in places; it has a depth of 1·5 m at half tide except towards the head; the best berth is just within the E pier. **Supplies.** Water at the dock. Petrol, diesel, provisions at Fethard, 1 mile.

Baginbun bay also offers excellent shelter and holding. Watch out for lobster pots up to a mile offshore between the Hook and Baginbun Point, a salmon net extending from this point and more pots about 2 miles SE of it.

HOOK HEAD

is the end of the low peninsula at the E side of the entrance to Waterford Harbour. A rocky ledge extends 2 cables SW of the point. There is a dangerous wreck $1\frac{1}{4}$ cables W of Doornoge Point, or about $\frac{1}{2}$ mile NW of the Hook. Light. The Hook lighthouse is very distinctive consisting of a massive 12th century tower, 24 m high and about 12 m wide, white with two black bands, upon which stands a shorter modern light-tower. It shows Fl 3 s, 46 m, 24 M. Horn (2) 45 s.

Tidal Streams

From the Hook to the Saltees the tidal streams set E and W. The E-going stream begins at -0050 Cobh (+0545 Dover) and the W-going stream at +0553 Cobh (-0015 Dover). The rate near the Saltees is about 2 kn.

Off the Hook itself, especially in strong W winds there is a dangerous tidal race known as Tower Race, which extends about 1 mile S of the head. In general it is at its strongest from +0420 Cobh to -0455 Cobh (-0130 to +0140 Dover). If the race is expected to be bad a yacht should keep outside the 20 m line, when rounding Hook Point. (See also tidal streams Waterford Harbour entrance below.)

Distances

Carnsore Point to Coningbeg Light Vessel
.. .. 14 miles
Coningbeg Light Vessel to Pollock Rock buoy
.. .. $56\frac{1}{4}$ miles
Carnsore Point to Hook (via Saltee sound)
.. .. $21\frac{1}{2}$ miles

DUNMORE EAST *(see plan)*

is a small artificial harbour on the W side of the entrance to Waterford Harbour. The village of Dunmore East is a popular holiday resort. The harbour is the base for the important autumn herring fishery during which it is crowded with fishing boats. Recent major improvements have given it a depth of 2 m to 3·4 m and made it safe in all summer weather, though there may be a swell along the NW wall in S winds. It is a popular port of call for yachts which are made welcome, though owners are reminded that it is primarily a fishing port and they should take care not to inconvenience fishing boats.

Lights

The large granite lighthouse on the pier shows L Fl WR 8 s, 13 m, 12-9 M. W from 225° to 310°, R thence to 004°, obscured elsewhere. A pillar on the end of the breakwater which forms an extension of the pier shows Fl R 2 s from 310° through S to 000°. On the N point of the W quay a light Fl G 2 s shows from 165° to 246°.

Directions

By day the white pilot look-out on Black Nob just S of the harbour is conspicuous as is the ice plant and the pier itself. Enter under power or much reduced sail and berth at the E pier, then report to the HM for instructions. The Waterford Harbour SC has a club-house on the NW quay.

Anchorage

Alongside 2 timber baulks with tyre fenders on West quay. Alternatively yachts may lie alongside berthed fishing boats but must be prepared to move at the request of the Harbour Master or fishing skippers. 3m at LAT. Yacht moorings are laid outside the harbour in the bight N of the North West quay where good shelter is to be obtained in all but strong winds from NE to SE. Advice on vacant moorings can be obtained from WHSC on VHF 16 or 39.

By night approaching from the E, give Hook Head a berth of $\frac{1}{2}$ mile or more depending on the state of the sea. Alter course for Dunmore East light when in the red sector. From the W hold course for Hook Head until the red sector of Dunmore East light is entered then alter course for it. The white sector of the light shows across the estuary and up it and clears Creadon Head.

Facilities

Water from a tap at SE corner of quay and from tap at WHSC. Diesel obtained on E quay (phone V. Cobden - 051-83654). Good restaurants, pubs, hotels, shops and P.O. in village. WHSC has is Club House on the W quay. Visiting yachtsmen are made welcome and showers and toilets are available

10

during normal hours. RNLI lifeboat lies afloat. There are good public heads on the S quay at HM office and showers with plenty of hot water near the grid open at 0800.

WHSC .. .. 051-83230/83389 VHF 16/39
HM 051-83166
DIESEL - V. COBDEN 051-93654

Dunmore East has the Pilot Station for Waterford Harbour, telephone and fax 051-83261. VHF ch. 16, 14, 12.

Dunmore East, popular staging place looking N

DUNMORE EAST

Depths in metres

TRUE MERIDIAN

The drying harbour of Ballyhack on the Waterford Estuary, with the car ferry crossing to Passage East.

New Ross is the most northerly seaport on the River Barrow, though tidal waters extend beyond it to St. Mullins.

WATERFORD HARBOUR (see plan)

The passage up the River Suir to Waterford and that up the River Barrow to New Ross are both well worth while if time can be spared. The scenery is very beautiful in places and the pilotage presents no great difficulty, both rivers being well buoyed. Power is desirable, especially for the narrower part of the Suir which should not be attempted under sail as the wind is unreliable. In conditions when Dunmore East is uncomfortable and crowded with fishing boats good shelter can be obtained at Cheek Point, 9 miles up the estuary or further up in King's Channel behind Little Island.

The entrance between Hook Point on the E and Swine Head on the W is 3½ miles wide and free of danger up to Creadan Head. A bar with 4·7 m least water lies 1 mile inside Creadan Head. The best water across it is marked by 2 port hand buoys and 2 starboard buoys *see below*.

Light. Leading Lights

A light is shown, to seawards only, from a white tower with red stripe at Duncannon Fort exhibits a Dir. Oc WRG 4s 11/8M, G 353° - 356.75° W 356.75° - 357.25°, R 375.25° - 001°. Also this tower shows to N an Oc WR 4s 13m 7/9M R 119° - 149° and W 149° - 172°. The R sector covers Drumroe Bank. There are also 4 new port and starboard buoys marking the channel with characteristics -

No.1. Starboard hand buoy Fl G 2s.
No.2. Port hand buoy Q R.
No.3. Starboard hand buoy Fl G 4s.
No.4. Port hand buoy Fl R 3s.

Tidal Streams, Waterford Harbour Entrance

Outside the entrance the W going stream begins +0450 Cobh (-0100 Dover) and the E going stream at -0120 Cobh (+0515 Dover), the spring rate not exceeding 1 kn.

Inside the entrance the flood begins at -0425 Cobh (+0210 Dover) and the ebb at +0045 Cobh (-0505 Dover), the spring rate off Creadan Head being 2½ to 3 kn, decreasing outwards to mid-channel.

At Portally Head the harbour and coastal streams meet and separate. On the ebb the meeting results in a line of ripples E across the entrance and for ¾ mile S of the head.

Between Portally Head and Creadan Head the flood commences close in 1 hour earlier, i.e. -0525 Cobh (+0110 Dover), turning E and S off Creadan Head until the main flood sets in.

The W- going stream commences off Hook Head at +0350 Cobh (-0200 Dover) 1 hour earlier than offshore and changes in a rotary direction. SE at -0010 Cobh (+0600 Dover), E at +0250 Cobh (-0300 Dover), thence via N to W again.

The junction of the W-going stream from the Hook and the ebb from the harbour is marked by overfalls W from the Hook or by a race extending a mile S of the Hook, the Tower Race, which can be dangerous in strong winds. It is probable that the race and overfalls occur chiefly from +0420 to -0455 Cobh (-0130 to +0140 Dover).

In the entrance the flood runs mainly up the W side and the ebb down the E side and strongest near Hook Head. Within Creadan Head the streams in general follow the channels.

Directions

Duncannon Spit, which dries, extends ¾ mile SSE of Duncannon Point. A green conical buoy starboard side of channel and further up a Red Can buoy to port side of channel abeam Duncannon.

Quays

Duncannon. Berths inside N side of harbour wall alongside fishing boats. Do not attempt entry during the fierce ebb but before or at HW. The anchorage NW of the quay is in a tidal lop with poor holding. Shops about ¼ mile away. Berths inside N side of harbour wall alongside fishing boats. **Arthurstown** on the E bank opposite Passage light, dries. **Passage East** quay dries out. There is anchorage off it but the tides run hard and it can be uncomfortable, and dinghy work difficult. **Ballyhack.** Possible to lie alongside quay at old slipway. Keep clear of ferries using new slipway. Facilities - pub, shop, restaurant, boat yard.

Danger

A cable area 4 cables wide and shown on chart 2046 extends across the estuary from Duncannon Fort to a beacon on the W shore.

There are a number of fishing weirs on the estuary and river which are shown on chart 2046. Their position must be noted if turning to windward.

RIVER SUIR, DUNCANNON TO CHEEK POINT

Above Duncannon Fort the channel runs close to the E bank. Drumroe Bank dries to the W and is marked by two R Can buoys moored on its edge. At night keep in the white sector of Duncannon light until the red sector of Passage light is entered.

Light

Passage Point light pile, red with white top, shows Fl WR 5 s, 7 m, 6-5 M. White from the W bank of the river NW of the light to 127° leads W of Seedes Bank. R thence over Seedes Bank and to 302°. Obsc. elsewhere.

Leave Passage light to port and then close the W bank of the river above Passage Harbour. By night keep in the white sector of Passage light. This will leave Seedes Bank to starboard.

Once past Seedes Bank there is plenty of water in mid-channel for a yacht to round Cheek Point.

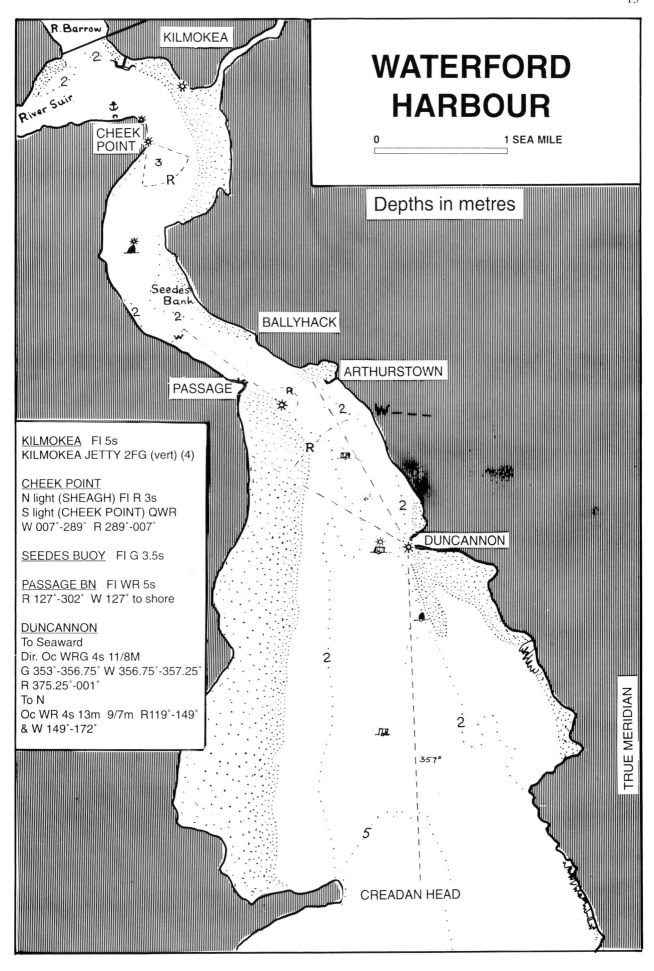

WATERFORD HARBOUR

0   1 SEA MILE

Depths in metres

R.Barrow

KILMOKEA

River Suir

CHEEK
POINT

R

Seedes
Bank

BALLYHACK

ARTHURSTOWN

PASSAGE

R

R

DUNCANNON

KILMOKEA   Fl 5s
KILMOKEA JETTY 2FG (vert) (4)

CHEEK POINT
N light (SHEAGH) Fl R 3s
S light (CHEEK POINT) QWR
W 007°-289° R 289°-007°

SEEDES BUOY   Fl G 3.5s

PASSAGE BN   Fl WR 5s
R 127°-302° W 127° to shore

DUNCANNON
To Seaward
Dir. Oc WRG 4s 11/8M
G 353°-356.75° W 356.75°-357.25°
R 375.25°-001°
To N
Oc WR 4s 13m 9/7m R119°-149°
& W 149°-172°

357°

TRUE MERIDIAN

CREADAN HEAD

14

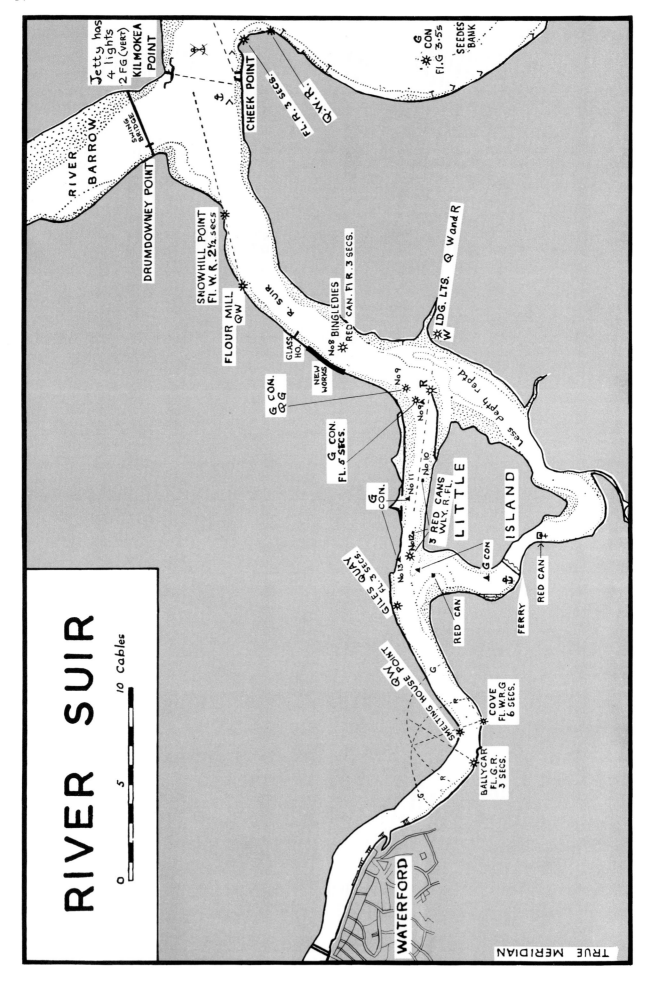

RIVER SUIR

0   5   10 Cables

Scale

KILMOKEA POINT

Jetty has 4 lights 2 FG (VERT)

RIVER BARROW

SWING BRIDGE

DRUMDOWNEY POINT

CHEEK POINT

FL.R. 3 SECS.

Q.W.R.

G CON F.L.G 3·5s

SEEDES BANK

SNOWHILL POINT FL.W.R. 2½ secs

FLOUR MILL Q.W

R. SUIR

No8 BINGLEDIES

RED CAN. Fl R. 3 SECS.

W. LDG. LTS. Q W and R

GLASS HO.

NEW WORKS

G CON. Q G

No9

R

Less depth reptd

G CON. FL. 5 SECS.

No9

No10

No11

G CON.

No12

3 RED CANS WLY. R FL.

LITTLE ISLAND

G CON

RED CAN

No13

GILES QUAY FL. 3 SECS.

RED CAN

FERRY

SMELTING HOUSE POINT Q.W

G

COVE FL.W.R.G 6 SECS.

BALLYCAR FL.G.R. 3 SECS.

R

G

WATERFORD

TRUE MERIDIAN

15

A car ferry crosses the estuary between Passage East and Ballyhack.

Buoy, Lights

A G Cone light buoy, Fl G 3 s, is moored at the N end of Seedes Bank. On Cheek Point a light is shown, Fl R 3 s, 29 m, 3 M. Two cables S of Cheek Point a light is shown, Q WR 6 m, 5 M. The white sector leads in the channel close to the W bank and over Carter's Patch in 3·6 m. Red covers the remainder of Carter's Patch. Campile River on the E bank shows Fl 5 s. Kilmokea Power Station shows a group of FG lights.

Dangers

An area from the power station to Cheek Point is a Prohibited anchorage. Its position is shown on chart 2046 and the plan. There are fish weirs N and W of Cheek Point. Yachts may lie alongside the outside of quay at Cheekpoint or anchor off - vacant moorings are often available enquire from James Doherty at Pier Head. Tides run hard and dinghy work can be difficult. Cheekpoint is however a sheltered anchorage in all but strong N winds and a yacht can be left on a mooring in safety, enquire from James Doherty.

Facilities

2 restaurants, pubs and bus to Waterford.

RIVER SUIR ABOVE CHEEK POINT

Above Cheek Point a yacht will be safe on a mid-channel course until the training wall at the NE end of Little Island is reached. By night the chart and plan shows the position and characteristics of the lights which make pilotage in this reach quite straightforward.

Dangers

The Bingledies on the SE side of the river are composed of mud and boulders and dry. They are in the red sector of Snowhill light. A training wall, 4 cables long, extends from the N shore of Little Island in an ENE direction. Its extremity is marked by a Lt beacon, Q R 8 m, 5 M. There is a drying patch 1½ cables ENE of this beacon.

Queen's Channel

runs N of Little Island and is straightforward. The plan shows the position of the two unlit G Cone buoys marking the N side of the channel and the two unlit and one lit R Can buoys on the S side. Leading lights at the E end of the channel, Q R and Q, 8 and 15 m, 5 M. lead through bearing 098°.

King's Channel

is the old bed of the river and leads S of Little Island. It is silting up at its E end and is crossed by submerged wire cables for the ferry and submerged

power lines at its W end. It should not be used except for the approach to the anchorage at its W end.

Anchorage

There is a secure and very well sheltered anchorage in the King's Channel. Approach through the W end of the channel leaving the G Cone buoy well to port, the next R Can buoy to starboard and the G Cone buoy inside the channel fairly close to port as the dredger discharges mud in the bight SW of this buoy. Between this bight and the mainland ferry slip there is a restricted width with 6 to 8 m between the drying mud and the much deeper channel. Land at the gangway beyond the slip. No facilities. Main road ¼ mile. The castle on the island is an hotel. Contact the ferry on VHF 16 to obtain information on this anchorage. There is a telephone cable between a gate on the island and a sluice on the shore. It is possible to cross the ferry chains and ropes if the tide is not too strong - the tide lifts these.

Queen's Channel to Waterford

There are no dangers in this section of the river and plenty of water for a yacht except close to the banks.

Lights

On the N bank Giles Quay shows Fl 3 s, 3 M. On the S shore Cove shows Fl WRG 6 s, 6 m, 2 M. Green down river and red up river. White along the S bank down river. Ballycar shows Fl RG 3 s, 5 m. Red downstream and green upstream.

WATERFORD

is a busy commercial port with quays both sides of the river. There is a strong tidal stream past the city and yachts must not attempt to anchor but should be prepared to moor alongside the pontoon on the S side opposite Reginalds and above Adelphi Quay -1.6m LAT. Report for instructions to the harbourmaster's office on the quay or, if closed, to the customs office. HM phone 051-74499. VHF ch. 16 and 14.

Facilities

A visit to Waterford is a good opportunity to obtain supplies of food or other requirements. All services are available except sailmaker and boat repairs; the latter can be done at Ballyhack (see above) where there is a patent slip. EC Thur. Rail to Dublin. Water - contact Wharf Foreman at 051-32095. Launderette at Dooley's Hotel.

The River Suir is navigable for 9 miles above Waterford, but there are two bridges to be passed and local advice should be sought if considering this; just above the first bridge there are cables with 38 m clearance.

16

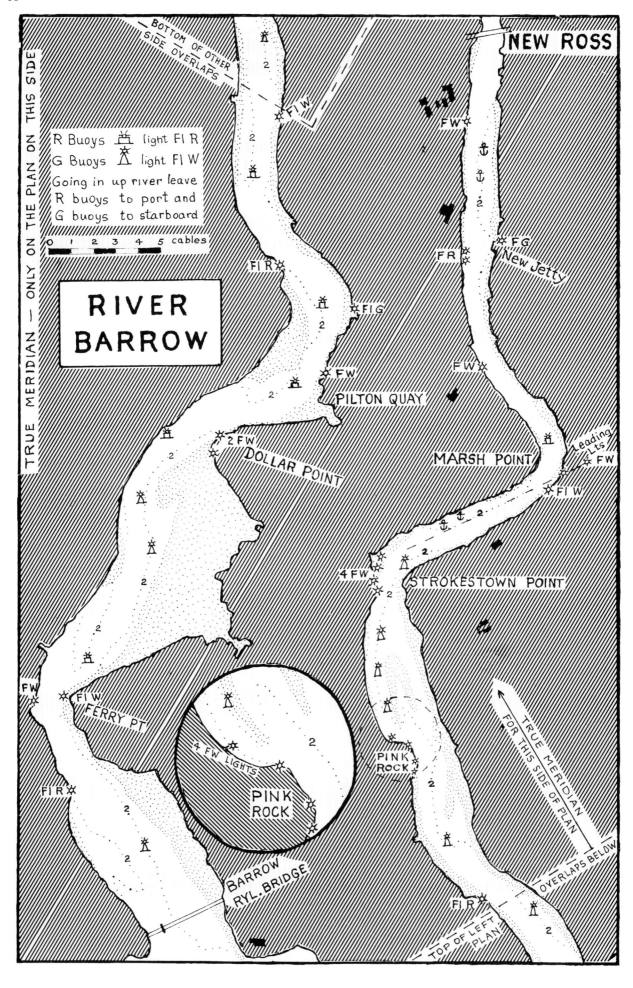

NEW ROSS

RIVER
BARROW

R Buoys [symbol] light Fl R
G Buoys [symbol] light Fl W
Going in up river leave
R buoys to port and
G buoys to starboard

0 1 2 3 4 5 cables

TRUE MERIDIAN — ONLY ON THE PLAN ON THIS SIDE

BOTTOM OF OTHER
SIDE OVERLAPS

Fl W

FW

FG
New Jetty

FR

Fl R

Fl G

FW

FW

PILTON QUAY

MARSH POINT

2 FW

DOLLAR POINT

Leading
Lts
FW

Fl W

4 FW

STROKESTOWN POINT

TRUE MERIDIAN
FOR THIS SIDE OF PLAN

OVERLAPS BELOW

FW

Fl W
FERRY PT

4 FW LIGHTS

PINK
ROCK

PINK
ROCK

Fl R

BARROW
RYL. BRIDGE

Fl R

TOP OF LEFT
PLAN

THE RIVER BARROW (see plan)

is navigable by large ships to New Ross where it is crossed by a fixed bridge. Only shallow draft motor cruisers can proceed beyond the town where in 2 miles they have the choice of going 7 miles up the Nore to Inistioge or following the Barrow for 4 miles to St. Mullins where the Barrow navigation is entered. This links with the Grand Canal giving communication with Dublin and the Shannon for boats drawing not more than 1 m.

Yachts going to St. Mullins or Inistioge are recommended to leave New Ross 2 hours before High Water (+40 mins Barrow bridge), and may lie safely, 1·1 m draft, at the Steamerhole, St. Mullins or with 0·9 m draft can anchor W of the New Quay, Inistioge.

The trip to New Ross is well worth while for yachts visiting the estuary; the river scenery is most attractive and the town is useful for supplies. New Ross is a busy port with traffic in fertilisers, an oil depot and Ro-Ro berth.

Tides

The spring rate on both flood and ebb is around 2 kn most of the way; the maximum encountered, during winter floods only, is 4 kn. The flood starts at -0420 Cobh (+0215 Dover), and the ebb starts at +0030 Cobh (-0520 Dover) . S winds can raise the river up to 0·6 m above normal level and N winds can lower it by 0·6 m.

Bridge

The Barrow joins the Suir just above Check Point; immediately above the confluence it is crossed by a railway bridge with an opening near its W end. The clearance under the bridge at LWN is approximately 10 m and 6 m at HWS. Three long blasts of a ship's siren brings out the keeper to open the bridge. However he might well not hear a yacht's fog-horn so it is advisable, if circumstances permit, to give advance notice by phoning the bridge-keeper at (051) 88137. There is a 24 hour service. As he cannot always be by his phone it may be necessary to try more than once. Vessels enter by the E opening and come out by the W opening of the bridge. The clearance under the wires which span the opening is 33 m HWS.

Plan — Lights — Caution

The plan shows the position of the lights in Jan 1983. The LW and 2 m lines are based on surveys from 1951 to 1976. Going upstream G Cone light buoys show a Fl G light and should be left to starboard, R Can light buoys show Fl R and should be left to port. There are two unlit leading beacons, in line 328½°, for the reach immediately above the bridge. The leading lights, in line 095°, for the reach S of Marsh Point are W, the position of the buoys is altered from time to time to indicate the deepest parts of the channel.

Directions

The bridge should be approached eastward on the flood tide to allow for set as the flood sets strongly to the W. Vessels must enter by the E opening. Kilmokea Point on the E side of the river with its power station and jetty is steep-to but Drumdowney Point on the W side has shoal water just off it and to the S.

In the river there is ample width almost everywhere for a yacht drawing 1·8 m and it is not necessary in many places to follow the buoyed channel strictly. However buoys should be left on their correct side if the plan shows them to be close to shoal water. Any ship must follow the correct channel closely so keep well clear of any which are met. Note that there are wrecks just N of the line joining the 4·4 m sounding off Dollar Point and the buoy off Pilton Quay and also off Pilton Quay. These wrecks are well clear of the main channel.

The only narrow part is at Pink Point, 3½ miles below New Ross (see inset on plan). Here the channel is very close to the W shore going round the bend and then continues between groynes on the W and Red Bank, which dries 1 m, on the E. The bank is marked by 3 G Cone Lt buoys, Q. There are floodlights on Pink Point and two R triangles, apex up, lead clear of the bank.

Anchorage

The best berth near New Ross is on the E side a little below the town, as shown on the plan. Depth is 2 to 2·5 m. With fresh SE to SW winds and the ebb tide there can be a nasty lop in the town reach. In these conditions anchor clear of the leading line on the N side of the down-stream half of the next reach which runs E and W. A riding light is essential and it is important to ensure that the yacht will not swing into the channel. The S side of this reach is much deeper, 7 to 12 m. There is no good place for a yacht to berth alongside though sometimes a berth may be available alongside the light-vessel which is moored on the E side. Apply to HM. There is a private landing stage near a house owned by Mr James Stewart who is very helpful. There is a slip on the W side above the bridge, and also a public landing stage near the Boat Club where boats can be slipped at half-tide.

Facilities

Harbour Office on the town quay with landing at a pontoon below. If in any doubt phone the HM, Captain L. J. Foley, phone 051-21303 or 21889. VHF Ch. 16 and 14, c/s "Ross Station". Fresh water, shops, banks, hotels etc, near at hand. Sail repairs at Barrow Valley Marine. Early closing Wed. Bus to all parts. In summer a cruising restaurant operates daily, phone 051-21723, and is highly recommended.

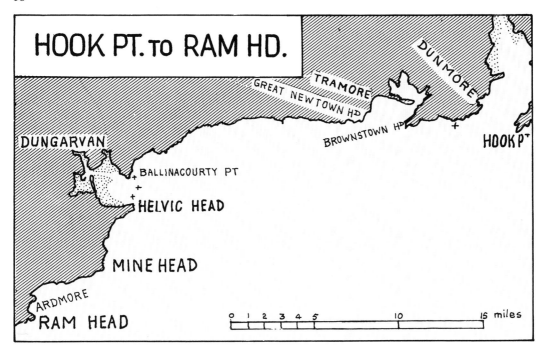

COAST WEST OF WATERFORD HARBOUR

Dangers West of Dunmore East

Falskirt Rock 2¼ cables S of Swines Point, covers at ¾ flood. It is usually obvious by day, but as it is on the direct course of a yacht bound W from Dunmore East care should be taken at night to steer well clear of it, and arriving from the W after dark to keep a good offing. Swede Rock ¾ mile E of Brownstown Head and 1 cable offshore has 2·7 m over it.

Tramore Bay

offers no shelter. It is nearly 2½ miles wide at the entrance between Brownstown Head on the E and Great Newton Head on the W side. The spire of the church at Tramore is conspicuous from seaward. The RNLI operates an inshore lifeboat in Tramore Bay from April to October. Brownstown Head has two black towers on its summit while Great Newton Head (45 m) is distinguished by three white towers, on one of which, called the Metal Man, there is a large figure of a man with his right arm pointing out to sea.

Tramore to Dungarvan

The shore is generally bold and uninteresting and calls for little description. There are no hazards far enough off the shore to be dangerous. Glass, Sheep and Burke islets are all close to the shore to the W of Great Newton Head.

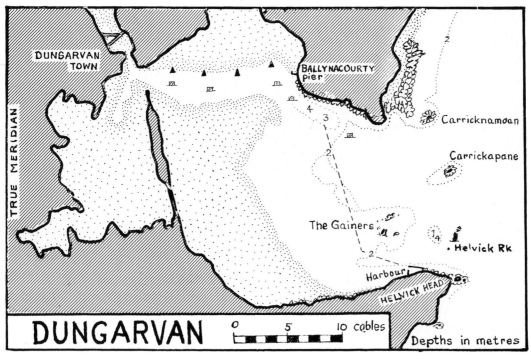

Dungarvon Town Harbour from NW.

DUNGARVAN HARBOUR

is a large bay whose entrance lies between Helvick Head on the South and Ballynacourty Point on the North The West side of the bay completely dries at low water. Carrickapane Rock, 2m high with shoal soundings extending 1½ cables west of it, lies nearly in the middle of the entrance and can be passed on either hand. Helvick rock and nearby shoals have from 1.4m to 2.3m and lie 3.5 cables North of Helvick Lodge, a conspicuous house on the edge of the cliff just West of Helvick Head. They are marked by an East Card. Lt. Buoy, Q(3), 10s, moored 1 cable NE of them. The Gainers are an extensive, rocky patch which dries 0.8 m in places. It lies between the limits of 5 and 8 cables South West of Carrickapane Rock and between 2 and 5 cables North of Helvick Pier. A Red can buoy marking it permanently removed in 1991. A Red can buoy approx 2¾ cables SSE of Wyses Point leads to the buoyed channel to Dungarvan Town Quay. Chart 2017 is essential.

Helvick Head (67m) is a steep, bluff headland, the ruins of a small watch tower on its summit have now disappeared. There is a rock 15m high close to the head and some other rocks off this, but they all show and are steep to. Ballynacourty Point is low; there is a lighthouse on it with a large disused chemical works just NW of it. A reef, which dries extends ½ mile ENE of the point terminating in a rock called Carricknamoan which is 1m high. The building marked on chart 2017 as Clonea Castle in position 52° 06'N 7° 32'W is really only a large house and bears no resemblance to a castle, furthermore it is no longer conspicuous. The building shown as "Castle (ruins)" East of it is now completely demolished. There is a golf club at Wyse's Point but the conspicuous golf club house was destroyed by fire in 1989

CAUTION

In summer keep a sharp look-out for salmon nets, which may be up to 1 mile long, in this area. Local fishermen operate on Channel 6 VHF and may give advice on position of nets if requested.

Light

A light, Fl (2) WRG 10s, 16m, 12-9-9 M is shown from a white tower on Ballynacourty Point. G from 245° to 274° covering the rocks off Ballynacourty Point. W from 274° to 302° leading NE of Carrickapane Rock. W from 325° to 117° covering Helvick Rock and the Gainers and the rocks E of Helvick Head. Obsc. elsewhere.

Approach

There are no difficulties in the approach to Ballynacourty Point or to Helvick Harbour by day or by night. Note, however, that there may be some difficulty in identifying Ballynacourty Point light against the background of the bright factory lights. There is a passage from the Helvick shore West of the Gainers which is useful when going from Helvick to Dungarvan. It carries 1.7m least depth of water. Keep the entrance to Helvick Harbour in transit with Helvick Lodge (103°), until Ballynacourty Pier transits with the conspicuous Crohaun (Cruachan) Mountain (345°). See chart 2049. Steer on this transit if close to low water when Carrickapane Rock nears 090° alter towards Ballynacourty Point and leave the outer channel buoy to port to avoid the tail of the Deadman's Sands.

DUNGARVAN TOWN HARBOUR

Yachts entering this harbour and lying alongside must be prepared to take the ground. A stranger should not attempt to enter during the last 2½ hours of ebb. Anchor 1 cable South of Ballynacourty Pier, and WSW of the Golf Club House in about 4m and await the flood. The channel from Wyse's Point to Abbey Point is clearly marked with Green and Red buoys. At half tide there should be at least 1.8 m between the buoys. Approach along the shore from Ballynacourty Point past Wyse's Point towards Ballinacourty Pier, keeping ¾ cable offshore. Just before coming abeam of the pier alter to 263°. The bar between Ballynacourty Point and Wyse's Point can be rough in strong SE winds though there is plenty of water in the channel between the buoys and the shore. The leading lights are exhibited from black and white striped poles located near Ballynacourty Pier and these will give a transit for this part of the channel when kept in line astern.

There are two conspicuous latticed steel radio masts visible on the skyline over the town and when the Northernmost bears 298° midway between Cunnigar Point and Abbey Point steer this course until between the points then alter to 350° keeping on the East side of mid channel until the quay is entered.

Berths and anchorage

The berths alongside the quay dry at springs. Check that the chosen berth is not foul before drying out. It is advisable to moor Port side to as the ebb sets strongly along the quay wall.

A yacht drawing 1.8 m could easily lie afloat at low water. Sound until a suitable hole is found. There is a small area of deep water West of Cunnigar Point where there is up to 4m LAT. It is sometimes possible to borrow a mooring in this area. Do not leave a yacht unattended at anchor here as the holding is very poor.

Approach by night

Keep the leading lights at Ballynacourty Pier in line astern, 083° - 263°. These are white synchronised occulting lights Oc. every 5 sec. and must not be confused with other bright lights ashore and on the pier. When the Dungarvan leading lights transit bearing 298° alter to this course. These lights are usually fixed Red but occasionally one or both of them may be white. The Dungarvan lights are mounted on ordinary ESB poles. Night entry is not recommended to those entering for the first time.

Supplies

All stores are available in the town. Large supermarket near quay. Hardware, gas, banks, post office, hotels and bus services. Petrol at quayside, garages 9-5 Monday to Friday. Duty free diesel from Esso Filling Station on the Cork Road.

Tourist Information

Dungarvan is located on the Colligan River. King's John's Castle an early 13th century Anglo Norman castle is situated on the quayside. Details of town trail from the Museum located in the Old Market House. Beaches at Cunnigar, Clonea and Ballinagoul. Other activities include board sailing, golf, squash, pitch and putt, sea and shore angling, forest and mountain walks and bird watching. Several good restaurants within walking distance of the quay. Car hire and numerous taxis available.

Tides

On the S side of Dungarvan Bay the tides are weak but they run strongly from Ballynacourty Point to and from Dungarvan . The flood runs from -0520 to +0040 Cobh (+0115 to -0510 Dover). Maximum spring rate in the pool is 1½ kn increasing to 2½ between Cunnigar Point and Abbey Point.

Helvick Harbour looking SE.

HELVICK

is a small artificial harbour on the South side of Dungarvan Bay, ¼ mile West of Helvick Head. It is approached by keeping half way between the Helvick Rock buoy East Card. Q(3), 10 s and the South shore of the bay. The entrance faces West and there is easy access to the harbour and good shelter alongside the quay except in strong West or North West winds when a yacht would be better off at Dungarvan Town Quay. There is a small patch with 0.5 m extending West from the North pier which should be given a berth of at least 30m and the entrance should be approached with the North pier open. The depth in the entrance is only about 1m despite recent dredging and the deepest water is close up to the South breakwater. So many fishing vessels now use this harbour that there is only limited space for yachts and consideration should be given to going to Dungarvan if the tidal conditions allow. The South side of the harbour is very shallow and if there are a lot of fishing vessels alongside it can be difficult to turn around inside the pier near low water. It is advisable for a member of the crew to remain on board in case the yacht has to be moved to accommodate the fishing vessels coming and going.

Light.

A FW light is shown from the pierhead.

Supplies

Limited groceries at Post Office 2 miles. Pub ½ mile.

Anchorage

With South or South West winds anchor in about 2.5m 2 to 4 cables West of the harbour away from any traffic. A riding light is advised.

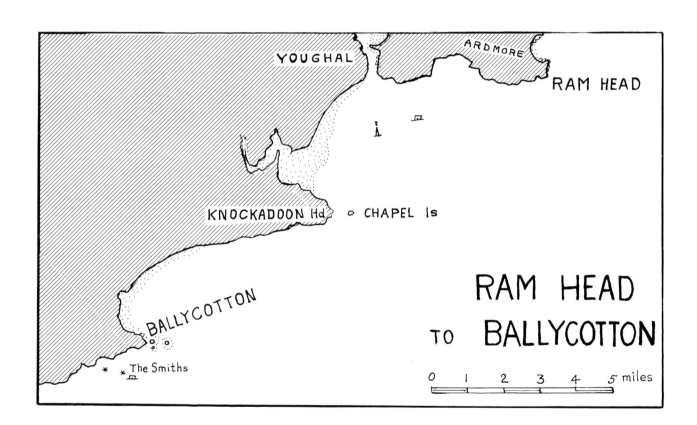

MINE HEAD

is a bold head 78 m high, steep to but with two outlying rocks. The Rogue lies about ⅓ mile E of the head and ¼ mile from the shore and dries 2·7 m. The Longship, dries 4 m, is about 1 mile SW of the head and 2 cables offshore. The shore between Helvick and Mine Heads is free of dangers.

Light

From a white lighthouse with a black band 21 m high, Fl (4) 20 s, 87 m, 28 M.

Tidal Streams

Off Mine Head the E-going stream begins -0215 Cobh (+0420 Dover), and the W-going stream at +0235 Cobh (-0315 Dover). Maximum spring rate 1·2 kn.

22

Ardmore Bay

lies to the W of Mine Head and is open and exposed but is free of danger, except for the Black Rocks, which dry and are 2 cables off the shore nearly 1 mile to NNE of Ardmore Head. Temporary anchorage may be found in fine weather off the pier. There are one or two shops in the village where limited supplies may be obtained. PO. There is a round tower on the slope of the hill near the village.

Ram Head

is 5¹/₂ miles W of Mine Head, and should not be approached too close as there is a rock with only 1·6 m over it ¹/₂ cable SE of the head. Ardmore Head is less than ¹/₂ mile N of it and is free of danger. Ram Head separates Ardmore and Youghal Bays.

Distances

Hook to Dunmore	2³/₄ miles
Hook to Helvick	23 miles
Hook to Ardmore	30³/₄ miles
Dunmore to Helvick	21³/₄ miles
Dunmore to Ardmore	29¹/₂ miles
Helvick to Ardmore	10 miles

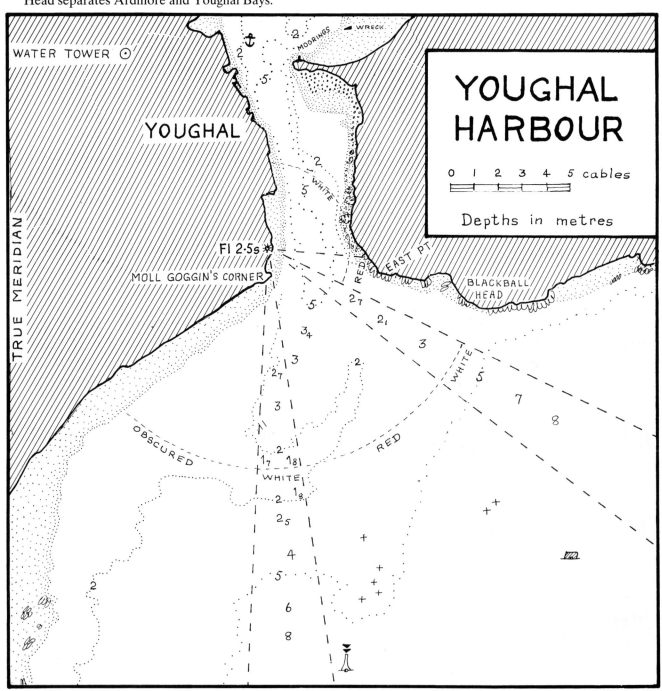

YOUGHAL HARBOUR *(see plans)*

New Chart 2071 issued 11.10.91. This historic harbour is formed by the estuary of the River Blackwater which enters the sea at the head of Youghal Bay. The bay is 6½ miles wide between Ram Head on the E and Capel Island. The W side of the bay is very shoal and the centre is occupied by an extensive bar. Bar Rocks, on the outer edge of the bar, consist of a very dangerous patch of rocks with a least depth of 0·6 m. They are marked by an unlit S Card buoy moored 3½c SSW of them. This buoy is very small and hard to pick up against the land.

Blackball Ledge is ½ mile NE of Bar Rocks and consists of several shoal heads with 3·4 m over them. It is marked by an unlit, R Can buoy moored 4 cables SE of the ledge. In 1986 the E bar had 2 m and the W bar 1·7 m. Neither should be attempted if there is a big sea running or in S or SE winds of Force 6 or over.

Because of the bar and the roll which enters in S weather Youghal has not been popular with yachts, but in moderate weather conditions it is an interesting and convenient anchorage with plenty of room and suitable depths. It is possible to enter by night. There is now a drying bank about 18 metres off the quays from the S end of market dock North to the point where 'crane' is marked on chart. Less water everywhere in the Youghal Harbour area has been reported.

Caution

During the salmon season nets may be set anywhere in the bay and particularly in the harbour entrance where 2 or 3 nets may be set so that they overlap requiring great care to find the way through. Remember that these nets may be drifting in or out on the tide at 2 to 3 kn. Care should be taken in following the fishermen's instructions for the avoidance of nets in confined waters that there is sufficient water for the draft of the vessel. They are often people with limited knowledge of a yachts requirements.

Light

A light is shown from a white tower on the W side of the entrance. Fl RW 2·5 s, 24 m, 9-12 M. W from 003° to 351°, R thence to 307°, W thence to 295°, R thence to 273°, W thence to 183°. Obsc elsewhere. The red sectors cover the offshore rocks and East Point and Blackball Head, the white sectors lead in across the bars and also shows white inside the harbour.

Directions — East Bar

Coming from the E, steer direct for the lighthouse when it comes well open of Blackball Head and bears about 300°. A convenient transit is the lighthouse and the right-hand edge of a group of trees on the summit of the hill behind it; Blackball Ledge red can buoy will be left to port. Coming from the W give Capel Island a birth of 2 cables and steer a course of 035° to leave both buoys to port. When the lighthouse bears 300° alter for it and hold this course until the estuary open up. By night this bearing is the centre of the white sector leading over E bar.

West Bar

has only 1·7 m but is 1½ miles shorter for yachts coming from the W. Having rounded Capel Island (see below) make for S Cord. Bar Rocks buoy, leave it about 2 cables to starboard and then steer direct for the entrance, about N true. Note: Bar Rocks buoy is often difficult to establish. It bears 020° distance 2M from the old lighthouse on Capel Island. From Bar Rocks buoy steer direct from the entrance about N true. By night get into the West White sector of the lighthouse (003° - 351°) and hold this until over the shallowest part of the bar, then alter to leave the light well to port, as the water is shoal to seaward of, and under the lighthouse.

Entrance

Keep a mid-channel course until abreast the light, then alter towards the W side to keep in the best water. Note that the W bank shoals very steeply to a drying height of 3 m just near the prominent red band-stand 2½ cables N of the light. From there on, keep about 1 cable off the W shore to avoid the shallow Dutchman's Ballast on the E side.

Tidal Streams

About ½ mile S of the W bar the stream is rotary, clockwise, commencing SSW at -0605 Cobh (+0030 Dover) through W and N to NNE at +0020 Cobh (-0530 Dover). The stream commences SSE at +0035 Cobh (-0515 Dover) and continues until +0320 Cobh (-0230 Dover). The maximum rate throughout being 0·5 kn . From +0320 Cobh to +0500 Cobh, however, the rate increases to 1½ kn . On the E bar the rates are about the same and the times about 10 mins later. In the entrance the flood runs from -0505 Cobh to +0130 Cobh (+0130 Dover to -0430 Dover). The maximum spring rate is 2½ kn flood and 3 kn ebb. The ebb runs hard off Ferry Point forming an eddy in the bight to the S of the point. N of Ferry Point the flood runs first in the channel E of Red Bank and later in the channel to the W of the bank.

Anchorages

All Youghal's quays dry at LW except the pile landing Jetty at the S entrance to Market Dock which has 1m LWS and the commercial quay which has 2m alongside at its N end, and 3m at its S end at LWS. The commercial quay is only dredged offside

Youghal Harbour and River Blackwater from the SE.

itself being particularly shoal if approached obliquely from the S it is best approach at Rt. angles. This quay may be used by yachts with the permission of the Shipping Co. when not in use. A yacht should not be left here unattended towards LW as the quay is not of suitable construction for yachts to lie against near LW. A yacht should not be left unattended at the landing jetty.

Caution

There is a mussel bank, which dries 1 m, S of the Red Bank which now extends further to S and which is not marked on chart 2071. Its position is marked on the plan. The flood tide sets across it. The prominent water tower in line with the NE corner of the quays, bearing 260°, leads S of it. A line joining the water tower to the church tower, on the E side of the harbour near some trees, leads S of it bearing 265°-85°. Also note on the plan the new drying bank running NE from Ferry Pt. which is not marked on the charts. The gap between the tail of this bank and Ferry Pt. is less than ½ a cable.

(1) Anchor off Town Hall just N of lifeboat slip as space permits. Also off Market Dock where one can land.

(2) If troubled by swell some shelter from it can be found behind Ferry Point about 50 m offshore and no further E than the concrete slip.

When approaching this anchorage the flood tends to set onto the shoals close N of the point. There are local moorings E of the jetty. These moorings have long ground chains running NW-SE. Inside the moorings there is a wreck which dries 1·3 m and lies ¾ cable NE of the old pier. Do not go inside the line of moorings when looking for a berth.

(3) Further N than the last anchorage and above the line of moorings with the prominent water tower in transit with the NE corner of Youghal quays bearing 260°.

(4) In NW winds, better shelter can be obtained further up the harbour. The main channel is on the E side of Red Bank but there are dangerous stakes near the old fish weir which runs out into the channel. These stakes are very hard to pick up.

There is a very remote anchorage off the mouth of the Tourig river just S of Youghal Bridge which is sheltered in strong winds from NW through N to NE. If making this anchorage use the W channel which is always usable with about 2 hours of the flood made. On leaving Youghal quays bring the convent Tr onto the Town Hall bearing 175°. Hold this course until the chimney of the port bow bears 293° or the old Mill on the starbound bow bears 065° then alter to steer 003° until the end of the causeway is in line with Rincrew Hse 290°. Then alter to port for the centre span of the bridge. Anchor on the W side of the river at the mouth of the Tourig River in 3m.

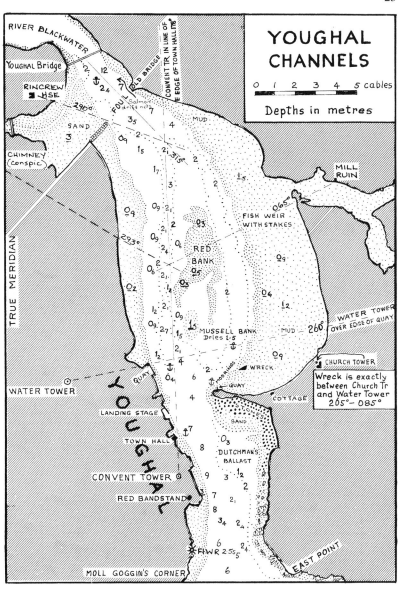

From this anchorage yachts capable of lowering their masts or motor cruisers can proceed up river for some 10 miles amongst fine scenery. By starting early on the flood with a dinghy powered by an outboard, and returning on the ebb the passage to Cappoquin 12 miles inland is possible from this anchorage. (Until the late 1950's three masted schooners made this passage to collect pit props). The river is not buoyed but by keeping towards the outside of bends depths of no less than 3m can be expected. Yachts should not go North of Villierstown Quay without local pilotage. The quay is recognised by being 1M North of the confluence of the River Bride coming in from the W and the only Quay on the left bank with a corresponding slip on the offside side of the river.

Bridge clearance
above HWOST 6 4 m. Depth in channel 14·6 m.
above LWOST 10 2 m. Depth in channel 10·7 m.

Facilities
All stores are available. PO, bank, bus to Cork and Waterford. Boat yard at Ferry Point has facilities to repair GRP and wood hulls, engines and electronics, also chandlery. Several good hotels and restaurants. EC Wed. There is a small piled landing stage projecting out into the stream by the quay by the main dock. (Just N of "Ferry" on chart 2071.) The stage has 2·3 m at LW and there is a water point on it. A boat may only use it for a short period with the boat manned. The harbour office is located in the Town Hall and can be contacted on VHF 16 and 6. The HM Bernard O'Keefe, phone 024-92820 will be able to give additional information as regards depths of water in the area. All repairs at Ferry Point Boat yard. Launderette in North Main Street. Showers at the Sea Angling Club. Youghal Sailing Club issue a very useful small brochure giving items of local interest, telephone numbers and the names and telephone numbers of a number of members who are willing to assist at any time. It is supported by advertisers who give much additional information.

Capel Island

is 37 m high and on its summit is the base of an unfinished lighthouse which is painted white and looks like a beacon. The island should be given a berth of 2 cables as there are reefs all around it. Capel Island Sound lies between the island and Knockadoon Head. A mid-channel course is safest as there are numerous outlying rocks on its N side which narrows the channel to about half its apparent width. Sound Rock with 2·4 m over it lies 4 cables NNW of the old lighthouse on th. Island.

The tide runs through the sound with considerable force which forms overfalls with wind against tide. There is little saving in distance and it is not recommended.

Ballycotton Bay

lies between Capel Island on the E and Ballycotton Island on the W, distance 6 miles. The N shore of the bay is foul with shoal patches of only 1·2 to 2·4 m, extending nearly ½ mile offshore.

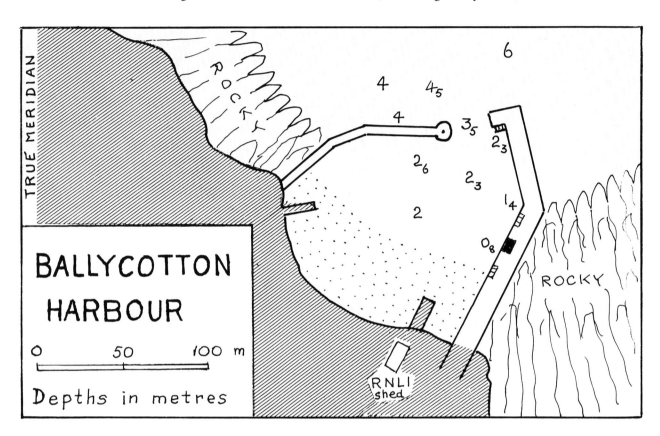

BALLYCOTTON HARBOUR

Depths in metres

BALLYCOTTON HARBOUR (see plan)

is artificial, formed by a pier and breakwater. It is not large and as there are numerous fishing boats moored in it there is no room to round up inside, so that yachts with no power should go in under very easy sail. Go alongside, if possible, rather than anchor as the harbour is a mass of mooring chains. There is a depth of 3 m at the entrance and not less than 1·5 m between that and the first row of fishing boats (or moorings). There is 1·8 m alongside at the first ladder.

Supplies

There are some good hotels and stores are available in shops in the village. PO, bus service to Cork. Water from tap on pier. (see photo)

Anchorage

As the islands afford excellent shelter there is a good anchorage in offshore winds in 6 m to NE of the breakwater without going into the harbour. The

harbour is subject to some sea with winds with N in them, and to considerable scend in strong SE winds. The RNLI lifeboat lies afloat in the harbour.

Tides

In the bay the streams are very weak, but in Ballycotton Sound and round the islands the streams are appreciable.

Ballycotton Island

The island is 50 m high and has a black lighthouse enclosed within white walls on its summit. It is steep-to all round.

Light

Fl WR 10 s, 59 m, 22-18 M. Horn (4) 90 s. W from 238° through N to 063°, R elsewhere except where obscured by land. The red sectors cover Capel Island and Power Head, but not Smiths Rock, see below.

Ballycotton Harbour and Island from W.

Ballycotton Sound

lies between Ballycotton Island and Small Island
(16 m) and has a rock called the Sound Rock, which
dries at LW and lies almost midway between the
two islands. Keep closer to Ballycotton Island when
going through the sound, and if coming from the W
do not haul up for Ballycotton Harbour until the
entire pier is opened clear of Small Island. The
latter island is foul all round and at LW the rocks
between it and the shore dry. After passing
Ballycotton Island there are some rocks to the W of
it which must be cleared before heading for Power
Head. This sound is not advised in SW winds.

The Smiths

are a dangerous group of rocks which lie about 1½
miles WSW of Ballycotton Island and are ½ mile
offshore. There are three distinct pinnacles, one of
which dries. They are marked by a R Can Lt Fl R
(3) 10 s moored SE of the shoal. Do not pass N of
Wheat Rocks, which dry 1 m and lie between the
Smiths and the shore to the NW. Capel Island open
S of Ballycotton Island clears all these dangers.

Tidal Streams

From Ballycotton to Cork Harbour the streams are
very slack inshore and off the Smiths are scarcely
perceptible.

Ballycroneen Bay

is on the E side of Power Head and has rocks 4½
cables offshore in places, so if beating along here do
not go too close inshore. Keep Ballycotton Island
open all the time until you come to Power Head.

Power Head

The disused, white fog-signal station on the head is
conspicuous as is a radio mast 1¼ M north of the
head which shows fixed red lights . Hawk Rock with
2·7 m over it lies about 2½ cables S of the head and
Quarry Rock, which dries 0·3 m lies 1½ cables
offshore ESE of the head. Pollock Rock has 7·5 m
over it and lies 1 ¼ miles ESE of the head; a R Can
Lt Buoy Fl R 6 s, Bell, is moored to the S of it.
Keep 3 cables offshore between Power Head and
Roche's Point.

Distances

Youghal to Ballycotton Harbour	11¾ miles
Youghal to Roche's Point	22 miles
Ballycotton to Roche's Point	11½ miles

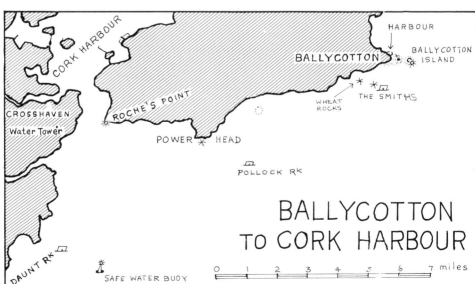

28

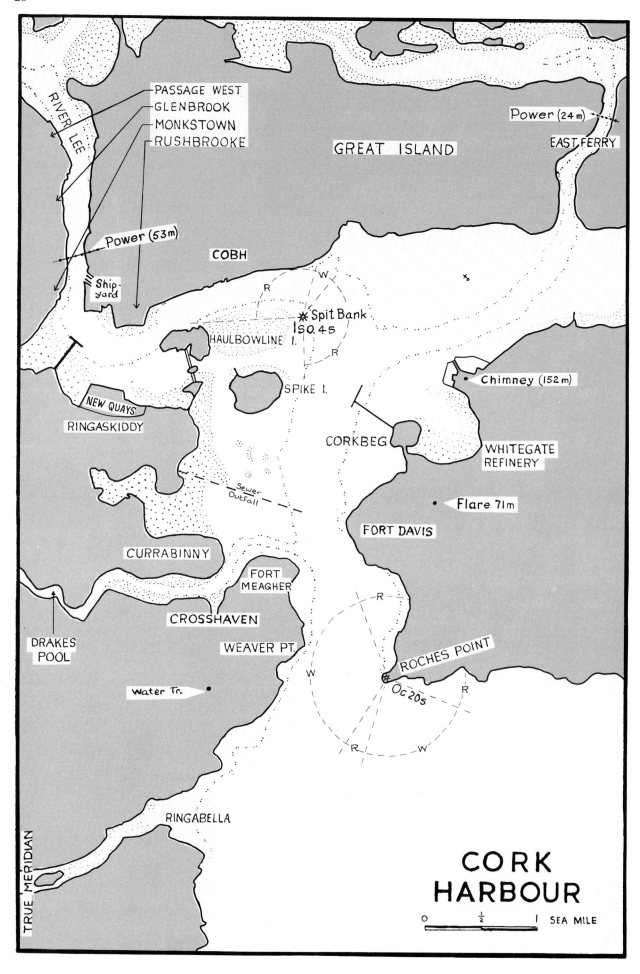

CORK
HARBOUR

0   ½   1   SEA MILE

CORK HARBOUR *(see plan)*

on the estuary of the River Lee is one of the finest, easiest approached and safest harbours in the world. The entrance between Roche's Point and Weaver's Point is ³/₄ mile wide. There are no dangers to worry a yachtsman in entering. Harbour Rock has 5·2 m over it and Turbot Bank, on which the tide often causes a disturbing looking ripple or sea, has a least depth of 5 m. The entrance narrows to a little over ¹/₂ mile between Fort Meagher (Camden Fort) and Fort Davis (Carlisle Fort). These forts are over 1 mile inside Roche's Point and beyond them the harbour opens out into a large expanse. The main channel lies in a N by E direction for a distance of over 2 miles, passing to the E of Curlane Bank, Spike Island and Spit Bank, after which it turns to the W, leads N of Spit Bank, past the town of Cobh and also to the N of Haulbowline Island. The channel swings around to the N again in Monkstown Bay, and is navigable for large ships right up to Cork City, a distance of 10 miles from Cobh. A second channel branches off to the E, opposite to Spike Island, and leads up to the E of Great Island. On the W side there are two separate channels; one, of great importance to yachtsmen, leads up to Crosshaven, and the other branch, known as the West or Back Channel goes to the W of Curland Bank and Spike Island, then turns W separates into two branches to pass either side of Rocky Island, and after passing S of Haulbowline Island, rejoins the main channel. This latter channel is narrow, has less than 1·1 m in places and is not recommended to strangers. At Rocky Island it is spanned by HT cables 21 m above HWS and by a low level bridge with a clearance of 7·1m above HWS which gives access to Haulbowline Island. In the area to the E and South of Roches Point there is an Army firing area. Red flags are shown and notices put in local papers and onshore when it is likely to be used. Great care is taken not to interfere with all shipping.

Landfall Mark

There is a 24 m high hammer-headed water tower about ³/₄ mile S of Crosshaven village and 1¹/₂ miles W of Roche's Point. It is not particularly conspicuous from close inshore but approaching the coast from the S it shows up very distinctly as the land is raised. A high chimney with red bars and red lights NE of Corkbeg in the harbour shows up through a limited arc.

Roche's Point

is fairly low and has a white lighthouse on it, also some old watch towers E of same. There are two rocks extending a cable S of it, called Cow and Calf. The Cow always shows but the Calf, which is the outer rock, dries 1·4 m. Close S of the Calf there is a wreck with 4 m on it. In strong S or SE gales the sea will break for a cable S of the Calf.

Weaver's Point

has high ground (50 m) behind it and on this and on the slope to the point there are a number of houses and bungalows. The point itself is clear, but drying rocks, 2 cables NNE of the point extend 1 cable offshore. To clear these rocks keep Cork Head open of Weaver Point, 198°.

Tidal Streams

In the entrance the flood makes -0540 Cobh (+0055 Dover) and the ebb at +0010 Cobh (-0540 Dover). Spring rate 1 to 1¹/₂ kn, but more over Harbour Rock and Turbot Bank. It increases to 2 kn between the forts.

Light. Fog Signal

From a white lighthouse on Roche's Point a light is shown, Oc WR 20 s, 30 m, 20-16 M. Dia (1) 30 s, R from land to 292°, W thence to 016°, R thence to 033°, W thence to 159°, R thence to land. This gives red sectors covering Pollack Rock, Daunt Rock and Dognose Bank.

Leading Lights

Two sets of leading lights are shown in the entrance, both being sited below Fort Davis on the E side of the entrance. While the two channels are applicable to large ships the leading lights are mentioned to avoid confusion.

    1. Oc R 5 s, 11 and 21 m high, 5 M in line bearing 034° lead NW of Harbour Rock.

    2. Oc 5 s, 29 and 37 m, 10 M, in line bearing 354° lead E of Harbour Rock.

Entrance — Buoyage

The buoyage follows the Lateral system except for the N side of Harbour Rock which is marked by a N Card Lt buoy, Q. Both ship channels are marked. However yachts may ignore the buoys in the entrance and stand boldly in between the forts. If the tide is ebbing some of the stream may be avoided by keeping to the W side but do not go too close in between Weaver Point and Fort Meagher and keep at least 1 cable off Rams Head below Fort Meagher.

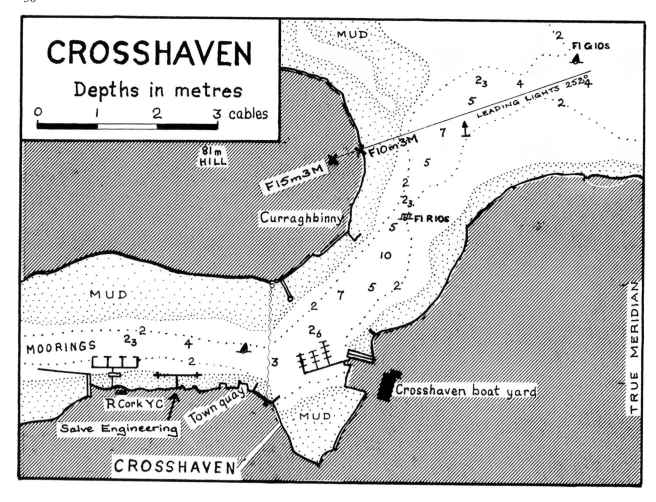

CROSSHAVEN
Depths in metres

CROSSHAVEN (see plan)

is on the Owenboy River with its entrance on the port hand after passing the forts. It is the best anchorage for yachts in the harbour and the Royal Cork Yacht Club has its station there.

From abreast Rams Head alter course for the G Cone buoy Fl G 10 s which marks the end of the spit separating the Back Channel from the Crosshaven Channel. At night, Roche's Point light on Rams Head will bring a yacht 1 cable E of the buoy. Leave the buoy to starboard and pick up the leading lights on Curraghbinny Hill F 15m 3M and F 10m 3M 252° which leaves a red perch to port and then steer for a R Can buoy Fl R 10 s to port. Do not go much W or NW of the buoy as the channel is very narrow at this point. The channel widens beyond this buoy but there is a lull under Currabinny Hill which makes beating in or out difficult. Make short tacks and do not go N of the face of Currabinny Pier (wooden, piled). Leave a G Cone buoy N of Crosshaven town pier to starboard.

The channel is now marked with lit buoys, however at night and in doubt a skipper can anchor in the mouth of the river and wait for daylight.

Note that submarine telephone cables cross the river from E of the town quay to W of the slipway on the N bank. They are marked by diamonds at each end. Note also that it is very shoal on the N side abreast of and above the ferry slip.

Anchorage and berthing

1. There are three marinas in the river. The Crosshaven Boat Yard marina (tel. 831161) is on the S shore opposite the yard. There is 2 m at most berths. It is marked by 2 vert FR lights at its E and W ends. Water and diesel are available. No showers or heads. Apply to Crosshaven Boat Yard for a berth. In strong W or NE winds this marina can be uncomfortable.

A new small marina is situated between the RCYC and the Town Quay operated by Salve Engineering Marine (Tel. 831145). 40 berths.

The Royal Cork Yacht Club (tel. 831023) marina is opposite the club on the S bank and consists of an E and W pontoon with fingers extending into the river. It is marked by FR lights at each end. There is 2 m at most berths and the visitors moorings are at the W end. In addition there is a second pontoon running upstream from the slipway to the W of the club. There is less water alongside parts of this pontoon. Diesel and water are available. Apply to RCYC for a berth.

2. Large yachts can anchor S of Curragnbinny Pier in 6 to 9 m but room is limited due to moorings. There is fishing boat and yacht traffic in this area so the channel from the town pier past Curragnbinny Pier must be kept clear. A riding light is essential. Land at the slipway or the marina.

3. Small yachts can sometimes find space to anchor above the RCYC but the area is very congested and there are many old chains on the bottom. It is usually possible to pick up a mooring by arrangement with the Club boatman or the Crosshaven Boat Yard.

4. In bad N or NW weather when anchorage near the club can be most uncomfortable, especially during the flood, good shelter can be obtained in the reach above the first bend or in Drake's Pool above this. Again there are many moorings. The small quay at the bend dries and is foul.

Facilities

Water at three marinas and at the town quay, tap by the WC. Diesel fuel at CBY&SE. Petrol by can. A yacht should not be left unattended at the town quay. All yacht repairs, boat lift, laying up and mooring hire at Crosshaven Boat Yard (Tel 831161). Repairs, Salve Engineering (Tel 831145). Sail making and repairs by MacWilliams Sails (Tel 831505). Customs clearance through Garda Station (Tel. 83122) near the Yacht Club. There are a number of shops, including butcher, PO, Kosangas,

Camping Gaz and chemist in the village. Frequent buses to Cork. Supermarket at Carrigaline, 4 miles, on bus route to Cork. Doctor (Tel. 831716). Car hire - Johnson and Peroth (Tel. 273295). Taxi (Tel. 373883 or 371741). There are no harbour dues, but marina charges average about £12 per night. Showers in RCYC, also food. Launderette in Crosshaven village.

Drake's Pool

There is a delightful sheltered anchorage about 1¼ miles upstream from Crosshaven with steep wooded banks on both shores. Two metres can be carried to the anchorage. Follow the line of moorings keeping closer to the N bank near the first bend and to the S bank near the next bend.

Communications

Most of the marinas and yacht clubs in this area monitor VHF 16 and M during normal working hours and weekends during the summer season. Cork Harbour is on permanent 24-hr. watch on 16, 12 and 14.

Crosshaven viewed from the West showing the three Marinas, with Roches Point and the entrance to Cork Harbour in the background.

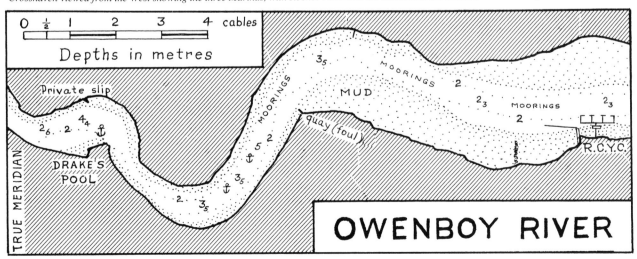

COBH

If bound for Cobh steer to pass E of the piled Spit Light, Iso WR 4 s, 10 m, 10-7 M; W sector over Bar Rock, R elsewhere. There is a "T Head" pier serving the refinery which extends 4 cables from Corkbeg on the starboard side of the main channel. It is marked by 2 FG Vert lights. **Caution**. It is prohibited to pass within $\frac{1}{2}$ cable of this refinery pier.

One mile E of the pierhead is a power station with a very prominent chimney. Some tide may be avoided by keeping just inside the line of Nos 8 and 10 R Can buoys and there is no need to go out to Nos 14 and 16 R Can buoys. A straight course from No 8 buoy to No 18 or Bar Rock buoy, R Can, will just clear the Spit Bank which projects a little 2 cables S of the Spit Light. After passing the lighthouse head for the spire of Cobh Cathedral for $\frac{1}{4}$ mile after which head for No 20 R Can buoy. The town of Cobh is situated on Great Island and fronts the water for a distance of 1 mile with deep water close in. The cathedral spire is conspicuous.

Danger

Note that there are both power and telephone cables from the NW end of Haulbowline Island to the shore.

Anchorage

West of the town near the deep-water quay, abreast the steps near the railway bridge, about $\frac{1}{2}$ cable offshore in 7 m. The tides are strong and there are eddies which make a kedge advisable. For a berth alongside apply at the Port Operations Stations which is always open and maintains a continuous watch on VHF Channels, 16,14 and 12.

Facilities

Garage, good shops, ship chandlery, hotels PO and bank. Rly to Cork. Water from Rly station. Customs clearance at Customs Office, Lynches Quay (tel. 811311).

RINGASKIDDY

(S shore opposite Black Point). Deepwater quay and car ferry terminal. No facilities.

CORK

Berths are available, if desired, but before starting up the river consult Port Operations Office, (tel. (021) 811380), Channels 12, 14, 16, for permission.

Unless instructed to do otherwise small craft should berth on the N. side of the N. arm of the River (Penrose Quay) and should not be left unattended.

Customs Office (tel. 831587) to rear of Cork Harbour Commissioners.

East Ferry Marina with The Marlogue Inn, Restaurant & Bar.

GLENBROOK

is the best anchorage in West Passage, the narrow reach of the River Lee W of Great Island; this is entered between the large shipbuilding yard at Rushbrooke on Great Island and Monkstown on the opposite W shore; Glenbrook is on the W shore ³/₄ mile above Monkstown; between them there are overhead power cables with ample clearance. Anchor in line with or very close outside the moored craft and clear of the main shipping channel. A riding light is essential. Note that there is one floating dock moored immediately S of the shipyard and a pier extending to deep water on the S bank E of the prominent chemical factory.

Facilities

Small shops. Buses to Cork.

East Ferry

The passage E of Great Island is most attractive with pleasantly wooded shores. NE of Fair Rock (perch) which dries 0·2 m there is an extensive shoal with 0·2 m in places. It is prohibited to go nearer to the oil refinery pier at Corkbeg Island than ¹/₂ cable.

Anchorage at East Ferry

1. Berth at the marina on the W shore. S Coast Cruisers Ltd. E Ferry Cobh, Co Cork (021) 811362. Water, diesel and electricity available. Very good pub and restaurant is now in the marina complex.

2. On the W side above the marina and clear of the moorings in 3 to 6 m.

3. On the E side near the pier in 3 to 4 m. Pub. Take care as this anchorage may be foul.

4. Just outside the N end of the passage in 4 to 5 m, outside the moorings. No facilities.

Tides

The general rate of the tidal stream in the main channels in the harbour is 2 kn, but off Harbour Rock, White Point and between Monkstown and Rushbrooke it increases to 3 kn. In the entrance and harbour the duration and rates are affected by the wind, S'ly winds increasing the flood, and N'ly winds the ebb.

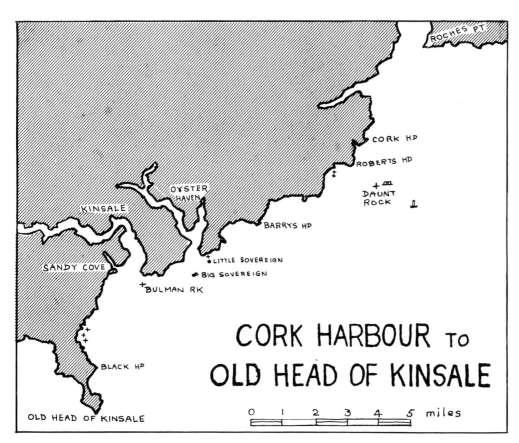

GENERAL DIRECTIONS

When leaving Cork Harbour and bound W there is no need to go out to Cork pillar buoy. Little Sovereign Island in one with Reanies Point 241°, leads NW of the Daunt Rock, 3·5 m. The tide is slacker inshore.

Tidal Streams

From the Old Head of Kinsale to Cork Harbour the E-going stream (NE) begins -0550 Cobh (+0045 Dover) rate 1 kn springs. The W-going stream (SW) begins +0050 Cobh (-0500 Dover) rate 1·2 kn springs. Off the Daunt Rock the rates are 0·7 kn, springs and 0·4 kn neaps.

Oysterhaven.

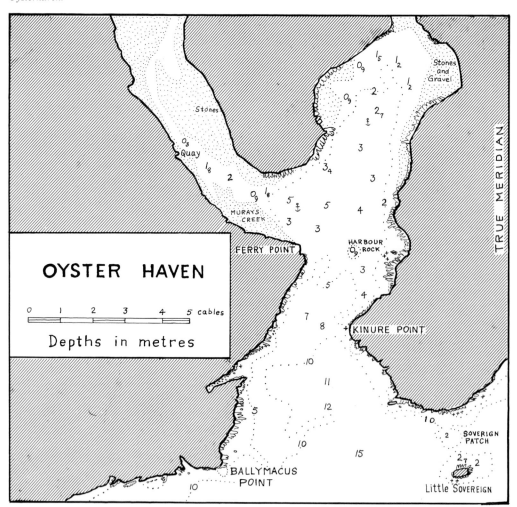

OYSTER HAVEN

0   1   2   3   4   5 cables

Depths in metres

Stones and Gravel

Stones

Quay

MURAYS CREEK

FERRY POINT

HARBOUR ROCK

KINURE POINT

TRUE MERIDIAN

BALLYMACUS POINT

SOVERIGN PATCH

Little SOVEREIGN

Daunt Rock

a pinnacle with 3·5 m over it and which frequently breaks in bad weather, lies 7 cables SE of Robert's Head. It is covered by a red sector of Roche's Point light. There is a R Can Lt buoy, Fl R (2) 6 s, moored 1 cable E of the rock.

Cork, safe water pillar buoy, RWVS, Spherical Topmark, Racon, Fl 5 s, is moored 1½ miles SE of the rock.

Cork Airport light

about 10 miles N of the entrance to Kinsale is sometimes visible at sea, Fl WG 7½ s.

WEAVER POINT TO ROBERT'S HEAD

Templebready Fort is just outside Cork Harbour on the W shore beyond Weaver Point, and extending from the shore for a distance of 1½ cables under this fort is Carrigabrochell (Carrig Rock, locally called The Dutchman) which dries 1·8 m.

Ringabella Bay is a sandy inlet ¾ mile wide and is shoal to the N of Ringabella Point (Lawn Point). It offers temporary anchorage in fine weather and offshore winds. Fish Point, off which there is a sunken wreck, at the S of the bay is low and should not be approached closer than 1½ cables. One mile to the S of Fish Point is Morris Head which, while clear itself, has 3 rocks, the Foal, the Mare and the Horse, 3 cables N of it but they are close inshore and show at LW.

Cork Head is clear and between it and Robert's Head, 1 mile beyond it, lies Robert's Cove, where small yachts could make a very short stay with offshore winds. There is 2 m at the entrance and a sandy bottom. Robert's Head is steep-to, 73 m high, and has an old telegraph on its summit.

Robert's Head to Oyster Haven

Reanies Point which is easily identified by the large gate posts on its summit, is the next headland, 1½ miles beyond Robert's Head, and between them is Carrigadda Bay (Rocky Bay). This bay is foul, Carrigadda, a reef which dries, stretching 3½ cables from the shore in the centre of the bay. Flat Head is only 6 cables beyond Reanies Point and the coast is clear between them. There is a 5·2 m patch 2 cables S of Flat Head. Reanie's (Jordan's) Bay lies between Flat Head and Barry's Head, 1½ miles away, and is also clear. Newfoundland Bay, which is free of danger, lies between Barry's Head and Blinknure Point E of the entrance to Oyster Haven. Big Sovereign consists two rocks 28 and 22 m high separated by a narrow cleft. There are some small outlying rocks but they are not dangerous as they all show. Little Sovereign, 16 m high, is clear all round and lies 2 cables offshore and there is a rock called Sovereign Patch with only 2·1 m on it between Little Sovereign and the shore. Ballymacus Point (58 m), NW of Big Sovereign and at the W of the entrance to Oysterhaven, should not be approached closer than ¾ cable.

OYSTER HAVEN (see plan)

is a good harbour but is subject to roll in S winds. Its NW arm is wooded and very attractive. The entrance to the harbour which is to the N of Big Sovereign Island is clear as far as Ferry Point on the W side, but opposite this point lies Harbour Rock with only 0·9 m over it. This rock is about halfway between Ferry Point and the opposite shore and must be passed on its W side.

Anchorages

1. In 2 to 5 m NNW of Ferry Point in soft mud and weed which can choke a CQR anchor. Keep Kinure Point on the E side of the entrance open of Ferry Point and anchor midway between N and S shores. Do not be tempted to go further up the NW creek as it shoals suddenly.

2. Up the N arm of the harbour and off the W hank and just below two cottages on the shore. Do not go any further up as the holding becomes poor with much weed.

Oyster Haven to Kinsale

Keep a cable clear of Ballymacus Point and do not go too close inshore between Ballymacus Point and Frower Point 1 mile SSW of it. There is no danger on the direct course. The Bulman Rock lies 2½ cables S of Preghane Point. It is a three-headed rock with a least depth of 0·9 m and with deep water all around it. It is marked by a S Card Lt buoy, Q (6) and L Fl 15 s, moored 1 cable SSW of the rock. There is a passage inside the rock. Keep the N end of the Big Sovereign in line with Frower Point, 091°, and if turning to windward give Preghane Point a berth of 1 cable and do not go S of the 081° line.

Kinsale Harbour.

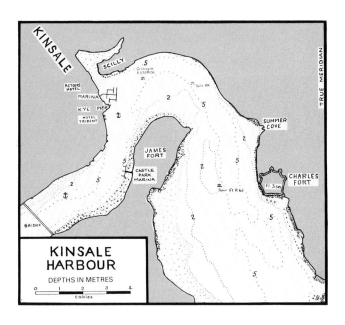

KINSALE HARBOUR *(see plan)*

This splendid harbour at the estuary of the River Bandon is easily entered by day or night. The entrance lies between Shronecan Point on the W and Preghane Point on the E. Shronecan Point has rocks extending off it for nearly ½ cable but there is plenty of water close up to these rocks. Farmer Rock is ¾ cable offshore, 3 cables NE of Shronecan Point, and dries 0·6 m. There are no dangers on a mid-channel course up the harbour and the bar below Charles Fort has a least depth of 3 m. If beating in or out note that Carrignarone, dries 1·5 m, lies 1 cable offshore at Middle Cove on the E side.

Do not go within ½ cable of the E shore between Middle Cove and Charles Fort ½ mile N of it, as there are a number of rocks there, and note that the W side of the harbour from Money Point, opposite to Middle Cove, up as far as Blockhouse Point, over ¾ mile N of it, is very shoal. There are three red can buoys marking the W side of the channel, which must be left to port. The first, the Spur buoy, Fl (2) 6s is opposite Charles Fort, the second, the Spit, QR is two cables N of Blockhouse Point, and the third Crohogue, Fl (3) R 10 s is 2 cables WNW of the second buoy.

Lights

A light is shown from a small white tower on the ruins of Charles Fort, Fl WRG 5 s, 18 m, 9-6-6 M. G 348° to 358°; W thence to 004°; R thence to 168°. The narrow, white sector leads clear into the entrance. The green sector is to starboard and the red sector covers the rest of the harbour. Note that this light is obscured E of the entrance and over the Bulman Rock.

Anchorage and berthing

1. The Kinsale Yacht Club has a marina to the N of the town quay. It is marked by 2 FG Vert at each extremity. Apply to yacht club or HM for a berth. HM - Eddie Hurley (021-772503) VHF 16/14.

2 . On the bank N of Blockhouse Point clear of the moorings in 2 to 3 m. The bottom is shell.

3. One cable offshore E or SE of the town quay, in 13 m. There is a strong tide in this position.

4. Further up the harbour in 4 to 10 m. Keep clear of the channel leading to the town quay and use a riding light at all these anchorages.

5. New marina at Castle Park.

Bridge

A bridge crosses the estuary above the town. Clearance is about 5 m at HW springs and 7 m at half tide and 8-7 m at low water.

Facilities

All supplies are available, banks, hotels, seventeen restaurants and good shops and pubs. There is a bus service to Cork and to the airport. There is a yacht yard up the river. Petrol and diesel from the Trident Hotel, just S of the quay, water and diesel available on the quay where the harbour master's office is situated. There is a good slipway at the quay and the Kinsale Yacht Club is across the road opposite the quay. Kinsale is an attractive old town with a good museum. There is also a Tourist Trail. The marina has water and electricity. Diesel at Gibbons quay. The YC (tel. 772196) has bar, showers and a welcome with meals on Wed. and Thurs. Doctor (tel. 772253). Police (tel. 772302). Repairs at Kilmacsimon Boat Yard (tel. 021-775134). Hull, engines and electrics. Robert Fry (tel. 021-772681) - engines only. Also Aquafix (tel. 023-40170). Car hire (tel. 021-273295) - delivery from Cork. Taxi (tel. 021-772642).

Kinsale Yacht Club and the HM Office monitor VHF Channel M when open. Charles Fort in the process of being restored is worth a visit.

Tides

The tide in the harbour runs in the direction of the channel. The flood begins -0600 Cobh (+0035 Dover) and the ebb at -0010 Cobh (-0600 Dover). Spring rate is 1½ kn off the town and Blockhouse Point, 1 kn elsewhere.

KINSALE HARBOUR TO THE OLD HEAD OF KINSALE

When leaving the harbour the entrance to the small inlet of **Sandycove** will he seen on the W side. There is good shelter in this cove except with SE winds. Enter midway between Shronecan Point and Sandy Cove Island and after 2 cables The Pill Creek opens up to starboard. Small Point is on the E side of the entrance to this creek, which dries out. Anchor in 2 to 4 m to SW of Small Point, however less water than is marked on the chart has been reported in the bay. The passage W of Sandy Cove Island is a mass of rocks and practically dries out at LW.

Bullen's Bay (see chart 2081), on the W shore about half way between Kinsale entrance and Old Head, is foul for 3 cables offshore, the principal dangers being Solomon's Rock which uncovers at LW, Carrignarone which always shows and Bull Rock which dries 0·9 m. These rocks form a group which is a little to the S of the centre of the bay. Black Head at the S end of Bullen's Bay has a small islet off it called Cush or Minane Island. There is a rock 1½ cable E of this islet. Holeopen Bay, with the subterranean passage through the head from which its name derives, is S of Black Head. The ruins of a De Courcey castle are on the narrow isthmus ¾ mile from the head. Bream Rock is close to the shore at the E side of the head and dries about 3 m.

OLD HEAD OF KINSALE

is a fine, bold projecting headland which is quite steep-to. **Light.** A light is shown from a black lighthouse with 2 white bands, 30 m high. Fl (2)10 s, 72 m, 25 M. **Fog signal:** Horn (3) 45 s. **Radio Beacon.** (Appendix 6).

Distances

Weaver Point to Old Head .. .. 15¾ miles
Weaver Point to Oyster Haven .. .. 11¼ miles
Weaver Point to Kinsale Harbour .. 14¾ miles
Oysterhaven to Kinsale Harbour .. .. 5 miles
Kinsale Harbour to Old Head .. .. .. 6½ miles

Tidal Streams. — Dangerous Race

Off the head the W-going stream makes +0120 Cobh(-0430Dover), and the E-going stream at -0520 Cobh (+0015 Dover). The spring rate is 2½ kn. The stream probably runs continually S on both sides of the head. These streams form a race which extends over 1 mile from the head, to the SW during the W-going stream and to the SE during the E-going stream. This race can be dangerous to small craft. The race can be avoided by rounding the head close up except in S winds and any strong winds when the broken water extends right up to the head. Under these conditions give the head a berth of over 2 miles.

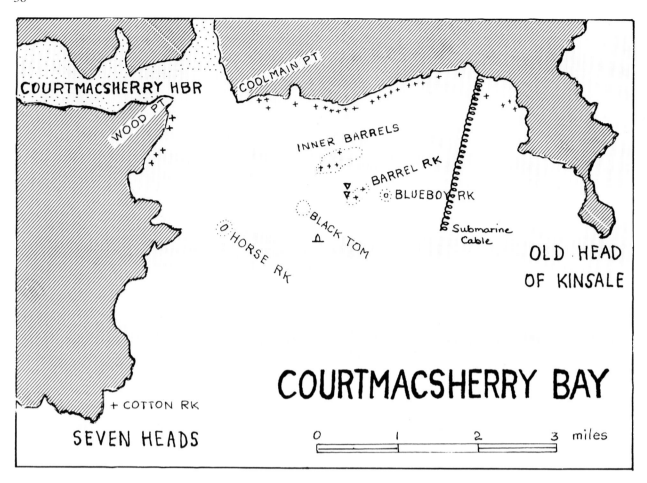

COURTMACSHERRY HBR

COOLMAIN PT

WOOD PT

INNER BARRELS

BARREL RK

BLUEBOY RK

Submarine Cable

OLD HEAD OF KINSALE

BLACK TOM

HORSE RK

COURTMACSHERRY BAY

COTTON RK

SEVEN HEADS

0   1   2   3 miles

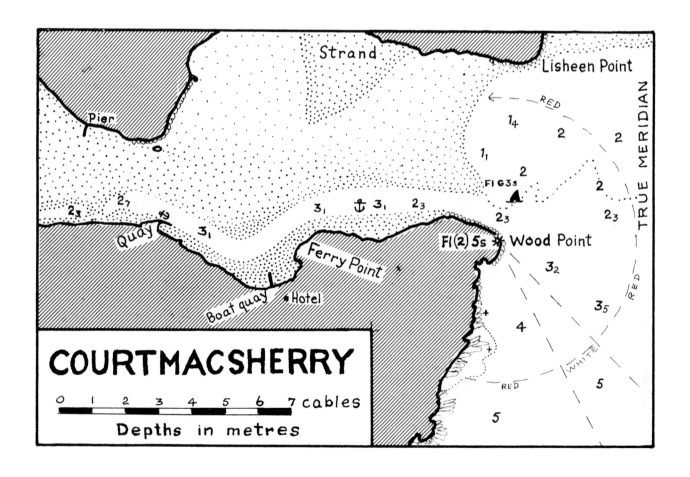

Strand

Lisheen Point

RED

Pier

TRUE MERIDIAN

1_4 2   2

1_1

FI G3s   2

2

2_3 2_7 3_1 3_1 2_3 2_3

Quay

3_1

Ferry Point

FI(2) 5s   Wood Point

Boat quay   Hotel

3_2

RED

WHITE

3_5

4

RED

5

5

COURTMACSHERRY

0 1 2 3 4 5 6 7 cables

Depths in metres

Chapter 2

OLD HEAD OF KINSALE
TO CAPE CLEAR ISLAND

Tidal Streams, Old Head to Seven Heads
The E-going stream makes at -0420 Cobh (+0215
Dover) and the W-going stream at +0205 Cobh (-
0345 Dover) . Springrate 1½ kn. There is little
stream in Courtmacsherry Bay. Spring rate off
Seven Heads reaches 2 kn.

COURTMACSHERRY BAY (chart 2081)
lies between these heads and the inner portion of
the bay has a number of dangerous rocks.
Courtmacsherry Harbour in the NW corner of the
bay with its bar and narrow channels between
sandbanks and strong tides has never been a
popular port for yachtsmen. It is, however a pretty
and friendly place. The bay itself can be a
dangerous place in strong onshore winds and in
poor visibility.

Dangers in the Bay
Barrel Rock, which dries 2·6 m, lies near the middle
of the bay, 1¼ miles from the N shore. It is marked
by an unlit S Card perch, the topmark was reported
missing in 1992. Black Tom buoy is now in position
51° - 36' 37N 08° - 37' 80W. There is a submarine
cable which runs S from Garretstown bay, i.e. the
bay which is 3M NNW of the Old Head of
Kinsale.There is a sunken rock 2 cables NE of the
perch. Blue Boy has only 0·2 m over it and lies 4
cables E of the Barrels perch. Black Tom with 2·3 m
over it lies 6 cables W of the perch; it breaks in bad
weather and has a green conical about 5 c SSE. Half
a mile N of the Barrels lies an extensive patch
called the Inner Barrels which dries 0·5 m in one
place. The N and E shore of the bay are foul in
places for over 3 cables from the shore. Horse

Rock, dries 3·6 m, lies 4½ cables off Barry Point on
the W shore. There are no dangers on the direct
course from the Old Head to Seven Heads.

COURTMACSHERRY HARBOUR (see plan)
This harbour is entered between Wood (Land)
Point on the W and Coolmain Point on the E and is
formed by the estuary of Argideen River and offers
good shelter. There is however, a bar at the
entrance between Wood and Coolmain Points
which has least water 2·3 m and which breaks in
strong to gale S or SE winds and entrance should
not be attempted in these conditions.

The plan has been amended to delete the
channel to the North shore which has filled in.
North of Ferry point is shoal for about a cable off
the old Lifeboat House. One should give a berth of
a cable to Ferry point all round it, well outside the
small boats moored to the west of it. The boat quay
is derelict and deep water well away from its end.
The deep water outside the trots of moored boats is
about 50 yards wide. During the summer many sea
angling boats leave about 0900 and return 1600 to
1800 and will happily act as a guide.

Light — Light buoy
A light Fl (2) WR 5 s, 15 m, 5 M is shown from a
white pillar on Wood Point. The W sector between
315° and 332° leads in between Black Tom and
Horse Rock with R sectors on either side. A Lt
buoy, G Cone, Fl G 3 s, is moored off the spit
extending from the N shore towards Wood Point.
Despite these lights a stranger would be advised not
to consider entering by night.

Courtmacsherry from E.

Approach from Old Head

A course should be set from Old Head to a position 1 cable S of Horse Rock which will clear S of all the inner dangers. The high ground between Barry's Point and Carrigrour Points will be seen ahead on this course. After 3½ miles the Barrel Rock perch will be seen ½ mile to the N and course can be altered for Lisheen Point, bearing 312° in the centre of the entrance. Barrel Rock is steep to on its W side. By night continue on the course towards Horse Rock until the white sector of Wood Point light is entered when keep in this sector until Wood Point can be rounded. Note that the Barrel perch is difficult to pick up against the land.

There is also a passage inside the Inner Barrels, which is not recommended to a stranger in bad weather. From close up to the Old Head steer 302° and keep on this course for about 3 miles until the extreme low point of Wood Point is in line with Coolmain Point. When these points are in line bearing 280° alter course to that line and this will lead N of the Inner Barrels, and clear of dangers off the N shore. Approaching Coolmain Point, give it a berth of 2 cables, and continue on course towards Wood Point until 2 cables off. If beating in or out it is safer to go outside the Barrels, but if working inshore do not go within ½ mile of the NE corner of the bay or within ¼ mile of the N shore.

Approach from Seven Heads

Steer for Horse Rock and pass half way between the rock and Barry's Point, the latter being foul for 1½ cables offshore. Note the position of Cotton Rock off Seven Heads and also the shoal water which extends 1 cable offshore 4 cables S of Wood Point. By night, make good a course to pass ¼ mile SE of Horse Rock until the white sector of Wood Point light is entered, then keep in that sector until Wood Point can be rounded. To enter in daylight between Horse Rock and Black Tom bring the summit of Burren Hill over Coosnalacka, by Wood Point, 313°, and approach on this line. This leading line can be difficult to pick up in which case keep over to Horse Rock to avoid Black Tom.

Entrance — Directions

Inner Bar. There is, in 1992, an inner bar with 2·8 m least water where the wood at Wood Point ends and gives way to open fields and a caravan park. This is just E of the anchor on charts 2092 and 2081. Leave Wood Point 2 cables to port and alter course gradually to round the shoal water NE of the point, leaving the buoy to starboard. Then keep ½ to ¾ cable offshore until Coolmain Point is just touching the wooded shore W of Wood Point when steer to pass ½ cable off the old Life Boat house, now a residence. Except for the inner bar there will be 1·8 m on this course. It is advisable to watch your echo sounder or use the lead continuously once

Wood Point comes abeam. A gravel spit runs out W and N of Ferry Point.

Anchorage 1 *(see plan)*

There is a reasonable anchorage NE of the Ferry Point in about 2·8m. There is weed on the bottom and a strong tide so it is important to check that the anchor is holding. If staying over a change of tide it is advisable to moor with bower and kedge anchors up and down stream, especially in fresh W winds.

Directions *(continued)*

A yacht can go right up to the pier, but it is advisable to do this on a rising tide on a first visit. The lead should be used continuously. Keep ½ cable N of Ferry Point and make for the main line of moorings. There are small boat moorings to the E but they are for shallow draft craft only and should not be approached closely. Turn to starboard and keep close N of the main line of moorings until the quay is reached. There is no room to anchor N of these moorings as the ground chains run NW-SE and the channel is very narrow.

Anchorage 2

The area N of the quay is kept free of moorings to allow room for visitors to anchor. The pool extends 100 m or so in length, varying somewhat with heavy fresh-water floods, big tides and W'ly gales. Moor with two anchors up and down stream. Strong tide.

There is a small wooden staging which projects out from the pier and has 1·8 to 2·4 m alongside. A yacht could lie alongside but it would be unwise to leave it untended. There is a sheltered dock E of the quay which has been dredged and just dries at neaps. There is a good but steep slip W of the quay. Sometimes a mooring may be available.

Tides

These are strong in the harbour, the flood making at -0600 Cobh (+0035 Dover) and the ebb at -0010 Cobh (-0600 Dover).

Facilities

Fresh water and diesel (pump) on the quay. Apply to the Sea Anglers who have a house (Tel. (023) 46427) on the quay to whom queries as to possible vacant moorings could be made. Phone box at approach to quay. Sea fishing tackle for sale or hire on quay. Shops, Butcher Tues/Sats, PO and hotel in village, also pubs with bar food. Bus. Taxis. RNLI lifeboat lies afloat. Pilot M. L. Hurley (Tel. (0232) 46218). Repairs see appendix 12.

Warning

This can be a dangerous bay in bad weather especially near LW.

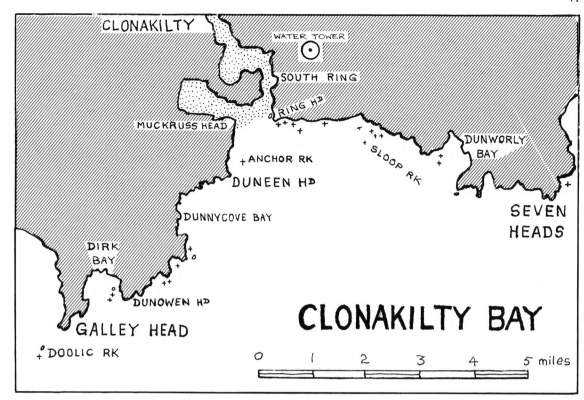

COURTMACSHERRY TO SEVEN HEADS

There is an anchorage shown on chart 2081 or 2092 in Broadstrand Bay which gives shelter in SW to NW winds. Avoid the local moorings. Anchor in the middle or the NW side of the bay as the SW side is foul with stones and thick weed. In Blindstand Bay in SW winds, anchor NE of mooring buoys. Generally in winds S through W to N these two bays offer better overnight shelter than Courtmacsherry. Holding is reasonable. Both of these are useful passage anchorages and were frequented by the sailing coasters and the Sherkin Island lobster boats which had no engines. The anchorage in Seven Heads Bay is more exposed and subject to roll.

There are two dangerous rocks close to the E side of Seven Heads. Cotton Rock which dries 3·6 m is 2 cables offshore and $^1/_2$ mile ENE of Leganagh Point; Carrigashoonta Rock which uncovers 3 m and is $^1/_2$ cable offshore and $2^1/_2$ cables ENE of Leganagh Point.

SEVEN HEADS

Leganagh Point, the most S of the Heads, is 40 m high, and has a tower on its summit. There are rocks extending $^1/_4$ cable off the point. There are not seven heads here, the name being shortened from Seven Castles Head. With wind against tide there can be a bad sea close in to the heads.

Distances

Old Head to Seven Heads	..	..	..	..	7 miles
Old Head to Courtmacsherry	..	..	..	7 miles
Courtmacsherry to Seven Heads	..	..	$5^1/_2$ miles
Seven Heads to Galley Head	..	..	$9^1/_4$ miles

Tidal Streams

At Galley Head and between it and Seven Heads the E-going stream makes at -0420 Cobh (+0215 Dover) and the W-going stream at +0205 Cobh (-0345 Dover). Spring rate is $1^1/_2$ kn, but reaches $2^1/_2$ kn off Galley Head and 2 kn off Seven Heads. There is little stream in Clonakilty Bay.

CLONAKILTY BAY

lies between Seven Heads and Galley Head and is very uninteresting from a yachtsman's point of view as it contains no good harbour. With a head wind and foul tide a yacht can stand well into the bay as it is free of dangers except for Sloop Rock, 3·2 m, 3 cables offshore near the middle of the bay and with drying rocks inside it and Anchor Rock with 2·3 m over it which lies $3^1/_2$ cables to the NE of Duneen Head on the W side. In addition Sheep Rock with 0·9 m over it lies 2 cables offshore, $^1/_2$ mile E of Ring Point.

SEVEN HEADS TO CLONAKILTY

After rounding Dunworly Point, on which there is the ruin of a castle, steer for Ring Head at the E side of the harbour entrance, distant 4 miles. After passing Dunworly Point and Dunworly Head (55 m) with Bird Island close to it, Dunworly Bay will open to starboard. This bay is exposed to the prevailing winds and is obstructed by rocks. Cow Rock, which uncovers 2·6 m lies in the middle of the bay and Horse Rock which is awash is $1^1/_4$ cables N of Cow Rock. If beating up Clonakilty Bay do not go within $^1/_4$ mile of the N shore to avoid the rocks mentioned above.

CLONAKILTY HARBOUR

is only suitable for small draught auxiliary yachts which can take the ground at LW, and as the sand shifts, the lead line should be kept going all the time when entering or leaving the harbour. The entrance is between Muckruss Head on the W and Ring Head on the E side. Inchydoney Island occupies the greater part of the harbour and there is only a very narrow channel which lies close to the E shore. Wind Rock lies just inside Ring Head and is marked by a green perch, and there is a bar at the entrance on which there is only 0·5 m in places at LW. Enter at ³/₄ flood and keep very close to Wind Rock, after which keep following the line of the E shore, keeping about ¹/₂ cable off all the way, as far as South Ring (this is ³/₄ mile from Ring Head), ³/₄ mile within the entrance. Moor alongside the quay at Ring and take the ground at low water. There is a good hotel on Inchydoney Island and stores can be obtained at Ring and Clonakilty. The depths in the harbour are varying, but in some places is only 0·5 m at LW. The tidal streams in the harbour are strong.

CLONAKILTY TO GALLEY HEAD

When leaving Clonakilty and making for the Galley, Anchor Rock, 3¹/₂ cables to NE of Duneen Head must be avoided. From Ring Head a course of 200° will lead clear E of the rock, and when abreast of Duneen Head alter course for Ringlea Point, distant 1³/₄ miles. Dunnycove Bay lies between these heads. Dunnycove, at the S side of the bay, would afford shelter in W winds Keameen Point, nearly ¹/₂ mile to WSW of Ringlea Point and Dunowen Head, or which there is the ruin of a castle, and lying over ³/₄ mile beyond Keameen Point, should not be approached closer than 1 cable. Dirk Bay lies just beyond Dunowen Head, and affords no shelter except for a short stay in very settled weather with light N or W winds, when one could anchor 1¹/₂ cables offshore on the W side in 4 to 6 m sandy bottom. On the E side of the bay, 2 cables off the shore is Carrigduff, a rock which dries at ¹/₂ ebb, and has foul ground 1 cable SW of it.

GALLEY HEAD

separates Glandore Bay from Clonakilty Bay and seen from a distance, particularly from the E the head looks like an island. It is 37 m high at its S end and slopes N to about 12 m where there is the ruin of Dundeady Castle. The head is fairly steep-to, and there are only the rocks you see, but about ¹/₂ mile SW by W of the head there is the very dangerous Doolic Rock, which is awash at HW. This rock is steep-to on its N side but 1¹/₂ cables to the SSW there is the Sunk Rock, with less than 0·4 m over it. Both the flood and ebb streams set across the Doolic and Sunk Rocks, so it is necessary to give them a wide berth. If passing inside the rocks keep closer to the head. With wind against tide there can be a bad and even dangerous sea close to the head.

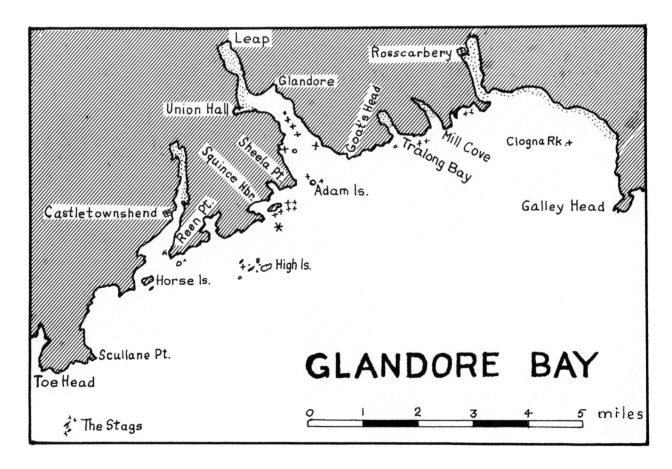

GLANDORE BAY

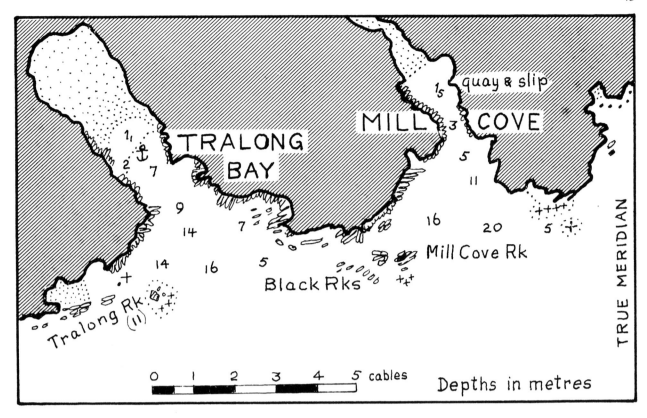

Light

A light is shown from a white lighthouse, 21 m high, on Galley Head, Fl (5) 20 s, 53 m, 28 M. The light is not visible inside the line of Seven Heads on the E side or inside the line of the Stag Rocks off Toe Head to the W. (Visible from 265° through N to 065°.)

Distances

Seven Heads to Galley Head .. .. .. 9¼ miles
Seven Heads to Ring Head .. .. 5½ miles
Ring Head to Galley Head .. .. 5¾ miles

Tidal Streams

Between Galley Head and Toe Head the E-going stream makes at -0420 Cobh (+0215 Dover) ,and the W-going at +0205 Cobh (-0345 Dover). Springrate 1½ kn. The stream runs 2½ kn off Galley Head with, probably, S-going eddies on both sides of the head from which the stream sets continuously on the Doolic Rock.

GLANDORE BAY (Chart 2092)

lies between Galley Head on the E and Toe Head on the W and has two good harbours, namely Glandore and Castle Haven, and also some coves that could be visited by small yachts under power.

GALLEY HEAD TO GLANDORE

Rounding Galley Head give it a berth of at least ¾ mile to clear the Doolic Rock. Alternatively pass inside the Doolic keeping closer to the head than the rock. In fresh winds keep well outside the Doolic. There are three inlets in the coast between the Galley and Glandore, namely, Ross Carbery, Mill Cove and Tralong Bay. Ross Carbery should not be attempted as it dries out to the line of the pier inside Downeen Point, and is only used by coasters that lie on the sand. Clogna Rock is well out of the usual track, but its position should be noted if beating out of the bay as it has only 0·9 m over it. It lies ½ mile off the centre of the long sandy beach at the E side of bay. There are rocks extending 1 cable S of Downeen Point and also off the point to the W of it at the entrance to Mill Cove. **Mill Cove** is very narrow but affords shelter for a small yacht to SW of the pier in offshore winds. Water is obtainable but no stores. Mill Cove Rock and Black Rocks, forming one cluster, are conspicuous and extend nearly 2 cables offshore to the W of Mill Cove. **Tralong Bay** would afford shelter in offshore winds. Keep midway between the E and W shores, but do not go too far in as the N side dries out. Anchor in 3 m in middle of harbour. Tralong Rock (14 m) at the W side of the entrance to Tralong Bay has rocks ½ cable SE of it and it is foul between Tralong Rock and the shore NW of it. The shore between Tralong and Goat's Head is foul for a distance of 1 cable nearly all the way.

44

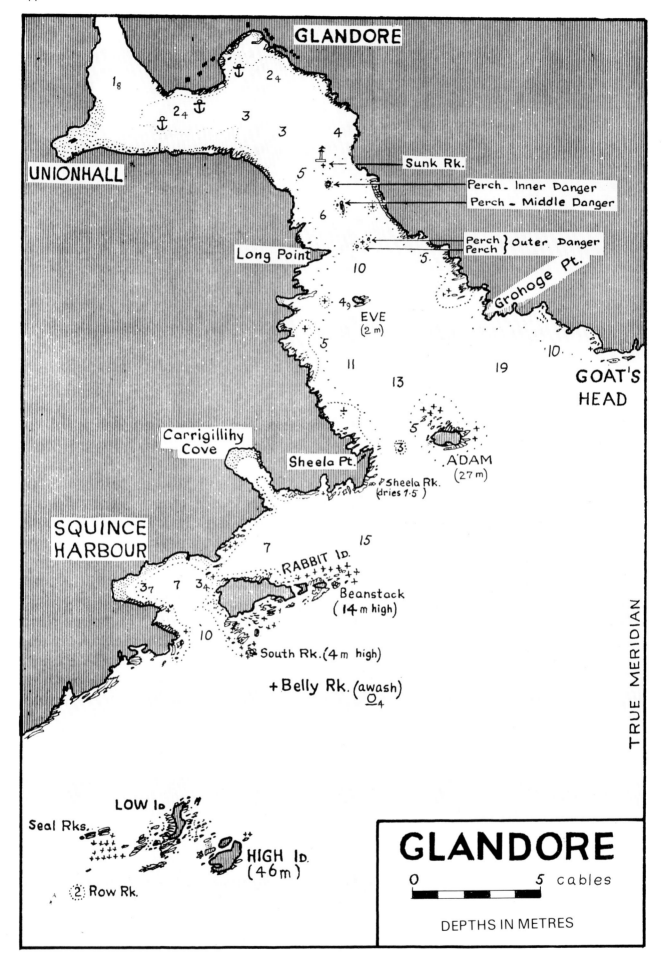

GLANDORE

UNIONHALL

Sunk Rk.

Perch - Inner Danger

Perch - Middle Danger

Perch } Outer Danger
Perch }

Long Point

Grohoge Pt.

EVE
(2 m)

GOAT'S
HEAD

Carrigillihy
Cove

Sheela Pt.

ADAM
(27 m)

Sheela Rk.
(dries 1·5)

SQUINCE
HARBOUR

RABBIT Id.

Beanstack
(14 m high)

South Rk.(4 m high)

+ Belly Rk. (awash)

TRUE MERIDIAN

LOW Id

Seal Rks.

HIGH Id.
(46m)

Row Rk.

GLANDORE

0   5 cables

DEPTHS IN METRES

Glandore Harbour with Adam and Eve clearly showing.

GLANDORE HARBOUR *(see plan)*

The entrance lies between Goat's Head (Foilnashark Head) on the E and Sheela Point on the W. Goat's Head is a bluff headland, 79 m high. Sheela Point is fairly steep-to, but has a rock called Sheela's Rock, which uncovers 1·5 m a cable SE of the point.

Adam's Island (27 m) which divides the entrance into two channels is foul for 1 cable off its N and E sides. There is a rock with 3 m over it at LW almost in the middle of the sound between Adam's Island and Sheela Point. Eve Island (7 m) over ½ mile N of Adam's Island, is bold on its W side. There is a rock 1¼ cables W of Eve Island, which does not show at LW, and another which dries 1·5 m 1½ cables to the SW of the first rock, but both of these are close to the W shore. The local saying is "Avoid Adam and hug Eve".

Just N of Grohoge Point, which is ½ mile inside Goat's Head on the E side, there is foul ground extending a cable offshore which shows at LW. The Dangers are three separate rocks in the middle of the channel which show at ¾ ebb and are marked by 4 perches. The Outer Danger is marked by 2 perches, one on its E side which is red and the other on its W side which is green; The Middle and Inner Dangers are marked by 1 perch each and these perches are green.

Enter the harbour between Adam's Island and Goat's Head or between Adam's Island and Sheela Point, and then head to pass 1 cable to the E of Eve Island. The best course after passing E of Eve is to pass midway between the W perch with green triangle topmark on the Outer Danger and Long Point and continue so as to pass midway between the Inner Danger perch with green cage topmark and the W shore. Sunk Rock, with 1·5 m over it at LW, lies nearly 1 cable N of the Inner Danger and is marked by an lit N Card Q buoy moored just to the N of the rock.

The Dangers may also be passed on the E side but when doing so do not go closer than 1 cable to the E shore as there is a rock ¾ cable offshore about midway between the Inner and Outer Dangers. There are also passages between the Dangers which may be used if beating in or out of the harbour, but note that the Middle Danger perch is on the N end of the rock, which is ¾ cable long. The E extremity of Eve Island in line with the W extremity of Adam's Island leads clear to the W of the Dangers. Having passed the Dangers keep on towards the bay opposite Glandore village, even if bound for Union Hall; a mud bank with at least depth of 0·9 m extends over 1 cable off the S entrance point of the W arm of the harbour so do not turn to enter this arm till half way across its mouth.

Anchorages

1. To the S and SW of the pier at Glandore but nearer to the W side of the bight in 2-3 m. The shelter is not good here in S to SE winds. Water at top of slip. Hotel with showers and meals. Stores in shop 1M up hill to E.

2. One cable NE of the Union Hall quay in 2·5 m, good holding ground. This is safer in S winds but rather exposed to blasts of NW wind funnelling down the estuary.

2A. 6 cables E of pier out of trawler traffic, in 3m, sheltered from S & SW.

Blind Harbour.

3. Close off the bluff on the N side gives the best all-round shelter but without convenient access to the shore, the nearby rough slip being on private property. A riding light would be advisable in these anchorages as there is fishing boat traffic in the early morning. Land to E of pier and walk ½ M to village with garage.

Tides

Tidal stream in all anchorages is slight.

Facilities

Water on piers at Glandore and Union Hall (Kilbeg). Shops with all supplies at both places, also gas at Union Hall. Good chandlery at Glandore. Doctor (023) 48255. Coastal Rescue; engine and electrical repairs see appendix 12. Hotel in Glandore with showers. Pubs with bar food in both places. Taxi at Union Hall. Bus at Leap 2M. Fuel can be arranged at Glandore if quantity is suitable for sending a road tanker. Yacht Club with H.Q. in Glandore Inn, proprietor Kiernan O'Donaghue, provides contact with all local facilities.

GLANDORE TO CASTLE HAVEN

Rabbit Island, 17 m high, which lies close to the shore ½ mile SW of Sheela Point and has a mass of rocks off it. At its E end lies **Stack of Beans**, 14 m high, which is conical in shape and must be given a berth of over 1 cable on its E side. There are numerous rocks extending to the S of Rabbit Island ending in South Rock which is 4 m high with deep water close up to its S side. 1½ cables further S lies the most dangerous **Belly Rock**, awash at LW and lying athwart the course to Castlehaven. If passing to the S of it keep Castlefreake open of Downeen Point -060°. Castlefreake is a large, grey and roofless mansion above Ross Carberry Bay. As this

line is not always easy to see a second clearance line is to keep the tower on Scullane Point (near Toe Head) open between Low Island and Seal Rock bearing 243°. To pass inside the rock sail close up to South Rock with the Big Stag just open N of Seal Rock bearing 230°. The safest way to clear Belly Rock in poor visibility is to keep Sheela Point open E of Stack of Beans, 008°, altering course to the W when High Island comes close aboard. When clear of Belly Rock steer for Skiddy Island at the entrance to Castle Haven.

Carrigillihy Cove

to the N of Rabbit Island is very narrow and exposed to S and E winds. There is 2·4 m half way up the cove and the inner part dries out. **Squince Harbour** lies to the W of Rabbit Island, but is a dangerous place in onshore winds. Keep midway in the centre of the entrance and anchor in 3·5 to 4 m, 1½ cables from the W shore inside.

High Island

is 46 m high, and with **Low Island**, 10 m high, and **Seal Rock** further to the W of the latter, may be regarded as one cluster which should not be approached too close as there are rocks off and between them. Note that Row Rock lies 2 cables SSW of Seal Rock and has only 2 m over it.

Blind Harbour

lies 1 mile W of Squince Harbour and like the latter is dangerous with onshore winds. Keep slightly to the W shore when making the narrow entrance and anchor in the middle of the harbour in 1·5 m. No stores available.

Mill Cove, Tralong Bay, Squince and Blind Harbours while unsuitable for overnight anchorage are all pleasant spots for a daytime visit.

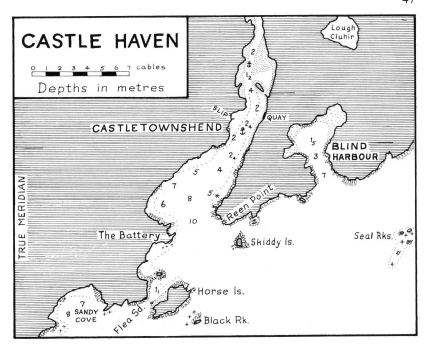

CASTLE HAVEN

0 1 2 3 4 5 6 7 cables

Depths in metres

GLANDORE TO TOE HEAD

On this course pass either inside or outside High Island. If going down inside follow the directions (above) for clearing Belly Rock and when past it steer to pass W of Seal Rock. There are no dangers W of the rock so when abreast of it head for Scullane Point distant 3 miles and giving this point a berth of 1 cable then steer for Toe Head, distant ³/₄ mile. To pass outside High Island steer to clear it by 1 cable, then alter course for Toe Head.

GALLEY HEAD TO CASTLE HAVEN

There is little saving in distance in passing inside High Island, so it is safer to pass outside. If passing inside High Island, do not go too close to the NE corner of Low Island, and keep clear of Belly Rock (see above), S of Rabbit Island. When passing S of High Island do not haul up immediately for Skiddy Island as Row Rock with only 2 m over it lies 2 cables SSW of Seal Rock. Keep outside the line joining the S sides of High Island and Horse Island at the entrance to Castlehaven; this will lead clear of Row Rock, but do not alter course until Seal Rock is well abaft the beam on this line. Battery Point and the S side of Skiddy Island in one, bearing 282° clears the rock.

CASTLE HAVEN *(chart 2129) (see plan)*

Light. A light is shown from a small white framework tower on Reen Point at the E side of the entrance. Fl WRG 10 s, 9 m, 5-3 M. G land to 338°, W thence to 001°, R thence to land. This gives a green sector over Skiddy Island and a red sector over Horse Island and Black Rock. The white sector leads in between. There are two islands outside the entrance. Skiddy, which is flat topped, and 9 m high, and lies 2 cables S of Reen Point. There are ledges and rocks off it for a distance of 1 cable all round. Horse Island with a tower on its E

side is close to the W shore, is 35 m high and nearly 4 cables in length. It is generally foul all round and Black Rock (21 m) is 1³/₄ cables SE of it and is steep-to on its S side. There is a boat passage inside Horse Island called Flea Sound, but it is very narrow and obstructed by rocks.

Enter Castle Haven between Reen Point and Battery Point. Inside these points the harbour opens out but later narrows again and then trends away to the NE. Keep the Stags (S of Toe Head) and Flea Island, N of Horse Island, in line dead astern bearing 208° to lead clear up the harbour. The N shore is beautifully wooded. Note the position of Colonel Rock, which has 0·5 m over it, and lies about ¹/₂ cable off the E shore about 2 cables N of Reen Point.

Anchorage

In mid-channel SE of the slip in 2·5 to 3 m, good holding and good shelter. In strong S wind there is better shelter above Cat Island (NE of the village) where there is 3 to 4 m in mid-stream, but the available space here is mostly occupied by moored fishing boats. Further upstream again (where an anchor is marked on the plan) there is adequate room if a yacht is moored with a kedge; the wooded shores here are very attractive and a dinghy trip to the head of the navigation is well worth while. Both quays at the village dry at LWS but the slip at the N one can be used by dinghies at all tides. The pier at Reen on the E side of the harbour has 0·4 m at LAT at its outer end; it is used by local fishing boats. **Caution.** A heavy telephone cable has been laid across the harbour from the village slip to the slip just N of Reen Pier; avoid anchoring near this line. **Tides.** The stream is slight off the quay but stronger above Cat Island, though a yacht will be tide rode at times.

Castlehaven.

Castletownshend is a quiet village climbing the western shore of Castlehaven.

Facilities

Castletownshend is a most attractive and unspoiled village. There are a few shops, PO and 2 restaurants, also good pub, - 'Fergus' is the contact for local facilities. Restaurant at Rineen 2M. Water from tap on village slip, also on Reen Pier.No diesel.

CASTLE HAVEN TO TOE HEAD

Scullane Bay between Horse Island and Scullane Point has some sunken rocks in places 1 cable offshore. Scullane Point has a small islet off it which is steep-to but there is a ledge called Red Rock extending for 1 cable offshore 2 cables SW of this islet.

Toe Head

is a barren headland 25 m high with an old tower on its E side. There is foul ground extending nearly 1/2 cable from the head.

The Stags

are a cluster of rugged rocks 20 m high, lying 3/4 mile S of Toe Head. Viewed from a distance, either from E or W they present the appearance of a ship under full sail. The four rocks which form the group are called Big Stag, Little Stag, White Mare and Strologue. The sound between them and the mainland, over 6 cables wide, is free of danger. The wreck of the "Kowloon Bridge" lies off these rocks and is marked by a South Cardinal Buoy Q(6) + L Fl 15 s. There is a 1,000 metre exclusion zone around the wreck.

Tidal Streams

Between Toe Head and the Stags the E-going stream makes at -0435 Cobh (+0200Dover) and the W-going stream at +0150 Cobh (-0400Dover). The stream runs 2 kn at springs off Toe Head and the Stags and there is usually a confused sea in Stag Sound, especially in W winds.

Distances

Galley Head to Toe Head	10 3/4 miles
Galley Head to Glandore—Union Hall ..	7 miles
Galley Head to Castlehaven	9 1/2 miles
Glandore—Union Hall to Toe Head	8 miles
Glandore—Union Hall to Castlehaven ..	6 miles
Castlehaven to Toe Head	3 3/4 miles

TOE HEAD TO BALTIMORE

There is foul ground extending 2 1/2 cables from the shore just W of Toe Head ending in the Belly Rocks which show. There are two bays W of Toe Head, namely, Toe Head Bay and Tragumna Bay, but both of them are completely exposed to the prevailing winds and their shores are foul in places.

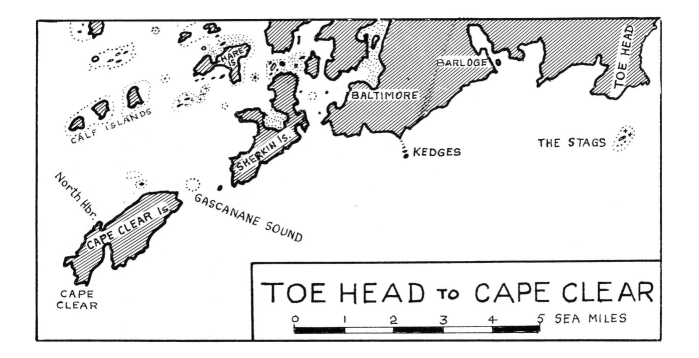

Barlogue Creek with the Rapids leading to Lough Hyne.

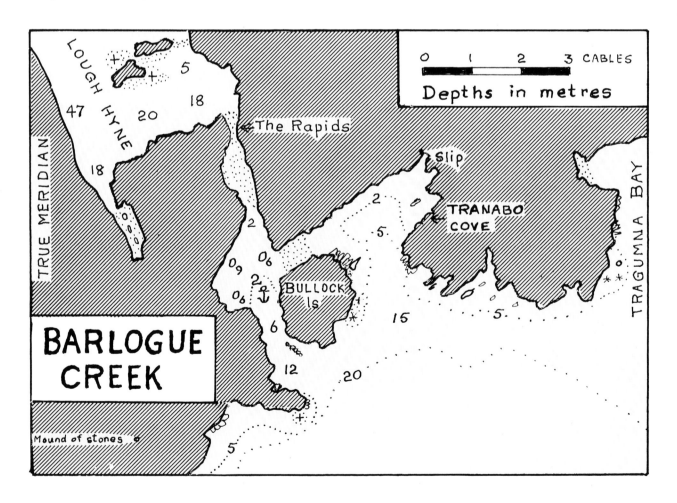

Barlogue anchorage during an ICC cruise in company, very seldom as crowded as this!

BARLOGE HARBOUR (*see plan*)

has a very narrow entrance so is not recommended to a sailing yacht without any engine owing to the difficulty of beating in or out. The entrance, which is very hard to distinguish until you are close in, lies between Bullock Island on the E and Carrigathorna (Lalawn Point) on the W. The Stags just closed by Gokane Point bearing 122° leads to the entrance. Do not be tempted to make for the wider entrance to Tranabo Cove which lies E of Bullock Island, as this little cove is very exposed. Enter midway between Carrigathorna and Bullock Island, but then keep closer to the W shore as there are some rocks S of the island. Follow a mid-channel course W of the island, but do not go in too far as it shoals pretty quickly once you have opened up the NW face of the island.

Anchorage

W of Bullock Island in 3 to 4 m in good shelter except in S or SE winds. No stores are available.

Lough Hyne

This lovely lake is connected with Barloge by a narrow channel which becomes a scour at half-tide. The ingoing stream makes at -0320 Cobh (+0315 Dover) and the outgoing at +0245 Cobh (-0305 Dover). A visit to the lough by dinghy is strongly recommended as the scenery is very beautiful. If using an outboard wait till 3/4 flood and beware of seaweed.

BARLOGE TO BALTIMORE

There are two rocks just S of Carrigathorna, so give it a berth of at least 1 cable before making for the Kedges, distant 2³/4 miles. The coast here is quite steep-to and free of dangers.

Kedge Island

is 34 m high and rocky and there are detached rocks extending from it towards the shore. There is a narrow passage between the inner rock, called Carrigatrough, and Spain Point on the mainland, which is 7·3 m deep. Do not attempt this passage without a fair wind and tide without auxiliary power as it is very narrow. Do not attempt if the sea is high. Spain Point is high. Telegraph Tower (ruin) on a hill behind it is 125 m high. It is conspicuous and is 1¹/4 miles from Baltimore Harbour. There are rocks, a wreck and a tide race off the SW end of Kedge Island so keep 2 cables S and SW of it. The coast W of Kedge Island is steep-to and the only danger on the course to Baltimore is Whale Rock, which uncovers 1·8 m and is ¹/2 cable offshore and ¹/2 mile E of the entrance. Lot's Wife Beacon in line with the SW face of Black Point, 318°, leads outside Whale Rock.

52

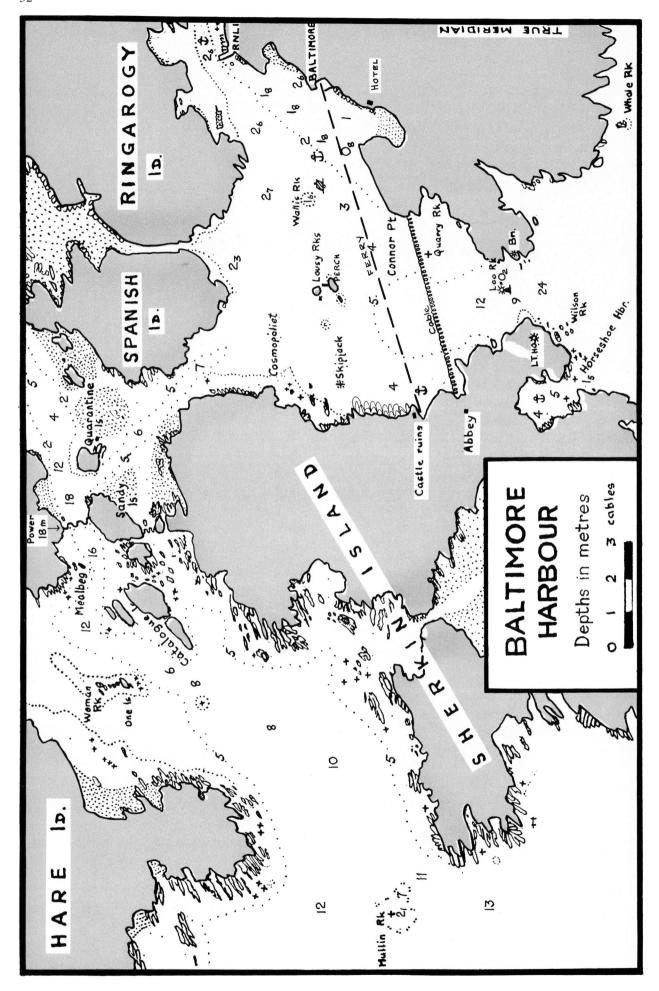

BALTIMORE HARBOUR

Depths in metres

0   1   2   3 cables

BALTIMORE HARBOUR (see plan)

a fishing port and yachting centre, is 1 mile across each way, mostly between 2 and 6 m deep, subject to swell but safe. Its S entrance is straightforward and can safely be used in any weather. The metric editions of charts 3725 and 2129 are based on a recent survey. New edition of chart no. 3725 issued 8.11.91

Light

A white lighthouse 9 m high on Barrack Point shows a light Fl (2) WR 6 s, 40 m, 6-3 M. Red from 168° through S to 294°, white thence to 038°, obsc elsewhere (unreliable). This is white to seaward and red over Kedge Island and in the harbour.

Beacon

A conspicuous, pointed white beacon 8 m high, known as Lot's Wife, stands 50 m high on Beacon Point, the E side of the entrance. **Buoy.** Loo G Cone buoy, Fl 3 s, marks the rock of that name on the side of the entrance.

Entrance

On the starboard hand there is a drying rock 65 m off Beacon Point and further in, ¹/₂ cable offshore is Loo Rock (dries 0·2 m), marked by its buoy. Barrack Point with its lighthouse on the port hand is foul for ³/₄ cable on its E side and S of it rocks extend ³/₄ cable to the SE ending in Wilson Rock awash at HW. Quarry Rock, about 2 cables NNE from Loo Buoy and 1¹/₄ cables from the shore has 2 1 m over it. A ferry crosses from Baltimore to Abbey Strand on Sherkin Island every hour in summer and every two hours in winter.

Directions

Approach the entrance with Loo buoy bearing about N and leave it fairly close to starboard. If beating in do not approach either side of the entrance nearer than ¹/₂ cable, unless with chart 3725 in the hand. If entering with a big sea do not pass more than 65 m W of Loo buoy. To avoid Quarry Rock steer N (or towards Lousy Rocks perch) till Baltimore quays come in sight.

The positions of a number of other rocks in the harbour must be noted if beating in or out or using the N entrance. Lousy Rocks lie near the middle of the harbour and dry 0·6 to 2·4 m. They are marked by a S Card perch, 12 m high, and extend ¹/₂ cable N and WSW of the perch. Ransome Rock lies over 1 cable WNW of Lousy Rock perch and has 2·3 m over it. Skipjack Rock, dries 0·9 m, Great Globe Rock, 0·6 m high, with ledges off it and Globe Rock, 2 m high, and Cosmopoliet Rock, dries 0·6 m, lie close together off the W shore of the harbour to the W of Lousy Rocks. Wallis Rock with 1·6 m over it and about midway between Lousy Rocks and the pier at Baltimore is marked by a R Can buoy on its

E side. The N entrance is described at the end of this chapter.

Anchorages

1. N or W of the N pier of the harbour, quite close if desired, in 1·8 m. A ferry plies frequently from the harbour to the slip near the Abbey ruin on Sherkin Island and also to North Harbour Cape Clear so keep well clear of the line from harbour to Sherkin slip. A riding light is advisable if anchored W of the harbour.

2. The safest place in strong NW winds is in Church Strand Bay beyond the RNLI slip in 1·5 to 3 m. There are a number of moorings in this area and a clear channel must be left to the N of these. Do not anchor between the two buoys off the RNLI slip. A yacht will be tide rode in this anchorage. The water shoals E of the moorings but it is possible to anchor just to the E of them and a yacht drawing up to 1·6 m will only touch at low tides on a mud bottom. Good holding and very secure anchorage with little tidal stream.

3. In W winds there is a good anchorage off the slip near the ruined Abbey on Sherkin Island.

4. A yacht of 1·5 m draught will lie afloat alongside the inner side of the S pier of the harbour. The motor boats to Sherkin and Cape Clear berth alongside the steps just inside the pierhead so keep just clear of these. Do not approach the outside of the S pier off which there is a rock.

5. In fine weather it is possible to berth outside the harbour at the NW side of the N pier towards its outer end. This is the most convenient berth for water as the hose and tap are close by. Note that rocks project from the head of the N pier. The inside of the N pier is used by fishing boats and yachts should keep clear of it.

Facilities

Water on N. pier. P.O. Shops with meat and dairy produce. One hotel with showers, many restaurants and pubs. Yacht chandlery, diesel, petrol and gas. Repairs to hulls, engines and electrics see appendix 11. Harbour Master - Chris Collins (028) 20123 Ch. 16 & 6. Glenans Sailing School in old railway station at N end of village. Baltimore S.C. (Ch. 16) on the quay is active in July and August and has showers. Ferries to Sherkin and Cape Clear Islands (see above). RNLI Lifeboat (028) 20143. Visitors mooring and boat keeper, Vincent O'Driscoll (028) 20125. Taxi, J. Nolan (028) 20397. Bus to Skibbereen.

Tides

In Baltimore Harbour the streams run in and out through both the N and S entrances, the meeting and separating place of these streams being near the Lousy Rocks. The flood stream runs E and SE

Approach to Baltimore Harbour.

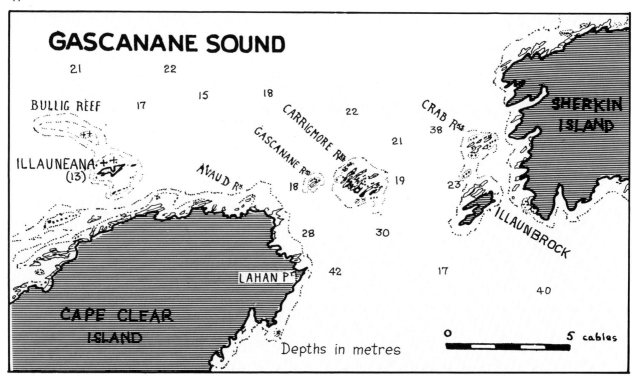

GASCANANE SOUND

21   22

BULLIG REEF   17   15   18

CARRIGMORE R^s 22

CRAB R^{ks} 38

SHERKIN ISLAND

GASCANANE R^{ks} 21

ILLAUNEANA (13)

AVAUD R^s 18   19   23

ILLAUNBROCK

28   30

LAHAN P^t 42   17   40

CAPE CLEAR ISLAND

Depths in metres

0   5 cables

on the N side of Sherkin Island and N on its E side commencing at +0545 Cobh (-0005 Dover). The ebb stream runs W and S in the same respective places, commencing at -0025 Cobh (+0610 Dover). Through both entrances to Baltimore the streams move inwards towards, or outwards from the Ilen River.

BALTIMORE TO GASCANANE SOUND
Sherkin Island is 2½ miles long and is 98 m high at its SW end. The S shore is steep and the few rocks there always show and are close inshore.

HORSESHOE HARBOUR
is on the SE shore of Sherkin Island, just outside the entrance to Baltimore, and has a very narrow entrance (¼ cable) but as the name implies opens out inside. There are rocks at the E side of entrance, which extend 75 m off the shore. Keep close to the SW point of the entrance, but then swing across to the other side, as there is a rock just inside the entrance, close to the inner SW point. Anchor in middle of harbour in 4 to 5 m. The anchorage inside in Baltimore Harbour, close to the Sherkin shore, is preferable to Horseshoe Harbour.

GASCANANE SOUND

lies between Cape Clear Island and Sherkin Island. It is divided into two main channels by Carrigmore and Gascanane Rocks. Carrigmore Rocks are 6 m high and lie almost in the middle of the sound. Gascanane Rock uncovers 1·8 m, lies more than 1 cable W of Carrigmore Rocks and is a danger as both streams set on to it. The E channel is wider and safer and Illaunbrock (Badger Island), off Sherkin, is quite steep-to on its S and W sides, but has a ledge of rocks called Crab rocks 2 cables N of it. A mid-channel course should be steered as tides are very strong, running up to 3 kn at springs.

The W channel is much narrower and the position of Avaud Rocks, which extend for ³/₄ cable off the NE corner of Cape Clear Island must be noted. There is a channel between Illaunbrock and Sherkin Island which should not be attempted by a stranger as although quite deep it is obstructed by rocks on the Sherkin side. If coming from the E and having passed through the sound bound for Crookhaven do not head for that port until clear of the Bullig Reef N of Cape Clear Island. Directions for clearing the Bullig are given under "North Shore of Cape Clear" below. A strong S or SE wind creates a nasty sea in the sound, especially when the tide is flooding. This sea can be dangerous and the sound should not be attempted in strong to gale force winds.

Tidal Streams

In the Gascanane Sound the streams run with considerable strength at springs, reaching a maximum rate of 3 kn and causing dangerous eddies especially near the rocks in the centre. The SE-going stream makes at +0520 Cobh (-0030 Dover) and the NW-going stream at -0055 Cobh (+0540 Dover).

CAPE CLEAR ISLAND

(NB not Clear Island as on metric chart) is nearly 3 miles long and 1 mile broad. The three headlands on the SW side are known as Bill of Cape Clear, Cape Clear and Blananarragaun (Bream Point) respectively, the latter 32 m high, being the most S point, and all are steep-to and free of danger. The old lighthouse (ruin), standing at a height of 133 m near the centre of the SE side of the island, is conspicuous. The Lure Rocks (Carricklure on metric chart) lie ¹/₂ cable offshore just under the old lighthouse.

SOUTH HARBOUR

lies just to the E of Blananarragaun. The entrance is wide, but the harbour narrows inside. There is nearly always a roll of a sea there and a considerable draw, so it is not safe for anchoring except for small yachts in settled N winds. The anchorage is in the centre of the harbour in 4 to 6

m. The holding is good - it would need to be as it is entirely exposed to S winds. Pointanbullig on the E side of the entrance, has rocks ¹/₂ cable off it.

Tidal Streams

These have not been observed near Cape Clear, but it is probable that they run E and W between Cape Clear and the Fastnet Rock. The E-going stream probably makes at -0420 Cobh (+0215 Dover) and the W-going stream at +0150 Cobh (-0400 Dover) . Spring rate 2 to 2¹/₂ kn . Off Blananarragaun the streams are confused . It is thought that the E-going stream divides at the Bill of Cape Clear setting NE along the N shore of the island and S to Blananarragaun, forming a large eddy E of Blananarragaun. The W-going stream forms an eddy W of Blananarragaun Point. The result of this is usually a heavy and confused sea between the Bill of Cape Clear and Blananarragaun off which a race on both streams are formed. With strong tides and often a big W swell and light airs a yacht without auxiliary power should keep well clear.

Distances

Toe Head to Cape Clear	11¹/₄ miles
Toe Head to Gascanane Sound	8¹/₂ miles
Toe Head to Baltimore	6¹/₂ miles
Toe Head to Barloge	2¹/₄ miles
Barloge to Baltimore	4³/₄ miles

NORTH SHORE OF CAPE CLEAR

Bullig Reef, which extends 3 cables NW of Illauneanna (Bird Island) is a danger as it is on the course from Gascanane Sound to Crookhaven. There are two rocks in the reef which are awash at LW. The grey chapel on Sherkin Island kept in line with the conspicuous Telegraph Tower SE of Baltimore 082°, leads clear N of the reef. Illaueana is 2 cables off the N shore and has foul ground all round it and between it and the shore, and to the SW of it is a reef called Lacklahard, and to SW of this again is another reef called Carrigierah. Generally all this part of the shore is foul, so be sure to keep more than 3 cables N of Illauneana and do not attempt to go S of that island. Keep the pub in North Harbour in sight to clear the Ballig Rocks to W when making to the N.

NORTH HARBOUR (see plan)

is a small inlet on the N shore of Cape Clear which should be approached with caution as the harbour is very small and the entrance narrow. By keeping the grotto on the S head of N harbour on the line of the outer pier, this leads clear of the rocky plateau just N of the outer pier head. If approaching North Harbour from the W, note that Tonelurga Rock lies 1 cable offshore near the ruins of Doonanore Castle ³/₄ mile from the Bill of Cape Clear, and that Illaunnagart Rock extends ³/₄ cable offshore, just to

North Harbour Cape Clear.

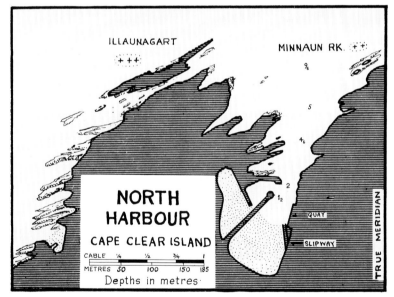

Based on the Ordnance Survey by permission of the Government (Permit No. 2191)

the W of the harbour entrance. The E side of the entrance is rocky and must not be approached too close until inside the cove when it becomes the safer side.

The harbour inside the pier is shallow and a yacht should not go much beyond the end of the pier. In bad weather, especially from the NW, a heavy swell sets into the harbour; it is possible to avoid this by going into the inner basin which dries out. Balks of wood may be placed across the entrance to this to break the swell. The Post Boat calls from Baltimore and a tourist boat from Skull.

These berth at the steps on the SE side of the pier which must be kept clear when they are expected which, in summer, is frequently. Lie alongside beyond the steps where a yacht of 1·5 m draft will take the ground for an hour or so each side of LW at or near spring tides. It is possible to anchor just below the slip and quay on the E shore. There is no room to swing and a yacht should moor with anchors fore and aft and a warp to the slip, allowing room for the Post Boat and fishing boats to come alongside and to turn around. A limited amount of stores are available. Water.

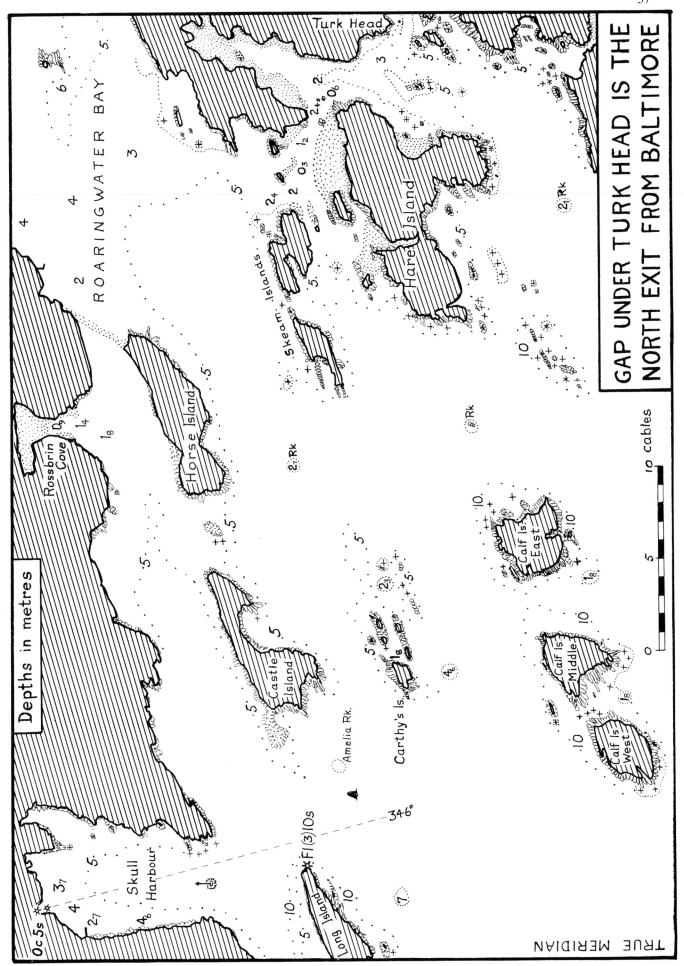

GAP UNDER TURK HEAD IS THE
NORTH EXIT FROM BALTIMORE

Turk Head

ROARINGWATER BAY

Skeam Islands

Hare Island

Rossbrin Cove

Horse Island

Depths in metres

Castle Island

Amelia Rk.

Carthy's Is.

Calf Is. East

Calf Is. Middle

Calf Is. West

Skull Harbour

Long Island

Fl(3)10s

346°

Oc5s

10 cables

TRUE MERIDIAN

NORTH ENTRANCE TO BALTIMORE

There is a passage N of Sherkin Island which is very intricate and not recommended for yachts without engines. **Caution.** It is spanned, N of Sandy Island, by HT cables 18 m above HWS. The first part of the passage lies between Hare Island and Sherkin Island. If making for the channel after coming from Long Island Bay note that Toorane Rocks, which cover at HW, extend for ³/₄ mile to the SW of Hare Island so keep well S of them. Steer for Drowlaun (Truhane) Point on the NW part of Sherkin Island and keep close up to it so as to avoid the Mullin Rock which has only 2·1 m on it and often breaks. It lies 2¹/₂ cables NNW of Drowlaun Point. Doonanore (Dunamore) Castle on the W side of

Cape Clear Island open SE of Illauneana (Bird Island) off the N shore of Cape Clear Island bearing 230° astern leads clear between the Mullin Rock and Drowlaun Point. From close up to Drowlaun Point steer 041° for the Catalogue Islands, which are ¹/₄ mile long and are N of Sherkin Island and are distant 1 mile from Drowlaun Point. There is a rock with 1 m over it lying 1³/₄ cables W of the SW tip of the largest Catalogue Island, and the channel lies between this rock and the Catalogue Islands. The rock is avoided by keeping Mt. Lahan (77 m) on the E end of Cape Clear Island, just overlapping Drowlaun Point and bearing 212° astern. This line only just clears E of the rock so go nothing to the W of the line.

Hare Island in Roaring Water Bay. The best anchorage is at the NE corner immediately SE of the little pier.

The famous Fastnet Light on a calm day!

When up to the SW end of Catalogue Islands alter course so as to pass midway between Catalogue Islands and Two Women's Rock. The latter islet and rock are together 1 cable long and are 3 cables off Hare Island shore. The next part of the channel lies between Catalogue Islands and the mainland N of them. When hauling round to the N of Catalogue Islands do not go too close to their NW corner as there is a sunken rock ½ cable off it. There is a rock called Mealbeg ½ cable off the point of the mainland, N of Catalogue Islands. Mealbeg is a two-headed rock, the inner head showing at half-tide and the outer at LW. To avoid it keep close to the line joining the N points of the Catalogue Islands and Sandy Island. In summer there may be a small buoy moored directly over Mealbeg. After passing Mealbeg steer midway between Sandy Island (20 m) and shore N of it, giving NE corner of Sandy Island a berth of over ½ cable; it is necessary to keep to midchannel passing under the HT cable, thus passing beneath its lowest point, because there is a rock which covers at HW on the N side. Having passed the NE corner of Sandy Island (as above) alter course to pass midway between Sandy Island and Quarantine Island E of it, and continue on a midchannel course between Spanish Island to port and Sherkin Island to starboard until Baltimore Harbour is opened. Keep to the N of Wallis Rock buoy when making for the anchorage off the pier. If making for the anchorage on the Sherkin side note the positions of various rocks on the W side of Baltimore Harbour previously mentioned.

An alternative approach is to pass N of Mullin Rock by keeping the Catalogue Islands just open S of the S point of Hare Island. Thence give Hare Island a good berth and leave Woman Rock to starboard; or pass between S Woman Rock and the 1 m rock to S of it. In good visibility the Fastnet just open of Cape Clear Island 227° leads N of both the Mullin and the 1 m rock, but this transit must be closed when passing the reefs at the SE end of Hare Island.

Anchorage

There is reasonable anchorage in 1·5 to 2·5 m in good shelter N of Woman Rock and between Hare Island and the mainland. No supplies, but pleasant sandy beaches. Restaurant (028) 38192.

Passage between Hare Island and Frolic Point

After passing Mealbeg keep close to the E side in 1 to 2 m; at half tide only one of the Corrignamoe group of rocks, which are N of the NE point of Hare Island, will be showing. When Frolic Point is bearing W alter course to leave it 50 m to starboard and steer for the N side of Grogh Island. It will be seen that the N shore of Illaunagrogh (Grogh Island) and the SW corner of E Skeam Island are just open with a small sandy beach on W Skeam Island showing between them and bearing 270°. There is a drying outlier about 20 m S of Frolic Point otherwise that side is clean.

After passing Frolic Point make between Goose Island and E Sheam, avoiding the drying spit SE of Goose Island. The centre of Goose Island touching the NE point of Hare Island clears the rocks off the NE point of E Sheam Island. There is good anchorage off the beach on E Sheam Island. The Passage S of E Sheam Island, between it and Illaunagrogh, is clear but there are many half-tide rocks S of Illaunagrogh.

Ilen River

It is possible with a rising tide and the use of the lead to go a long way up this river, which is of course accessible to a tall-masted yacht via Baltimore Harbour. If weather-bound in Baltimore this makes a pleasant day sail and there are sheltered reaches in which to anchor according to wind direction.

FASTNET ROCK

is an isolated rock, 28 m high, which lies 3¾ miles WSW of Cape Clear and 9 miles SE of Mizen Head. There is a rock with 3·4 m over it ¾ mile to the NE of the Fastnet. With the exception of this latter rock the channel between Cape Clear and the Fastnet is free of dangers.

Light — Fog Signal

A light Fl 5 s, 49 m, 28 M, is shown from a grey granite tower on the rock. Horn (4) 60 s. Automatic.

Traffic Lanes

If approaching from seaward note that W by S going traffic runs from 2 to 4 miles S of the Fastnet and E by N going traffic 6 to 8 miles off it. The lanes should be crossed as near to right angles as possible. The inshore zone extends 2 miles S of the rock.

Tidal Streams

See also above for streams off Cape Clear. Within 1 mile N and S of the rock the streams run SSE and NNW, the E-going stream making at 0405 Cobh (+0230 Dover) and the W-going stream at +0200 Cobh (-0350 Dover). Spring rate 2·2 kn. With W winds the E-going stream runs 7 hrs and increases speed by ½ kn, and the converse with E winds. There can be a tide race with the E-going stream extending for 1 mile SE of the rock.

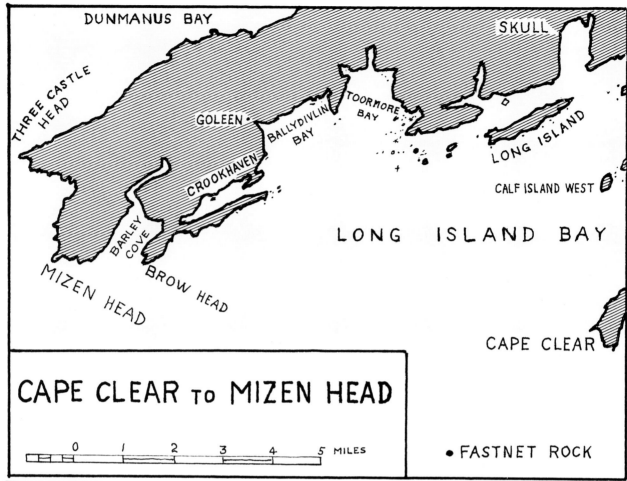

DUNMANUS BAY

SKULL

THREE CASTLE HEAD

GOLEEN

BALLYDIVLIN BAY

TOORMORE BAY

LONG ISLAND

CALF ISLAND WEST

CROOKHAVEN

LONG ISLAND BAY

BARLEY COVE

MIZEN HEAD

BROW HEAD

CAPE CLEAR

CAPE CLEAR TO MIZEN HEAD

0   1   2   3   4   5 MILES

• FASTNET ROCK

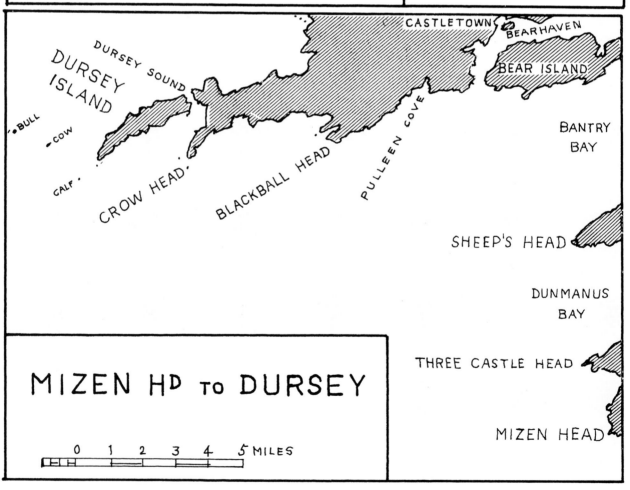

CASTLETOWN

BEARHAVEN

DURSEY SOUND

DURSEY ISLAND

BEAR ISLAND

• BULL

— COW

BANTRY BAY

CALF •

CROW HEAD

BLACKBALL HEAD

PULLEEN COVE

SHEEP'S HEAD

DUNMANUS BAY

MIZEN HD TO DURSEY

THREE CASTLE HEAD

MIZEN HEAD

0   1   2   3   4   5 MILES

Chapter 3

LONG ISLAND BAY TO
DURSEY ISLAND

LONG ISLAND BAY

General
Long Island Bay lies between Cape Clear and the Mizen Head. It extends NE as Roaring Water Bay. The area offers innumerable anchorages and fascinating pilotage. Sailing N from Gascanane Sound three islands will be seen ahead, the West, Middle and East Calf Islands, while to starboard will be seen the entrance to the Ilen River, already described and bounded on the N by Hare Island. Beyond Hare Island are the West and East Skeam Islands and the expanse of Roaring Water Bay. North and NW of the Calf Islands are the reefs of Carthy Island, then Horse Castle and Long Islands, with Long Island Sound and Castle Island Sound and Skull Harbour inside them. Further to the W are Goat and Turf Islands, Crookhaven and the Mizen.

Long Island Bay, East Side
Making N from Gascanane Sound course can be set W of West Calf Island or between the East and Middle Calf Islands. The only danger on the course W of West Calf Island is the Bullig Reef described on p ??. Directions for courses to the Mizen or Crookhaven from Gascanane Sound are given below. If making for Calf Sound after coming through the E channel of Gascanane Sound steer 305° for the highest point of Middle Calf (11 m) . There is a sunken rock with 1·8 m on it 1½ cables SW of the SW point of East Calf Island. The N shore of Hare Island just open S of the S shore of East Calf Island, 052°, clears this rock to the SE. Long Island Point, White Tower closed in behind the NE point of Middle Calf Island, 320°, clears it to the W. Amelia buoy G Cone, touching the same point 323°, gives better clearance but the buoy is not easy to pick out at this distance against the land.

On no account attempt the passage between West and Middle Calf as it is all obstructed by rocks. Middle Calf has a sounding of 2·7 m ¾ cable off its NE corner, and there is a rock which uncovers at LW 1 cable S of this island. East Calf is foul for 1 cable on its N and S side and for 1½ cables on its E side but its W side is clear except for the isolated rock already mentioned.

Keep midway up the sound and when clear head for Amelia buoy, 313°, distant nearly 1¼ miles. The buoy and Long Island Point will be almost in line on this course which passes to the W of the Carthy Islands, a dangerous group with foul ground extending ¾ mile to the ENE and ESE of them. The Carthys should not be approached closer than 1 cable on their W side. Amelia Rock, 4 cables WSW of Castle Island has 2·1 m over it and is marked by a G Cone buoy which must be left on the starboard hand. Castle Island has foul ground extending nearly 3 cables W of it, known as the Castle Island Grounds. Long Island Point, the E end of Long Island, is low and marked by a white round tower, Q(3) 10 s, 16 m, 8 M. There is a reef off the point so give it a berth of over 1 cable.

GASCANANE SOUND TO MIZEN AND CROOKHAVEN
As already mentioned the Bullig Reef, 3 cables NW of Illauneana (Bird Island) N of Cape Clear, is a danger on these courses. From the W channel of Gascanane Sound steer 295° for the W end of West Calf Island. From the E channel steer 290° for the same point - in each case until the Bill of Cape Clear bears 218° - and then alter course to 265° for Brow Head, distant 10½ miles or if bound to Crookhaven to 276° for its entrance, distant 8 miles. There are no dangers on these courses across the bay.

ROARING WATER BAY
It is also possible to pass E of East Calf Island. Bring the conspicuous Barnacleve Gap just E of Mount Gabriel, 404 m high and N of Skull, open W of two roofless grey cottages with a small clump of trees on the E point of Castle Island, bearing 335°. This will lead W of Toorane and Anima Rocks, but only just clears Toorane Rocks, so borrow nothing to the E of the line abreast Toorane Rocks. If bad visibility prevents this line being seen steer for East Calf Island and come to a cable off its SE point before rounding it. Note that Mount Gabriel has two conspicuous white radar domes on its summit.

Toorane Rocks

The main bulk of these rocks is usually marked by breakers but the most W heads only show at extreme LW. It is most important to be quite certain of a yacht's position before rounding these rocks and under no circumstances cut corners.

Anima Rock

which shows at LW but frequently does not break or show when just covered is a very dangerous rock. It may be passed on its S side by keeping the S shores of Middle and West Calf Islands just open S of East Calf Island, 250°. It may be passed to the N by keeping the N side of Middle Calf Island just open N of East Calf Island, 245°.

To clear it to the W keep Cape Clear Chapel, the largest building in the centre of Cape Clear Island, in one with the W point of Illauneana, 190°. Illauneana is hard to distinguish against the mass of Cape Clear Island. It is a long, low rock slightly darker in tone than its background; its N side, low slate cliffs, show fairly clearly; its W point is a low cliff with a rounded top.

To pass E of it take safe bearings on Trawbawn Rock which always shows.

There is a deep channel N and NW of Toorane and Greymare Rocks but this is not recommended without local knowledge.

Rowmore Rocks, N of West Skeam Island and which rarely show are dangerous. They have less than 2 m on them. If turning to windward past them, Telegraph Tower, 125m and SE of Baltimore, in one with the E point of West Skeam Island, bearing 116° leads E of Rowmore Rocks. Reenabulliga (Curra Point) at the E of Gascanane Sound open W of West Skeam Island bearing 160° leads W of Rowmore Rocks. There are no good clearing marks to pass safely N or S of them. To pass N of them keep half way between Horse Island and West Skeam Island and to pass S of them keep ½ cable off West Skeam Island.

Ballydehob and Poulgorm (Skegamore) Bays both offer good shelter in W winds. Truchare (Trickery) Rocks at the entrance to the latter always show. P.O., Bank (occas), Restaurants.

Leamcon (Lemon) Tower, 107 m and 1½ miles N of Goat Island, in one with Long Island Point beacon bearing 281° leads between the rocks W of Castle Island and Amelia Rock, but leads very close to the rocks SW of the SW point of Castle Island.

There are a number of anchorages in Long Island Channel and Castle Island Channel but most of them have weed on the bottom and a yacht should be given a good pluck astern after anchoring to make sure that the anchor has gripped.

The channel between Castle and Horse Islands is straightforward. Bring a ruined chimney near the disused copper mine to the NE of Rossbrin Cove in line with the small point NW of the 1·2 m sounding and the "R" of Rossbrin Cove on chart 2129, bearing 041°. This line will lead SE of Castle Island Spit. Rossbrin Castle, ruined, in line with the same chimney, bearing 047° will pass NW of the same spit. If passing between Horse Island and the mainland known as Horse ridge, keep to the N. There is a large amount of weed near the surface. Chart 2129.

If passing between the Carthy Islands and East Calf Island the position of a number of rocks must be noted. Foal Rock uncovers 2 m, and Sharragh's Rock, dries 2·8 m, to the E of it which usually shows. A rock 1 cable N of Sharragh's Rock uncovers at LW. There is a rock with 2·1 m on it half way between Foal Rock and East Calf Island. Rincolisky Castle (ruins) touching the S side of West Skeam Island, 057°, leads between the 2·1 m rock and East Calf Island. It is possible to pass N of Foal and Sharragh's Rocks. Keep Carthy's Islands (South) close aboard and alter course to the NE as soon as the island and the spit to the E of it has been passed.

Rossbrin

This cove is a safe place to leave a yacht but is fully occupied by moorings. To find if a mooring is available phone A. Stott, Ballydehob 61.

Anchorage, Carthy Islands

There is a delightful, daytime, anchorage inside the Carthy's Island group. Approach through the narrow channel SE of Carthy Island which carries 3 m or else by the channel between N and S Carthy Islands, which carries 1·2 m. If using this entrance keep the N face of S Carthy Island open to avoid the rocks mentioned above. This anchorage is subject to some swell if there is a sea running in the bay. It is also exposed to NW winds when the rocks NE of Carthy's Island cover as the tide rises.

Tidal Streams

In the entrance to Long Island Channel, between the Alderman Rocks and the Fastnet, the streams set E and W, the E-going stream making at -0455 Cobh (+0140 Dover) and the W-going at +0115 Cobh (-0435 Dover). Spring rate is 2½ kn decreasing in strength towards the head of the bay. The E-going stream sets SE and S through the channels between the outer islands. The W-going stream runs in opposite directions.

The small rock girt anchorage under Black Castle.

The peaceful anchorage of Rossbin.

Southern approach past Long Island to Schull Harbour.

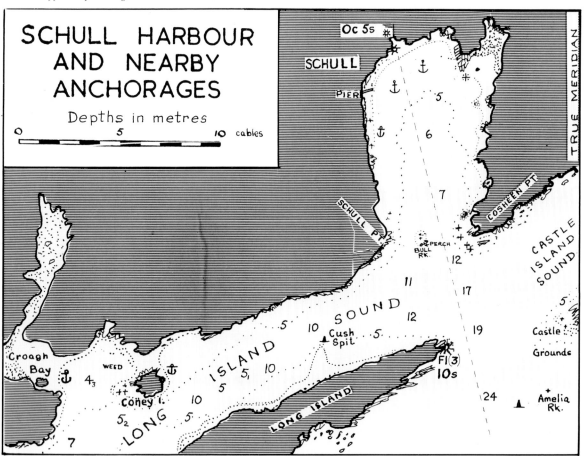

SKULL HARBOUR (see plan)

is a good-sized harbour affording splendid shelter except in strong S or SE winds. The entrance lies between Skull Point on the W and Coosheen Point on the E. There is a rock called Bull which covers at half-tide, and is marked by a red iron perch, and lies almost in the centre of the entrance; its E, S and W sides are steep-to however, and it can be left on either hand, but it is foul 3/4 cable N of the perch. Baker Rock which is awash at LW lies about 1/2 cable off the W shore, 1 1/2 cables to N of Skull Point. The rest of the W shore is clear, but the E shore should not be approached closer than 1 cable. The village of Skull lies in the NW corner of the harbour.

Lights

A light is shown from the E Card beacon on Long Island Point (Copper Point), Q (3)10 s, 16 m, 8 M. Leading lights are shown from, white, lattice steel masts NE of Skull pier. In line 346° they lead E of Bull Rock and W of Amelia Rock. Both show Oc 5 s. Front 5 m, rear 8 m, 11 M.

Anchorage

One cable SE of the extended pier in 2 to 4 m, good holding ground. A riding light is essential. S of the pier and close in to the W shore of the bay in depth to suit draft. There is 1·5 m alongside the seaward end of the pier at LAT. The head of the pier is usually used by fishing boats when they come in in the evening. The S side of the pier is used by a motor boat which takes passengers to Clear Island. It is usually possible to lie alongside a fishing boat on the N side of the pier. Be sure you are clear of the main fairway to the pier.

Supplies

There are hotels and good shops with butcher and dairy produce. PO, bank. Bus connections. Water from a tap on the pier. Ice and fish sometimes from the cold store by the pier. Showers at hotel, see HM for diesel. Excellent bookshop.Fuel and gas. 2 restaurants. Golf clubs.

Schull Harbour.

SKULL TO MIZEN HEAD (outside Long Island).
Long Island is over 2 miles long, ¹/₂ mile wide and low. There is a safe passage inside the island which is dealt with in the next paragraph. After rounding the point at the E end of the island, the course for Mizen Head will lead close to the S shore of the island so the position of some rocks off it must be noted. The Garraun Rocks form a ledge just W of the point but are close to the shore. Over ¹/₂ mile to the W of the E point lie the Carrigeenwaun Rocks which are always visible and extend 1 cable offshore. Generally give the S shore of the island a berth of over 1 cable. At the W end of Long Island is Goat Island Sound, then Goat Island and Little Goat Island with a white beacon on it, height 23 m. W of this is Man-of-War Sound and then Illaunricmonia (Turf Island). After passing Long Island and if bound for Crookhaven there is a dangerous rock called Bulligmore which must be avoided. This rock has only 0·9 m on it and lies ¹/₂ mile WSW of Illaunricmonia and is almost S of Castle Point. Unless there is some swell coming in it does not show as the tide rises. Keep Carrigduff (Duff Islet) open of Little Goat Island, 250°-70°, and this will lead S of Bulligmore; Carrigduff is close up to the SW end of Long Island. Do not haul up for Crookhaven entrance until Duharrig Rock (5 m) is abeam.

Skull to Crookhaven (inside Long Island)
This is a shorter course and a nice sail down the sound. After leaving Skull Harbour a G Cone buoy will be seen which marks Cush Spit extending 1³/₄ cables N from Long Island and over ¹/₂ mile W of its E point. This buoy must be left on the port hand when sailing W down Long Island Channel. There is an anchorage, if desired, in perfect shelter except in E winds, E of Coney Island, on the N side of the sound in 3·5 m. Croagh Bay, W of Coney Island, can also be used as an anchorage. Do not go far in as it is shoal to the W. The W side of Coney Island has rocks off it for over a cable and there is a drying rock 70 m S of it. There are three W exits from this sound, namely, Goat Island Sound, Man-of-War Sound and Barrel Sound.

Tidal Streams
In Lough Buidhe, Long Island Channel and Castle Island Channel the streams make E and W at a maximum rate of 1¹/₂ kn at springs, but through the E and W of Goat Island they set N and S. The course of these streams is as follows: The stream starts S through Man-of-War and Goat Island Sounds and E through Long Island Channel at -0530 Cobh (+0105 Dover); it starts W through Long Island Channel and N through Goat Island and Man-of-War Sounds at +0030 Cobh (-0520 Dover) . The E-going stream S of Long Island runs towards Sherkin Island and the N entrance to Baltimore .

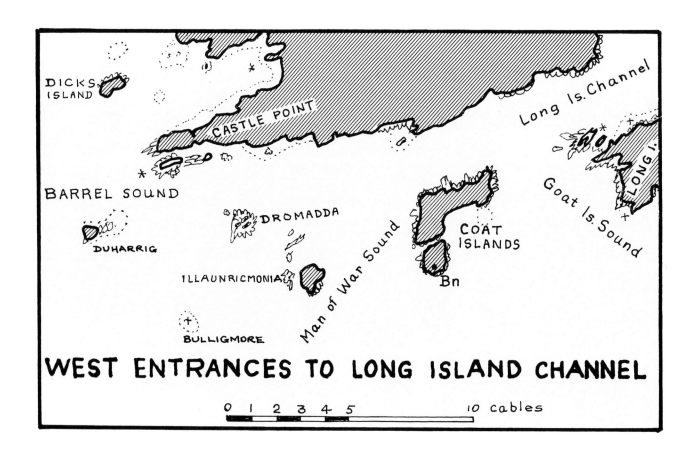

WEST ENTRANCES TO LONG ISLAND CHANNEL

0 1 2 3 4 5   10 cables

GOAT ISLAND SOUND

is between Long Island and Goat Island and is over 2 cables wide at its N end. It is obstructed by Sound Rock which covers at half-tide and lies 1 cable W of Garillaun off the W end of Long Island, so keep closer to the Goat Island side. Note that there is a rock with 0·2 m on it in the bight on the E side of that island. Do not head for Crookhaven till the Bulligmore has been cleared as previously mentioned.

MAN-OF-WAR SOUND

lies between Goat Island and Illaunricmonia (Turf Island). It is wider than Goat Island Sound (3 cables) and is free of danger. Illaunricmonia (7 m) is clear on its S and E sides but foul to N and W. Goat and Little Goat Islands, the latter with its white beacon, are clear on their W sides. Carrigduff Island, off the SW point of Long Island, just open S of Little Goat Island, 70°-250° leads S of the Bulligmore.

It is possible to pass between the N and S Barrels and Dromadda but this is not advisable unless the sea is smooth and both Barrels are showing.

BARREL SOUND

lies between Castle Point, on which there is a conspicuous square castle, and a number of rocks to the NW of Illaunricmonia of which Dromadda Rock (12 m high) is the furthest N, and Duharrig Rock (5 m high) is the furthest W. There is foul ground for 2½ cables E of Duharrig of which the N and S Barrel Rocks dry 1·4 and 1·8 m respectively. Green Island, S of Castle Point has foul ground E of it and for ¼ cable S of it. After passing down Long Island Channel continue a mid-channel course through Lough Buidhe which lies between Goat Island and the mainland. Then steer to leave Green Island 1 cable to starboard and pass N of Dromadda, the Barrels and Duharrig Rock. There are no dangers on the course from Duharrig Rock to Crookhaven.

TOORMORE BAY

Amsterdam Rocks, which always show and Amsterdam Reef which dries 0·3 m and is 2 cables SSW of it, lie on the W side of the approach to the bay. The clearing line to pass SE of Amsterdam Reef given on chart 2184 is no longer identifiable as the 32 m tower has fallen down. Bring Brow Head Tower (111 m) well open S of Sheeman Point, 238°, and this will lead clear. The E shore is foul and should be given a berth of 2 cables.

Anchorage

There is a delightful fine weather anchorage in the bay N of Reenard Point sheltered from SW to N but it would become untenable in fresh S to SE winds. Bring up off the beach in 3 m.

Goleen.

Goleen from E.

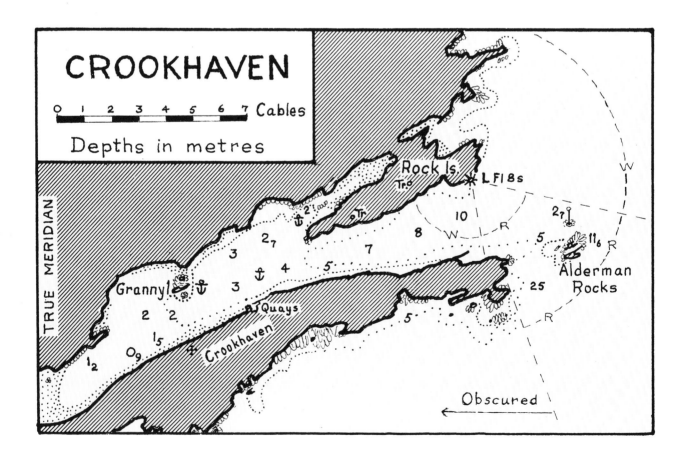

CROOKHAVEN

Depths in metres

Approach to Crookhaven from the East with Alderman Rocks in the foreground.

The waterfront village of Crookhaven.

GOLEEN

One mile N of Crookhaven lighthouse there is a narrow cleft in the rocks, named Kireal-coegea on chart 2184, which a yacht may enter in quiet weather. It leads to Goleen village whose two churches can be seen from some distance off though the existence of the cleft does not become apparent till very close. The high sides provide excellent shelter from offshore breezes but it is open to the SE. There are no dangers in the approach but in the entrance itself there are rocks awash at HW on the N side, so keep over to port. Moor to two anchors in the pool below the quay, there is not room to swing. It may be possible to berth at the quay. The wide expanse beyond the quay dries. Land at steps on quay, or at HW at slip nearer village. Shops and pubs. Petrol.

CROOKHAVEN (Chart 2184) *(see plan)*

The white lighthouse on Rock Island at the N side of the entrance is conspicuous. Alderman Rocks lie from 2 to 3$\frac{1}{2}$ cables offshore E of Streek Head at the S side of entrance. These rocks are 9 m high and Black Horse Rocks, which dry, extend $\frac{3}{4}$ cable N of them, and are marked by a N Card BY Beacon which should not be approached closer than $\frac{1}{2}$ cable. The passage W of Alderman Sound is not worth attempting as it is narrowed by rocks on both sides. Crookhaven affords splendid shelter, and is very easy to enter by day or night. It is 2 miles long and at its entrance is 2 cables wide, but it narrows to 1$\frac{1}{2}$ cables about $\frac{1}{2}$ mile from entrance and then opens up again to about 3 cables W of Rock Island. Both shores are steep-to. There are a number of old watch towers on the shores. Sail right up the harbour until abreast of the village. If beating in you can go quite close to either shore.

Light

L Fl RW 8 s, 20 m, 11, 13 M, is shown from a white lighthouse on Rock Island R over the Aldermans, W elsewhere. (Outside the harbour, W over Long Island Bay to 281°; R thence to 340°. Inside the harbour R from 281° to 348°; W thence towards the N shore.)

Anchorages

1. Abreast of the village and well out in the middle of the bay in 3 m, good holding but sometimes weed may be found.

2. With E winds N of the W point of Rock Island.

3. In fresh W winds some shelter may be had in the lee of Granny Island on the N shore, NW of the village; beware of Row Rock, dries 0·3 m, close S of Granny Island. **Note** that there is usually a lot of weed in any anchorage close in to the piers.

4. A yacht drawing 1·5 m or less could get good shelter in W winds in the bay W of Granny Island; this is a long way from the village.

Supplies

Though the village is small the usual village shop stores can be obtained. There is a PO with telephone. Two pubs, 3 restaurants and a cafe. Water taps on both quays.

Tides

There is only a slight tidal stream in the harbour. The tide sets strongly through Alderman Sound and care should be taken not to be drawn into it in calm weather.

CROOKHAVEN TO MIZEN HEAD

Streek Head at the E end of the peninsular forming Crookhaven Harbour is 44 m high and rises steeply from the sea. It has rocks off it, the outer rock, Gokane, being 6 m high. There are a number of old watch towers on this stretch of coast. If beating along the shore do not stand in too close as some of the bights are foul and the inner ends of the drift nets are very close to the land. **Warning.** Salmon drift nets set at right angles to the land will frequently be found between Alderman Rocks and Brow Head.

Brow Head

is 1$\frac{3}{4}$ miles E of the Mizen. It is 111 m high and slopes at a steep gradient seaward but gradually inland. There is a ruined signal tower near its summit. Between Brow Head and the Mizen lies Barley Cove. It affords no shelter and is rather remarkable for the wide expanse of sand at its head. Devil's Rock (Barley Rock) is in the middle of this bay and is awash at HW. Carricknagower, a rock awash at HW which nearly always breaks, lies 1 cable offshore $\frac{1}{2}$ mile about ESE of Mizen Head. Both the flood and ebb streams set on to the rock.

Mizen Head

is the SW extremity of Ireland. The actual head known as Cruachan Island is low, but it is readily identified from a distance on account of Mizen Peak, 229 m high, 1 mile NE of it. A graceful bridge connects Cruachan Island to the mainland. A spit with 3·8 m least water at its outer end extends $\frac{3}{4}$ cable SW of the Mizen and due to the strong tide frequently breaks.

Light

A light is shown from a white building on Cruachan Island, Iso 4 s, 52 m, 16 M. (Metric chart does not show Cruachan Island.) It is visible from 133° through E to 313°. Radio Beacon, see Appendix 6.

Mizen Head, the most Southerly point of the Irish Mainland.

MIZEN HEAD TO THREE CASTLE HEAD

Dunlough Bay lies between Mizen Head and Three Castle Head, and the coast here is very rugged, but steep-to. Caher Rock, 3/4 mile N of the Mizen, shows above HW, and is close inshore.

THREE CASTLE HEAD

marks the S end of the mouth of Dunmanus Bay. It is 111 m high and has sunken rocks extending 1 cable W of it, while South Bullig with 4·6 m over it and lying 4 cables off the head, breaks in bad weather. The red sector of Ardnakinna Point light on Bere Island shows over these dangers; the white sector leads clear of them. There are ruins of three castles in the hollow on top of the head.

Tidal Streams

Off the Mizen Head and Three Castle Head the E-going stream runs S and the W-going stream NW to N forming eddies off Three Castle Head. The E-going stream makes at -0505 Cobh (+0130 Dover) and the W-going at +0120 Cobh (-0430Dover). Between the Mizen and Crookhaven the streams set E and W. The spring rate off the Mizen is 4 kn and off Three Castle Head 3 kn, decreasing to 1½ kn 4 to 5 miles offshore. This results in a dangerous race off the Mizen especially with wind against tide. There is also a race off Brow Head, and the Mizen race may extend the whole way across Dunlough Bay to Three Castle Head. The broken water

extends right into the land. As Brow Head is 111 m high, Mizen Peak 229 m and Three Castle Head 111 m there is often a lull under the heads with onshore winds. It is not advisable to go too close to the heads without auxiliary power in case the strong tides and onshore swell take charge.

Distances

Crookhaven to Mizen Head .. .. .. 7½ miles
Cape Clear to Mizen Head .. .. .. 11½ miles
Cape Clear to Crookhaven .. .. 8½ miles
Gascanane Sound to Mizen Head .. .. 14 miles
Gascanane Sound to Crookhaven .. .. 10 miles
Skull Harbour to Mizen Head .. .. 12¾ miles
Skull Harbour to Crookhaven Harbour via
 Long Island and Man-of-War Sounds 8¾ miles

72

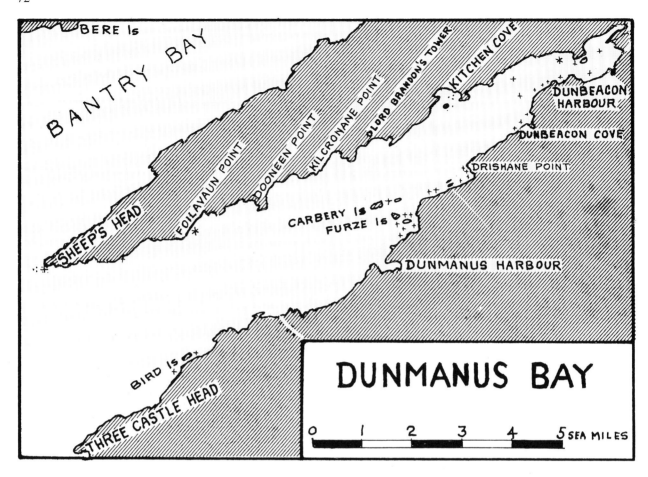

BANTRY BAY

BERE Is

SHEEP'S HEAD

FOILAVAUN POINT

DOONEEN POINT

KILCRONANE POINT

LORD BRANDON'S TOWER

KITCHEN COVE

DUNBEACON HARBOUR

DUNBEACON COVE

DRISHANE POINT

CARBERY Is

FURZE Is

DUNMANUS HARBOUR

BIRD Is

THREE CASTLE HEAD

DUNMANUS BAY

0 1 2 3 4 5 SEA MILES

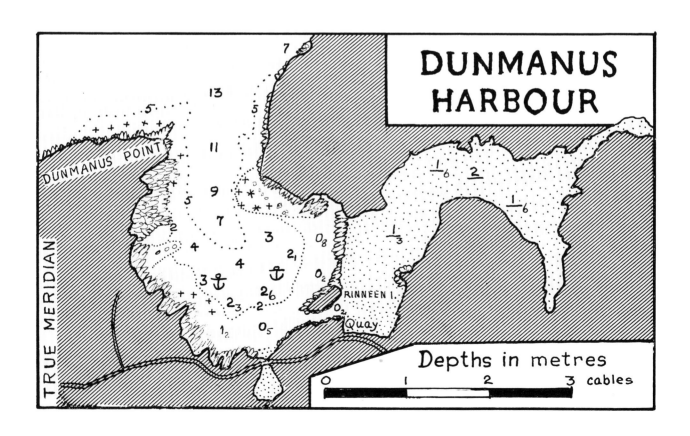

DUNMANUS HARBOUR

TRUE MERIDIAN

DUNMANUS POINT

RINNEEN I.

Quay

Depths in metres

0 1 2 3 cables

DUNMANUS BAY

is 3^1/$_2$ miles wide at its entrance between Sheep's Head on the N and Three Castle Head on the S and extends 13 miles in an E by N direction. The bay contains three harbours. Dunmanus is halfway up the S shore, Kitchen Cove two-thirds of the way up on the N side and Dunbeacon Harbour at the head of the bay, and there is also an anchorage at Dunbeacon Cove on the S shore, near the head of the bay. Kitchen Cove is the best of these harbours. As far as Carbery Island, 7 miles within the entrance, the bay is free of danger, and both shores, which are steep, can be approached close in. There are no navigational lights in the bay. **Tidal Streams.** There is no perceptible tidal stream in the bay.

THREE CASTLE HEAD TO DUNMANUS HARBOUR.

Generally the shore between these places is free of danger, but 1 mile W of Dunmanus Point there are some sunken rocks extending 1 cable offshore. Bird Island is 51 m high and is 3 miles from Three Castle Head. It is close to the shore, and the passage inside it is foul.

DUNMANUS HARBOUR *(see plan)*

There is usually a bad breaker on the shore near the harbour which is rather frightening approaching the narrow entrance. There are a number of sunken rocks off the E side just inside the entrance which possibly extend further than on the plan or on chart 2252, (reports please), and the W side is also foul so restricting the entrance to ^{1}/$_2$ cable. Enter on a mid-channel course heading 50 m W of the ruins of Dunmanus Castle on the S shore. Anchor in the centre of the harbour in 4 to 6 m, sand and soft mud. The E side of the harbour dries out. There is sometimes a roll in the harbour if the swell is running up the bay outside. No supplies but a road runs past the head of the bay. A wild and attractive place.

Carbery Island

is 15 m high, lies in the middle of the bay, and is 4 cables long with foul ground all round it. There is a patch called Carbery Breaker, with only 2·3 m over it, extending 3 cables from W end of the island, and the NW and SW shores are foul for 1^1/$_2$ cables off. The gap in Knockaughin (Cushalawn) Mt open N of Carbery Island bearing 080° clears Carbery Breaker to the N. Three cables E of Carbery Island lies Cold Island (4·3 m) and the passage between them is nearly all foul. 2^1/$_2$ cables to the SE of Carbery Island lies Furze Island (15 m). This island also has rocks off it, and while the passage between Furze and Carbery Island is clear, the passage between Furze and the mainland is very foul. It is possible to go S of Carbery Island in fine weather. If doing so keep midway between Furze and

Carbery Islands giving the W point of Furze a berth of at least 1 cable. Continue in mid-channel between Furze and Cold Islands and between Murphy Rocks and Cold Island. Do not attempt in bad weather.

CARBERY ISLAND TO DUNBEACON COVE

Between Carbery Island and Drishane Point the S shore of the bay is foul and should not be approached closer than 2 cables. E of Drishane Point the shore is clear until Carriglea Rock (dries 3·2 m) is reached at the W entrance to Dunbeacon Cove.

DUNBEACON COVE

is easily distinguished by the wall of a ruined castle NE of the cove. The inner portion of the cove dries out so that a yacht cannot go in far enough to get any real shelter in bad weather. Anchor midway between the E shore and Carriglea Rock in 4 m mud. Landing at quay up the cove, which dries at LW. No stores are available.

THREE CASTLE HEAD AND SHEEP'S HEAD TO KITCHEN COVE

There are no dangers on the direct course from Three Castles Head to Kitchen Cove, 10 miles up the bay on the N shore. If approaching from Sheep Head (the N entrance point to the bay), the N shore is steep-to until reaching Pointabulloge, 8 miles up. Give Pointabulloge a clearance of over 1 cable to the S and 2 cables to the W to avoid the reefs off it. The point 1 mile NE of Pointabulloge should also be given a berth of 1 cable as the rock off it, which dries 1·5 m appears to be further out from the land than charted; it is quite a large rock. Lord Brandon's Tower, 49 m, in the bay W of Pointabulloge is conspicuous.

Temporary anchorage in fine weather is possible E of Dooneen Point, but the water is deep and the holding is reported to be poor with a foul bottom in places. There is a small quay with deep water close to it but there are running moorings across the gut to the shore. Above the temporary anchorage E of Kilcronane Pt. there are two pubs and restaurant in the village. See chart 2552.

KITCHEN COVE *(see plan)*

is 1^1/$_2$ miles beyond Pointabulloge. The entrance, 2 cables wide, is between Owens Island and the W shore. Owens Island is a low grassy islet in front of the cove with rocks which are awash at HW extending ^{3}/$_4$ cable off its W side and for ^{1}/$_2$ cable off its E side. All the E side of the harbour is strewn with rocks, and there is also a dangerous rock which dries 0·2 m ^{1}/$_2$ cable off the inner point on the W side. The N shore is wooded.

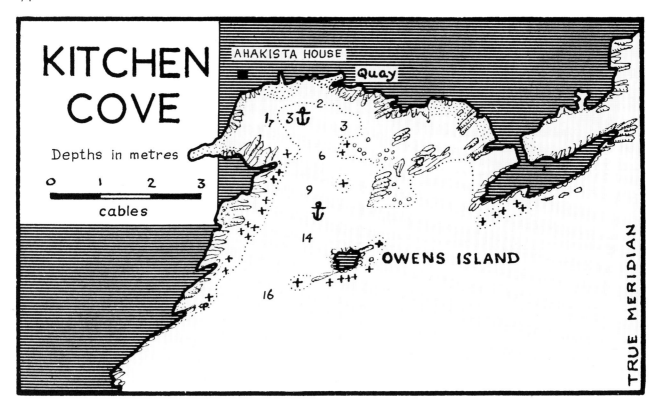

KITCHEN COVE

Depths in metres

0 1 2 3

cables

AHAKISTA HOUSE

Quay

1₇ 3 ⚓ 2

3

6

9

⚓

14

16

OWENS ISLAND

TRUE MERIDIAN

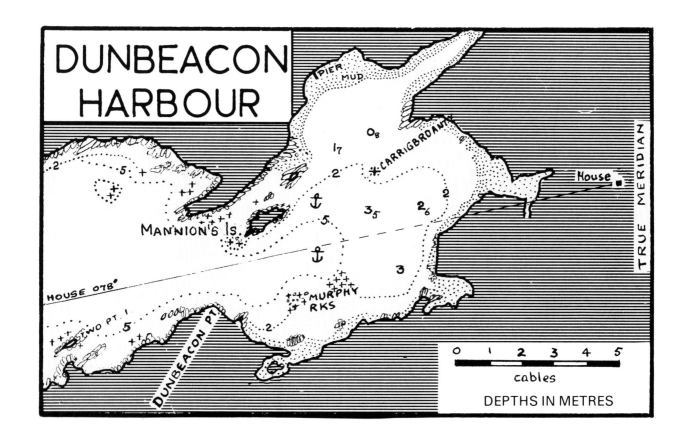

DUNBEACON HARBOUR

PIER

MUD

O₈

1₇

*CARRIGBROAN

2

⚓

3₅

2₆

2

2

5

5

MANNION'S Is

⚓

3

HOUSE 078°

MURPHY
RKS

TWO PT. 1

5

DUNBEACON PT.

2

House

TRUE MERIDIAN

0 1 2 3 4 5

cables

DEPTHS IN METRES

Anchorage

The best anchorage for a large yacht is to NW of Owens Island and midway between it and the W shore in 9 m, mud bottom, but smaller yachts could get a more sheltered anchorage in less water by keeping 1 cable off the W shore and letting go clear of the moorings when the little cove in the W end of the harbour opens up. This anchorage is exposed in S winds. The holding is good. Land at the quay. There is one small shop, two pubs and a small restaurant. Small fishing boats remain on moorings all winter.

KITCHEN COVE TO DUNBEACON

There is a passage N of Owens Island, which could be used, but it is narrow, so it is safer to go to the S of this island. There is a landlocked bay just beyond Kitchen Cove and to the W of Reen Point, but its entrance is almost completely blocked with rocks. The water starts shoaling after passing Reen Point, and there are patches which must be avoided in bad weather.

Three-quarters of a mile E of Reen Point and off the S shore is Doona Rock with 4·9 m on it and 2 cables W of Doona Rock there is another rock with 4·1 m over it. Off the N shore and ½ mile NE of Reen Point there is a third rock with 1·7 m on it. The tower on Sheep Head open of the tangent of Reen Point and bearing 248° just clears the 1·7 m rock. The S shores of Illaunacushla and Reen Point in line bearing 244° leads OVER the latter rock.

Three Castle Head, Bird Island and the N tangent of Carbery Island in transit and bearing 232° leads between Doona Rock and the 1·7 m rock. Good visibility is necessary for this clearing mark.

When clear of these dangers you can then steer for entrance to Dunbeacon Harbour, which lies between Dunbeacon Point on the S and Mannion Island on the N keeping the large grey house at far side of harbour midway between Dunbeacon Point and Mannion Island, bearing 078°. Do not go close to the S shore where Twopoint Island, ½ mile W of Dunbeacon Point, has rocks off it. If turning to windward up or down the bay, keep at least 2 cables off the N shore, and 1 cable offshore between Twopoint Island and Dunbeacon Harbour on the S shore. Unless there is a swell running there will be no danger on Doona Rock or the patches W of it.

DUNBEACON HARBOUR (see plan)

looks large but is very shallow in its N and NE sides, and is obstructed by the Murphy Rocks, awash at LW on its S side. Halfway between Mannion Island and the E shore there is a rock called Carrigbroanty, which uncovers 0·5 m at LW. By keeping Two Point Island open N of Dunbeacon Point you will avoid Murphy Rocks.

Anchorage

Large yachts should not go far in and are advised to anchor 1 cable SE of Mannion Island in 5 to 7 m, but small yachts could get better shelter close to the E side of Mannion Island in 2 to 4 m. The pier is not in great shape. A good mark is Two Point Island or the shore S of it in line with the S side of Mannion Island. Durrus village is about 1¼ miles from the harbour and has two restaurants, 4 pubs, P.O., fuel and gas.

Distances

Mizen Head to Dursey Head	17½ miles
Mizen Head to Dursey Sound	15 miles
Mizen Head to Three Castle Head	2 miles
Three Castle Head to Sheep's Head ..	3¾ miles
Three Castle Head to Kitchen Cove ..	10¼ miles
Kitchen Cove to Dunbeacon Harbour ..	3½ miles
Dunbeacon Harbour to Dunbeacon Cove	2 miles
Dunbeacon Cove to Dunmanus Harbour (inside Carbery Island)	4½ miles
Dunmanus Harbour to Three Castle Head	7¾ miles

SHEEP'S HEAD

or Muntevary is the SW extremity of Bantry Bay. It is 168 m high with fine cliffs. The North Bullig Rock with 6·2 m over it lies 1½ cables SW of the head and would break in severe weather. There is less tidal stream round this head than round any of its neighbours.

Light

A light is shown from a white tower, 7 m high, on Sheep's Head. Fl (3) WR 15 s, 83 m, 15-18 M. R from 007° to 017° W from 017° to 212°, obsc elsewhere. The red sector leads W of the South Bullig off Three Castles Head.

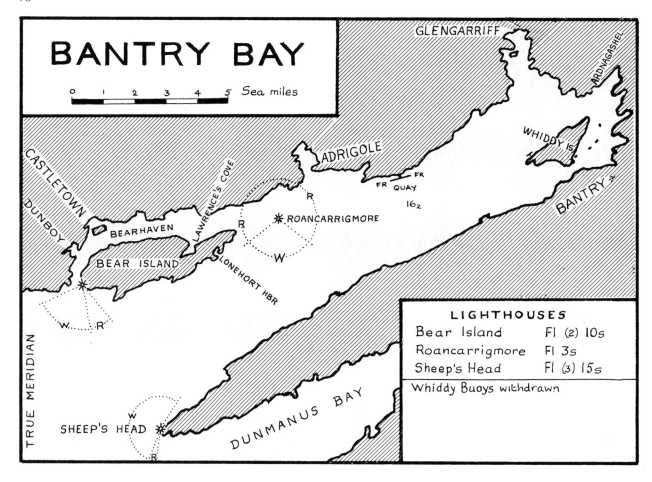

BANTRY BAY

0 1 2 3 4 5 Sea miles

GLENGARRIFF

ARDNAGASHEL

WHIDDY IS.

CASTLETOWN

DUNBOY

BEARHAVEN

BEAR ISLAND

LAWRENCE'S COVE

LONEHORT HBR

ADRIGOLE

FR QUAY

FR

16₂

ROANCARRIGMORE

BANTRY

TRUE MERIDIAN

SHEEP'S HEAD

DUNMANUS BAY

LIGHTHOUSES	
Bear Island	Fl (2) 10s
Roancarrigmore	Fl 3s
Sheep's Head	Fl (3) 15s
Whiddy Buoys withdrawn	

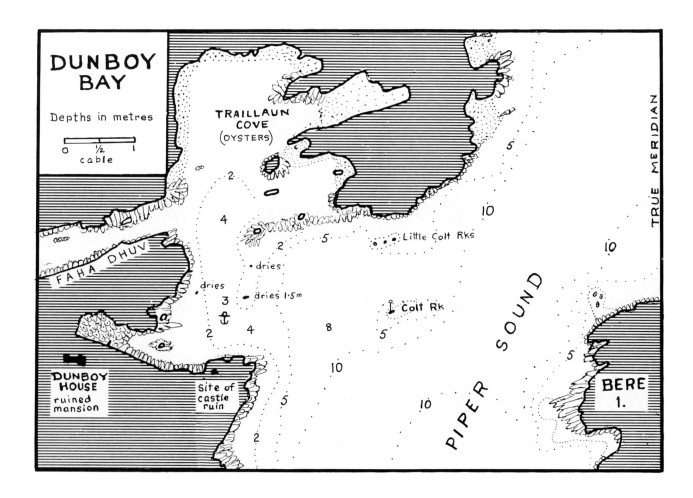

DUNBOY BAY

Depths in metres

0 ½ 1 cable

TRAILLAUN COVE (OYSTERS)

FAHA DHUV

DUNBOY HOUSE ruined mansion

Site of castle ruin

Little Colt Rks

Colt Rk

PIPER SOUND

TRUE MERIDIAN

BERE I.

dries 1·5m

BANTRY BAY *(see plan)*

extends 18 miles inside Sheep's Head and is 3 to 4 miles wide. There are some good yacht harbours in it. Castletown, Bearhaven and Bantry arc best for stores. Adrigole and Glengarriff are very beautiful. Lawrence Cove and Lonehort, both on Bear Island, and Dunboy are all well worth a visit. The land on either side of the bay is high, flat-topped Hungry Hill on the N shore being 682 m high and Sugarloaf Mountain near Glengarriff 571 m . Generally the bay is free of dangers and the shores can be approached close in except in the vicinity of Bear and Whiddy Islands.

Tidal Streams

The tidal streams are barely perceptible except in the entrance to Bearhaven and Bantry Harbours. With strong S or SW winds a current sets into the bay around Sheep's Head.

BEARHAVEN

on the N shore of the bay, is bounded by Bear Island on its S side and has two entrances. Bear Island is over 5 miles long, its highest point (270 m) being about 2 miles from its W end and from this point it descends gradually to Lonehort point, its E extremity. The main entrance is round the E of Bear Island, but if coming from the S or W, the W entrance is the shortest passage to Castletown, which is the best yacht anchorage.

DUNBOY BAY *(see plan)*

is on the W side of Piper Sound and there is sheltered anchorage there for small yachts except in E winds. There is a pier at the inner end of the cove in front of the prominent ruined Dunboy House. The inconspicuous ruins of Dunboy Castle are close to the point. Approach midway between Colt Rock, which has a red beacon with can topmark, surmounted with a horse and rider, and Dunboy Point, the latter being foul for ¼ cable off. There is a rock which dries 1·5 m 1 cable N of Dunboy Point; the perch which previously marked this rock has gone. Enter halfway between the rock and the point or ½ cable from the point. A mark to avoid the rock is the front door of Dunboy House open to the left of the small tree on the edge of the grass above the sea wall; this tree is at the right-hand end of a group of trees and bushes. Anchor in 2 m ½ cable SW of the rock or ½ cable NW.

There is another rock which dries 1 m ½ cable to the N of the 1·5 m rock. When the tide is out and these rocks are showing it is easy to pass between them and approach the anchorage safely from the N. There are oyster beds in Traillaun Harbour to the N of Dunboy Bay and in the SW corner of Dunboy Bay.

Dunboy House marks the Dunboy anchorage in the approach to Castletownbere.

Castletown Harbour looking towards Piper Sound and the Western entrance.

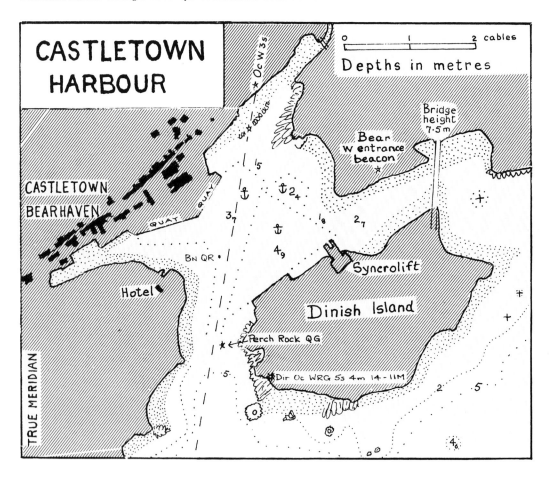

CASTLETOWN HARBOUR

Oc W 3s

0   1   2 cables

Depths in metres

Bridge height 7·5 m

Bear W entrance beacon

CASTLETOWN BEARHAVEN

QUAY

QUAY

5

2₄

3₇

1₈

2₇

4₉

BN QR

Syncrolift

Hotel

Dinish Island

Perch Rock Q G

5

Dir Oc WRG 5s 4m 14-11M

5

2

5

4₆

TRUE MERIDIAN

CASTLETOWN (see plan)

Dinish Island, 8 m high, and 4 cables long forms the SE boundary of Castletown Harbour which is one of the major fishing ports on the W coast. Walter Scott Rock, 2·7 m over it, lies almost 2 cables S of Dinish Island. It is marked by a S Card Lt buoy Q 6 + LF 15 s on its S side. The RC church at Castletown in line with Perch Rock beacon in the entrance leads W of this rock. Carrigaglos, 0·6 m high, lies ¹/₂ cable off the SW point of Dinish Island. The entrance is very narrow so that it is often advisable to motor in; the total width between the 2 m line and Perch Rock and the 2 m line off Came Point is only 36 m wide and has been dredged to 3·7 m and passes immediately W of Perch Rock. The rock is marked by a light beacon with a large green square. The narrow E entrance is crossed by a low-level fixed bridge, height 7·5 m and is only suitable for motor boats. There is now a Directional Lt. on the SW shore of Dinish Island, it shows over the W entrance to Bearhaven. Characteristics: Oc WRG 5 s 4 m 14-11 M. It is in line with a beacon on the mainland shore 024°.

Leading Lights

are shown on R marks on a W stripe Oc W 3 s. In line 010° they lead through the entrance. **Perch Rock Light** is Q G.

WESTERN ENTRANCE

This is called Piper Sound and lies between Fair Head (45 m) on the W and Ardnakinna Point, on which stands a lighthouse, on the E of Bear Island side. Inside Ardnakinna Point the entrance narrows to 1³/₄ cables between Piper Point on the W and Naglas Point on the E. Piper Rocks, which lie close to the S extremity of Piper Point, are high, but there is a rock with only 1·5 m over it ¹/₄ cable E of them, therefore give Piper Point a berth of 1 cable. The leading marks, consisting of a red and white beacon on the SW shore of Dinish Island and the gable end of a hut on the mainland, white with a vertical red stripe, will then be identified. These marks in line 024° lead right up the sound clear of everything. If beating in or out note that Bullig Bay, just N of Piper Point, has a number of rocky islets in its N part known as Traneen Islands, and there are rocks called Traneen Rocks, one of which is awash, over ¹/₂ cable outside these islets.

Lights
Ardnakinna Point

shows Fl (2) WR 10 s, 62 m, 17,14 M, from a white cylindrical tower. R from 319° to 348° (covering the dangers off Sheep's Head and Three Castle Head), W from 348° to 066°, the safe approach from seaward, and R from 066° over the land and Castletown Harbour until obscured by Bear Island.

Leading Light

From the front leading mark on the SW of Dinish Island there is a directional light, Oc RWG 5 s, 10 M, the narrow white sector of which, from 024° to 024¹/₂°, leads through Piper Sound and clear of dangers till the Castletown leading lights are picked up (see below). It shows R from 024¹/₂° to 027¹/₂°, which covers Piper Point, and G from 020¹/₂° to 024°, which covers Naglas Point. The old rear beacon E of Castletown is unlighted and kept for day in line with front mark.

Harbour Rock has a depth of 3·7 m, and lies in the middle of the channel, over ¹/₄ mile inside Piper Point; the leading line takes you to E of it. Fort Point is on the island side ³/₄ mile inside Naglas Point and the shore S of it is foul for ¹/₂ cable off and there are three rocks drying 1·8 m called Foilnaboe ¹/₂ cable N of the point. There are detached rocks, with 2·4 m over them, lying 1¹/₄ cables to the NE of Foilnaboe Rocks. Colt Rock lies on the W side of channel above Dunboy Point, 2·1 m, and is marked by a red perch - with a can topmark. Little Colt Rock (unnamed on new chart) is a reef which dries 0·9 m and lies between Colt Rock and the land N of it, but much nearer to the mainland. Drom Point also on the W side is foul off its point for ¹/₂ cable. Sheep Islands on the Bear Island side are a group of flat grassy islands which have a rocky ledge, which is awash at HW, called Long Point (unnamed on new chart), extending 1 cable W of them. A salmon drift net has been met in the main channel.

Anchorage

The harbour limits include all of Bearhaven Sound from W and E entrance, it is well sheltered and the holding in the 2·4 m area is good mud. The plan shows the dredged area. Yachts should anchor in the part dredged to 2·4 m, or in a heavy SE blow might go nearer to Dinish Island; but keep well clear of the quay on the island which is used by large fishing boats. There is a landing slip near the NW corner of the dredged areas and steps at the NE end of the quay. There is often a fishing boat undergoing repairs at the W end of the quays and a yacht could lie alongside her conveniently. The NE quay is also frequently available for berthing. Do not go alongside the central part near the ice plant as this is in continuous use by fishing boats. For water at the NE quay apply to the HM office on the quay. Harbour Master, Captain Jones, (027) 70220, after hours (027) 70128 also fax (027) 70329. VHF Ch.16 and 14. Ice plant now on Dinish Pier.

Supplies

Shops, hotels, banks, gas and PO. Petrol from garage in square. Water and diesel are available on the pier. Locally owned bus to Bantry Mon, Tue, Fri and Sat. Limited chandlery, marine electronics

Lawrence's Cove from NE.

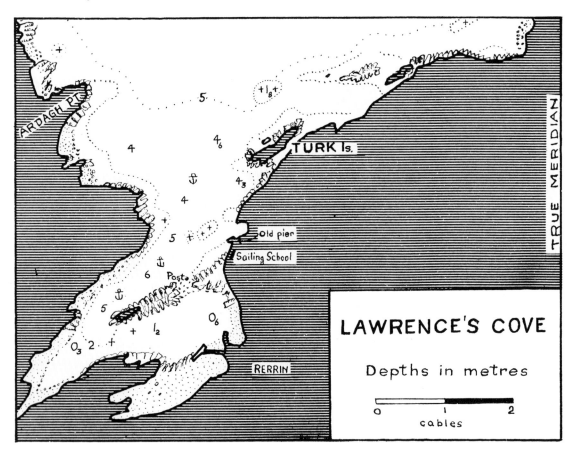

ARDAGH PT

5

+ 1/8 +

4 6

TURK Is.

4

4 3

Old pier

Sailing School

5

Post

6

5

I 2

O 6

O 3 2

RERRIN

TRUE MERIDIAN

LAWRENCE'S COVE

Depths in metres

0   1   2

cables

sales/service on main quay, (027-70016). Marine Engineers, John O'Sullivan (027-70129) and Richard Power (027-70298). There is also a marine lift. Harbour dues are payable to lie alongside. Showers at boatyard.

Tides

In the entrances to Bearhaven the tidal streams run in from +0550 Cobh (HW Dover) and out from -0025 Cobh (+0610 Dover). Max spring rate E entrance ½ kn, W entrance 2 kn.

Leaving Castletown and sailing E it is possible to pass between the Walter Scott Rock and the Privateer Rock on a mid-channel course if Privateer Rock, which dries 1·5 m is showing. It is safer to leave the Walter Scott buoy to port. There are no dangers on the S side of Bearhaven if the shore is given a berth of 1 cable. On the N side Volage Rock, which has 2·4 m over it lies 1¼ cables S of Minane Island (5 m) which is 4 cables E of Dinish Island. Hornet Rock, with only 1 2 m over it, is over 1¼ miles E of Walter Scott Rock and is marked by a South Cardinal Buoy VQ(6) + Fl 10 s moored ¾ cable S of it. George Rock, 1½ miles E of Hornet Rock has 7·3 m on it and is also marked by an Isolated Danger Buoy Fl (2) 10 s.

MILL COVE

on the N side of Bearhaven and to the N of Hornet Rock buoy has no particular attraction but would afford some shelter in N winds. Illaunboudane is a 1·5 m high islet close to the E side of the entrance and there are rocks which dry 1·2 and 2·4 m ¼ cable W and S of this. There is also a rock which dries 0·9 m 1 cable SW of Carrigagannive Point at the W side of the entrance. All the N part of the harbour dries out so anchor immediately inside the line of the E and W points of the entrance. There are oyster beds in the cove. There is a conspicuous white flagstaff at Sea Point E of Mill Cove and also a stone pier. **Beal Lough** is a small cove E of Sea Point which has a narrow entrance and a depth of 1·2 m, soft mud bottom. There is a sunken rock ½ cable SSW of the entrance. Also a stranded wreck 5 cables S of Beal Lough is marked by a N Card Pillar Q. Pass well to the S nearer the island shore.

LAWRENCE COVE *(see plan)*

on the S side of Bearhaven affords good shelter except in N winds. Coming from the E, Palmer Rock must be avoided; it has only 1·8 m over it and lies 3 cables NE of Turk Island and 1½ cables offshore. The cove narrows suddenly by reason of a patch with only 0·3 m over it; this lies W of the ruined army pier and there is foul ground between. Further in a rocky ledge extends from the E shore; near the end of this is a 0·9 m high islet on the W end of which is a large, rusty tank.

Larger yachts should anchor W of Turk Island in

4 m, mud. Smaller yachts may go further in and get better shelter by keeping close to the W shore and anchoring N of the 0·9 m islet. There is not much swinging room and it is advisable to moor to two anchors if staying overnight. A small motor ferry runs from here to Castletown.

There is a channel through the rock ledge which dries 0·5 m and is marked on its E side by a post with triangular topmark. It is only suitable for motor boats. There are two sunken rocks S of the inlet and no suitable marks to avoid them. If going right up to the quay it is advisable to have sufficient rise of tide to clear the rocks. Pass S of the rocks within 20 m of the shore. The channel has been dredged to 1·8 m, but this cannot be relied upon.

Facilities

Glenans sailing school operates from this harbour and its headquarters is the building S of the old army pier; this pier is dangerous but at HW it is possible to land at the wall in front of the school. There are shops, PO and a pub at Rerrin opening unreliable. Restaurant. A boatyard with slipway can undertake some repairs.

EASTERN ENTRANCE TO BEARHAVEN

This is the main entrance and lies between Lonehort Point and Roancarrigmore. Lonehort Point is the E end of Bear Island, and is a long low point with a shelving rock running out for a distance of ½ cable beyond it. There are the remains of an old pile lighthouse on the point. Carrigavaddra, 2·7 m high, is a rocky patch extending for almost ½ mile SE of Lonehort Point. There are a number of rocks on the patch, some of which show and some of which arc awash . A perch BY S Card marks these rocks, but do not go closer than 1 cable N or E of the perch. Between Lonehort Point and Carrigavaddra there is a rock called Wrinkle, which is awash at LW, and also a 2·1 m sounding, and other rocks which dry 1 to 1·5 m, so do not attempt this passage.

Roancarrigmore

lies 1¼ miles E of Lonehort Point. It is a flat-topped rock 6 m high and 1½ cables in length from W to E and ½ cable in breadth. The N and E sides are clear but there is a rock which dries 0·6 m ½ cable off its S side and other shoal patches near this.

Light

A light Fl WR 3 s, 18 m, 18, 14 M is shown from a white lighthouse with a black band on Roancarrigmore. W from 312° through N to 050°, R elsewhere. The red sector covers Carrigavaddra, Roancarrigbeg and Doucallia Rock.

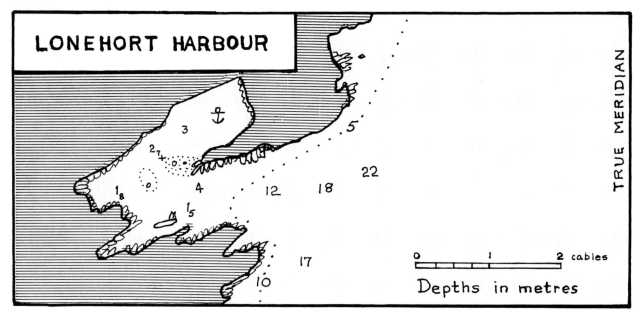

LONEHORT HARBOUR

TRUE MERIDIAN

Depths in metres

0   1   2 cables

Roancarrigbeg

is an irregular patch of rocks, 2 cables long and 1 cable wide, 3 cables N of Roancarrigmore. At HW it forms four flat-topped rocks 6 m high. There are sunken rocks 1½ cables S of it and its remaining sides arc foul for ½ cable. It must be given a wide berth. There is a fish farm 6 cables to the W of this patch.

South Shore of Bear Island

Bear Island is over 5 miles long, its highest point, Knockanallig, is 270 m high and about ¾ mile W of this is another peak (209 m) with an old watch tower on it. There are also two Martello towers on heights E of it. Between Doonbeg Head (84 m), its most S point, and Cloonaghlin Head, 2 miles E of it and with a Martello tower on its summit, lies Feagh Rock, 0·9 m high. It is 3¾ cables offshore to the S of Greenane Rock (12 m high) and as it lies 1 cable outside the direct line of the heads it is important to keep well out from and between Doonbeg and Cloonaghlin Heads, especially at night. There is an islet close S of Doonbeg.

Lonehort Harbour *(see plan)*

¾ mile to the SE of Lonehort Point, is a little cove which offers splendid shelter in reasonable weather, but as there are no marks to avoid the rocks in the entrance it must be entered with the greatest caution. The soundings on the plan indicate the course to follow. Carrigavaud, the rock E of the 1·8 m sounding, is sharp tipped and dries about 1·2 m; its position when covered is often indicated by seaweed. There is a long rock, which rarely covers, on the S side of the entrance and separated from the shore by a very narrow channel. This rock runs out below water at its E and W ends and extends as a half tide reef about 30 m N into the channel at its E end.

    Keep in mid-channel until the E point is abeam

then steer to pass 50 m E of the long rock to clear its half tide extension. As its W end comes abeam and the small creek on the W shore opens up close the W shore N of the creek to clear Carrigavaud and then keep close to the N shore to avoid the half tide reef extending ½ cable NW from the E point. There is a least charted depth of 1·8 m in the entrance but it is believed to be slightly less, so keel boats should not enter at LWS. Trammel nets may be set completely closing the entrance or the narrows so approach with caution. There will probably be no orange buoys to mark these nets so only the small cork floats must be spotted.

    Anchor in the centre of the E end of the cove in about 1·5 m. There is not much room. Stores at Rerrin, 1 mile.

BEARHAVEN TO ADRIGOLE

After passing Lonehort Point course can be set to pass between Roancarrigbeg and the shore. As Roancarrigbeg is foul all round, keep closer to the mainland. Alternatively, pass between Roancarrigmore and Roancarrigbeg keeping closer to the former rock. If passing S of Roancarrigmore keep 1 cable clear of the islet.

Bulliga Ledge and Doucallia Rocks

After passing the Roancarrig Rocks the position of the Bulliga Ledge and Doucallia Rock must be noted as they are in the direct approach to Adrigole and Doucallia is on the course up Bantry Bay to Glengarriff. There is now a fish farm just S of Bulliga Point. Doucallia Rocks are 6 cables ENE of Roancarrigmore, and cover at 2 hours flood. Although usually breaking, in smooth water and near HW there may be no indication of their whereabouts. To pass W of Doucallia keep not more than 3 cables from the Lighthouse. To pass S of it steer 090° for 1 mile. To pass between Doucallia and Bulliga Ledge bring Leghern Point, S

Ardigole Harbour.

of Lonehort Harbour, just open S of Roancarrigmore bearing 238°. To pass E of Doucallia identify Orthon Island in Adrigole Harbour; this is not easy as it is low and hard to distinguish against the background. Bring it just open W of Pointamore (Drumlave Point) bearing 351°. If Orthon Island cannot be identified bring the centre of the entrance to Adrigole Harbour bearing N. In addition, Mehal Head just open S of Shot Head, 077° leads between Bulliga Ledge and Doucallia.

Bulliga Ledge has 3·7 m over it and would only break in bad weather. It is 3 cables SE of Bulliga Point and is best avoided by keeping 1½ cables offshore rounding Bulliga Point or using the Mehal Point and Shot Head line above to pass S of it until it is safe to enter Adrigole.

ADRIGOLE HARBOUR *(see plan)*
The entrance just to the NE of Bulliga Point is 2 cables wide and the harbour then opens out but is obstructed by a low islet called Orthon Island, which lies in the middle of the harbour. The passage between this island and the W shore is obstructed by rocks. Enter on a mid-channel course and then, giving the S end of the islet a berth of 1 cable, steer to pass midway between the islet and the E shore. There are rocks extending 1 cable off the N, W and S sides of the island. The portion of the harbour near the N shore dries out. This is one of the most beautiful anchorages on the W coast. Commercial quay reported with FR light at each end.

Anchorage
Depending on direction of wind, in 4 to 5 m ½ cable NW of the pier on the E side or 1½ cables N of Orthon Island in 4 m or in strong W winds closer to the W shore NW of the island. Holding of soft mud. The anchorage is sheltered except that in bad weather with winds from W to N very heavy squalls come down from the high hills which almost surround the harbour. Some stores are available at Drumlave village which is ½ mile from the pier. Bus to Bearhaven and Bantry Mon, Tue, Fri and Sat. The N side of the pier which is ruined; is best for dinghy landing; yachts should not go near it.

South shore of Bantry Bay
is generally very clear of danger. There is one rock whose position should be noted, however, if beating out of the bay. It has 2·6 m over it, and lies ¾ mile

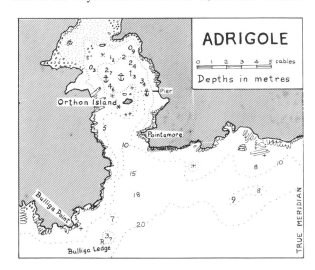

84

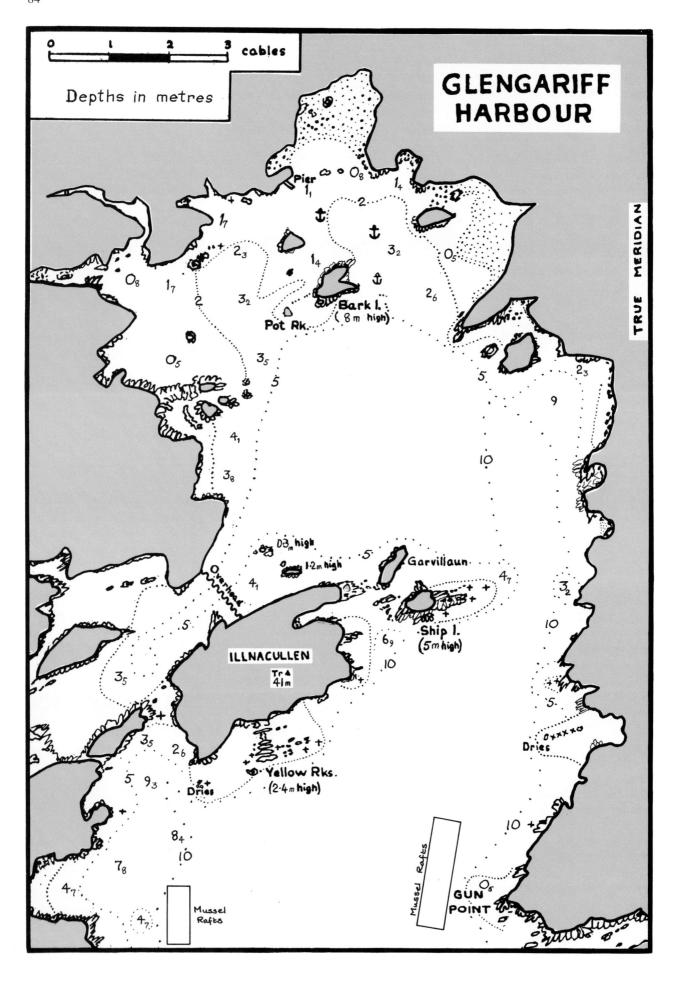

GLENGARIFF HARBOUR

Depths in metres

0   1   2   3   cables

TRUE MERIDIAN

Pier
1₁   1₄
        0·8
                2
1₇
    2₃   3₂
0₈   1₄   0₅
    1₇   Pot Rk.   Bark I.   2₆
    2   (8 m high)
    3₂
0₅   3₅
            5   5   2₃
                                            9
    4₁
    3₈   10

            0 3 m high
            0 1·2 m high   5   Garvillaun   4₇
    Overhead 4₁   3₂
        5   Ship I.   10
                        6₉   (5 m high)
    3₅   10
        ILLNACULLEN   5
            Tr▲
            41m   Dries
    3₅   2₆   0××××0
    5   9₃   Yellow Rks.
        Dries   (2·4 m high)
                                        10
    8₄
    7₈   10   GUN
    4₇   Mussel   POINT
        4₇   Rafts   Mussel Rafts   0·5

to W of Reen Point (2 miles SW of Whiddy Point W), and 2½ cables offshore. If beating down Bantry Bay it is possible to make full length tacks right across the bay and right up to either shore as there are no submerged rocks any distance from the shore except the Doucallia, off Roancarrig, usually marked by a big breaker.

ADRIGOLE TO GLENGARRIFF

When leaving Adrigole and proceeding E note that there is a rock awash at LW 1½ cables offshore and nearly ½ mile E of the entrance. Do not alter course for Shot Head until it is bearing 090°. This low, jutting head is free of outlying dangers as are the bluff heads of Mehal, 1 mile further E and Leahill Point (43 m) 1¼ miles beyond that. Sheelane Island is ¼ mile off the shore and is 12 m high with sunken ledges off its E, S and W sides. The larger island inside this is West Garnish, 14 m high. There is a passage between Sheelane Island and the shore, but if using it note that Carrigathowder Rock lies ½ cable off the mainland N of Sheelane Island, and not also Coulagh Rocks which extend nearly 3 cables in a SE direction from the shore ¾ mile NE of Sheelane Island and the 0.5 m patch 2 cables E of West Garnish Island. Coolieragh (Seal) Harbour to the NE of Sheelane Island offers no particular attraction and its E side is foul for 1½ cables. Muccuragh Rock, 1½ cables ENE of Sheelane Island, dries 1·1 m and lies nearly 1 cable off.shore. Four Heads Point is a little over 2 miles E of Sheelane Island and has rocks which show, ½ cable off it. There is deep water close up to these rocks.

GLENGARRIFF HARBOUR

(Chart 1838) *(see plan)*
is the birthplace of the Irish Cruising Club which was founded by 19 yachtsmen who happened to meet there on 13th July, 1929, aboard five cruising yachts. It would be hard to exaggerate the beauty of Glengarriff and it is rightly called the "Madeira of Ireland" on account of the mildness of its climate. No one cruising on this coast should miss calling to this lovely harbour. After passing Four Heads Rocks, the entrance to the harbour is clear and course may be shaped to leave Gun Point to starboard. Note Tinker Rock, N of Crowdy Point and Carrigbuy, NW of Big Point, both on the W side. Illnacullen is 41 m high with a conspicuous Martello tower on its summit. It is marked Garinish on the chart.

There is a reef called the Yellow Rocks, 2·4 m high, with foul ground near them 1 cable S of this island. Ship Island (5 m), which is close to the E side of Illnacullen, is foul on its E side and should be given a berth of 1 cable. Keep closer to the E shore than to Ship Island, and then alter course for Bark Island (8 m). Do not go between Bark Island

and the island ½ cable NW of it as there is a rock which dries S of the NW island. Also keep away from drying Pot Rock ½ cable WSW of Bark Island; it used to have a post, shown on the chart, but it no longer exists. (This island NW of Bark Island is locally known as Carrigeen and so named on the old chart but the metric chart has no name on it and calls a rock Carrigeen which is 2½ cables W of the N end of Bark Island.)

Danger, Overhead Cable

There is a HT electric cable from the centre of the N side of Illnacullen to the nearest point of the mainland to the NW, height 15 m.

The passage round the W end of Illnacullen should not be attempted as there is a large uncharted rock drying 0 3 m right in the middle near the narrowest part.

Anchorage

There is a most delightful anchorage in perfect shelter in 3 m NE of Bark Island and yachts less than 1·8 m deep can go further NW and quite close to the wooden pier, where however it is advisable to buoy the anchor. Yachts can anchor anywhere S of Bark Island but it is 7 or 8 m deep. Near Illnacullen anchor about 50 m N of its NE point, E of Otter Island Rock, depth 4 m. Fuel and fresh water at dinghy pier. Excellent harbour to leave a yacht in safety. Moorings available.

Supplies

There are a number of hotels and a PO. Stores may be obtained from shops in village, but not fresh meat, which, however, can usually be obtained from the hotels or ordered from Bantry. Water from Eccles Hotel. Most helpful with showers and baths at all times. Landing at pier or at steps between the pier and Eccles Hotel. These steps are used by the local outboard boats which ply for hire so care should be taken not to obstruct them when leaving a dinghy. New concrete pier replaces old timber one. Two water taps on quay. Glengarriff is a tourist resort with bus service to Killarney, Cork, etc. Illnacullen is a State-owned garden, open to the public, beautifully laid out and containing many rare plants. Pat Somers of the Perrin Bar (027-63226) about 3 mins. walk from the harbour is an excellent contact for fuel, supplies and repairs. He will keep an eye on an unattended yacht. Can be called of VHF 77 c/s "Perrin". Also - Vincent O'Sullivan, Island View Guest House (027-63081) or VHF 7 HRO, Bantry Radio Control..

GLENGARRIFF TO BANTRY

After passing Gun Point, steer to clear Carrigskye islet by 1 cable. This islet is only 1·2 m high. This course will clear Morneen Rocks (dry 1·1 m), Lion Rocks and Yellow Rocks. After passing Carrigskye

Glengarriff Harbour.

Glengarriff — where the ICC was founded in 1929.

do not alter course immediately for Whiddy Point East, the NE corner of Whiddy Island, as half-way on the direct line between them and ¼ mile SW of Ardnamanagh Point on the mainland there is a rock called Castle Breaker with only 3·8 m over it. Whiddy Point East is clear of danger and may be rounded close in. Whiddy Island has a large oil terminal towards its SW end which is no longer operating.

WHIDDY ISLAND

2³/₄ miles long, lies NE and SW in the SE corner of Bantry Bay, forming Bantry Harbour under its lee. The island had a large oil storage depot near its W end with an isolated jetty 2 cables N of the shore. This jetty has been damaged by fire. The coast from the jetty to the NE corner of the island is clear given a berth of 1¹/₂ cables. SW of the island lie the East, Middle and West Gerane Rocks extending ¹/₂ mile WSW of Whiddy Point West (Reenanick Point). West Gerane is 1 m high. Lousy Island is 2¹/₂ cables offshore on the S side of the island and the North Beach extends 1¹/₂ cables at the SE corner of the island. The E shore of the island is dealt with under Bantry Harbour.

BANTRY HARBOUR *(see plan)*

North Entrance. The islands in the harbour are generally foul all round and should be given a berth of 1 cable and of 1¹/₂ cables W of Horse Island. To pass between Horse Island and Carrignafeagh bring the ruined house at the E end of West Chapel Island in line with a prominent white house among trees beyond the S shore, bearing 181°. There is a rock, 0·6 m high on the spit N of Horse Island. There are now a number of unlit Mussel Fishing

rafts in the N entrance. Rafts may be encountered anywhere in the area E of Whiddy Island, particularly outside the buoyed channel. Rafts may extend in strings or consist of lines of barrels only. They are low, unlit, unmarked and sometimes difficult to see. Do not pass close as floating mooring lines extend beyond them. Their approximate positions are shown in the accompanying plan. If approaching in poor visibility, be sure to turn to starboard as soon as the channel buoys can be picked up as to go too far towards Snave Village lights leads over Carrignagappul Rock which is very dangerous. Unfortunately the lights of Bantry Town are always obscured by islands or land.

Directions

Pass about midway between Whiddy and Horse Island (as above), and when Horse Island bears E steer for Chapel G Cone Lt buoy, Fl G 2 s. Alternatively leave Horse Island G Cone Lt buoy, Fl G 6 s to starboard Gurteenroe R Can Lt buoy, Fl R 3 s to port and Chapel G Cone Lt buoy Fl G 2 s to starboard.

West Entrance

S of Whiddy Island, is locally known as The Beaches. It should only be used in moderate sea conditions because the bar, which is just seaward of the narrowest part, has a least depth of 2 m and sometimes breaks. Outside the bar is Cracker Rock with only 1·7 m. There are leading marks on the shore to the S of South Beach about 1¹/₂ cables. Back mark W post with FR lt. Front mark RW post with W lt. Follow these in on the bearing 091° until the next set of leading marks on the S of Whiddy Is.

The Pier in Bantry Town.

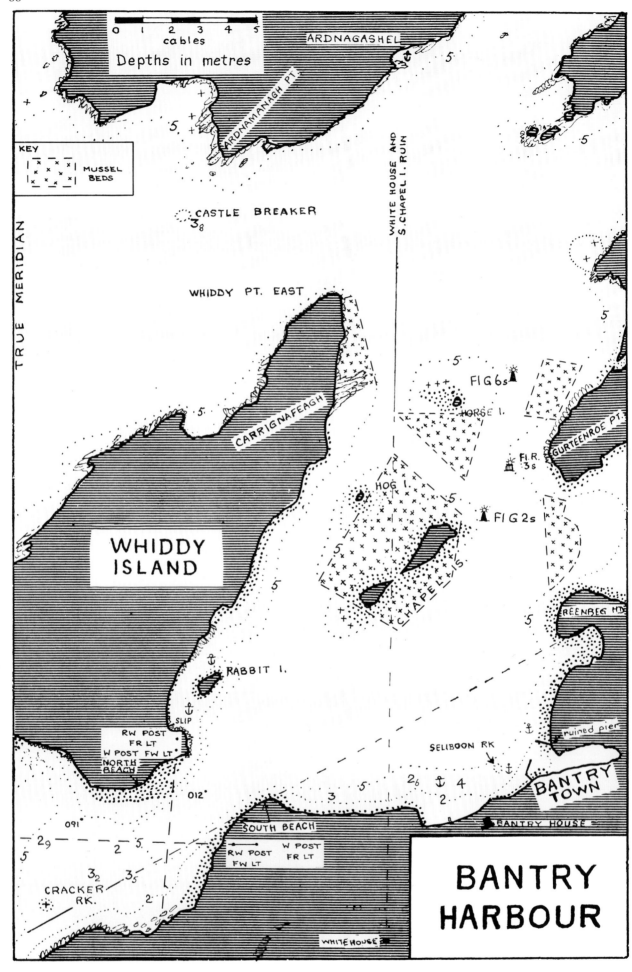

0 1 2 3 4 5
cables

Depths in metres

KEY

MUSSEL BEDS

ARDNAGASHEL

5

ARDNAMANAGH PT.

5

WHITE HOUSE AND S. CHAPEL I. RUIN

CASTLE BREAKER
3_8

5

TRUE MERIDIAN

WHIDDY PT. EAST

5

FIG 6s

HORSE I.

5

CARRIGNAFEAGH

GURTEENROE PT.

Fl.R. 3s

HOG I.

5

FIG 2s

WHIDDY ISLAND

5

CHAPEL IS.

5

GREENBEG HD

RABBIT I.

SLIP

ruined pier

RW POST FR LT
W POST FW LT
NORTH BEACH

SELIBOON RK

BANTRY TOWN

2_6 4

012°

2

3 5

091

SOUTH BEACH

BANTRY HOUSE

2_9 2 5

RW POST FW LT W POST FR LT

3_2 3_5

CRACKER RK.

2

WHITE HOUSE

BANTRY HARBOUR

at North Beach come in transit on 012°. The back mark is RW post with FR lt. the front is W post with FW lt. Follow this transit in until the bay opens up. However, do not approach N Beach closer than ³/₄ cable as the shoal is extending. The lights have approx. 1 M range. The sounding off Bantry House 0₃ on Admiralty Chart marks a drying rock, so be careful if approaching the shore to land as it looks quite clear close to the slipways. The tide in this entrance may reach 1¹/₂ kn. Shrimp pots appear in the autumn season; the W entrance may be thick with pots having small buoys of bottles or plastic floats.

Anchorages

1. One and half cables NNW of Town Pier, soft mud. Keep over 1 cable from the demolished pier on the N side as it is foul. There is also a berth to the W of the Town Pier between it and Seliboon Rock (2·3 m). Not recommended for yachts alongside as the outer berth and steps must be kept clear for fishing boats and Whiddy ferry. The inner part of the pier dries, however there is 2 m at the second and third berth, the dredged area of the basin is narrow so keep close to pier. Visitors moorings by arrangement. Contact Bantry Bay S.C., Gordon Harwick (027-50081) or The Anchor Bar (027-50012).

2. A better place is NW of Bantry House outside local yachts in 3 m, fair holding. The slips can be approached by dinghies at all states of the tide except LSW. The W slip is beside a public beach and it is inadvisable to leave a dinghy there during holiday time. This W slip (Abbey Slip) is the best for launching boats up to 5 tons having a gentle slope and straight approach. Beware of drying rock which has 0₃ marked on it on the Admiralty Chart.

3. It is quieter, also safer in W or NW wind, ³/₄ cable SW of Rabbit Island in 1·5 m, soft mud, or N of Rabbit Island, or best of all if draught permits inside Rabbit Island.

4. It is possible to go into the inner quays at Bantry for storing ship 1·5 m to 2 m at HW Neaps. Mud and rubbish bottom.

Tides

The streams are slack in the harbour and off the NE end of Whiddy do not exceed ¹/₂ kn but they reach a rate of 1¹/₂ kn in the W entrance to Bantry Harbour.

Supplies

There are good shops in Bantry where all kinds of stores are obtainable. Bus services to Cork. Water, diesel from Town Pier, PO, banks and hotels, EC Wed.

COAST WESTWARD OF BEAR ISLAND

From Fair Head at the W entrance to Bearhaven past Black Ball Head to Crow Head there are no dangers.

Pulleen Harbour

1¹/₂ miles W of Piper Sound is a small cove only suitable for exploration by the smallest yachts, of moderate draught, and in calm or very settled weather. If motoring in beware of lobster pots. The outer anchorage is between the 4·6 and 8·2 m soundings on chart 1840, bottom weed, fisherman type anchor recommended; this gives no shelter in any onshore wind. There is a very restricted inner anchorage NE of the 4·6 m sounding which can be entered after half flood by a yacht drawing 1 m, passing between two rocks (grass-topped) and anchoring immediately beyond them.

This inner pool has about 2 m, clean bottom, but there is scarcely room for even a small yacht to swing safely to one anchor. It is sheltered except from due S and normally swell-free except near HW. It would be prudent to reconnoitre the inner anchorage by dinghy and then, to avoid weed round the propellor, to tow or sail the yacht in. There may be open boats moored in the most N corner to an endless wire, to which the yacht's sternline might be taken. This corner is the best place to land. No facilities, except spring water.

Black Ball Head

is a bold, dark headland 81 m high with an old watch tower on its summit. Off this head there is sometimes a tidal race with both streams but more particularly with the W-going stream opposed to the wind. There is a small cove on the W side of the head called Black Ball Harbour but the anchorage is unsafe and there is a rock which narrows the entrance. **Crow Head** is 74 m high and has a small islet off it called Crow Island, 62 m high. Leamascoil Rock, 18 m high, lies very close to the S tip of the head and almost indistinguishable from it from the S. Two cables S of Crow Island is Cat Rock which covers at HW springs on which there is nearly always a big breaker. There is a passage between the Cat Rock and Crow Island. Bull's Forehead lies 1¹/₂ cables to the W of Crow Island and has 0·9 m over it. It is a dangerous rock as it so often does not break. A berth of 3 cables will clear the dangers off Crow Island. Having passed outside the Cat Rock a course towards Dursey Tower (250 m) leads well clear of the Bull's Forehead. There is a boat passage between Crow Island and the mainland; on a calm day with complete absence of swell, which is unusual, it is amusing to go through in a dinghy.

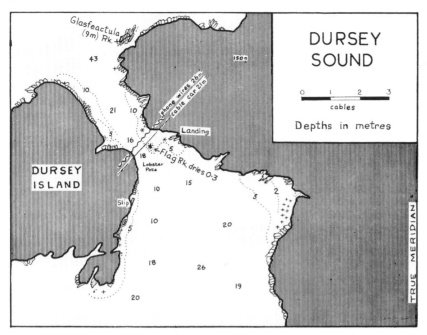

Dursey Sound

Glasfeactula
(9m) Rk.
43
10.
21   10
phone wires 26m
cable car 21m
5
16   Landing
18   ←Flag Rk. dries 0·3
Lobster
Pots
DURSEY
ISLAND
10   15
Slip   5   2
5   10   20
18   26   19
20

DURSEY
SOUND

0   1   2   3
cables

Depths in metres

TRUE MERIDIAN

Dursey Island & Sound viewed from the East.

A Western View of The Bull Rock.

DURSEY SOUND (see plan)

is a narrow and useful channel between Dursey Island and the mainland, but as the tides run up to 4 kn at springs it is advisable to go through with a favourable tide or at least before it reaches its maximum rate. Entering the sound from the S a peculiarity about which strangers should be forewarned is that having rounded Crow Head the bay presents the appearance of a cul-de-sac as the similarity of colour of the island and the mainland shores prevents contrast where they overlap.

Having cleared the Bull's Forehead off Crow Head steer for Illanebeg on the island shore. Look out for lobster pots SW of the entrance. Keep very close to the island shore going through the narrows which are only 1 cable wide. Flag Rock with only 0·3 m over it at LW lies almost in mid-channel in the narrowest part of the sound, thus limiting the navigable part to 90 m. The N-going tide sets directly on to the rock. There is deep water close to the shore of the island so a yacht should keep very close in. The E extremity of Scariff Island in line with the E shore of the island, 339° leads W of the 0·3 m rock. Note that Scariff Island, 252 m, and Deenish Island, 141 m, are the same shape viewed from the S. There is a cable car across the sound also a telephone wire; the least clearance at HWS is 21 m under the car itself with 24 m under the cables and 26 m under the telephone wires. There is usually a disturbed sea at the N entrance which could become dangerous in strong to gale force winds. The sea rebounds from the cliffs of Glasfeactula Rock, 9 m high, at the E side of the N entrance. Quite frequently a different wind is met on either side of the sound. Be prepared for sudden changes in wind direction going through the sound, especially near the N entrance where heavy squalls from the high ground may be met. On a glowering day with a Force 6 or better NW wind and a long, high swell the N entrance to the sound is a most impressive place. Salmon nets may be just N of the N entrance and it would be very dangerous to get onto one. If the conditions are suitable it is possible to anchor off the slip marked on the plan in 10m while waiting for the tide.

Tidal Streams

in the S run in about the direction of the channel. The N-going stream makes at +0135 Cobh (-0415 Dover) and the S-going stream at -0450 Cobh (+0145 Dover), springs rate in the narrows 4 kn, setting across the 0·3 m rock and forming eddies and overfalls there. There are eddies on both sides of the S entrance during the S-going stream.

DURSEY ISLAND

is 3½ miles long and its highest point, on which stands an old watch tower, is 250 m high. Its shores are clear of danger except off Dursey Head. The Cuckoo Rock (Culloo) is close in to the head but Lea Rock, which is awash at HW, is 1½ cables SW of the head. The N side of Bull Rock open S of the Cow, 300°, leads S of Lea Rock and Scariff Island, 9 miles N, open of Mealbeg Point (2 cables NW of Dursey Head), bearing 003°, leads W of it. In fine weather it is possible to land on the island at the boat slip in Dursey Sound shown on the plan. Telephone 50 m from the slip.

THE BULL

lies 2½ miles WNW of Dursey Head and is 89 m high. It is perforated in a SE and NW direction by an arched cavern through which the breaking seas roll in bad weather. There is a small gannetry on the rock. There are two detached rocks W of The Bull, one of which, the Gull, is 6 m high.

Light

A light Fl 15 s, 83 m, 23 M is shown from a lighthouse on the rock, visible from 220° through E to 186°.

The Cow

lies between the Bull Rock and Dursey Head, but slightly closer to The Bull, and is 62 m high. It also has arched caverns. The passages between these rocks and between the Cow and Dursey Islands are quite clear.

Calf and Heifer

are two small rocks lying very close together ¾ mile SW of Dursey Head. Calf is 21 m high and Heifer about 10 m. There is a red iron pillar on the Calf, the base of a lighthouse destroyed in 1881. There is often a considerable rebound of the waves in the channels between Dursey Island and the Cow and Calf.

Tidal Streams

Between Dursey Head and The Bull the S-going stream makes at -0350 Cobh (+0245 Dover) and the N-going at +0235 Cobh (-0315 Dover). Springrate about 3 kn. The streams run in about the directions of the channels between the rocks, causing a turbulent sea and often a race near Gull Rock S of the Cow.

Distances

Sheep Head to Dursey Head	14½ miles
Do. Dursey Sound	13¾ miles
Do. Castletown	7¼ miles
Do. Adrigole	9¾ miles
Do. Glengarriff	17½ miles
Glengarriff to Bantry	5¾ miles
Do. Adrigole	10 miles
Do. Castletown	16¾ miles
Do. Dursey Sound	28½ miles
Bantry to Adrigole (via W entrance) ..	10¼ miles
Do. Castletown	16¾ miles
Do. Dursey Sound	28¾ miles
Castletown to Dursey Sound	13¼ miles

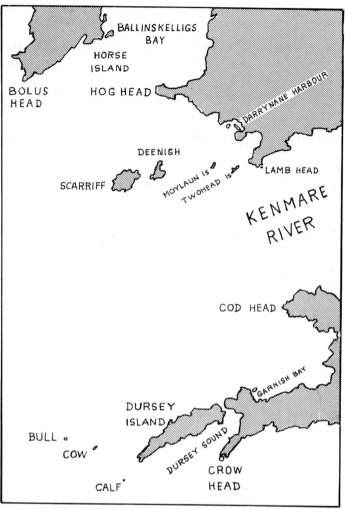

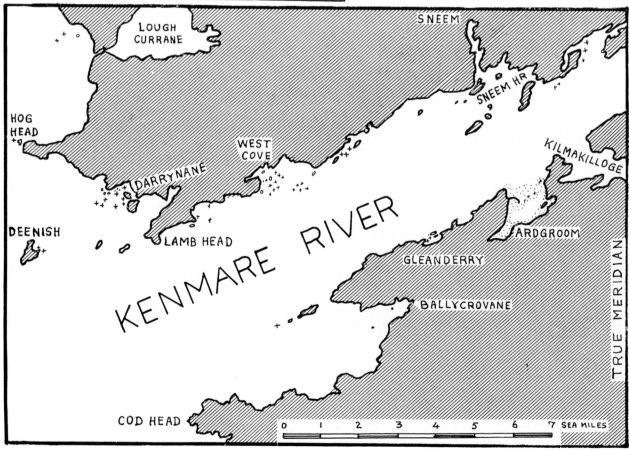

Chapter 4

KENMARE RIVER
TO VALENTIA

KENMARE RIVER
This beautiful large inlet extends about 28 miles ENE of the line of Scariff Islands and Dursey Island, at which point it is 7½ miles wide. The land on either side is mountainous and the scenery is magnificent. It contains numerous harbours and anchorages with varying degrees of shelter and accessibility. Its shores are generally foul and must be approached with caution but there is no danger in a mid-channel course as far as Sneem and Kilmakilloge, the favourite anchorages, some 16 miles from the entrance. The S shore until Kilmakilloge Harbour will be described first followed by the dangers and anchorages up to the head of the bay. This will be followed by the dangers and anchorages on the N shore of the bay. An intending visitor should carry the Kenmare River chart 2495 which has insets of some harbours and of the head of the inlet.

Tidal Streams
set fairly in and out of the Kenmare River. The ingoing stream makes at +0505 Cobh (-0045 Dover) and the outgoing at -0120 Cobh (+0515 Dover). Spring rate 0·5 to 0·8 kn in the outer bay, increasing to 1½ kn in the inner bay with turbulence off Dinish and Dunkerron Islands with the ebb and strong W winds. Between Scariff and Dursey Islands the streams run N and S, running N with the ingoing stream.

Coast — Dursey Head to Ardgroom
The N side of Dursey Island is steep-to except for a rock which always breaks ½ cable off Rutheen Point which is ¾ mile from Dursey Head. Ballydonegan Bay, between Dursey Sound and Cod's Head, is entirely exposed and only offers limited shelter in Garnish Bay, see below. There is a sunken rock, Tholane Breaker drying 0·3 m, 1½ cables offshore and ½ mile S of Cod's Head. Beyond Cod's Head is Coulagh Bay with Ballycrovane Harbour in its NE corner and many breakers SE of the direct course to that harbour. The N side of Coulagh Bay is formed by a series of islands and rocks which extend for 2 miles W from Kilcatherine Point. The first of these is Inishfarnard with a channel between it and Kilcatherine Point which is navigable with smooth water. W of Inishfarnard is Bridaun and W of that Bulligabridane which dries 1·2 m. Six cables SW of

Bridaun is the very dangerous Stickeen Rock with 1·5 m over it and which is frequently breaking. It is almost on the direct line from Cod's Head to Sneem. Dursey Island tower well open of Cod's Head, 220° leads N of it. Carrigeel, 2·4 m high, in line with the bottom of the valley between Miskish and Knockoura Hills and bearing 135° just clears Stickeen to the W. In line with the summit of Knockoura, bearing 146° it leads between Stickeen and Bulligabridane. In clear weather Miskish and Knockoura Hilla are easily recognised but Carrigeel can be hard to pick out against the land. Note that in a heavy sea the breakers extend W and N of Stickeen so give it a berth of at least 2 cables in these conditions.

A fish farm lit with buoys is positioned S of Inishfarnard just West of the channel between Inishfarnard and Kilcatherine Point.

GARNISH BAY (see plan)
is an open roadstead in the SW corner of Ballydonegan Bay. It can only be used for anchorage in settled weather and with the wind in the W sector. There are two anchorages.

1. W of the Carrigduff concrete beacon. It is important to find an area clear of weed and the water is usually clear enough to allow this. There is the least swell in this anchorage and it is convenient for landing. The approach N of Carrigduff beacon is kept clear of pots and nets.

2. A cable S of the beacon in 5 to 7 m, sand bottom. There is more room in this anchorage and the holding appears to be good.

Land at the slip in the boat harbour beside which there is a shop and a PO. There are so many nets, lobster, crab pots, shrimp pots, and fish pots set in this sector of Ballydonegan Bay that it is becoming unsuitable for yachts to use it. There is a real risk of getting hooked up. There appears to be a channel kept open N of the beacon which would allow access to anchorage 1. The harbour is not suitable for a yacht to berth alongside as there are spikes half way down the pier.

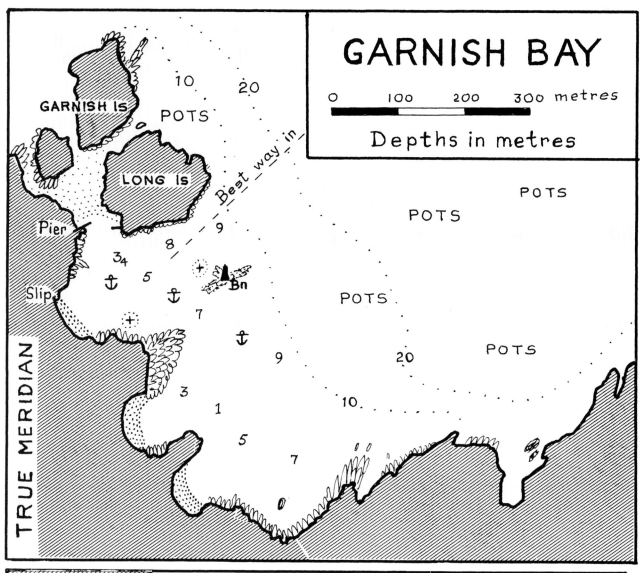

GARNISH BAY

0   100   200   300 metres

Depths in metres

GARNISH Is

POTS

10   20

LONG Is

Best way in

Pier

POTS

POTS

9

8

3 4

5

Bn

Slip

7

POTS

9

POTS

3

20

1

10

5

7

TRUE MERIDIAN

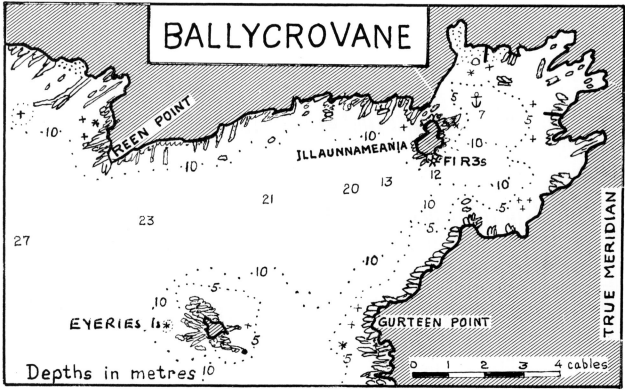

BALLYCROVANE

REEN POINT

10

10

10

ILLAUNNAMEANLA

5

7

10

5

Fl R 3s

10

12

13

10

20

21

10

5

23

10

5

27

10

10

5

EYERIES Is

10

5

GURTEEN POINT

5

Depths in metres 10

0   1   2   3   4 cables

TRUE MERIDIAN

BALLYCROVANE HARBOUR
(see plan and inset on chart 2495)

Coming from Cod's Head steer 057° with The Bull just showing astern till the summit of Inishfarnard is abeam, then steer to pass midway between Ainrush or Eyeries Island and the mainland N of it. Coming from the E use the passage between Inishfarnard and Kilcatherine Point in fine weather. Clearance lines for Stickeen Rock have already been given. Eyeries Island is 4 m high and has rocks all round it for a distance of 1½ cables. After passing it Illaunameanla, or Bird Island (2·3 m) will be seen at the NW side of Ballycrovane Harbour. There is a red beacon on the S side of Bird Island with a Fl R 3 s light. Gurteen Rock is ¾ cable off the S shore and dries 3·4 m. The N and E shores of the harbour are foul for over 1 cable. Fish farming temporarily stopped in this area. Reports to contrary please, however a new farm is reported SE of Inishfarnard.

Anchorage

Half a cable NE of Bird Island in 4 to 5 m, holding stiff mud. Exposed to W winds and subject to roll. In and after bad weather a big sea rolls in. Land at the pier. No supplies.

CLEANDERRY HARBOUR *(see plan)*

lies 3 miles E from Kilcatherine Point. Its entrance is concealed behind the low lying Illaunbweeheen (Yellow Island), which is long and grass-covered. It can be identified by Shamrock Hill to the W and a big patch of scrubby trees on the hillside above it. The actual entrance is only 8 m wide at LW with low rocks on either side and has 2 m at LW. There is a considerable pool inside with depths up to 13 m. The W end of the harbour is exposed at HW when the rocks cover and the best shelter is at the E end where there is space to anchor clear of a few moorings; but not much room to swing. Smooth water and a very careful, slow approach is essential. There are two reefs, which cover, just inside the entrance and to port. The course to the E end lies between them. The N reef is a continuation of a narrow point which forms the S side of a small creek. There are no convenient supplies. Fish farming reported.

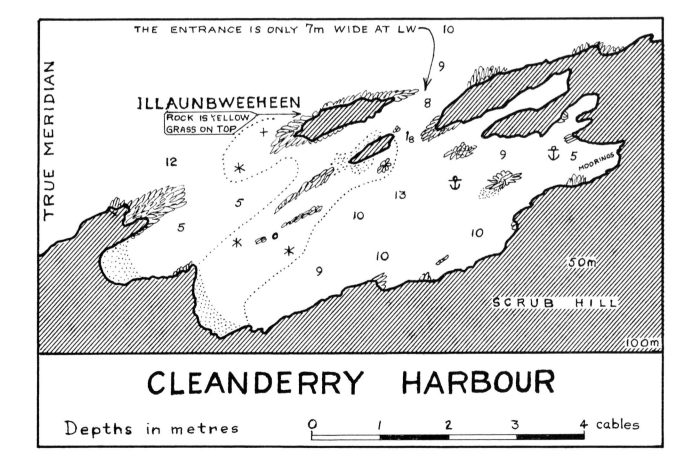

CLEANDERRY HARBOUR

Depths in metres

Cleanderry on the Kenmare River

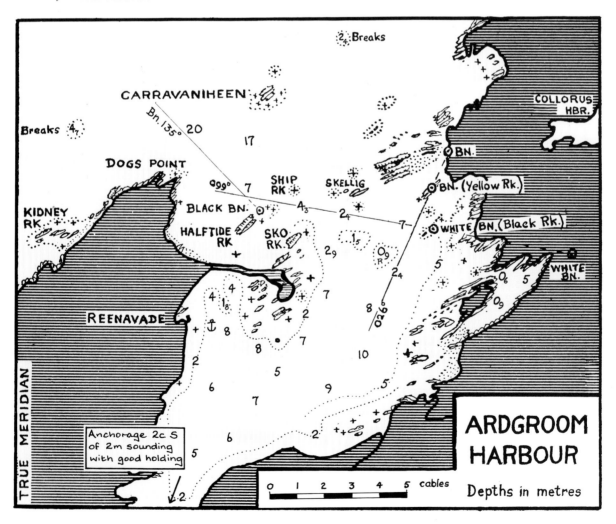

2₄ Breaks

CARRAVANIHEEN

Bn. 135° 20

COLLORUS
HBR.

Breaks 4₇

17

DOGS POINT

099° 7

SHIP
RK.

SKELLIG

BN.

BN. (Yellow Rk.)

KIDNEY
RK.

BLACK BN.

4₃

2₄

7

WHITE BN. (Black Rk.)

HALFTIDE
RK.

SKO
RK.

1₅

O₉
R

2₄

5

WHITE
BN.

4

4 1₈

7

2

2₉

8
026°

O₆ 5

O₉

REENAVADE

8

8

7

2

5

10

5

6

9

5

7

Anchorage 2c S
of 2m sounding
with good holding

6

2

5

TRUE MERIDIAN

↓ 2

0 1 2 3 4 5 cables

ARDGROOM HARBOUR

Depths in metres

ARDGROOM HARBOUR *(see plan)*

on the S side opposite Sneem has good shelter but the entrance channel is so narrow and intricate that a large yacht should not attempt it without auxiliary power. Carravaniheen, a rocky ledge the top of which shows 1 m above HW, stretches across in front of the entrance and 3 cables NE of this rock is a 2·4 m rock which sometimes breaks. There is another breaker (in gales) 4 cables NW of Dogs Point and ½ mile SW of this point is Kidney Rock, just showing at HW. See inset chart 2495. Enter between Carravaniheen and Dogs Point on the W side steering SE towards the beacon on Halftide Rock and identify the leading marks for the bar. The whole place is a mass of rocks and spits so the leading lines must be carefully followed.

The leading marks across the bar are white beacons. One is on the E shore near a new white building and the other on Black Rock, which dries 2 m. These beacons in line 099° lead clear over the bar in 2·4 m passing Ship Rock (awash at LW) and Skellig Rock 1 m high to port and Halftide Rock and Sko Rock to starboard.

The shore (back) beacon is sometimes obscured by bushes which have grown up around it and which are cut at intervals. It may only appear just as the 099° bearing is reached. A stranger would be advised not to attempt the entrance in bad weather if this beacon cannot be recognised. However approaching the front beacon on a bearing of 100° from a position just N of Halftide Rock would be safe in good conditions. Borrow nothing to the N of this line abreast Skellig Rock.

About ½ mile beyond the beacon on Halftide Rock the second set of leading marks will be picked up. These marks are dark, concrete in colour with faded black bands painted on them and are on the port hand side. The front beacon is on the Yellow Rock (awash at HW) and the other on the mainland to the NNE of it. The moment these two marks come in line bear hard a-starboard and keep them in line astern bearing 026°. Continue on this course for ¼ mile and then haul around slowly to the W, keeping about 2 cables off the S shore. Do not alter course for the anchorage until the quay bears 300° so as to avoid the mass of rocks extending nearly ½ mile S from the bar.

A white chimney to the North of the white beacon on the shore could easily be mistaken for the beacon which was obscured by bushes but was not very white. The second set of beacons are very difficult to distinguish from the surrounding rocks.

The one on Yellow Rock has a pointed top and faded fine black bands. The one on the shore has a light coloured square facing the bearing line (easy to see coming out, but difficult to see coming in until on the bearing line).

Anchorage

½ a cable E of the quay at Reenavade in 4 m. No stores are available nearer than Ardgroom village, distance about 2 miles. Holding is fair.

The anchorage inside Bird Island looks attractive but the bottom is grass on soft mud and the holding poor. The safest anchorage is taken up by moorings.

An area in which there is a large amount of fish farming reported. The approach bearings may have been encroached on. Also there is a large amount of waste plastic about.

Ardgroom Harbour from NE.

Kilmakilloge Harbour from NW.

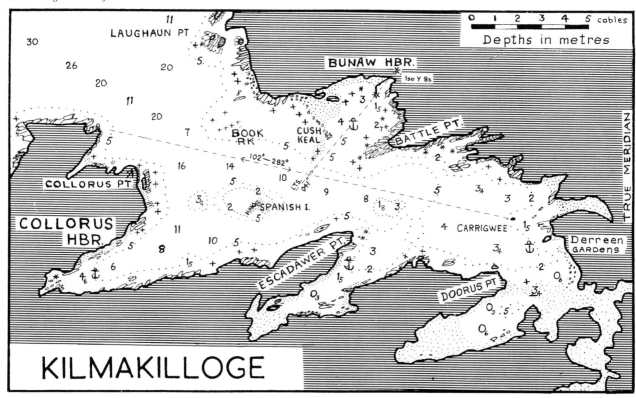

KILMAKILLOGE HARBOUR *(see plan)*

just E of Ardgroom, has three different anchorages where good shelter can be obtained amid lovely scenery. This is one of the most lovely harbours on the coast. However there are now fish farming operations in the main bay and a platform is anchored to the S of Escadawer Point. If approaching from the E give Laughaun Point on the E side of the entrance a berth of over 2 cables. A berth of 1 cable will keep you clear at the W side of entrance. Enter on a mid-channel course and steer slightly W of Spanish Island, a heap of large pebbles 4·3 high, in the centre of the harbour. Book Rocks, which is awash at LW, extends for nearly 3

cables off the E shore near a grassy precipice 52 m high. Collorus Point, just inside the entrance to starboard, must not be approached closer than 1½ cables. When past Collorus Point alter course to 102° for the woods near Dereen House. Give Spanish Island, to starboard, a berth of over 1 cable and note that the dangerous rocks fronting Bunaw Harbour, to port, extend 2½ cables SW from Battle Point. There is a rocky patch with only 1·8 m over it 1½ cables NE of Escadawer Point on the S side. Nearly 1 cable SE of Escadawer Point there is the very thin stump of a perch which covers and which marks the extremity of another reef off the point.

Carrigwee (Yellow Rock) is awash at HW and

has deep water close up to it. The perch on it is missing and the jagged stump previously remaining is reported missing in 1992. Note that a straight line from the W side of the entrance to Carrigwee clears all dangers within the harbour. Even at LW Carrigwee is hard to pick up against the land but its position is marked by a small hut on the shore which can be picked up in sunny weather through binoculars. There are leading lights in position 51° 46·74'N 9° 48·40'W showing Iso Y 8 s.

Anchorage

in 3 to 4 m 1 cable SW of Carrigwee or in 1·5 to 3 m S of Escadawer Point avoiding the broken perch mentioned above. When the tide is up landing may be made by dinghy near a road bridge SE of Dereen. There is a shop nearby at Lauragh, 1½ miles E of Dereen House. Dereen gardens can be visited. Fish farming reported mouth of entry bearing and in the coves. Two pubs, fuel at Luragh.

COLLORUS HARBOUR

is within Kilmakilloge on the W side and offers good shelter. After entering midway between Collorus Point and Book Rocks head SSW giving the shore on the W side a berth of over 1 cable, and note that there is a sounding of 0·3 m 1 cable W of Spanish Island and a patch with 3·4 m 2 cables W of that island. Keep at least 1 cable clear from either shore. Anchor in the middle of the harbour in 5 m abreast a small disused boat slip on the S shore. The holding is rather soft and unreliable with weed. No shops.

BUNAW HARBOUR

is also within Kilmakilloge and is on the NE side. In NW winds the shelter is poor. The entrance is 1 cable wide between unmarked rocks. Cushkeal to port shows at LW and both sides of the harbour are foul. Enter with the pierhead bearing 041°. There are poles coloured yellow and black bands with orange leading lights on this bearing and it is possible to see the glasses of the lights by day. The front light is on the pierhead. Anchor on the leading line between the pier and Cushkeal in 3 to 4 m and show a riding light if spending the night. There is 0·4 m alongside the pier (village side) at LW, bottom clean gravel but 0·8 m N of the steps a good berth for a shallow draft yacht. Limited stores available, pub on quay with meals, accommodation and showers. Water, fuel, gas and moorings.

INNER PART OF THE KENMARE RIVER

The following are the principal dangers. Chart 2495 is necessary.

Carrignawohill

is a ledge which dries 0·5 m and extends 2 cables offshore ½ mile NE Kilmakilloge.

Maiden Rock

dries 0·5 m and lies in mid-channel due S of the summit of Rossmore Island. there is a G Cone buoy 2½ cables NW of the rock.

Church Rocks

with 1·7 m over them lie ½ mile S by E of Maiden Rock and there are dangerous rocks extending WSW towards Church Rocks from Leaghillaun.

Lackeen Rocks and Hallissy Rock

are spread out in mid-channel just E of Blackwater. They have least depths of 2·4 m so with calm sea may be ignored by small yachts, but with any sea running should be avoided, which is not difficult as both shores are relatively clean in their vicinity.

Feagh Rock

which dries 0·2 m, lies 1 cable offshore about 3 cables E of Reenafeagh Point which is S of Hallissy Rock. A white pillar on the point bearing 245° leads just N of the rock.

Carrignaronebeg

dries 2·6 m and stands at the SE corner of a large foul area. A large tripod beacon on the rock marks the N side of the navigable channel.

Brennel Island (or Horse Island)

is surrounded by unmarked rocks, those bordering the channel being awash or submerged at HW. The three perches shown on old editions of Chart 2495 no longer exist, but the jagged stump of the perch on William's Rock, W of the island, covers at HW.

Bowlings Rock

with 0·8 m over it, lies just to the N of the line from Carrignaronebeg beacon to Illaungowla at the entrance to Dunkerron Harbour.

Note that a course of 066° from Maiden Rock buoy leads clear of all dangers to the mouth of Dunkerron Harbour. The clear channel past Brennel Island is 2 cables wide. Carrignaronebeg beacon will show and should be passed at a distance of between ½ and 1 cable.

ANCHORAGES IN THE KENMARE RIVER ABOVE SNEEM
Lehid Harbour

is a small cove SE of Church Rocks and should therefore be approached from the W. It has an extremely narrow entrance between rocky ledges on either side. A small boat might attempt it on a good day. There is anchorage in the centre of the harbour in 3 m.

Ormond's Harbour (inset chart 2495)

is sheltered by Ormond's Island on its N side and by Hog Island on its SW side. Ormond's Island (10 m) has rocks extending 1½ cables to the W of it and there are also rocks ½ cable off its S and N sides while the bar between it and the E shore only covers at last quarter flood. Hog Island is 1½ cables off the S shore, and there is foul ground between it and the shore, and also rocks ½ cable NE of it. The entrance is 1 cable wide, and is obstructed by a rock which, however, has 2·3 m over it. Keep midway between Ormond and Hog Islands and when 1 cable past Hog Island Head SE and anchor E of Hog Island in 5 m, mud bottom. No stores are available. Landing on S shore.

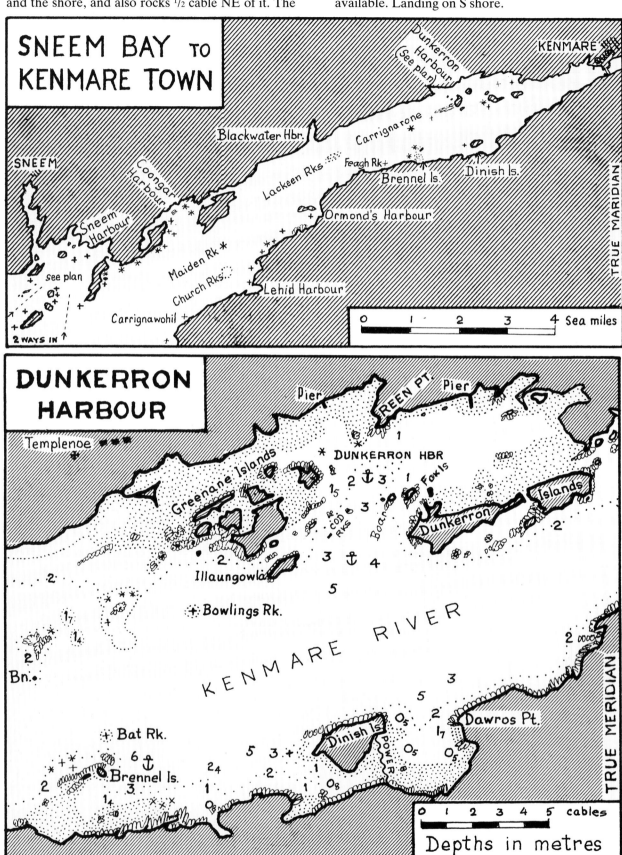

SNEEM BAY TO KENMARE TOWN

KENMARE

Dunkerron Harbour (See plan)

SNEEM

Blackwater Hbr.

Coongar Harbour

Carrignarone

Feagh Rk

Brennel Is.

Dinish Is.

Lackeen Rks

Sneem Harbour

Ormond's Harbour

see plan

Maiden Rk

Church Rks.

Lehid Harbour

Carrignawohil

2 WAYS IN

TRUE MARIDIAN

0   1   2   3   4 Sea miles

DUNKERRON HARBOUR

Pier

REEN PT.

Pier

Templenoe

DUNKERRON HBR

Greenane Islands

Fox Is.

Dunkerron Islands

COD RKS

Boar

Dunkerron

Illaungowla

Bowlings Rk.

KENMARE RIVER

Bn.

Bat Rk.

Dawros Pt.

POWER

Dinish Is.

Brennel Is.

TRUE MERIDIAN

0   1   2   3   4   5 cables

Depths in metres

Dinish Island

With wind between SW and E there is good shelter halfway between the quay on the E of the island and Dawros Point, 2 m. With NE wind there is shelter SW of the island in 2 m but there are sunken outlying rocks on either side of the approach. Fish farming reported just off bay to E, with amber flashing lights.

Kenmare Quay

1/2 mile from the town, may be reached at HW but it is not recommended especially for drying out. The bottom is mud which dries. Good supplies in the town. Anchorage SE of Quay in the Pool. Kenmare Town, good hotels and restaurants, fuel and gas, all supplies. Local information from Mr Jerry Hanley, Kenmare (0667-41143).

Dunkerron Harbour *(see plan)*

on the N side offers good shelter. It is a very pretty harbour with woods on Dunkerron Island. The entrance is between Illaungowla on the W and Dunkerron Island on the E. Cod Rocks on the W

side have foul ground behind them. They are 2·4 and 3 m high respectively. Fox Island 4·9 m high on the E side and inside the harbour has a reef extending 1 cable W into the harbour terminating in the Boar. Anchor (1) Between Cod Rock and the Boar in 2·5 to 3·5 m. (2) Midway between Reen Point on the N shore and Fox Island in 1·8 m. Landing at Templenoe pier NW of Reen Point which dries at LW. Stores from Kenmare, 3 miles along the main tourist road. (EC Thurs.) Templenoe village, 1 mile W along the road has PO, bar and limited stores.

Blackwater Harbour

is a very pretty river mouth on the N shore 2³/₄ miles NE of the Maiden Rock buoy. There is a good stone pier on the W side with 1·2 m at the end, dries at the steps and further in, sand bottom. In the channel there is 3·5 m just beyond the pier but no room to swing and many small boat moorings. If entering, keep about 10 m off the head of the pier because there is a sandbank further out in the middle of the apparent channel. It is much simpler

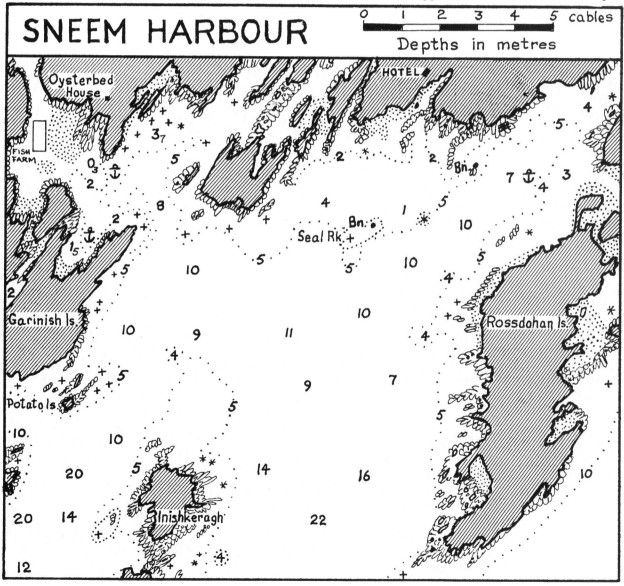

SNEEM HARBOUR

0 1 2 3 4 5 cables

Depths in metres

to anchor just outside the point S of the pier in 3·5 to 7 m, where there is good shelter in W winds. No stores but the main road and a PO close at hand.

Coongar Bay

provides sheltered anchorage in 3·5 to 9 m except in S or SW winds. Its shore are foul for a considerable distance especially at the head of the bay and there is no convenient landing. The much more attractive harbour of Sneem 2½ miles further W is usually preferred.

Sneem Harbour

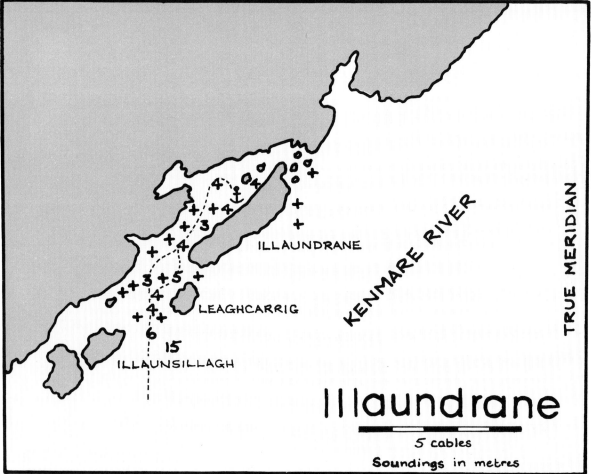

ILLAUNDRANE

KENMARE RIVER

TRUE MERIDIAN

LEAGHCARRIG

15

ILLAUNSILLAGH

Illaundrane

5 cables

Soundings in metres

SNEEM HARBOUR (see plan)

This lovely harbour on the N side of the Kenmare River is, like Glengarriff, one that should not be missed by yachtsmen cruising on this coast. The main entrance lies between Sherky Island (34 m) on the W side and Rossdohan Island (36 m) on the E. Sherky Island and Illaunanadan to the NE of it are both clear on their S shores, but Inishkeragh, the third island of the group, must be given a berth of 1½ cables. Rossdohan on the E side must be given a berth of over 2½ cables as Bullig Point, its SW extremity, is foul. From a position 2 cables off Inishkeragh alter course to 336° for the NE corner of Garinish Island. Parknasilla hotel is conspicuous.

There is also a passage N of Sherky Island, but if using this the Cottoner Rock, which dries 0·6 m and lies 1¼ cables to the N of the middle of Sherkey Island must be avoided. Derryquin Castle, at the NE corner of the bay, in line with the sharp peak of Derrygariff Mt, 051°, was the line to clear N of Cottoner Rock and also N of rocks which cover and lie 1 cable N of Inishkeragh. The line also leads S of the Murin patch which extends 1 cable E of Potato Island, a small islet to the S of Garinish Island. Derryquin Castle has recently been demolished so this transit is only of use to those familiar with its position. A check on this is that it was immediately below a pronounced "V" notch in the trees on the hillside above. However, the grey, stone mass of its foundation remains and is used as a rubbish dump and can be identified with care through field glasses. If it cannot be spotted or visibility prevents Derrygariff Mt being seen, keep close to Inishkeelaghmore (Pigeon Island) which is clear on its S side and then 1 cable S of Potato Island. Do not haul up for Garinish Island until 2 cables past Potato Island. When rounding the NE corner of Garinish Island give it a berth of ½ cable. Note that there is a rock, awash at LW, 1¼ cables SW of Illaunslea on the E side of the approach to Garinish Island.

Anchorages

There is a delightful and perfectly sheltered anchorage in the bight NE of Garinish Island in 2 to 4 m. There is a heavy, old chain across the mouth of the bight so anchors should be buoyed in this position. Landing at the Oysterbed House pier on the mainland N of Garinish Island. Water tap. There is 1·5 m LAT alongside this pier but there are no ladders on the S face and the steps on the W side is a bad place to leave a dinghy. Fish farming reported SW Oysterbed House.

There is another anchorage in 6 to 8 m N of Rossdohan Island, but the shelter there is not so good in SW winds. The hotel maintains a mooring suitable for a 35 ft yacht. If making for this anchorage note that Seal Rock (Carrignarone) lies in the middle of the NE part of the harbour. It covers at HW but is marked by a stone beacon. There is a rocky patch nearly awash at LW 1¼ cables E of Seal Rock beacon. There is another perch on a rock which also covers off Long Point NE of Seal Rock. The N and NW sides of Rossdohan are very foul everywhere and should be given a berth of at least 2 cables. There is 2·5 m at HWN at Parknasilla hotel pier.

Supplies

There are good shops, hotels and PO in the town of Sneem which is about 2 miles from the harbour. At half flood it is possible to row a punt to a small slip near the town. With slightly more flood an outboard can be used with caution. Bus connection to Kenmare, Killarney etc. Large hotel (Parknasilla) with landing slip NNE of Seal Rock. Information on area from Paddy Breen (0667-5129).

Tidal Streams

Between Scariff and Lamb Head the stream makes to the S at -0110 Cobh (+0515 Dover) and to the N at +0500 Cobh (-0050 Dover). The rate of these streams is about 1½ kn.

Sneem to Lamb Head

A course of 250° from S of Sherky Island to Lamb Head at the W entrance to Kenmare River and distant 8½ miles is clear of all danger. However if beating down river the shore to the N of this line is foul with many rocks and breakers. Carrigheela is only 2 cables N of the course from Sherkey Island to Lamb Head and covers at HW. It is over ½ mile offshore and 4 miles E of Lamb Head. West Cove lies inside it. Beara Rocks cover at HW and are 3 cables offshore SW of a sharp peak 116 m high at the W side of West Cove. Brigbeg dries 0·3 m and lies 3 cables E of Illaunaweelaun (1 mile E of Lamb's Head) and there are other rocks inside it. Lamb's Head is 101 m high and Lamb's Island very close E of the head is 34 m high and there is a rock called Blackhead Rock (6 m) close S of the island. Close SW of Blackhead Rock is Carrigatemple, a rock which covers at HW.

Illaundrane

anchorage lies 3 M due W of Skerky Island. Enter between Leaghcarrig and Illaunsillagh, giving each a good berth, pass N or S of the patch which is awash at LW about 1 cable N of Leaghcarrig then head for the NW shore of Illaundrane which is clean and anchor half way along the island in 4 metres. Well sheltered from all winds. The N passage is only available by dinghy as is the lagoon at Loughan. No supplies.

West Cove from SE

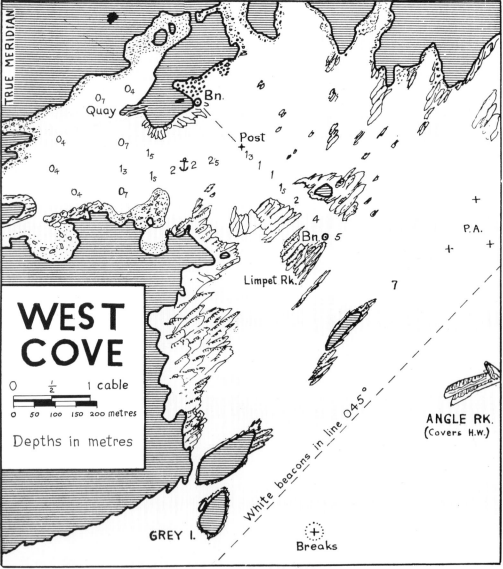

Based on the Ordnance Survey by permission of the Government (Permit No. 2191)

WEST COVE *(see plan)*

is a very well sheltered but a rather shallow harbour lying in the NW corner of the rock-strewn bight behind Carrigheela, mentioned above, and some 6 miles SW of Sneem. The approach is well marked by beacons. The entrance is very narrow, but receives some shelter from the rocks further out and a yacht with reliable power should always be able to get in. At LAT there are depths of 1m sand just inside the entrance.

Directions

The sharp peak already mentioned 3 miles up from Lamb's Head should be readily identified and the shore finally approached just E of its summit between Illaunroe and Grey Island till two white beacons about 1 mile away come in line bearing 045°. Enter on this line between Grey Island and the breaker 1½ cables E of it and clear of other rocks further in. There is no beacon on Grey Island, as shown on the old fathom chart 2495; the front white beacon just mentioned is on Burnt Island and the rear beacon on the mainland just NE of it. The quay at West Cove will be seen to port with a house in trees above it and a white beacon E of it; there is also a stone beacon on Limpet Rock at the SW side of the entrance. When the white beacon comes open to the right of Limpet beacon and in line with the rock on the opposite side of the entrance swing round to port and steer for Limpet beacon. An iron post with ring topmark inside the entrance kept central on the white beacon leads safely through, but very close to Limpet beacon, passing which it is permissible to bring the post just to the left of the beacon. Then keep them in line and turn to port when 18 m from the post. A safe course up the cove is with the post in line with the rear approach beacon.

Approach may also be made from the NE passing between Noon Island (about 2 cables W of Daniel's Island) and Coosane (Grampus) Rock 3 cables SW of it. Coosane Rock never covers but there is a sunken rock 100 m N of it. From here steer to pass 1 to 2 cables SW of Burnt Island and join the 045° leading line, the front beacon being on Burnt Island. Keep closely to the line till on the marks for the entrance above.

Anchorage

The only place with over 1·5 m at LAT is abreast the cottage E of the quay; the deep area here is narrow. The big house in line with the tank on the quay gives about 1·5 m. Further up is mostly 0·4 to 0·7 m, sand in the middle or mud NW of the quay. A yacht might berth at the quay and dry out, but the lower part of the vertical wooden fenders has rotted away. Landing at the steps beyond the quay at all tides. No facilities, but main road ¼ mile, leading E to Castlecove, 1 mile, shop and petrol, and W to Caherdaniel 2¾ miles.

Temporary anchorage: White Strand Bay 2M E of West Cove, Good for lunchtime in offshore winds. Bar and restaurant on beach

HOG ISLANDS

Scariff or Great Hog Island 252 m is steep-to all round except for a rock which always shows, called Farbregagh, close in on its N side, and a reef called Scariff Hedges, which extends for about 2 cables off the W side. Deenish or Little Hog (141 m) is foul on its NE side for a distance of 1 cable. Moylaun Island (21 m) 1½ miles E of Deenish has a rock 1½ cables SW of it, called Moylaun Rock, which always shows. Two Headed Island (40 m) close to Lamb Head is steep-to all round. The passages between all these islands are clear. The bay E of Deenish Island (marked "Landing" on old chart) is a good temporary anchorage in S and W winds.

Distances

Dursey Head to Puffin Island	16½ miles
Dursey Head to Sneem	18¾ miles
Dursey Sound to Puffin Island	16¼ miles
Dursey Sound to Sneem	16½ miles
Sneem to Dunkerron Harbour	11 miles
Sneem to Kilmakilloge	4½ miles
Sneem to Ardgroom	4¼ miles
Sneem to Puffin Island	21¾ miles
Dunkerron to Kilmakilloge	10½ miles
Dunkerron to Dursey Sound	24½ miles

Course from Scariff Island

If making for Valentia from the Kenmare River you can either go outside the Scariff Islands or use one of the passages inside it, the shortest course being between Moylaun Island and Deenish.

Darrynane photographed on line of leading marks into Harbour.

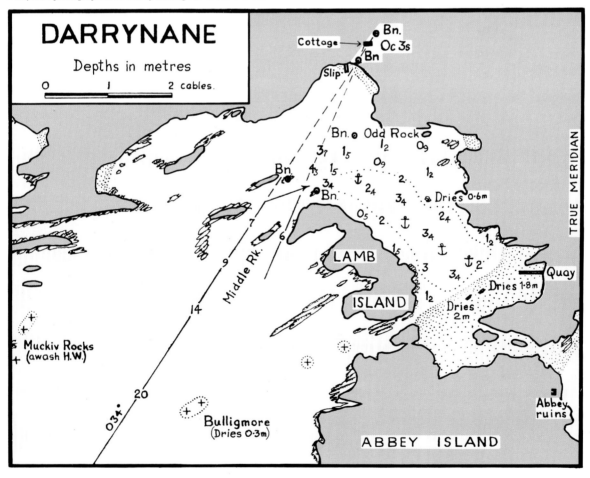

DARRYNANE

Depths in metres

0   1   2 cables.

Cottage →

Bn.
Oc 3s

Bn

Slip

Bn. Odd Rock
1₂   0₉
1₅   0₉
Bn   1₂
4₃ 1₅
3₄   2₄   2   Dries 0·6m
Bn   2₄   3₄   2₄
0₅   2   3₄
3₄
1₅   2
Middle Rk.   3   3₄   2   Quay
6   LAMB   3₄   Dries 1·8m
7
ISLAND   1₂   Dries
9   2m
14

Muckiv Rocks
(awash H.W.)

20

Bulligmore
(Dries 0·3m)

Abbey
ruins

TRUE MERIDIAN

ABBEY   ISLAND

DERRYNANE BAY

lies just N of Lamb's Head, and affords little shelter in the prevailing winds, but with settled offshore winds there is anchorage in 9 m to SE of the Abbey ruins on Abbey Island (45 m). The N and SE sides of the bay are foul for 2 cables off and the E side, which is sandy, dried out. To the N of Abbey Island is Derrynane Harbour. The huge sandy beaches stand out well.

DERRYNANE HARBOUR (see plan)

This beautiful little land-locked harbour provides good shelter, free from swell and amid delightful surroundings. The entrance is, however, extremely narrow and faces SW. Auxiliary power would frequently be essential. Entrance or exit is impossible in bad weather, especially from the SW. There are squalls in the anchorage in N winds.

Beacons

There are two conspicuous, white, leading beacons, lights Oc 3 s, on the shore opposite to the entrance. In line, bearing 034°, they lead just NW of Moylaun and between Muckiv Rocks and the Bulligmore and clear into the entrance N of Middle Rock. There is a beacon with a dark red top on a rock on the NW side of the entrance. There is another beacon with a blackish top on Lamb Rock off Lamb's Island on the E side of the entrance. The only way in is between these two beacons. There is a grey concrete beacon on a rock on the N side of the harbour. If lights can not be seen do not attempt to enter in the dark.

Dangers

Muckiv Rocks, awash at HW and which always show, extend 3½ cables SW from the shore WSW of the entrance. Bulligmore, with less than 1·5 m, lies 3½ cables SW of Lamb's Island which shelters the harbour. Middle Rock, which always shows, lies in the centre of the entrance. It is long and low, steep-to on its SE and NW sides, but runs out under water NE and SW.

Lamb's Island is foul to the SW with ledge and a sunken rock off its SW tip. It is steep-to on its NE side, except for Lamb Rock, marked by a black beacon. On the N side of the channel there are several rocks which show and which are steep-to on their SE side. The inner of these is marked by the red beacon.

Approach

Approaching from the S pick up Moylaun Island (21 m) and having passed it bring The Bull (W of Dursey Island) open just W of Moylaun Island. This line leads direct to the entrance, and the leading marks will be picked up ahead. Bring them in line bearing 034°. From the N, do not close the shore within ¾ mile until the leading marks come in line.

These marks lead between the outer dangers, Muckiv and Bulligmore, and up to the usual entrance NW of Middle Rock. At the entrance however the line leads too close to the outlying Halftide Rock on the NW side and a middle course should be taken. Having passed Middle Rock, alter course to starboard, enter between the beacons, the best water being close to the SE beacon, and steer immediately towards the quay at the SE end of the harbour.

Should there be considerably less swell S of Middle Rock than N of it, when definitely past Bulligmore alter course to bring the near leading mark in line with the W chimney of the cottage between the two leading marks or keep a little closer to Middle Rock than this transit. When past Middle Rock enter as already described. At night a good torch is needed to identify the two dark beacons and to find a safe position to anchor. Bulligmore is considered to be very dangerous - be sure you are on the correct transit during approach.

Anchorage

Anchor clear of local moorings and of the sunken rock on the NE side. The Lamb Island side is usually preferred. The SE end of the harbour has least swell, but the edge of the beach near the quay is fairly steep-to. There is a new quay beside the slip below the leading lights; a yacht could berth across the end of it at HW provided there is no swell, but she should not dry out there. The bottom is sand which dries at LWS. Land at either quay. Water tap, privately owned, beside a shed 200 m from the quay on the right. Milk from Keating's Hotel, ½ mile. Stores from Caherdaniel, 2 miles. No fuel.

Ballinskelligs Bay

is a large bay N of the Scariffs. Hog's Head at the SE end of the bay is 162 m high and has two rocks called the Pigs 1½ cables NW of it. These are always visible but there is a reef which uncovers at LW lying 1 cable W of them. Horse Island is close to the W side of the bay and the sound between it and the shore is choked with rocks and there are two sunken rocks close to its E end. Blue Boy Rock, which has foul ground inside it, lies ½ mile off the NE shore of the bay and is awash at LW. Bay Rock with 1·2 m over it lies ¾ mile NE of Horse Island. All the centre of the bay is a prohibited anchorage owing to telegraph cables.

Anchorage

In settled weather there is temporary anchorage just N of Horse Island. Anchor in 4 m to the N of the island with the S to the W of the island just closed in. This is a little to the S of the permanent mooring of a lobster boat and is surprisingly swell free in SW winds. Nearest stores, with butcher, from Waterville, across the bay. This is a long, often rough and dangerous way by dinghy.

108

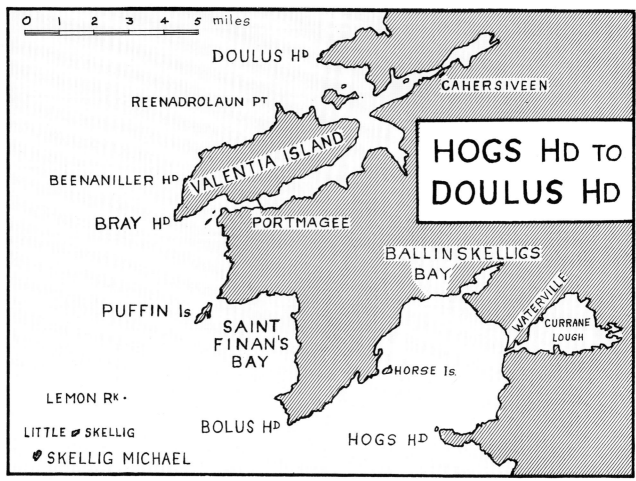

O 1 2 3 4 5 miles

DOULUS H^D

CAHERSIVEEN

REENADROLAUN P^T

HOGS H^D TO DOULUS H^D

BEENANILLER H^D

VALENTIA ISLAND

BRAY H^D

PORTMAGEE

BALLINSKELLIGS BAY

WATERVILLE

CURRANE LOUGH

PUFFIN Is

SAINT FINAN'S BAY

HORSE Is.

LEMON R^K ·

BOLUS H^D

HOGS H^D

LITTLE SKELLIG

SKELLIG MICHAEL

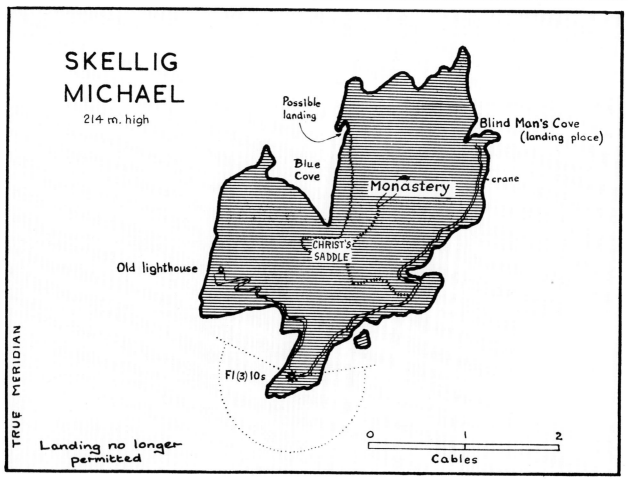

SKELLIG MICHAEL

214 m. high

Possible landing

Blind Man's Cove (landing place)

Blue Cove

Monastery

crane

CHRIST'S SADDLE

Old lighthouse

TRUE MERIDIAN

Fl (3) 10s

Landing no longer permitted

0 1 2

Cables

Bolus Head to Puffin Island

Bolus Head is a bold headland with high land (407 m) behind it and has a tower on its top. Ducalla Head, 1 mile N of it, is foul for 1 cable offshore. St Finan's Bay lies between Ducalla Head and Puffin Island and is completely exposed to the prevailing wind. There is a landing slip at Carriganea on the N shore but there is a rock in the entrance and it is only suitable for small, open boats in fine weather.

Skellig Michael from E.

GREAT SKELLIG OR SKELLIG MICHAEL

so called on account of a legendary appearance of St Michael on the island, lies 6 miles SW of Puffin Island. It is nearly ¹/₂ mile long and rises to a pinnacle of 214 m.

Light

A light Fl (3)10 s, 53 m, 27 M is shown from a white lighthouse on the S point of the island. Visible from 262° through N to 115°. Partly obscured within 6 miles between 110° and 115°. High on the SW point there is a disused lighthouse.

The Washerwoman

a rock 1·8 m high, lies 3 cables SW of Great Skellig and has two sunken rocks ¹/₂ cable off its N end.

LITTLE SKELLIG

lies 1 mile to the ENE of Great Skellig and is 131 m high. There is a small sunken rock less than ¹/₂ cable off its S side. Lemon Rock is 20 m high and lies about midway between Little Skellig and Puffin Island. Little Skellig has no easy landing place and is the second largest gannetry near Britain. In Spring there are 20,000 pairs of gannets flying in and out from the island, diving all around and perched in serried ranks on every ledge. It is a marvellous sight.

Tidal Streams

Between the Skelligs and the shore the N-going stream makes at +0500 Cobh (-0050 Dover) and the S-going stream at -0110 Cobh (+0525 Dover). Spring rate 1¹/₂ kn. W of the rocks the tides are complex but do not exceed 1 kn.

GREAT SKELLIG *(see plan)*

High on the slope of the ridge which runs out to the NE of the island are the remains of a very early Christian settlement. Despite 1400 years of summer and winter gales and the ravages of Viking raids and the occupation of centuries they are in a surprisingly good state of preservation and the beehive huts with their dry stone construction could be lived in to this day. Their worst enemy is the modern tourist with his trash and souvenir hunting.

There are five beehive cells and two oratories and three sets of steps leading up from the sea. The panorama of sea, island, mountain and rock from the monastery is superb and the climb up and visit there is an unforgettable experience.

Directions

About 1 cable S of the N point of the islands is a small gut called Blind Man's Cove. It faces NE and the inner part of its SE side is a concrete quay about 16 m long and with deep water alongside. The width between the quay and the rock face opposite is only 8 m so it is necessary to be able to manoeuvre out in reverse. In settled weather with little or no swell it is possible to lie alongside in a yacht. With even a slight swell the sea surges in and out of the cave at the head of the cove so good fenders and stout warps are essential. It would be most unwise to leave a yacht unattended for even a very short time.

The quay is used by the lighthouse authorities and by fishing boats and launches which bring tourists out to the rock, these boats come and go frequently. In addition conditions can change very quickly, easily within the time taken to reach the summit and return.

There are three sets of steps leading to the monastery. The easiest ascent to the top should be commenced from a point some 300 m along the path to the lighthouse whence a good flight of steps leads up to Christ's Saddle and from there on to the monastery. Another set leads from near Blind Man's Cove up the E face of the rock. The lowest part of this approach was blasted away when the lighthouse road was built so it is not easy to get on to it and it is not advised without local knowledge.

In E conditions it might be possible to land from a dinghy near the NE end of Blue Cove on the NW side of the rock. There is nowhere to leave the dinghy. A very steep and probably dangerous path leads from there up to Christ's Sadrdle. The lower part of this approach has been destroyed so a difficult scramble is needed at the start. In the event sea conditions for a landing there would be rare. Lobster pots are often set in the cove.

Salmon drift nets running from the W of the rock and extending to The Washerwoman may be found in summer.

Puffin Island

is nearly 1 mile long and is 165 m high with steep cliffs both on the island itself and on the shore behind it. Canduff, its SW extremity is steep-to. Puffin Sound is obstructed by rocks but has a narrow passage, 1/4 cable wide, through which the tides run rapidly. It is a very imposing place and quite possible in fine weather and little swell. Keep 1/4 of the width of the sound from the W side. It is not recommended without auxiliary power as the wind can be very flukey. In bad weather it breaks right across, a most formidable sight.

In fresh onshore winds and swell there can be a very disturbed sea between Bolus Head and Bray Head on Valentia Island.

VALENTIA HARBOUR

has two entrances. One, known as Portmagee Sound, which is narrow and intricate, is S of Valentia Island, and the main entrance is to the N of the island.

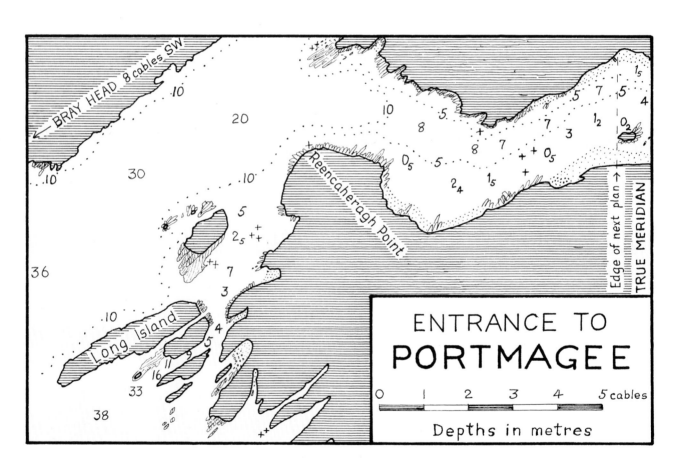

PORTMAGEE SOUND (Chart 2125) *(see plans)*

There is a safe anchorage at Portmagee but the sound beyond it, which leads to Valentia Harbour, has an intricate stretch with minimum depth of only 1·5 m so a fair wind or an engine are essential and a rising tide desirable. Immediately beyond Portmagee there is a road bridge with an opening span.

The shores at the entrance are mainly high cliffs and there is usually a bad sea at the entrance. There are some rocks and islets on the S side of the entrance but nothing dangerous as they all show. Long Island has a rock off its W end called Bull Rock (7 m) and to NE of it are Horse Island and the Deaf Rocks. Reencaheragh Point (21 m) on the

Portmagee Sound from W.

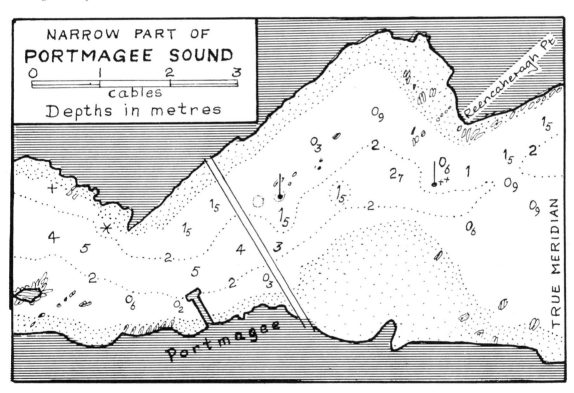

NARROW PART OF
PORTMAGEE SOUND

0   1   2   3

cables

Depths in metres

TRUE MERIDIAN

Reencaheragh Pt.

Portmagee

mainland is foul for a distance of ¼ cable, and Skuagh Point on the N side on which there is the ruin of a fort has rocks off it which show.

Enter midway between these points and steer 110°. The point on the island shore 4 cables beyond Skuagh Point is called Quay Brack, and the Anchor Rock, which is sunken, lies ¼ cable off this point. When abeam of Quay Brack alter course to 065°, and this will lead up parallel to the island shore and about ½ cable off and to the N of a shallow rocky patch, which lies 1¼ cables to ESE of Quay Brack. Loughan Islet (4 m) will be seen to starboard. There is foul ground around it. There is a large

bungalow (Coarabeg House) on the N side of the bight ahead; when this house and Loughan Islet are in line, alter course for the pier at Portmagee on the S shore. There is a good anchorage in 5 m off the pier. There is a strong tide in the anchorage.

While it is possible to approach between Short Island, S of Long Island and Black Rock to the S of Short Island this cannot be recommended. The passage is so narrow that any sea or swell would cause it to break and any obstruction from a lobster pot or trammel net could cause hitting the rocks on either side. The channel is used by small local fishing boats.

Berthing

From the SW end of the pier about ¾ of its outer side is shallow with a drying ledge extending out about 3·3 m and ending abruptly at the start of the deep NE quarter where the fishing boats lie afloat at LW. It is only really safe for yachts to berth around HW and they should not be left unattended. Near the SW end there are often lobster pounds. Shop with butcher, restaurant, two pubs, water on quay, visitors moorings on enquiring at quay side pub.

Valentia Harbour viewed from the East over Renard Point.

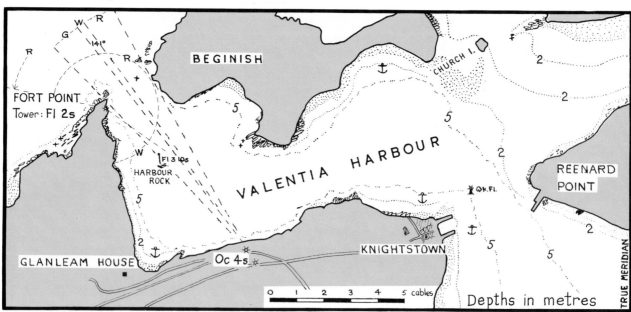

Portmagee to Valentia (Knightstown)

If proceeding to Valentia, anchor or berth near HW at the pierhead. **Communications:** Valentia Radio (066-76109); Lifeboat - Secretary (066-76126); Pilots - Workboats - Divers - Towage (066-76124); Repairs - Hulls - Valentia Marine (066-76184) with heavy duty slip; Repairs - Engines and Electrics - Nolan's Garage (066-76200). The bridge opening between 0900-1700 Mon-Fri is arranged through Mr. Rudd (066-72143) office or (066-74251) home or Mr. Courtney (066-77174). There is room to jill about or lie to at either side of the bridge. Having passed through the bridge a course for Luinga Rock perch leads clear of Doory Foot, a gravel spit which dries and extends for 2 cables off the shore. The perch to port just beyond the bridge marks Labyrodeen Rocks. Luinga and Labyrodeen perches are red.

Keep close to the perch on Luinga Rock, and note that there are shoal soundings for a distance of 3/4 cable E of it, and also shoal soundings extending NE from Doory Foot. After passing close S of Luinga Rock haul up slowly for the N shore until the perches on Labyrodeen and Luinga come in line, and keep on this line for a few cables until the channel widens out and you are clear of a sunken rock about 1/2 cable S of Reenanea point. Follow a mid-channel course up between the island and mainland as far as Reenglass Point, distant 3 miles, after which head for the anchorage off Knightstown, which is situated on the NE corner of Valentia Island.

Valentia Island

is 7 miles long with remarkable slate cliffs on its N shore. Bray Head is the SW extremity of the island and is a bold headland with high land, 338 m, 3/4 mile to the NE of it. Bearhaboy (Bray) Rocks, 1 1/2 cables off the head, are conspicuous, the outer rock showing 2 m and the inner one 6 m above HW. There are sunken rocks 1/2 cable offshore 1 cable and 3 cables N of Bearhaboy Rocks. Echala (Schala) Rock which is 23 m high, lies 1 1/2 cables SW of Beenaniller (Benilla) Head. 1 1/2 cables N of Beenaniller Head lies Gallaunaniller (Gillaun) Rock which covers at HW. There are WT masts near Reenadrolaun (Reenada) Point and at night there are fixed, dim, red lights on top of them. Cromwell or Fort Point with its lighthouse is at the W entrance to Valentia Harbour. There is a dangerous 3 m rock 1 cable W of Reenadrolaun Point.

VALENTIA HARBOUR (see plan)

Steer a mid-channel course between Cromwell (or Fort) Point on the W side, and Beginish Island on the E side, along the line of the leading marks ashore. Cromwell Point is low and has sunken rocks extending 1/2 cable NNE of it, on which there is always a big break, and there are rocks which show and a sunken rock extending 3/4 cable off the opposite shore. There is often a nasty sea at the entrance which can be dangerous in NW gales.

Light

A light Fl WR 2 s, 16 m, 15 M is shown from a white tower on Cromwell Point. R from 102° through S to 304°, W thence to 351°. Obscured from seaward from near Reenadrolaun Point and by Doulus Head when bearing more than about 180°.

Directional light and leading marks

The front mark is a white cone beacon, the rear mark a white triangle on a wall. In line, bearing 141° they lead in. The light is shown from the front leading mark. Oc 4 s, WRG 25 m, 11,8,8 M. G 134° to 140°. W 140° to 142°. R 142° to 148°. The white sector leads in. The back mark shows Oc 4 s, 5 M visible 133° to 233°'. Now painted orange and white stripes.

Harbour Rock 130 m long dries 2·6 m and is marked by an E Card BYB E Card Iron Mast Q(3) 10s, 4m, 5M, with an obscured sector from 040° - 080° (40°). It lies on the W side of the fairway. There is a rock with 3·4 m over it 1/2 cable NE of the perch. Beginish patch lies on the E side of the fairway between Harbour Rock and Beginish Island. It has 4·3 m over it on Racoon Rock. After passing the Harbour Rock the harbour trends to the E and is free of dangers. However note the ledges and sunken rocks up to 2 cables W of Cruppaun Point.

As Knights Town comes abeam note the position of the Foot, a gravel spit which dries 1·2 to 0·6 m in places and extends ENE from Valentia. Its extremity is marked by an E Card Lt buoy VQ(3) 5s. Unless there is a big N sea running a yacht beating in, or out may stand outside the leading marks, avoiding Harbour Rock and the Cruppaun ledges.

Anchorages

1. The most convenient for landing is 1/2 cable SE of the ferry pier at Knightstown in 4 kn, mud. This is well sheltered in W winds. The holding is poor so in strong wind a kedge is advisable. Avoid anchoring near the telegraph cable which runs from Reenard Point to the N breakwater.

2. Just W of the Foot, near the RNLI boat, good holding in 2·5 m. Well sheltered in winds from SE to SW. Land on the pebble beach at the back of the harbour pier.

3. In strong NW winds better shelter can be obtained by anchoring in the sandy bay at the SE end of Beginish Island, avoiding the buoys used by fishing boats.

4. Excellent shelter in winds from W to SE in the bay S of Harbour Rock. Anchor in 4 m 1 cable from

the head of the bay opposite Glanleam House. Land on pebble beach. Road to Knightstown, 1½ miles.

5. There is a pier at Reenard Point opposite Knightstown. It projects 100 yards from the shore in a SW direction at the site of the old ferry slip which remains on the NW site of the pier. Only the outer 35 m on the SE side is 3 m deep. There are steps on the SE side which is generally in poor condition. Subject to the requirements of fishing boats a yacht might moor here.

6. There are moorings available at times - contact Dermot Walshe in Knightstown or Des Lavelle – *see below*.

Supplies

Knightstown has limited shops including butcher (open 0900 to 1030 Mon to Thur, all day Fri and Sat). Petrol pump at the harbour. Water tap at N side of S pier. Good gash disposal at both piers on Thursdays at midday. Ferry to Reenard Point which is 2½ miles from Cahersiveen. Ice and sometimes frozen fish from the cold store at Reenard Point. RNLI lifeboat is moored N of the Foot. Boat repairs at Valentia Marine Ltd (066-76184). Gas at J. Reeds (066-76120). HM Des Lavelle (066-76124 Fax 76309) who can organise permanent moorings. Launderette at Knightstown Hospital. Minibus - R. Nolan Garage (066-76200). Taxi - D. MacCrohan (066-76412). Bus to Cahersiveen/Killarney and train to Dublin.

Tidal Streams

Valentia Harbour. The tides set fairly through both the N and S entrances to the harbour, meeting about half-way between Portmagee and Reenglass Point. The ingoing stream makes at +0450 Cobh (-0100 Dover) and the outgoing at -0135 Cobh (+0500 Dover). Spring rate at Portmagee, 2 kn and 1½ kn off Fort Point and Knightstown. The same times apply to the Caher River, where the tides run strongly in the channel and in the anchorage off the quay.

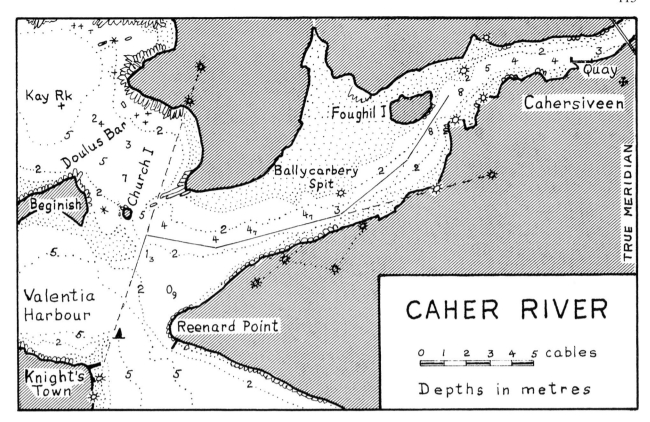

CAHER RIVER (VALENTIA RIVER)
AND CAHERSIVEEN *(see plan)*

Cahersiveen is a considerable market town which would be useful for supplies. It is situated 2 miles up the Caher River from Valentia Harbour and can be approached over Doulus Bar in 2·4 m or across the sheltered Caher bar in 1·4 m. The difficult pilotage of this river is aided by twelve FG leading lights whose position is shown on the plan, and also two FR, Nos 11 and 12. They are mounted on poles with B and Y horizontal bands and are discernible by day. There is also a light Fl R 3 s on Ballycarbery Spit. The lights cannot be relied on.

Directions

From Valentia a yacht is advised to start as early on the tide as she can cross Caher Bar. The plan shows the recommended course, following the five leading lines whose bearings are as follows (outwards in brackets): Nos 1, 2,13 and 14—019° (199°). Nos 4 and 5—100° (280°). Nos 7 and 8—076° (256°). Nos 3, 4, 9 and 10—053° (233°). Nos 5, 6,11 and 12—035° (215°). As soon as No 9 is past abeam steer 050° so as to pass nearer to No 11 than to No 10, then follow a mid-channel course till the quay at Cahirciveen is reached. Rocky spurs extend from both shores.

From Doulus Bay

at LWS the depth in the bar is not less than 2·4 m, but this entrance is not recommended if a big sea is running. Give Black Rocks (Doulus Rocks) a berth of ¹/₂ cable, then steer for the E end of Beginish as soon as Reenard Point opens to port of it; this line leads closer to Black Rocks than to Kay Rock with 0·9 m which is 2 cables E of them. When Lamb Island and the N point of Beginish are about to open alter course to keep them so astern till Reenard Point opens to the E of Church Island. Then steer to pass 50 m E of Church Island so as to avoid Passage Rock, which dries 1·5 m and lies under a cable E of the island. Then join the line of Nos 4 and 5 leading lights.

Anchorage

Anchor just S of midstream abreast the quay. The tide runs about 2 kn at springs. The projecting mole gives some shelter in W winds to the most W berth at the quay. There is a ring bolt on this mole. A yacht of 1·5 m draft would probably lie afloat at this berth at LW neaps. The best depth is at the W end near the mole. There is a small drying reef on the N shore opposite this mole. A yacht might be left here unattended if local fishermen who are friendly can be contacted. There is a bridge across the river just E of the town.

Supplies

Many good shops with all normal groceries and butcher. The town is ¹/₂ mile from the quay. Garage. Bus service to Killarney and Tralee. EC Thur. Water from a tap on the E side of the fishery building on the quay. The quay has 5m at LW springs at the W end. Summer tourist office. Marine Engineer Mr. J. Kelly (066-72502).

Part 2

WEST COAST

DINGLE BAY
to
BLOODY FORELAND

Introduction to Part 2

The Coast and its scenery

From seaward the whole coast of Ireland is beautiful. In the south, low cliffs are backed by green fields and distant views of mountains; the headlands are bold and rocky, often surmounted by a lighthouse or an old watch tower. North of the Fastnet the scenery becomes more dramatic. There are cliffs and headlands in great variety, and often on a majestic scale, with high mountains beyond them. Offshore, in many places, there are spectacular rocks and islands; there are golden sands and picturesque anchorages . The colouring in sunlight is superb. To quote the late H. J. Hanson, (from the Cruising Association handbook) there is: "The glory of the sea in fine weather at sundown, when it often resembles a lake of molten gold."

The wild and rocky west coast is fully exposed to the Atlantic swell and in unsettled weather is usually a lee shore. If a yacht is overtaken by bad weather and the low visibility which often goes with it, and if an anchorage known to her skipper is not near at hand, he will probably have no choice but to get clear of the land and await an improvement. As a cruising ground it can therefore only be recommended for well-found and not-too-small yachts capable of getting to windward in any conditions.

On the other hand, in fine weather the coast provides some of the most fascinating sailing imaginable, with many well-sheltered anchorages and endless scope for exploration. The sea is empty of shipping, except for local fishing craft. The scenery is varied and magnificent. The inhabitants are courteous and friendly.

A good selection of groceries and liquor is obtainable in most villages, and first class hotels are to be found within a few miles of most anchorages.

Fog is comparatively rare.

Tidal streams are to be found in appendix 3 and are not particularly strong except off salient points and in narrow entrances.

SYNOPSIS

The coast from Valentia to Bloody Foreland 240 miles NNE consists of cruising grounds offering shelter, in which a yacht may move around in comfort and pleasant surroundings even when the sea is rough outside, with intervening stretches of exposed coast which most crews will hope to pass

quickly and in good weather. Only two of these latter sometimes involve a night passage, namely Dingle to Aran and Mayo to Donegal, each about 75 miles. The weather can change extremely quickly and on either of these passages you might have to run up to 35 miles for shelter, so it is well worth waiting for suitable conditions. On most of the coast however distances between safe anchorages are of the order of 10 to 20 miles.

PASSAGE NOTES

BLASKET SOUND TO CONNEMARA
ACHILL TO NORTH CONNEMARA

If making a passage River: from Sybil Point in Kerry to the Aran Islands note that the course to Gregory Sound, 030°, 64 miles, passes 7 miles W of Loop Head and that there is no light between there and Inisheer Light 33 miles NE. If making for Galway the course to South Sound, 036°, 65 miles, passes only 4 miles from Loop Head and only 3 miles from Hag Head and the Cliffs of Moher. In poor visibility or at night it is important not to get to the E of the direct course. In clear weather Kilkee town lights show up surprisingly well to seaward.

If making a passage to the S the same conditions will apply and, in addition, there is no major light between Loop Head and Inishtearaght, a distance of 39 miles. The direct courses are outside the range of visibility of Little Samphire Light. Note carefully the limited arc of visibility of Inishtearaght Light.

Caution

Chart 2679 shows overfalls 4 and 10 miles NNW of Inishtearaght. In bad weather this area should be avoided altogether as the sea is very steep and confused. In 1975 a yacht lying a-hull there in a gale had her coach roof stove in by a huge breaker.

Set

In the prevailing W swell there will be a pronounced set to the E. In making a passage from the Aran Islands to the Blaskets it would be wise to allow 5° for this and possibly more with a light wind and a heavy swell.

Day or Night Passage

In good conditions and a steady wind there it is easy to make the passage in daylight in June or July. However, especially sailing S, a night passage is often advisable, giving a daylight landfall on the Dingle Peninsula and avoiding the possibility of having to beat out around the Blaskets in the dark.

At night, if rounding Tearaght, note that the rocks extend for 1 mile W of the light and that Great Foze Rock is 3¼ miles SSW of it. Again note the arc of visibility of the light to the S.

Working N by day, the low land and Magharee Islands E of Brandon Bay will not be sighted, but the high ground to the E of Kerry Head will be seen in clear weather, followed by Loop Head lighthouse with its conspicuous white wall running S to the sea.

Between Aran Islands and the Blasket Sound trawlers may be sighted and sometimes, especially at night, pair trawlers with the trawl between them. Off the mouth of the Shannon salmon drift nets may be met, in some cases several miles long.

If rounding Eeragh Island light at night give it a berth of at least ½ mile as the rocks to the W of the light dry out a long way with heavy breakers (this is the NW end of Aran Islands).

APPROACHES

To the Connemara coast from the South

In clear weather and in daylight the approach presents no difficulty. The Connemara Mountains will have been in view for sometime and the coastal hills will be easy to identify while still well offshore. Course can then be shaped for the Aran Islands, the Skerd Rocks or Slyne Head as required and a positive fix secured before reaching the offshore rocks.

Similarly in clear weather by night the lights on Slyne Head, Eeragh Island and Inisheer will give a good fix well clear of danger. However, a stranger would be prudent to heave to and await daylight rather than relying on picking up the somewhat dim lights on Croaghnakeela, Inishnee or Kiggaul Bay. The light on Straw Island at the entrance to Kilronan Harbour has recently been raised and is now visible S through Gregory Sound. Fishing boats use this sound by night employing a safe bearing on the light. A stranger should use it with caution.

In bad visibility the only possible approach would be to make the S side of the Aran Islands making certain that visibility will be sufficient to identify the landfall on the islands. By night it would be prudent to heave to and await daylight.

With driving mist and strong to gale force winds any approach to the outer dangers would be foolhardy. The coast from Inishbofin Island S and SE to the Aran Islands becomes a confused mass of breaking rocks and shoals and as the sea builds up it will break on shoals normally considered safe. The only seamanlike action would be to maintain course and offing safe W of all the dangers if that is possible or else heave to to await the clearance, remembering that in summer weather this will usually not exceed some 6 hours before the wind begins to veer W with the mist giving way to brighter weather.

To the Connemara coast from the North

Here conditions are somewhat different as no long approach passage is involved, a yacht will normally be day sailing S from Blacksod Bay or Achill. However if a yacht should be caught by a sudden and unexpected deterioration in the weather the same conditions as in the approach to the S would apply. It might be possible to make the Bills and then to Inishturk and so to Davillaun. From there it would be possible to make Inishbofin Harbour, Cleggan or Ballynakill Bay. With Clew Bay and Achill Sound to leeward it would probably be wiser to seek shelter there or keep to sea, rounding Slyne Head if necessary, until conditions improved.

PASSAGE MAKING

A yachtsman sailing round Ireland and not wishing to explore Donegal or Sligo Bay usually sails from Broad Haven to Aran Island or vice versa, almost 70 miles, so it can only be a day sail with a fresh suitable wind. If not going fast enough and anchoring for the night is desired, going either way, head in for Teelin or in bad weather to Killybegs. Going NE Rathlin O'Birne is the best landfall as it has no off-lying dangers and a good light and the cliffs of Slieve League are most above 500 m. If wishing to anchor before Aran Island, Church Pool is a safe place though uncomfortable in N and E winds, but be careful to avoid a rock and breaking shoals between it and the S entrance of Aran. Sailing down towards Erris Head the first local thing seen is The Stags of Broad Haven, 90 m high, and at night Broad Haven and Eagle Island lights. If the wind goes S of W and you approach the shore E of the Stags you might, in daylight, anchor in Portacloy or a further E bay, but Porturlin and Kilcummin Roads are bad in fresh S wind and Killala can only be entered above ½ tide. So it might be better to tack W for Broad Haven, which can be entered in the dark.

Caution

The direct course from Rathlin O'Birne N to Rinrawros Point on Aran Island leads clear of danger but there is a set, strongest on the flood, in towards the dangers of Boylagh Bay which must be guarded against. Continuing on passage to Bloody Foreland keep well to seaward of the Donegal Stags and the Bullogconnell Shoals, described later in chapter VII.

Ports of Refuge

If running for shelter into Donegal Bay in strong W winds and unable to fetch Broad Haven, Kilcummin Roads should be considered preferable to Sligo, and if the wind changed it would be possible to go into Killala towards high tide. But the best choice, though further E, would be Killybegs.

CHAPTER V

Fifteen miles from Valentia takes you to the Dingle Peninsula, where there is now a new marina at Dingle town, with most of the usual facilities. In settled weather there is fine scenery to be enjoyed and an unrivalled sense of remoteness. The Blaskets, though officially evacuated more than once, still appear to have a few inhabitants in summer and make an interesting visit. It is now a National Park, with Peig Syaerts House open to tourists at times.

The Shannon Estuary is seldom entered by passing yachts, but it has several good anchorages in pleasant pastoral surroundings; moreover it has fairly strong tides, so if it is a beat down river the ebb will shorten it.

CHAPTER VI

The most fascinating cruising ground is the 35 miles of the Connemara coast between Cashla Bay and Slyne Head with the Aran islands offshore . A glance at the chart of it will show the countless possibilities of day sailing in its large sheltered bays which meander miles inland, or along the coast outside them amongst islets and half-tide rocks with not a buoy and scarcely a day-mark anywhere. The sandy beaches between stretches of low rock in the foreground combine with the peaks of the Twelve Pins as a magnificent background to make some of the finest scenery in Ireland. Aran has the largest community of the offshore islands and its Cyclopean fort Dun Aengus is one of the most remarkable relics of pre-history in the world and attracts a steady flow of tourists.

CHAPTER VII

Next comes the 55 mile stretch from Slyne Head to Eagle Island which has a number of interesting islands and bays, but distances a little greater and passages more exposed than south Connemara. It has ideal yacht harbours at Ardbear Bay (near Clifden), Ballynakill harbour, Little Killary and Clew Bay, and many more from which to choose.

The islands include Inishbofin with the best natural harbour of any Irish island, guarded by a Cromwellian fort. Inishturk, high and rocky, the smallest and most isolated community of all the islands. Clare, larger but almost as isolated, once the stronghold of that remarkable pirate queen Grace O'Malley or Granuaile, whose castle dominates the harbour. Achill, Ireland's splendid largest island, is a complete contrast being a favourite holiday resort connected to the mainland by a short bridge. Finally the uninhabited small islands off the low Mullet Peninsula include Inishglora, where storm petrels nest in the early Christian relics, including a chapel dedicated to St. Brendan the Navigator who is believed to have reached America 1,000 years before Columbus.

One of the many bays on this coast Clew Bay is remarkable for its hundreds of rounded grassy islets while nearby Killary is reminiscent of a Norwegian fiord.

Achill Sound provides interesting pilotage and one or two good anchorages, but H.T. cables now rule out a through passage for most yachts. The passage between Blacksod and Broadhaven is open, the bridge at Belmullet canal is passable if you have a tabernacle or minimum draft.

CHAPTER VIII

The almost unbroken line of cliffs stretching for 24 miles between Broadhaven and Killala Bays fronts the most remote and sparsely inhabited part of Ireland. It is known to few because it is often a lee shore, also because those short of time usually prefer to cross directly from Broadhaven past Rathlin O'Birne to Church Pool, Boylagh Bay or Aran roads. Donegal Bay is a most attractive area of open sailing water with striking views of mountains all around and a choice of passages of between 15 and 30 miles across it. Its inner part has several interesting anchorages between Sligo and Killybegs; Inishmurray, no longer inhabited, is well worth a visit to see its unique collection of early Christian buildings.

From Teelin to Church Bay is a dog-leg passage 28 miles entirely without shelter past a most impressive variety of huge cliffs. Finally the Rosses, running 15 miles from Aranmore to the Bloody Foreland, is a delightful cruising area somewhat similar to Connemara, but with fewer breakers and isolated dangers. It is normally visited by a yacht sailing round Ireland as it is on the direct route and has several safe anchorages.

122

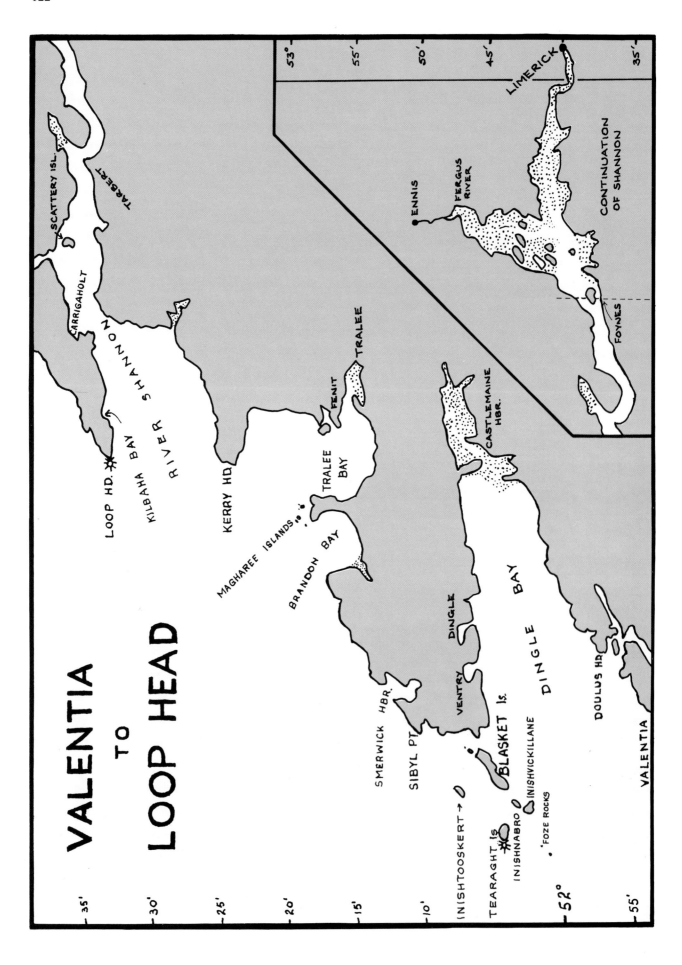

VALENTIA
TO
LOOP HEAD

Chapter 5

VALENTIA TO
THE SHANNON

Charts (for details see Appendix 1). It is quite possible to sail past this part of the coast, and to take shelter in Dingle or the Shannon if necessary, using only the small scale chart 2254. It is worth having 2790 if intending to visit Dingle, Ventry and the Blaskets. For the Magharees 2739 is required and this is also of help for Tralee Bay and Fenit. Four large scale charts 1819, 1547, 1548 and 1549 cover the Shannon to Foynes.

Tides
HW at Loop Head occurs at about the same time as at Galway, Valentia being at most 1 hour earlier. The rise on the coast is about 4 m at springs and 3·3 m at neaps. Up the estuaries and inlets the times are later and the rise greater. Some details are given in the text and in Appendix 3.

DINGLE BAY
This fine and picturesque bay is 10 miles wide at its entrance between Valentia Island and Great Blasket Island and extends E for 20 miles to Castlemaine Harbour at its head. It is exposed to the full force of the Atlantic but offers shelter near its entrance at Valentia Harbour on the S side, already described, and in Ventry and Dingle Harbours which now has a marina on the N shore, 4¹/₂ and 8 miles respectively inside Slea Head. Castlemaine Harbour at its head is fronted by a dangerous bar and yachtsmen are advised not to consider entering it except in very calm and settled weather.

Tides
Across the entrance to the bay the streams run N and S. There is little stream in the bay. The streams are strong in Castlemaine Harbour and entrance and in the entrance to Dingle Harbour.

Coast
The shores of Dingle Bay are singularly free from off-lying dangers. On the S shore there is a breaker 3¹/₂ cables NE of Canglass Point; Reenadrolaun Point, on Valentia Island, open NW of Doulus Head, bearing 223°, clears this breaker. On the N shore of the bay there is only Crow Rock in the approach to Dingle Harbour, see below.

CASTLEMAINE HARBOUR
This estuary is entered between Rossbehy and Inch Points; it is extensive in area and largely dries at LW. The entrance is about 1 mile wide. Rossbehy Point extends 2 miles from the S shore and Inch Point about 2¹/₂ miles from the N shore. Both points are formed of low and irregular sand dunes, partly covered with grass and fronted by sand beaches on which the surf breaks continuously. There is a stone beacon which is not conspicuous, on the N tip of Rossbehy Point.

Bar
Extensive drying sand banks extend W from both points for about 2 miles. The entrance channel lies between them and carries about 3 m on the bar at its outer end, gradually increasing to some 13 m off Rossbehy Point. There are no buoys or leading marks and changes in the channel may occur with W gales. The banks are marked by heavy breakers at LW or with any swell which defines the line of deepest water. According to the chart, which has not recently been amended, the channel lies close to Rossbehy Point and further in the best water lies 3 cables off the SE shore.

Tides
The tidal streams run at 3 to 4 kn at springs. The ebb sets over the N banks until they dry. There may be an eddy along the edge of the S banks. The ingoing stream makes at +0605 Galway (HW Dover) and the outgoing at +0005 Galway (-0600 Dover).

Entrance
In view of the above the harbour cannot be recommended to yachtsmen and no directions can be given. In any weight of sea stranding on the outer banks would probably prove fatal and with the ebb running, the sea on the bar and in the entrance would prove dangerous to small craft in fresh winds. **Anchorage.** The greater part of the harbour dries. The deepest water lies near the SE side and this makes the anchorage exposed in strong W winds and with the strong tide in the channels. **Facilities.** There are no convenient facilities.

Dingle Harbour and Marina.

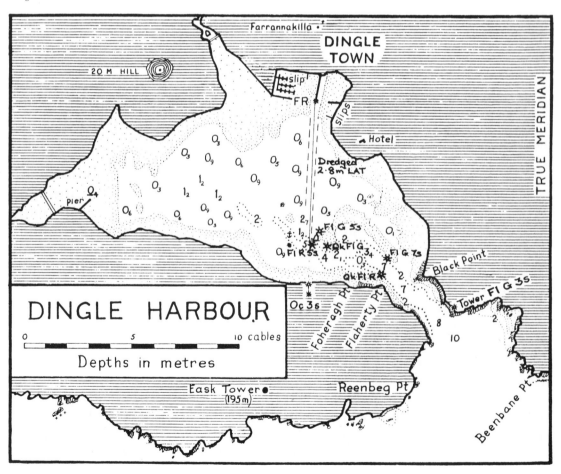

DINGLE HARBOUR

0   5   10 cables

Depths in metres

Farrannakilla

DINGLE
TOWN

20 M HILL

slip

FR

Hotel

Dredged
2·8m LAT

pier

TRUE MERIDIAN

Fl G 5s

Fl R 5s   QkFlG

Fl G 7s

QkFlR

Black Point

Oc 3s

Foheragh Pt

Flaherty Pt

Tower Fl G 3s

Eask Tower
(195m)

Reenbeg Pt

Beenbane Pt

DINGLE HARBOUR *(see plan)*

Chart 2789 shows where it is; chart 2790 which is due for amendment shows it twice as large as our plan. The harbour has a safe entrance and is landlocked and free from swell but most of it is very shallow. The harbour has a channel dredged to 2.6m LAT to the main pier. The inner harbour has a modern marine with facilities for visiting vessels.

Entrance

is ³/₄ mile E of the conspicuous Eask Tower, 195m above the shore. The only dangers on the approach are the Crow Rock (dries 3.7m) and its outliers which can be avoided by day or night by keeping the lighthouse open on Reenbeg Point, 024°. On the E side of the inner end of the entrance a rocky ledge, dry at LW, extends almost half way across from Black Point, marked by the square old Lough Tower. The harbour opens up and the channel is buoyed to the two breakwaters of the inner harbour.

Directions

Having passed between Reenbeg and Beenbane Points a berth of ¹/₂ cable clears any inshore dangers in the entrance. To avoid Black Point ledge, as soon as the lighthouse is passed steer 311°-312° towards a 20m hill on the far side of the harbour, or if it is not visible steer in this direction leaving twice as far from Flaherty Point. Enter the buoyed channel N of Flaherty Point. The channel 40m wide and is dredged to 2.6m LAT. The channel runs in a NW direction from the entrance buoys and then in a Northerly direction the turn on to the transits (two poles in field in Southern shore with black and white diamonds Occ Wh 3s). There are visitors berths available at the marina inside the Western breakwater.

Anchorages

Vessels should not anchor in the main channel. A suitable anchorage can be found approx. ¹/₂ mile S of the main pier, 1 cable W of the dredged channel. Care should be taken to avoid drying patch in this area approx 2 cables NNW of lower transit pole.

Lights, Buoys

On the NE side within the entrance the white lighthouse shows Fl G 3 s, 20 m 6 M. At the channel entrance the first leg of the dredged channel running in a WNW direction is marked by a Port Buoy Qk Fl. R and Starboard Buoy Fl. G 7 s. The turn on to the N/S leg of the dredged channel is marked by Stbd. Buoy Qk Fl. G and Port Buoy Fl. R 5 s and Stdb. Buoy Fl. G 5 s. Additional buoys may be laid in 1992/93 on the N/S channel Port Fl. R (2) 5 s. and Fl. G (2) 5 s.

Facilities

Harbour master Lt. Cdr. B. Farell, Ph/Fax 066-51629. Communications: VHF Ch. 16 and via Valentia Radio. Good victualling. Fuel: Diesel at main pier, petrol - local garages. Showers: Available close to marina and launderette. Chandlery: Some chandlery items available locally. O'Sullivans, Tralee - 30 miles. 24 hour delivery from chandlers in Dublin and Cork. Boat Repairs: Boatyard and repair services available locally. Contact H.M. Engine Repairs: Griffins Garage, Morans Garage,

Dingle Marine — entrance to right background.

R & S Engineering and Hans Engineering. Radio and Electronics Service: Tom Hand Electronics (066-51640). Reidys Green Street, Kennedys Green Street. Banks. Car Rental: Available Tralee. Hotels and Restaurants: Large selection, town is well known for its seafood restaurants. Airport: Farranfore Airport (30 miles). 066-64399. Taxis: Sheehys Spa Road, 066-51301. V. Flannery, Cooleen, Dingle, 066-51163. Buses: Tralee.

VENTRY HARBOUR
This delightful harbour consists of a broad bay with an entrance nearly 1 mile wide facing SE. It gives good shelter in SW to N winds though there can sometimes be a swell. It is also subject to heavy squalls from the high ground to the W in breezy weather. It is exposed to the SE. Its W shore is formed by a superb sandy beach.

Directions
The entrance is easily recognised as being 2 miles W of the prominent Eask Tower. Parkmore Point on the W side of the entrance is at the E end of a long line of diminishing cliffs. Valentia lighthouse open of Doulus Head leads to it. The only danger in the entrance is the 2·9 m ridge extending 2½ cables SSE of Ballymore Point. This ridge will break fiercely in a big swell. It can be avoided by keeping S of the line joining the conspicuous chapel W of the centre of the beach and the SE entrance point. Beware of marine farm at head of bay.

Anchorages
1. The traditional place is off the beach in about 45 m, sand, church bearing about W and village about NE.
    2. On the S side of the bay about 1 cable N of the pier in about 3 m, sand.
    Both these anchorages can be subject to swell and cannot be recommended in E or SE winds, though anchorage (2) gives shelter in S winds. The sand is hard in both anchorages but it is important to give a good pluck in.

Facilities
Anchorage 1. There is a slipway and winch below the village but this is on rock so landing on the beach is advised. Small shops and petrol. About 3 miles to Dingle. Occasional bus. Anchorage 2. Convenient landing at pier but no facilities ashore.

BLASKET ISLANDS (chart 2790)
These islands are the most W in Europe and in every way live up to their position. They extend 8 miles W from Slea Head, are bold and precipitous with strong tides and overfalls in the channels between them. Owing to their rugged nature, exposed position and lack of safe anchorages they are rarely visited by yachts. On the other hand in good conditions there is fine and majestic scenery to be enjoyed and an unrivalled sense of remoteness. A day of sunshine and sparkling seas spent running and turning to windward through the channels between the islands will never be forgotten. Under these conditions they present little difficulty. Chart 2790 is essential. In bad weather their appearance can be utterly forbidding and they should be avoided.

TEARAGHT ISLAND
179 m high, is the furthest W. It is divided into two parts and pierced by a tunnel running N and S. In appearance it is a pinnacle from E or W. There are steps both E and W of the S entrance to the tunnel, seldom usable because of the nearly continuous swell. Cables and hoists stretch across this area for landing stores. Tearaght Rocks, 13 m high, extend 7 cables W of the island with half tide rocks in between them and to the S.

Light — Fog Signal
A light Fl (2) 20 s, 84 m, 27 M, is shown from a white tower on the W side of the island. Visible only from 318° through N to 221° Racon.

Great Foze Rock
27 m, lies 3 miles SSW of Tearaght Island with Little Foze Rock, 7 m, a mile NE of Great Foze Rock. These rocks are steep-to and very dangerous by night or in bad visibility.

INISHTOOSKERT
lies 4 miles NE of Tearaght, is 171 m high and its NW side is steep cliffs with a pronounced coxcomb on the N end. There is no anchorage or landing place. In flat calm weather it is possible to jump onto the rocks from a dinghy, but even then the swell surges in and out of the gulleys making this difficult. It is a steep climb to the top of the island on which there is the ruin of an oratory. There are rocks awash 3 cables SW of the island.

INISHVICKILLANE
134 m high, in the shape of a long ridge when viewed from the SE and Inishnabro 174 m high, rising towards its N end, lie close together about 2 miles SE of Tearaght. The SW and SE sides of Inishvickillane are foul with stacks, rocks and breakers for 4½ cables. Chart 2790 gives transits to clear these dangers, the object of which is best studied on the chart. The NE and NW tips of Inishnabro are also foul for 2 cables. The tidal stream is always to the W at up to 2 kn in the sound between Inishvichillane and Inisnabaro.
    Anchorage is marked on chart 2790 in the bay on the NE side of Inishvickillane. Do not anchor much closer in than marked, as the bottom is foul

The anchorage on the NE side of Innishvickillane.

with weed and rocks inside the 10 m line. Fishermen regard this as the best anchorage in the Blaskets. It is sheltered in the prevailing winds, holding is good and the tidal stream weak. Departure, should it become necessary, is simple.

The owner of the house on the island reports being able to use the mooring all the year except in strong E winds. In fine weather landing is easy on the small single beach from which a steep path leads up the cliffs.

The island is privately owned with a dwelling house and there are vestiges of an oratory. There are two windmills on the high ground. On the NE end of the island there is an inflatable pontoon which can be swung up clear of the swell. The island is a traditional home of fairies and most attractive. Red deer have recently been introduced.

The anchorage off the village at Great Blasket looking NE across Beginish.

INISHNABRO

There is no easy landing on this island. There is, however, a possible landing in very settled weather through a cave in the middle of the SE side of the island between the 14·3 and 16·2 m soundings on chart 2790. The cave leads to a pool open to the sky. The entrance to this cave is N and S and it is just S of a larger cave entrance which runs in E and W.

The cave is about 2 m wide and 5 m high, not wide enough to use oars. It leads into a small, rocky pool just big enough to row and with enough flat rock to land on and pull the dinghy ashore. An inflatable dinghy is recommended. It is possible to scramble up a gulley above the pool and reach the flat middle neck of the island by a dry stone wall. Even on a very calm day there is a surge and scend in the cave.

The N tip of the island is formed by superb cliffs and arches. There is a strong tide rip on its NE side. Note that there is a rock which dries 0·8 m nearly 2 cables ENE of the tip of the island. The tide rip extends down SE of this rock.

GREAT BLASKET ISLAND

289 m high, and over 3 miles long is separated from the mainland by Blasket Sound, 1 mile wide. There is a landing place on its NE side with reasonable anchorage off it in good conditions. Land at the boat slip to the S of the strand. Impossible to see at LW, however if anchored off the strand, a ridge of weed covered rock shows the position. If you anchor in 5m off the S end of strand you should be out of the tide. The village is deserted though some of the houses are habitable. The population used to be about 200. A few people live there in summer, especially for the sheep shearing. There is a good well at the top of the village. N of Great Blasket lies a mass of rocks, breakers and islets.

Dangers in the entrance to
Dingle Bay — Barrack Rock

with 8·2 m over it and which breaks in gale conditions, lies 2½ miles SE of Inishvickillane; Clogher Rock in line with the site of Sybil Tower (015°) leads 2 cables E of Barrack Rock. The site of Sybil Tower is the highest point of Sybil Point, 206 m, and separated from the point by a slight dip. Sybil Point is 10 miles from Barrack Rock so this mark will often be invisible in the conditions in which the rock would be dangerous. Inishvickillane just touching Inishnabro, 303°, leads 2 cables N of the rock.

Wild Bank

(Three Fathom Pinnacle), lies 2½ miles SSW of Slea Head. There are frequently overfalls on this shoal. Clogher Rock (sharp pointed) off Clogher Head in line with the site of Sybil Tower (016°),

leads 1½ miles W of it. Tearaght seen over Canduff Point (the SW extreme of Great Blasket), bearing 274° leads ½ mile N of it. The S extreme of Tearaght touching the NE end of Inishnabro 287°, leads 1 mile S of it. The summit of Clogher Head, 113 m, in line with the W side of the Lure, 006°, leads ½ mile W of it. There is no good transit to pass E of the shoal, but a bearing on the Lure should prove adequate.

Tides

Among the Blasket Islands the N-going stream makes at +0505 Galway (-0100 Dover) and the S-going at -0120 Galway (+0500 Dover). Clear of the islands the spring rate is 1 kn, increasing to 2 kn as the islands are approached. In the narrow channels the stream reaches 4 kn. There are overfalls on Wild Bank and on the uneven bottom among the islands. In gale conditions these can become heavy breaking seas. N of Inishtooskert the N-going stream trends towards the mouth of the Shannon.

Magnetic Abnormality

A local magnetic abnormality is reported near the Blasket Islands.

BLASKET SOUND (chart 2790 or 2789)

This lies between Dunmore Head on the Dingle Peninsula and Great Blasket Island. It offers a considerable saving in distance when on passage between Valentia and the Shannon or Aran Islands. It is straightforward in daylight with a fair wind or tide or under power. There is plenty of room to turn to windward. Garraun Point, the NE corner of Great Blasket Island, is steep-to. With its exposed position, uneven bottom and strong tides it can be a rough and unpredictable channel. Temporary buoy Fl (5) Y 20 s 4 cables W of landing place at Dunquinn.

Tides

In Blasket Sound the N-going stream makes at +0445 Galway (-0120 Dover) and the S-going stream at -0140 Galway (+0440 Dover). The spring rate is from 2 to 3 kn. The duration of these streams can be much affected by the wind.

Dangers

Wild Bank already mentioned, is nearly on the direct course from Valentia Harbour to Blasket Sound.

A long and low ridge of rock extends SW from Dunmore Head ending in the sharp pointed and conspicuous Lure (44 m). The Lure appears as an islet from a distance. Scollage Rock, which covers at springs, lies ¾ cable W of the Lure. Over 3 cables WSW of the Lure are Stromboli Rocks with a least depth of 1·8 m, and between them and Scollage Rock there are shoal patches with 1·8 and 2·7 m over them. 1½ cables W of Stromboli Rock is another rock with 1 8 m over it. On account of the strong tides precautions must be taken to avoid these dangerous rocks which usually cause overfalls and which break in bad weather.

A yacht bound to or from Dingle through the sound may in good conditions take a short cut by passing ½ cable W of Scollage Rock provided that the rock is uncovered and has been identified in good time. One of the two Armada ships which were wrecked in the sound foundered on these rocks and the wreck has been located on the S side of them.

N of the NE end of Great Blasket Island a maze of rocks and breakers extends for a distance of 1½ miles and gives some shelter to the sound. There are deep passages between the rocks which should only be attempted in fine weather and with chart 2790. The passage out and N of Carrigfadda affords superb views of the fine N shore of Great Blasket Island. It is straightforward sailing NW but not so easy coming in from seaward. One of the largest Armada ships came in this way in an autumn gale, a wonderful feat of seamanship.

The principal islands Beginish (13 m) and Youngs Island (11 m) form the W side of the sound and appear as one island from N or S. Theogh Rocks extend SE of Beginish and there is a rock awash at LW 1¾ cables NE of Young Island. Local boats sometimes use the passage W of Beginish and Young Island where there is less tide and so, sometimes less sea than in the sound.

Leading Marks

Clogher Rock in line with the summit of Sybil Point, 015°, leads between Garraun Point and

Stromboli Rock. Note that this line leads close to Theogh Rock off Beginish and to the rock NE of Young Island, so steer nothing to the W of it while abreast these islands.

PASSAGE WEST OF GREAT BLASKET ISLAND

This passage is not difficult but with any sea running the relative shelter in the sound makes the latter preferable for yachts despite the nasty bit at Sybil Point, see below. It is also somewhat longer than through the sound, especially from Valentia. However it is very straight-forward with fine bold marks. Coming from the S, before closing Tearaght Island behind Inishvickillane get Canduff (the SW end of Great Blasket) lined up with the E side of Inishtooskert, 005°, and proceed on this transit then giving Canduff Point a berth of 2 cables. Steer then to pass ½ mile E of Inishtooskert. When Tearaght closes behind Inishtooskert steer 43° with this mark astern which leads NW of the tide rips.

Coast North of Dunmore Head

This is bold and precipitous until Clogher Head is reached. Off this head is the pointed Clogher Rock. There is a landing slip, only suitable for curraghs, near Dunquin village, the most westerly in Europe. The landing place with its winding path down the cliff is most impressive. There are rocks less than 1 cable S of the slip, and a few between ¼ and ½ mile NW of it; Carrigduff Rock there is 2 cables W of the shore.

Sybil Point

1½ miles N of Clogher Head is steep with overhanging cliffs near its summit which from the N

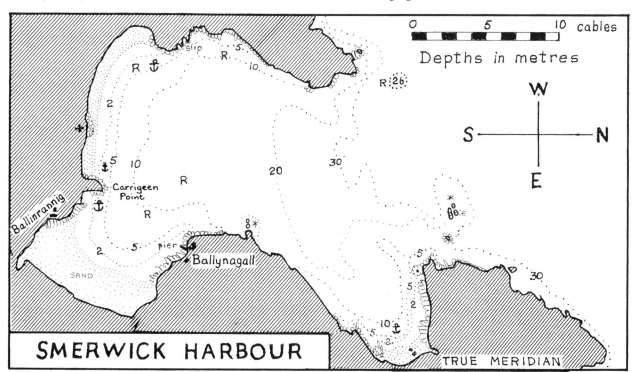

have the appearance of a coxcomb. The highest point, separated from the cliffs by a slight dip, is the site of the old tower mentioned on the old fathom charts and whose ruin can no longer be seen. Rocks and breakers extend 3½ cables W of Sybil Point. With a W or NW wind and swell and N-going tide there can be a most unpleasant sea between Sybil Point and Blasket Sound, with a race off Sybil Point. Similar conditions can be found S of the sound in S or SW winds and S-going tide.

NE and W of Sybil Point the coast has bold cliffs with Sybil Head (127 m) followed by the prominent cones of the Three Sisters, the highest 150 m. The conical hill, 251 m, above Ballydavid Head E of Smerwick Harbour is conspicuous. Rocks extend 1½ cables offshore off the Middle and East Sisters.

SMERWICK HARBOUR *(see plan)* (chart 2789)
This is just an open bay between the East Sister and Dunacapple Islets, 29 m 1 mile NE. The entrance faces NW. There are shoals and breakers between Dunacapple Islets and the shore to the E of them. The harbour is exposed to considerable ground swell and while not an ideal refuge in bad weather provides shelter from winds except those with N in them.

Anchorages
1. Smerwick Roads. In W or S weather anchor a little N of the slip marked "Boat Harbour" on chart, about 1½ cables off the cliffs in 10 m, good holding in stiff mud. A 10-tonner safely rode out a SE gale here in 1966. It is also possible to anchor further SSW in about 3 m. Landing at slip. No facilities. Guest house near slip.

2. In moderate or even fresh N winds some shelter can be found in the bay at the NE corner of the harbour, off the mouth of the stream there. Beware of lobster pots and trammel nets between Duncapple Islets and this anchorage. Anchor halfway between the 2 and 10 m soundings on the plan or chart. There are isolated boulders closer in.

3. With a S wind there is good holding, sand, just W of Carrigveen in about 2·5 m. There is a petrol pump beyond the sandhills.

Facilities
There is a pier at the village marked Ballynagall on the chart but confusingly known as Ballydavid locally. Here there are shop, pub, phone and bus service. The pier has only 0·5 m LWS near the head. If calm enough it would be convenient to berth here temporarily near HW. The bottom is rock in the vicinity of this pier.

Coast from Smerwick Harbour to Brandon Bay
A berth of 1 cable clears all dangers between Ballydavid Head and Brandon Point. This is one of the most impressive stretches of coast in the whole

of the W of Ireland, rising in great cliffs to the fine pile of Brandon Peak, 949 m. In fine weather with its wonderful scenery and abundant bird life it makes as fine a point of departure or landfall as anyone could desire. A dawn landfall on Brandon Mountain will never be forgotten.

BRANDON BAY (chart 2739)
This wide bay between Brandon Point and the low, sandy peninsular 4 miles to the E is quite exposed to the N and a heavy sea can set into it; it is well sheltered from SW to W. Cloghane Inlet, at the SW end, cannot be recommended. The approach to this inlet is over a sandy bar which practically dries and is more intricate than shown on the chart. The part of the creek which does not dry is narrow and shallow along NW shore. The best water is near the entrance and N of the small, grass-topped Lady's Isle. It is stated to be free from swell but is open to the whole fetch of the bay at HW. It could only be considered in an emergency.

Brandon Quay — Light
At Brandon village, 1¼ miles S of Brandon Point, there is a well-built quay which dries and provides dinghy landing. It is seldom calm enough for a yacht to go alongside the quay and never safe to dry out at it. The best anchorage is in 6 m, mud and sand just NE of the quay; there is a patch of rock just S of the line of the quay. The anchorage is not safe with the wind N of NW or with a heavy swell. A light, 2 FG (vert) is shown from the pierhead.

Facilities
Some groceries, meat, 4 pubs, PO and phone. Mechanic and taxi. Daily bus to Tralee. Petrol 1 mile. At Cloghane, 3 miles, RC Church and garage. There are one or two good restaurants.

MAGHAREE SOUND (chart 2739) *(see plan)*
This sound leads between the Magharee Islands and the end of the low, sandy peninsular which separates Brandon and Tralee Bays. The area should be avoided in bad weather or heavy swell which breaks on the banks N of the islands as well as in the sound, especially on the ebb. However in all normal summer weather the sound is quite safe. It is a pleasant spot and the sound provides a simple short cut to Fenit from the W. The W entrance is free of danger, giving the visible rocks a good clearance. Steer a middle course between the islands until abreast of Mucklaghbeg, 6 m high, to avoid Illaundonnell and Illaunlea on the S side which cover at half tide; between these the S side of The Rose Islet, Fenit Castle and Church Hill in line, 106° E of Tralee Bay, gives the best water. This transit can sometimes be difficult to see and an easier mark is the N side of Gurrig Island just open S of Illauntannig, 280°, having given the latter a

reasonable berth. Once through course can be set for Little Samphire Island.

If approaching Fenit from the W and passing N of the Magharee Islands, Illaunbarnagh, 9 m high and flat in shape, open twice its own length N of Mucklaghmore, 30 m high and pudding shaped, 110°, leads clear N of the banks. Kerry Head and Loop Head in line, 002°, leads clear E of them and W of Mucklaghmore.

Tides
The E-going flood through the sound starts +0505 Galway (-0100 Dover) and the W-going ebb at -0120 Galway (+0500 Dover) max 2 to 3 kn.

Anchorages
1. In fine, settled weather only, a yacht may anchor temporarily E of Illauntannig on which there are beehive huts and a stone cross. The anchorage is a pool with 2 m off the house on the island; the marks for it are the W point of Scraggane Bay in line with the E point of Illauntannig, and the S side of Illaunturlogh on the middle of Wheel Rock which dries 2·5 m and is steep-to. The point of Loop Head on the E point of Reenafardarrig leads W of the rock in 1·2 m.

2. Scraggane Bay on the tip of the peninsula is a reasonably safe anchorage. It has good holding and fair shelter, except in NE wind, when departure would not be difficult. Some swell may enter at high water when the rocks inside Doonagaun are covered. There is a pier on the W side which has recently been extended. The anchor on the metric chart is wrong. Anchor as close ENE of the pier as draft permits; there is 2 m with the pierhead 287° and the E end of Illauntannig 023°. A shoal runs out from the head of the bay nearly to its centre where it is awash at LAT. Lobster tanks are generally moored off the pier. The pier is unsuitable for berthing alongside due to swell and foul bottom. Good slip for landing. Small shop and pub at Fahamore, at Brandon Bay, 10 minutes.

3. In strong W winds there is good anchorage with very little swell on the W side of Tralee Bay. The best place about 3 cables offshore in 3 m is with Little Samphire lighthouse bearing 103°; this is just N of a rocky outcrop in the middle of the long reach.

TRALEE BAY (chart 2739)
Tralee Bay lies E of the Magharee Peninsula and has Fenit Port at its SE corner.

Lights
On Little Samphire Island from a stone tower a light is shown Fl WRG 5 s, 17 m, 16-13-13 M. W from 140° to 152°; R thence to 172°; obsc to 262°; R thence to 275°; obsc to 280°; R thence to 090°; G thence to 140°. The white sector leads clear into Tralee Bay with a red sector covering Mucklaghmore with its breakers and a green sector over the Magharee Islands and their breakers. A further red sector covers the shallow S side of Tralee Bay.

On Samphire Island a light is shown QR 15 m, 3 M.

On Fenit pierhead a light is shown 2 FR vert, 12 m, 3 M. Obsc from 058° to 148°.

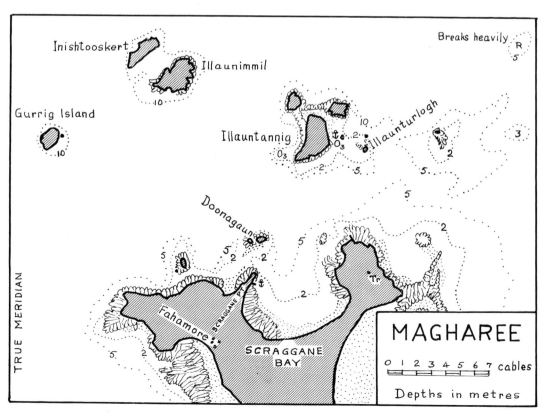

Fenit Harbour from S.

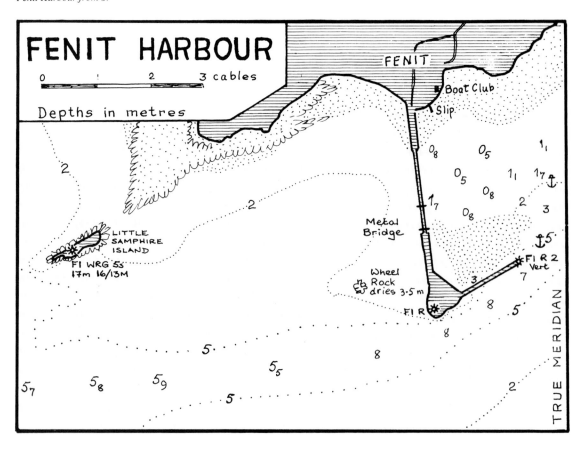

Dangers

Mucklaghmore, a pudding shaped rock 30 m high, stands in the middle of the entrance to Tralee Bay; E of it there are other rocks and shoals; 3 cables N of it is a dangerous rock which dries 0·9 m; there is a breaker almost 1 mile S of it; To keep safe W of these dangers Kerry Head should bear 354° or further W in line with Loop Head.

Approach by night

If coming from the W set course to pass 3 miles N of the Magharee Islands and hold this until the white sector of Little Samphire light is entered. If coming from the N get into the white sector of Little Samphire light as soon as it is picked up. When in the white sector alter course for the light. As soon as the 10 m sounding is reached alter course to 180° and hold this until the R sector is reached bearing 090° then stand in towards the QR light on Samphire Island. Give Little Samphire Island a berth of 2 cables and Samphire Island a berth of 1 cable. As Samphire Island comes abeam the 2 FR vert lights on Fenit pierhead will be seen and course can be altered to steer N to round the pierhead. Be on the lookout for any traffic coming out.

FENIT HARBOUR (Chart 2739) *(see plan)*

is formed by a causeway and a breakwater 520 m long connecting the shore southwards to Samphire Island. A further breakwater runs ENE from the island for 250 m and a narrow channel is dredged along the outer ²/₃ of its N side.

Entrance

To enter the harbour round the pierhead and steer N until Little Samphire lighthouse is visible under the viaduct to obtain the deepest water. The safest anchorage is inside the harbour with the lighthouse visible and near to the other moored boats. It is possible to tie up to the W end of the pier where several ladders and steps are available. This has a variable 3 m depth dredged close to the pier but shoals rapidly about 15 m out. The harbour is

exposed to E and NE winds but the holding ground is good. It is a safe harbour in almost any conditions with plenty of room. Two anchors are advised in strong to gale SE winds.

S of the harbour the bay becomes shallow and foul but there is plenty of room to tack. Wheel Rock is 1 cable W of Samphire Island but clear of the direct approach it dries 3·5 m. Samphire Island has a Fl R light and pier has F R (2 Vert) which is visible from 045°.

Facilities

Fenit village has groceries (066-36151), restaurants, hotels, guest houses, church, P.O. Bus to Tralee. Slip, a charge of approx. £3.00 is made for lying alongside pier. Fuel and water - contact Danny Doyle (066-36071). Gas in Strand Street (066-22018). VHF Ch. 16 & 14. Tralee Sailing Club C/S "Neptune". Hull repairs, Pat Browne (066-36046) also hulls, engines and electrics, O'Sullivan Marine at Monavalley Industrial Estate, Tralee (066-24524). Harbour Master (066-36046). Showers at Sailing Club and all possible support contact Tom O'Keefe. Club has bar facilities during season. Visitors moorings. Pontoon available 2 hours after LW for embarking, fuel, supplies, crew etc. Taxi - Barth Carmody (066-36287).

BARROW HARBOUR (chart 2739)

This delightful sandy lagoon is only for the inquisitive yachtsman not pressed for time. Entry and exit are only possible in settled swell-free weather, and must be made with the tide, which is strong, or at slack. Illaunnacusha Rock is about 6 m high and fairly conspicuous; it should be left ¹/₂ to ³/₄ cable to starboard when entering and course shaped for the centre of the gap between the point with a Martello tower (round) and the islet 1 cable off it. Just before bringing the islet abeam sheer across to starboard to pass close to it and then follow the slight curve in the channel along the beach on Fenit Island towards Fenit Castle, a square tower. Anchor opposite the castle in 3·5 m, very strong tide; this anchorage is ¹/₂ cable wide. Nearly all the inner expanse dries out.

THE SHANNON ESTUARY

From Loop Head to Limerick the Shannon Estuary is 50 miles long. From Carrigaholt to the River Fergus, a distance of 25 miles, there is a stretch of sheltered water 1 to 2 miles wide and of ample depth. There are several good anchorages giving protection from all but E winds. There is now a very good marina at Kilrush on the N side. There are many quays and creeks for those who like taking the ground. The natural harbour of Foynes gives complete protection, but the area with

suitable depths for anchorage is restricted and largely occupied. Above the River Fergus the channel becomes narrower and shallower, Least depth 1·8 m, and there is no provision for yachts in the Limerick dock, which has the usual drawbacks of a commercial basin. A yacht cannot be left there unattended as she may frequently be required to shift berth to facilitate shipping. The prevailing winds blow upstream, but the beat down river can be fast though somewhat wet if made on the ebb. The tides are strong, up to 4 kn.

Charts

The following charts cover the whole estuary:

1819 Approaches to the River Shannon. Kerry and Loop Heads to Carrigaholt.

1547 Kilcredaun Point to Ardmore Point. Includes Carrigaholt, Kilrush and Scattery Roads.

1548 Ardmore Point to Rinaleon Point. Includes Tarbert Island.

1549 Rinaleon Point to Shannon Airport. Includes Foynes Harbour.

1540 Shannon Airport to Limerick.

A yacht on passage from Kerry to Galway and wishing to take shelter can confidently enter the Shannon and with chart 1819 anchor at Carrigaholt in good shelter from the W. In emergency this could be done with chart 2254 but this chart shows none of the entrance buoys.

If going further up the river to Kilrush or Scattery Roads chart 1547 is required. This is the first point where any shelter from the E is obtainable.

DIRECTIONS — GENERAL

In view of the length of the estuary and its many buoys and leading marks detailed directions have only been given for the approach and anchorage at Kilbaha, E of Loop Head and for the approach and anchorage at Carrigaholt, Kilrush and Scattery inside Kilcredaun Point. From there on only limited and essential information has been given and a yacht should carry the necessary charts for the detailed pilotage.

Tides

The yachtsman should consult the Irish Coast Pilot for full details of the times and speeds of the main flood and ebb and of the many inshore eddies throughout the length of the estuary. It is approximately correct to reckon that between Foynes and the sea the flood starts about 5 hours before, and the ebb 1 hour after HW Galway. In most of this part the mid-channel ebb reaches 4 kn at springs, the flood somewhat less.

Lights and buoys

These are given on next page as far as Middle Ground in the order as they are met going upstream; the buoyage is to IALA system. Just N of the W entrance to Foynes Harbour there is a group of large mooring buoys, the two outer of which show light Q. Further up as the estuary narrows the buoys and lights are very numerous and the chart is essential.

DIRECTIONS FOR ENTERING THE SHANNON

The mouth of the Shannon is said to be between Loop Head and Kerry Head, but the real mouth is some 11 miles further in between Kilcredaun Head and Kilconly Point, and the ebb tide sweeps from this mouth in a SW direction forming a very bad tide race in strong winds between NW and SW or even S. A yacht running into the Shannon during the ebb should therefore keep along by the N shore E of Loop Head, which is free of offlying dangers thus avoiding the strong tide and obtaining some shelter from the swell. Coming in past the headlands at night in clear weather very bright vertical flashing lights will be observed to the E far up the river. These are the aircraft warning lights on the two chimneys at the ESB station just W of Money Point. (The steamer wreck shown W of Ladder Rock under Kilcredaun Head in the new metric chart is wrong. the wreck is situated just off rocky foreshore under Old Battery at Kilcredaun Point. All that remains shows about 1·2 m at LWS.)

From North or West

Loop Head should be treated with respect and given a berth of at least 2 cables (chart 1819). Between Loop Head and Horse Island (Dunmore Head) is an area of breaking water in heavy swells. Keept at least 1/2 M off shore. Pass N of Kilstiffin Bank which has 7 m LAT and is reported to be extending southward. Kilbaher cliff in line with Kilcloher Head, 260°-080°, leads through the Seven Fathoms Channel N of the bank. A buoy, R Can , Fl R 3 s, is moored 6 cables SSW of Kilstiffin Bank which breaks in bad weather or a big swell.

Keep 1 cable off Kilcredaun Head to avoid the race on the ebb and also the rocky ledge extending 1/2 cable from the head. Off Kilcredaun Point, 1/2 mile beyond the head, the ebb runs SW up to 4 to 5 kn at half tide, but having rounded the point fairly close to and turned N the tide off Carrigaholt Road is weaker and at Carrigaholt Castle is negligible. In poor visibility Kilcredaun Head can be distinguished by a white stain on the rocks beneath the lighthouse and immediately above the HW mark. There is a N Card Buoy V QK Fl 3·5M SSW of Kilcredaun Point.

Light

A light is shown from a white tower on Kilcredaun Head. Light Fl 6 s, 41 m, 13 M. Obsc within 1 mile between 224° and 247°.

From South

Should a yacht be beating in from Kerry Head there is no need to approach the Kerry shore too close, as there are some shoal patches, best seen on the chart. Chart 1819 shows a slip at the end of a road about 6 1/2 miles inside Kerry Head; this is only a slip which dries out, rocky bottom; it could be

Tidal rise and range from Kilbaha Bay to Limerick Docks.

Based on heights in metres above chart datum.

Place	MHWS	MLWS	Spring Range	MHWN	MLWN	Neap Range
KILBAHA	4·3	0·5	3·8	3·3	1·5	1·8
CARRIGAHOLT	4·9	0·7	4·2	3·7	1·9	1·8
KILRUSH	5·0	0·5	4·5	3·7	1·7	2·0
TARBERT Is.	5·0	0·5	4·5	3·8	1·7	2·1
FOYNESIs.	5·2	0·3	4·9	4·0	1·8	2·2
MELLON POINT	5·9	0·4	5·5	4·5	1·9	2·6
LIMERICK DOCK	5·9	0·4	5·5	4·5	1·2	3·3

SHANNON LIGHTS AND BUOYS FROM ENTRANCE TO MIDDLE GROUND

Ballybunion	N Card	Lt Buoy	V QK Fl. Racon 6m "M"
Kilstiffin	R Can	Lt buoy	Fl R 3 s, Whis.
Kilcredaun	W Tower		Fl 6 s, 41 m, 13 M.
Tail of Beal	W Card	Lt buoy	Q (9) 15 s.
Carrigaholt	R Can	Lt buoy	Fl (2) R 6 s.
Beal Bar	N Card	Lt buoy	Q.
Doonaha	R Can	Lt buoy	Fl (3) R 10 s.
Asdee	R Can	Lt buoy	Fl R 3 s.
Rineana	R Can	Lt buoy	QR
Scattery	White Tower		Fl (2) 7½ s, 15 m, 10 M.
Carrig	G Cone	Lt buoy	Fl G 3 s.
Tarbert tanker jetty	2 FG vert E and W extremities.		
Tarbert	White Tower		Iso WR 4 s, 6 m, 14-10 M.
	R from 277° to 287° over Boland's Rock.		
Ballyhoolahan Pt.	Leading lights in line 128°. Front. Iso 2 s, 13 m, 3 M. White Bn.		
		Rear. Iso 5 s, 18 m, 3 M. GWVS Bn.	
Garraunbaun	White beacon.		Fl WR 10 s, 16 m, 8-5 M. R shore to 072°,
	W thence to 242°, R thence to shore. R sectors cover Long and Carrigeen Rocks.		
Rinealon Point	BW Bn		Fl 2·5 s, 4 m, 7 M.

Entrance to Foynes.

Poultallin Point	G Cone	Lt buoy	Fl (3) G 6 s.
Battery Point	W Card	Lt buoy	Q (9) 15 s.
Carrigeen	R Can	Buoy.	
Weir Point	R Bn		VQ (4) R 10 s, 2 m, 2 M.
Colleen Point	G Bn		Q G 2 m, 2 M.
Leading lights	In line 106°		Front, Barneen Pt, BW Bn. Iso WRG 4 s.
			Rear, New Quay, BW Bn. Oc 4 s, 16 m, 10 M.
Elbow Rock	R Can buoy		E entrance to Foynes
Lony Rock	G Cone buoy		E entrance to Foynes
Tanker Jetty and mooring buoys			Lights. Q.
Inishmurry	R Can		QR
Aughinish Shoal	G Cone	Lt buoy	Fl G 2 s.
8 Metres	G Cone	Lt buoy	Fl G 3 s.
Beeves Rock	Stone Tower		Fl WR 5 s, 12 m, 12 M. R 091° to 238°.
	White elsewhere. R sectors cover rocks to the N.		
Flats	G Cone	Lt buoy	Fl G 3 s.
Rineanana Airport	W breakwater		2 FR

used for dinghy landing only in the calmest sea; temporary anchorage offshore in 7 m in S to SE winds.

In the middle of the entrance to the Shannon opposite Kilcredaun Point there is a W Card light buoy, Q(9) 15 s, marking the Tail Of Beal Bar, and 1½ miles NE a N Card light buoy Q marking Beal Bar. Yachts should always pass NW of these buoys.

Leaving the Shannon

With a fresh W wind, or with a W swell, it is best to pass Kilcredaun Head at slack water. A yacht leaving with the ebb in these conditions must be prepared to meet very steep short seas in the race and, even motor-sailing, may have difficulty in clearing the head; having passed it keep along the shore towards Loop Head to avoid the outer part of the race. (See above.)

KILBAHA BAY (chart 1819)

This is a useful passage anchorage 3 miles inside Loop Head, sheltered in winds from W to NE but with indifferent holding, exposed to swell and tidal eddies. A pleasant spot in fine weather, but if unsettled, Carrigaholt is much preferable. There are submerged rocky ledges on both sides of the bay so keep to the middle as you sound your way to the anchorage. This is in about 4 m in the centre of the bay with the pierhead bearing about 250°. It is completely exposed to SE winds which send in a nasty short sea. Wooden lobster tanks with buoys are moored in the inner part of the bay but there is still plenty of room for a couple of yachts to anchor.

Pier

The pier is good with clean sandy bottom. Abreast of 2nd bollard from steps it dries 1·4 m LWS. It is important, if drying out, to give the yacht a good list to the quay and take a halliard ashore, as there is a tiny stream which tends to scour the sand from under the keel; boats which have failed to take these precautions have fallen off the pier. In bad weather a swell enters the bay and causes a run along the pier. It is however possible to put a small yacht safely alongside in these conditions, due to the shelving bottom, by pulling her hard ahead as soon as she bumps, and when she starts to float again hauling into deeper water near the pierhead. In SE winds, when the bay is exposed, the pier offers secure shelter. Water.

Berths at the pier are now nearly always occupied by small lobster fishing boats which come and go at all times. Quite often a yacht could not berth there and she could only do so temporarily and could not be left unattended. There are new ladders at the berths.

Facilities

A pub close to the pier. Shop and pub, on the N side of the bay opposite the pier, has a petrol pump and water tap, PO and Phone. No meat or bacon. Bus from and to Limerick Saturday only. Mail car to Kilkee 2 pm daily could take a couple of passengers. (Daily bus service Kilkee Limerick). RC Church 15 minutes.

Buoys

Six cables E of Kilcredaun Point Carrigaholt Lt buoy is moored R Can Fl R(2) 6 s. Four cables N of Beal Bar buoy Doonaha Lt buoy is moored. R Can Fl R(3) 10 s. It is beside the 14·6 m wreck on chart 1819. Both these buoys are for the benefit of deep draft ships.

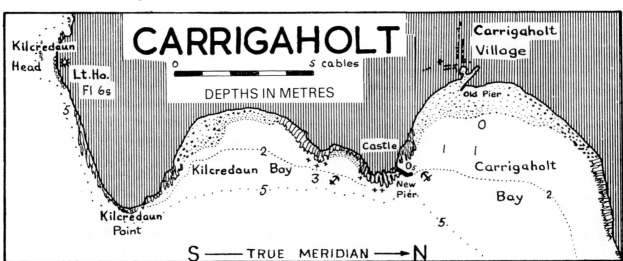

CARRIGAHOLT (chart 1547) (see plan)

This bay, 1½ miles N of Kilcredaun Point, gives good protection from all W winds and a yacht seeking shelter in the estuary need go no further. The most convenient anchorage is about ½ cable N of the new quay at the castle in 3 m, excellent holding and no tidal stream to speak of. It is exposed to wind and sea from S to NE. In S winds one can go alongside the new quay. In E to NE it is better to run up to the Old Quay at the village at

HW. A yacht can find better shelter in W or NW wind off the small bay S of Carrigaholt Castle and N of Kilcredaun Bay, good holding in 3 m sand.

The New Quay (Carrighaholt Castle)

This is a good quay with new ladders and a good sandy bottom alongside, but less depth than shown on the chart; there is 3 m LWS at the pierhead berth and 1-2 m just S of the steps. These steps are dangerous at night as they face the reverse way from normal and have no safety railing. Each side of the steps are usually taken up by lobster boats, so a yacht can only temporarily berth alongside, or possibly for the night, but be prepared to rise early next morning to let lobster boats leave. There is an underwater projection of approx. 0·3 m at the steps. Water.

Warning

Due to the drift across the bay and the short sea that gets up it is unsafe to lay alongside this quay in strong NW winds; a small yacht foundered alongside due to this. Even in moderate N to NE wind a yacht will pound a little when taking the ground. 12 minutes' walk to the village.

The Old Quay

This is at the village and is very snug and safe in all weathers, but only available for moderate draft. It is accessible only at HW and has a 1·7 m HWN at the deep berth, which is between the first two bollards you meet coming in. Between the projecting end of the quay and the first bollard a sandbank which dries 2·7 m has formed along the quay. There is another possible berth just inside the projecting part. Before going in, inspect the quay and approach channel at LW. Used by fishing boats.

Facilities

Groceries. Meat (good) only on Sunday. PO, Phone. Petrol at Mrs Keatings. Doctor resides in village. RC Church. There is a small restaurant in the village.

QUERRINBAY (chart 1547)

Querrin Creek, 4½ miles from Carrigaholt on the shore, can be identified by a handball alley above the quay. It is approached close inshore from the E at suitable rise of tide. The best depth is close to the S point of the entrance which is steep-to. The quay, just inside the entrance, dries 1 m, mud bottom. With fresh SW wind the S side is uncomfortable at HW and one can shift to the E berth. Both berths are exposed to the E. There is 1·6 m alongside the S side of the quay when 5 stones are showing below the SE corner of the quay. A mussel fishery is operating off Querin Creek. Its W end is 4¾ cables 103° from Corlis Point and its upstream end 2¼ cables to the Eastward. It is unlit and not on the chart. Its position is liable to change. A further mussel fishery is reported about 3 miles to the W just south of Trabawn Point. This is also unlit. Post Office and telephone 1¼ M.

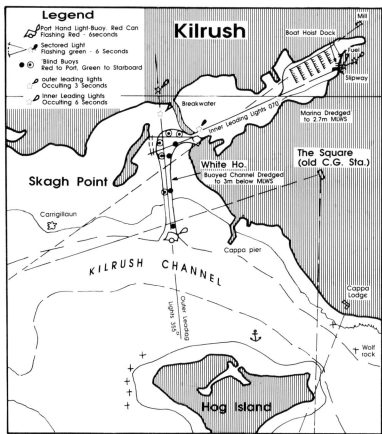

Shannon Marine Developments Ltd.

Kilrush Marina from SW.

Tide Race

In the steamer channel S of Scattery Island, between the Rineanna and Carrig Shoals, there are heavy overfalls on the ebb with strong W winds; these are worst near the Rineanna buoy. A yacht beating down can avoid most of this by keeping between the buoy and Scattery Island. Avoid the windward edge of Rineanna Shoal. Both shoals mentioned have 4 m least water.

KILRUSH AND APPROACHES

(chart 1547) *(see plan)*

Kilrush Channel lies between Scattery Island and the Co Clare shore and is the direct approach from the W to Kilrush and Cappagh Pier. Scattery Island needs a berth of 2½ cables and Hog Island beyond it a berth of nearly 2 cables. On the mainland side the channel is defined by two outlying dangers, Baurnahard Spit, dries 2·5 m, and Carrigillaun. On the road N of Carrigillaun there is a cottage at the level crossing; Kilrush chapel steeple open S of this cottage, 068°, clears the Baurnahard Spit in 1·1 m; for more water keep the marks well open. The line of the road running down from the cottage to the shore leads W of Carrigillaun; to pass S of the rock keep the tower of the disused CG Station, The

Square on the chart, open S of the very conspicuous residence just N of Cappagh Pier, 075°.

The transit ruled on chart 1547 is very useful, the high storehouse (Glynns Mill) in line 055° with the conspicuous white house on Watch House Point; this leads safely in until the line of the road from the level crossing is reached when course must be altered to starboard.

Approach from the SE Wolf Rock

This rock with 1 m is dangerous near LW and lies 1 cable offshore on the E side of the channel between Hog Island and the shore. Keep well over towards Hog Island; when Scattery Lighthouse is in line with the E part of Hog Island, the rock is abreast.

Kilrush

Kilrush Creek Marina - VHF Ch. 37 & 80. The new marina is now open for yachts. Enter as shown on plan through navigation channel and lock gates at all states of tide 3m. LAT. Marina channel dredged to 2·7m. LAT. Facilities available, 120 berths with water 220v AC, Diesel at boatyard pontoon, chandlery, showers/WC's, car park, 24-hour security, telephone.

Boatyard has 45 ton travel hoist, 16 ton crane with 60ft. hoist, covered storage, hard standing, repair facilities in GRP, wood, steel and aluminium, diesel and petrol engines, sails, spars, rigging, repairs and fittings. Marina Manager: John Hehir. Boatyard Manager: Adrian O'Connell. Tel No: 065-52072; International: 010-353-65 52072; Fax: 065-51692.

Kilrush Town

All facilities, hotels, banks, Church, Lloyd's Agents (M. Glynn & Sons Ltd.), good bus services, including connections to Shannon Airport via Ennis. EC Thur.

Cappagh Pier

This is the deepwater pier for Kilrush and lies in the channel NE of Hog Island. The pierhead berth abreast the iron ladder has 2 m LWS but is in constant use by the pilot boat for vessels entering the Shannon. Yachts should not use this berth nor should they lie alongside the pilot boat. The middle and inner berths dry about 0·6 m and may be used at suitable rise in reasonable weather; it would not be safe to dry out there. It is a mile walk to Kilrush. **Facilities.** Small shop and pub, water. Phone along road to left.

Anchorages

1. There is temporary or fair weather anchorage 50 m SE of Cappagh pier in 1·5 m, fairly good holding. In SW or W gales this anchorage is smooth during the ebb, but with the flood there is a heavy tidal sea caused by an eddy which shoots out from the anchorage against the wind. If remaining overnight a riding light is essential.

2. A better anchorage is in the bay on the NE of Hog Island with good shelter from SE to SW; the tide here runs SE both flood and ebb. Anchor outside yachts on moorings. The anchor should be buoyed. A large yellow buoy lies in the anchorage to NE of Hog Island. This is used by the pilot boat in SE gales.

3. **Scattery Roads.** There is good shelter from SW to N winds in the bay on the SE side of Scattery Island which is low Iying. Give the S end of the island a berth of 2 cables and choose a berth in 2 to 3 m between 1 and 2 cables NE of the slip near the lighthouse, sand bottom. Note that it shoals quite suddenly from 4 to 1 m. Just outside this anchorage there is an eddy on the flood which causes a sea in strong S wind.

4. Off the jetty on the E side of Scattery is convenient for visiting the island, but due to the tide is less comfortable than Scattery Roads. Good holding in 2 or 3 m 1¹/₂ to 2 cables from the jetty. S of the line of this jetty a shoal extends 2¹/₂ cables from the island shore. About 150 m NE of the jetty there is a patch of stones which, like Carrig Donaun further NE, is awash at LWS.

BALLYLONGFORD CREEK AND SALEEN QUAY (chart 1547)

The navigational buoy and beacons for the approaches to Salen Quay are now all missing. It is only possible to sound one's way up to the quay on a rising tide in a dinghy or very shallow draft yacht.

Facilities

Ballylongford village, 15 minutes walk, has shops, PO, Phone, RC Church and petrol.

The Bridge

about 3 miles E of Scattery Island and opposite Ardmore Point on the S shore, is a rocky ridge extending over half-way across the estuary from the N shore. Although its least depth is 16 m there are heavy overfalls with both flood and ebb in strong W winds. It can be avoided by keeping within ¹/₂ mile of Ardmore Point.

Anchorage East of Ardmore Point

This gives shelter from SE to SW and is useful if forced to leave Tarbert in SE wind and ebb tide. There is a solitary white house on the shore W of Glencloosagh (Glown Clonsagh) valley. Anchor somewhat nearer to Ardmore Point than to this house with Scattery Lighthouse just open of Ardmore Point, in 2 m.

Money Point (N side)

A new ESB Power Station and pier are in use. The pier has fixed vertical red lights.

Tarbert.

TARBERT (chart 1548) *(see plan)*

Tarbert Island on the S shore has a power station whose two chimneys can be seen from the mouth of the Shannon. The vicinity of the tanker jetty NW of the island is a prohibited area. Tarbert piers are situated 4 cables SE of the lighthouse which is on the N point of the island. At springs the ebb tide runs at 7 kn from the piers out past the lighthouse causing heavy overfalls in strong NW and W winds. Off the pier the tide always runs NW as there is an eddy on the flood. The outer pier has 4·5 m LWS at the outer berth on its S side, decreasing to 1·8 m just beyond the elbow, stony bottom. Yachts may berth at this outer part but not inshore of the elbow as the inner part must be left clear for the car ferry approaching its slip. The berth on the S side of the pier is dangerous in strong winds between E and S and uncomfortable in strong SW winds. Shelter from winds can be found by berthing on the N side of pier. A very strong tide sweeps past the pierhead on the ebb when great care must be taken in going alongside; the tide also sweeps through a tunnel in the pier beyond the second red shed, which should be avoided.

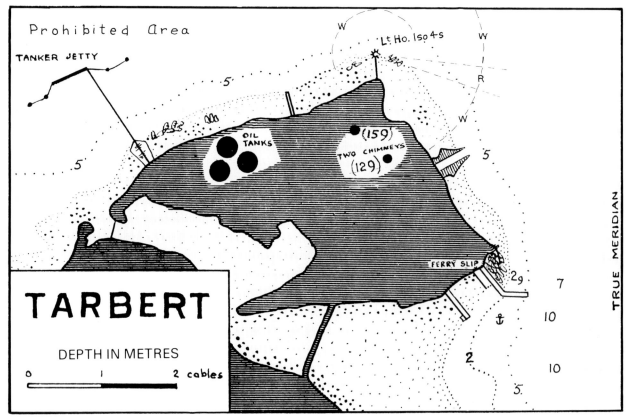

Anchorage

Either S of the elbow of the outer pier and E of the inner quay in 2 m or a bit further S with the inner quay in line and with Knock village on Clare in line with the end of the outer pier in about 3 m, sheltered water in winds between SW and NW, excellent holding; exposed however to W and NW winds due to Tarbert Island being low.

Ferry

In summer time two car ferries operate between Tarbert and Kilimer leaving simultaneously every half hour in summer daylight hours. Yachts should avoid obstructing them and should not expect it to give way if met in the estuary.

Facilities

There is a pub ¹/₄ mile from the pier. Tarbert village, nearly 2 miles by road, 1 mile by dinghy at HW, has shops, petrol, PO, Phone, bus to Limerick.

KNOCK PIER (chart 1548)

Clonderalaw Bay on the N side opposite Tarbert is a long inlet most of which dries. Knock pier is 1 mile within the bay on its NW side and is approached across drying mudflats. When the rock at the base of Tarbert Lighthouse covers, which corresponds to HW neaps, there is 1·8 m at the pier. **Caution.** The E pier shown on the chart is in ruins and covered at HW. Keep very close to the visible W pier when going alongside its E side. The bottom is mud over small stones and shelter good, subject only to a little discomfort in SE and E winds. **Facilities.** PO, Phone, 90 m from pier with public water tap beside PO. Two pubs, one with taxi.

Bowline Rock

(marked Boland's on chart and which dries 1·4 m) is 1 cable long and marked by a 10 m high red perch with topmark near its SE end. **Caution.** The flood sets SSE across the rock so do not pass N of it with the flood, unless with ample wind or power, to avoid being swept onto the rock.

GLIN (chart 1548)

Glin pier is on the S shore 3 miles from Tarbert lighthouse and NE of Glin Quay. It is a good stone pier, with a ruined iron extension on piles, having the berthage on the E side of the stone pier with clean muddy bottom and shelter with winds between SE and WSW.

Anchorage

Anywhere ENE of the pier in 4 m good holding, well sheltered in S winds, exposed from W to NE. At night Rinealon Point light just open of Garraunbaun Point light is a good anchoring mark. The first half of the ebb runs W but at half tide a strong eddy runs E until LW, when the flood commences and continues running E until HW. Be very careful not to be set onto the ruined staging by the tide.

Facilities. A few minutes' walk from the pier the town of Glin has RC church, small hotel, shops and petrol.

Labasheeda Roads (chart 1548)

This anchorage gives good shelter in W and NW winds with good holding. The best place is NE of Redgap Point as close as possible to the mudbank to avoid the SW-going ebb. Labasheeda village has RC Church, PO, petrol and pub, no bus. It is too far to row but can be reached by outboard when the tide is up; land in the creek SE of the village which has 1·5 m HWN. **Dillisk Rocks** (dry 0·3 m) at the E end of the bay must be avoided.

Kilteery Pier

This is on the S shore opposite Dillisk Rocks. It is in good condition and dries about 1·2 m. It can provide a sheltered berth alongside from SE through S to NW. It is foul with stones in two places on its SE side: immediately S of the elbow, and at the steps, inshore from the 7th step from the top; between these two stony places there is a good mud berth. There are no facilities nearby; it is half an hour's walk to Loughel, RC Church and pub. Just above Kilteery Pier, in the fairway is Loghill buoy Fl G 3 s, pass to N of this.

Anchorage

West of Rinealon Point. This is well sheltered in N and NE winds and is out of the strength of the ebb tide. It lies off Aillroe Hill which is conspicuous on the shoreline 6¹/₂ cables W of Rinealon Point with the road along its S slope. Anchor abreast the hill about ³/₄ cables from the shore in 4 m.

FOYNES HARBOUR (chart 1549) *(see plan)*

This is the channel between Foynes Island and the S shore. It is undoubtedly the best anchorage in the Shannon with shelter from all winds, easy access and quite good facilities. There is, however, a 3 kn ebb stream through the anchorage. It is now becoming the busiest port in the Shannon with greatly increased commercial shipping. As a result anchorage for visiting yachts is strictly limited. **Lights.** The W entrance is lit and the lights and leading lights are shown on the plan.

Directions for entering from the West

Approaching from the W there is shoal water extending 1 cable off the S shore as far as Poultallin Point at the entrance; this is marked by a G Cone Lt buoy, Fl (3) G 6 s. From the W end of Foynes island a shoal runs out for 2 cables with a rock on its S edge; these are marked by two red can buoys, the

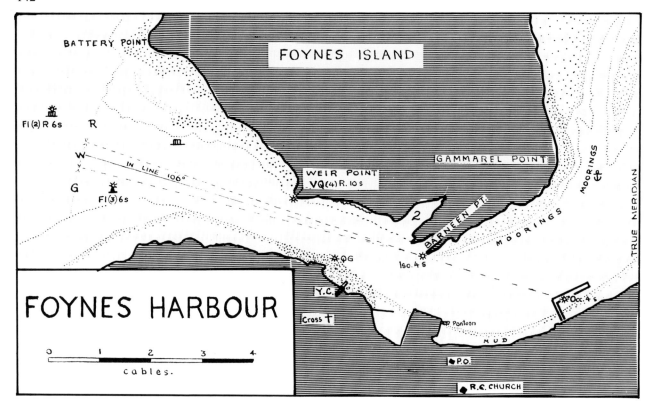

outer one showing Fl (2) R 6 s. Otherwise the
channel is clear; having passed the buoys a course
for the middle leads safely in.

Tanker Moorings
Note if approaching the W entrance from upstream
that there are now 7 large mooring buoys, of which
the outer two show lights Q. These are situated up
to 2½ cables N of the W end of Foynes Island with
a boom carrying an oil pipe extending 475 m out
towards them from the island.

Entrance from the NE
This is a long channel between mudbanks with
some rocks and requires more care than the W
entrance. A leading wind or power is necessary.
The shallowest part, 1 mile or so NE of Foynes
Island, has 2·1 m. Approach with St Senan's
hospital bearing 215°; the hospital is a very
conspicuous, flat-roofed building S of the railway
station. Long Rock lies in mid-channel with a G
Cone buoy on its W side; leave this buoy to port
entering. Two cables further on a Red Can buoy
marks the E side of the Elbow Rock; this must be
left to starboard. At this point the channel has
increased in width to 1 cable and from it steer for
the pier or the anchorage. After half-tide a yacht
drawing 1·8 m may approach the Long Rock buoy
direct from the N keeping both buoys in line
bearing 192°. To clear the rock on the end of the
spit E of Sturamus Island keep Foynes chapel open
its own width of Gammarel Point which gives 0·6 m
LWS. To clear the mud spit S of this rock and E of
Foynes Island, keep St Senan's hospital open half

its length of Gammarel Point, which gives 1·2 m
LWS, or open its full length gives 3 m.

Anchorage
There are local yachts moored under the SE shore
of the island half way down to Barneen from
Gammarel Point. Visiting yachts should **not** anchor
outside these W of Gammarel as they will obstruct
shipping. Instead they may find a berth SSE to E of
Gammarel Point close outside the yacht moorings.
In strong NW to SW winds it is best to anchor E of
Gammarel Point. Buoy the anchor. Yacht owners
are advised to consult the HM (Tony Murphy) as
there may be spare moorings.

There is now a marina pontoon 250m long off
the yacht club which has the usual facilities during
the season. Short stay IR£2.50. Overnight IR£5.00
which includes a welcome in the club. There are
also six offshore moorings for visitors. VHF watch
in summer Ch.6 & M. 069-65641. Taxis. Pat Moran
is in charge of marina.

Quay
The harbour W of the W Pier dries out. The berth
alongside this side dries about 0·6 m and has 4·2 m
HWS and 3·4 m neaps. The new concrete N side of
the quay has a continuous face down to 1·5 m above
LWS below which it is open between concrete piles;
it is therefore dangerous for a yacht near LW and
particularly with the first of the flood; this berth has
7·6 m LWS and is nearly always occupied by
coasters as is the outer part of the W side. The inner
(North facing) part of the W side has drying mud
and a good slip, the end of which is marked by a

white arrow, so a yacht might go there at HW for repairs or a scrub at LW. There is no berth on the E side of the quay, but there is a very convenient floating pontoon for dinghy landing.

Facilities

Water on the quay. Churches, doctor, PO, garage, petrol, diesel oil, grocers, butcher, bus to Limerick.

East Pier

This is always occupied by ships entirely unsuited for berthing yachts as it is built on widely spaced piles.

CAHIRACON PIER (Chart 1549)

This is behind Inishmurry on the Clare side N of Foynes. It is not a very good pier for yachts as it is unsuitable for drying out being built on a projecting rocky ledge. There are dangers in the approach from either direction. The best approach is from SW but there is a dangerous rock, the weed on which shows at LW, just over 1 cable SW of Inishmurry; the pierhead bearing 10° leads clear in W of this rock. The NE entrance is much more difficult and only possible at sufficient rise as the flats between the island and Colonel Rock only have 0·3 m; a drying spit extends 4 cables NE from the island and between its NE end and Ballynacragga Point there are rocks on the mud on the mainland side.

The best berth, which only just dries (rock) at LWS, is between the chain hanging from the middle bollard and second stone on the edge of the pier W of the E bollard. Elsewhere the rock dries 1·8 m. The ebb runs very strongly off the E corner of the pier and causes an eddy up the outer face of the pier. There are rocks immediately NE of the pier projecting somewhat outside the line of its face; to the SE the line of the face of the pier marks the edge of the mud. It is extensively used by a contracting company with barges and tugs lying alongside.

Anchorage

Between the pier and the island is not recommended as the spring ebb runs 4 kn and the bottom is stony. The best place is 1½ cables NE of the pier abreast the end of the reef running out from the island, good holding in 2·7 to 5 m, good shelter from WSW to N. **Facilities.** Landing at steps on NE end of pier at LW. Ladder on face of pier. Kildysart ½ hour on foot.

THE SHANNON ABOVE FOYNES

(charts 1549 and 1540).
Up to this point there are few dangers, except close to the shores, and these have been mentioned. Above Foynes the character of the river changes and there are many drying and submerged rocks, some in mid-channel, and especially around the islands in the mouth of the River Fergus, locally known as the Clare River. A yacht wishing to proceed to Limerick should follow the buoyed channel (*see end of Chapter*).

Auglinish Point

Yachts sailing in light winds are cautioned against the danger of being carried by the tide against the piles of the viaduct which stretches ¼ M from the point to the Alcan Jetty.

Herring Rock — Danger

There is a tail of rock with 0·6 m extending 2 cables N of this rock, which itself dries 2·7 m. This is particularly dangerous coming downstream as the strong ebb from Beeves Rock sets directly on to it. Hold well up N to clear the long Aughinish Pier.

Beeves Rock — Light — Dangers

There is a dark, stone light tower on Beeves Rock which provides welcome identification in this reach with its many ill defined dangers. A light is shown from the tower, Fl WR 5 s, 12 m. R from 091° through N to 238°, W elsewhere. The red sector covers the dangers on the N side of the river. Note that a dangerous ledge extends SE of Beeves lighthouse. It is locally known as Sheehan and dries 1·2 m at ¾ ebb. Keep not less than 1 cable S of the lighthouse. If beating in or out beware of the very dangerous tail extending 2 cables S of Horse Rock in the mouth of the Fergus River. This dries 0·3 m at its S end; a careful bearing of Beeves Rock is the only safe guide.

Deel River

2 miles E of Auginish Point, has 0·6 m at its mouth and somewhat more inside. It cannot be recommended, as the only mark for the channel is the perch at the entrance. When the Sheehan E of Beeves light is covered there is a depth of 2 m on the Deel bar NW of the perch.

Beagh Castle Quay

2¾ miles above Beeves Rocks, has 1·2 m alongside at HWN, mud bottom, but has old iron fastenings projecting from its face. No amenities. Not recommended.

RIVER FERGUS

locally known as **THE CLARE RIVER.** The mouth of this river is 3½ miles wide, obstructed by many islands and rocks on the W side, and by rocks alone on the E side where the main channel lies. Chart 1549 shows the mouth well. The river is navigable for 9 miles to Clare Castle.

Killadysert and Approach (chart 1549)

Killadysert lies at the head of a creek entered just within the W entrance to the Fergus River N of the Colonel's Point. The creek is sheltered by Inishcorker but the channel between this island and Inishturbrid is very narrow with a 5 kn tide and with its banks formed by boulders. The approach from the S to Colonel's Point is difficult and not recommended. The only mark to avoid the dangerous Colonel's Rock, which dries 0·3 m, and cross the bank on which it lies in the best water, 1·2 m, is to steer with the E summit of Inishcorker, 21 m high, bearing 000° until getting into deeper water. At the Colonel's Point, the E end of Inishcorker, the tide runs fast, spring ebb 5 kn. The passage past is narrow with 1 m and banks of boulders and no leading marks. There are a couple of large boulders NW of the point which must be given a fair berth when coming round for Killadysert Creek, but more particularly when leaving as the ebb sets down on them.

However, do not go too far from this side. The creek runs N of Inishcorker where there is a quay, and then SW to close to the village. It all dries at LW. There is a slip on the mainland point due N of the W of Inishcorker; just NW of this where the road joins the shore there is a quay.

It may be of interest to mention that at HWS it is possible with 1·0 m draught to proceed to Killadysert across the road which connects the W end of Inishcorker to the shore at LW. The approach is full of dangers for which no marks can be given and this is definitely not recommended to visitors.

Facilities

RC church, PO, pubs, chemist, doctor, hardware, butcher, petrol.

Channel North of Inishturbrid (Grady Island)

The rock shown N of Inishturbrid dries 0·3 m. E of this rock in mid-channel is a rocky shoal with 0·6 m on it. Both flood and ebb set across these rocks with increased speed and in the area generally there is a lot of turbulence. Carrignaragh further W covers at about 2 hours flood.

Channel West of Illaunbeg (O'Donnel Island)

There are dangerous rocks shown on metric chart 1549 on the mainland side of the channel one, a reef, just NE of the point of the mainland at the S end of the channel and the other ¾ cable further N.

Shore Island — Unmarked Rocks

Off the SW point of the island rocks dry out outside the LW mark of the island as well as 1½ to 2 cables further N. These are shown on metric chart 1549.

PARADISE ANCHORAGE

Carrigaduffy (Paradise Rock) which dries 1·8 m protrudes a little more into the channel than the chart shows. When approaching Inishmore (Deer Island) keep to the island side of mid-channel. There is good anchorage sheltered from the SW to NW 1½ cables E of the ruined landing stage at the boathouse in 2 m or more water. Watch out for a disused yacht mooring in this anchorage; it is fairly close to the mud above ruined landing stage. Do not anchor inshore SE of the ruined landing stage, for half-way between it and a small creek, is the N edge of a mussel bank which dries. Paradise House, now a ruin, was the home of Lt W Henn, RN, the owner of the cutter *Galatea* which he raced against *Mayflower* in a challenge for the America's Cup in 1886. The *Galatea*, which drew 13½ ft, was on a subsequent occasion sailed up to Paradise.

BALLYNACALLY ANCHORAGE

There is very nice shelter from either NW or SE about 4 cables NE of the Paradise stage off a landing slip where the road from Ballynacally meets the shore. Anchor not more than a cable from the island and not quite as far up as its quay. Do not anchor immediately upstream of the Ballynacally slip so as not to foul a new plastic water pipe which is across the bottom of the channel to the island. It is all right to anchor at the top of the chart between the two island quays, again not more than a cable from the island. It would be foolish to sail N of the chart limitations.

Facilities

Ballynacally, 15 minutes walk, is a tidy village N of Paradise and just outside chart 1549. It has a PO, petrol, pub and groceries. RC Church at Ballycorrick is 35 minutes from the slip.

Channel West of Canon Island (chart 1549)

Entering from the Shannon E of Inishtubbrid there is a clear channel between Canon Island and Inishmacowney (Horse Island). Beyond Inishmacowney there are some rocks to port to be avoided. This leads to a channel N of Inishloe (Low Island) by which the main Fergus Channel can be reached. It is very narrow between steep, drying banks and has least water about 1 m.

Anchorage

There are three hillocks NW of the N of the two hills on Canon Island. Opposite the middle hillock there is a boat harbour suitable for dinghy landing. The channel here is too deep for anchoring conveniently but there is 8 m a little further up.

RIVER FERGUS, Main Channel (chart 1549)

Considerable care is needed at the entrance because of the unmarked rocks. After half-tide a yacht drawing 1·5 m could ignore most of these, but then Horse Rock would be just covered and there is no mark to avoid it. It is therefore only safe to attempt this entrance when Horse Rock, which dries 2·8 m can be identified with certainty and used as a mark to avoid the others; this means within about 2 hours of LW. The three groups of rocks which show at LWS are shown on the chart. They are firstly a rock almost 3 cables S of Horse Rock and which dries 0·3 m and is on the W side of the channel. Secondly Moylaun's Children, a group on the E side of the channel and 3 cables E of Horse Rock and finally a group of rocks 2 to 3 cables N of Horse Rock and on the W side of the channel.

When Blackthorn Island (East Drynagh Island) comes abeam the last named rocks will have been passed and it is safe to keep over to the W side to avoid Outer Brecknish Rocks which dry on the E side of the channel. About 3½ cables upstream of these rocks there is a rock in mid-channel with 1·8 m over it which smaller yachts can usually ignore. From there the channel is clear until near Coney Island.

Anchorage East of Coney Island
Between Feenish and Coney Islands the middle of the channel is obstructed by Roadway Rock which covers about 2 hours after LW. The approach to the anchorage is between the rock and Coney Island. Anchor E of the island in 2·5 to 5 m, sheltered from W to NE. The tide here always runs to the S and is not strong. Good view from the top of the island.

Above Coney Island the river winds for 7 miles through extensive featureless mudbanks to Clarecastle; as no useful instructions can be given for this part it is not recommended. Furthermore 1 M due S of Clarecastle there are power cables with 18·2 m clearance at HWS. It may be noted that the channel now lies W of the Boorland Rock perch, not E of it as shown on the old chart, there is no chart available now.

CHANNELS TO LIMERICK
Chart 1540 with up to date corrections for lights and buoyage is essential for this passage which is straightforward with adequate rise of tide. It is important to note carefully the limited distances for which the leading lines shown on the chart remain valid and the precise purpose of each set.

A yacht may go up on either side of The Middle Ground which divides the river into two channels for a distance of 3 miles. The N channel which is used by shipping is well buoyed and carries a least depth of 2·7 m. The S channel has 1·8 m. Battle Island is 1½ miles beyond Middle Ground and should be passed S of it and the red buoys. At the entrance to the N channel is a harbour which dries. It is part of the Shannon Airport duty free area and landing there is strictly prohibited. Note that there

is only 1 cable between the end of the W breakwater and Carrigkeel Rock on the S side of the channel. Keep N of the line between the two G Cone buoys. It is 12 miles from Carrigkeal to Limerick. There is a new bridge from Russells Quay in a NW direction with 3·3 m clearance at LAT.

Limerick Docks
open from one hour before HW until HW. They are on the S bank below the city and it is entered heading SE. It is inconvenient for more than a short stay as a yacht may be required to shift berth frequently to facilitate commercial shipping movements. There is no slipway but yachts of less than 20 tons dead weight can be lifted out by crane if desired.

Limerick supplies all the facilities of a city including rail connections to Dublin and Cork and easy access to Shannon Airport. There is no sailmaker or boatbuilder. Limerick Harbour Authority require yachts entering the basin to sign an indemnity form. These can be obtained at the gateman's hut at the tidal gates or at the harbour office.

LIMERICK TO KILLALOE
There is no chart covering this 15 mile section of the river which is navigable by 1·6 m draught with 2·7 m headway. Anyone interested should consult the Shannon Navigation Office in Limerick Phone 061-44210, or the Limerick Harbourmaster, Phone 061-44914. There is no good anchorage immediately below Limerick and as a yacht would have to unstep her mast it is advisable to lock into Limerick dock temporarily. The passage through Limerick city is made during the second half of the flood and when the power station is on reduced or no load. The river is impassible in either direction during the ebb. The services of a pilot for this part are strongly recommended.

The Ardnacrusha Locks each rise 9 m and long lines are needed. Above the locks there are 7 miles of Head Race Canal where the stream may be 3 kn if the turbines are running. At Arch of Parteen Weir the navigation is on the W bank. Above this the Shannon broadens, the channel being along the E bank. The canal and lock at Killaloe are disused and the navigation arch of the road bridge is the steel span near the E side. The stream flows fast under the bridge.

Information about the Shannon and the canal system may be obtained from the Hon Secretary, The Inland Waterways Association of Ireland, Kingston House, Ballinteer, Dublin 4. Phone 01-983392.

146

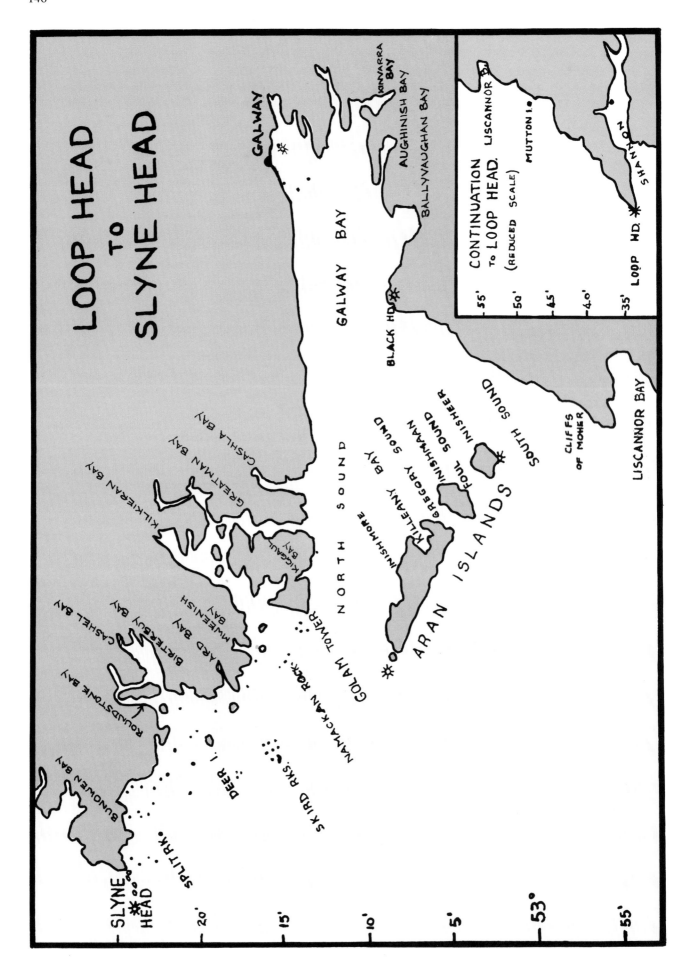

LOOP HEAD
TO
SLYNE HEAD

GALWAY

KINVARRA BAY

AUGHINISH BAY

BALLYVAUGHAN BAY

GALWAY BAY

BLACK HD.

CASHLA BAY

GREATMAN BAY

KILKIERAN BAY

KIGGAUL BAY

NORTH SOUND

INISHMORE

KILLEANY BAY

GOLAM TOWER

FOUL SOUND

GREGORY SOUND

INISHMAAN

INISHEER

SOUTH SOUND

CLIFFS
OF MOHER

LISCANNOR BAY

ARAN ISLANDS

MWEENISH BAY

ARD BAY

BIRTERBUY BAY

CASHEL BAY

ROUNDSTONE BAY

BUNOWEN BAY

NAVACKAN ROCK

DEER I.

SKIRD RKS.

SPLITRK.

SLYNE HEAD

20'

15'

10'

5'

53°

55'

CONTINUATION
TO LOOP HEAD.
(REDUCED SCALE)

LISCANNOR BAY

MUTTON I.

SHANNON

LOOP HD.

55'

50'

45'

40'

35'

Chapter 6

LOOP HEAD TO
SLYNA HEAD

Charts (For details see Appendix 1). Three are essential for the passage, 2254, 2173 and 3338, also three are essential for the Connemara bays and Slyne Head, 2096, 2709 and 2708. For the Galway Bay creeks 1984 is needed and 3339 is best for the Aran Islands. For Joyce's Pass 2708 is essential. The obsolete 2442 gives the Mutton Island, Co. Clare anchorage. This anchorage is also shown in the plan, p 148.

Tides (For details see Appendicies 2 and 3)
On all this part of the coast HW occurs at about the same time as at Galway, or 6 hours before HW Dover. The rise at Galway is 5 m at springs and 4 m at neaps. Elsewhere it is 0·3 to 0·6 m less. Where tidal streams are of significance they are mentioned in the text.

(See p119 for Passage Notes for the approach from the S and N to the Connemara coast).

LOOP HEAD TO BLACK HEAD

LOOP HEAD. Light, Radiobeacon, Danger. Loop Head, 68 m high marks the NW limit of the Shannon estuary. A light, Fl (4) 20 s, 84 m, 28 M is shown from a white lighthouse on the head. Radiobeacon (see Appendix 4). **Danger.** There is a breaker ½ cable N of the head.

Coast
The 45 miles of coast from Loop Head to Black Head at the entrance to Galway Bay has no safe anchorages and being exposed to the full ocean swell is best admired from a comfortable distance. A brief description of its main features is given for the benefit of yachts standing close in on the inshore tack. Goleen Harbour is a crack in the cliffs about 5M S of Kilkee. It almost all dries out at LW. At HW there is a small lagoon inside with some flat shore where a dinghy could be pulled up. A track connects to the main road. It is an attractive place for very small craft which can dry out in offshore winds. Moore Bay with the town of Kilkee at its head lies 13 miles N of Loop Head offers possible shelter in offshore winds. Leim Chaite (Leaconnor) Cliffs, 75 m high, are 3 miles N of Kilkee and are conspicuous. Mal Bay, 4 miles further N offers no secure shelter though there is a fine weather anchorage inside Mutton Island, see plan. Chart

3338 shows an anchorage open to the NW and N in the head of Doonbeg Bay on the S side of Doughmore Bay. Nothing is known about this anchorage.

MUTTON ISLAND *(see plan)*
1 mile long and 30 m high, extends 2 miles offshore and is 21 miles NE of Loop Head. It must be emphasised that this area is rock-strewn and offers no shelter in a heavy onshore swell and is also a lee shore in winds between NW and SW. It could be approached in suitable weather using this plan or chart 3338. (Note that Ballard Tower and the Atlantic Hotel, used for clearing marks on the old chart, no longer exist.)

Seafield Quay
From a position ENE of Carrickaneelwar (Lime Rock) steer exactly 196° for the seaward end of the pier which at HWS is only 1·3 m high. Anchor on this line in 4 to 5 m sand, when about 2 cables from the quay with the tower and bluff on Mutton Island in line, as shown on the plan. The shelter is uneasy at the best of times and wind from a N quarter sends in a bad swell, rendering dinghy work unsafe.

A straight channel 1·8 m deep and about 27 m wide runs in between drying rocks from almost ½ cable seaward of the pier to alongside the outer 40 m of the E side of the pier, beyond which it dries. Bottom is all rock. The pier points 351°.

Mutton Island Anchorage
There is an anchorage, sheltered except from the S, about 1 to 1½ cables off the ruined cottages at the SE end of the island, marked Tobacco Cove on the chart, bottom rock with patches of sand, 3 to 4 m. This is less prone to swell than the Seafield anchorage but is separated from the quay by ³/₄ mile of exposed water and a drying reef. It must be approached with due regard to the various rocks and shoals. Coming from the S, wait until Mattle (Battle) Island bears 070° before steering for it, then leave it 2 or 3 cables to starboard. Coming from the N, give the SW corner of Mutton Island a berth of 1½ to 2 cables to pass between it and Curragh Shoal (2·1 m), then steer E towards Mal Rock till the anchorage opens up. Pass halfway between the island and Mal Rock which, when covered is nearly always breaking.

Danger

Four miles NE of Mutton Island, Muirbeg Rock, with 0·3 m of water on it, lies 1 mile offshore.

Liscannor Bay with wide sandy beaches is 7 miles N of Mutton Island but offers no safe shelter. There is a drying pier in the NE corner of the bay but it is subject to such a scend in gales that craft in it will be broken up. Cancregga is the N point of Liscannor Bay. Working up this coast at night or in thick weather it is important to keep well clear of Mutton Island and Cancregga to prevent getting embayed inside them.

N from Cancregga the coast rises in the stupendous sweep of the Cliffs of Moher, rising sheer to 199 m near the prominent O'Brien's Tower on their summit. Below this tower the 61 m pinnacle of Branaunmore is dwarfed by the cliffs rising behind it. Off the cliffs are Stookeen and Carrickatrial Rocks, both 1½ cables offshore. To port the great, limestone cliffs of the Aran Islands echo the mainland cliffs. The N end of the cliffs terminate at Doonagore Bay and on from there the coast is bold to Black Head with the high and bare Burren Hills behind it. From Cancregga to Black Head is 15 miles.

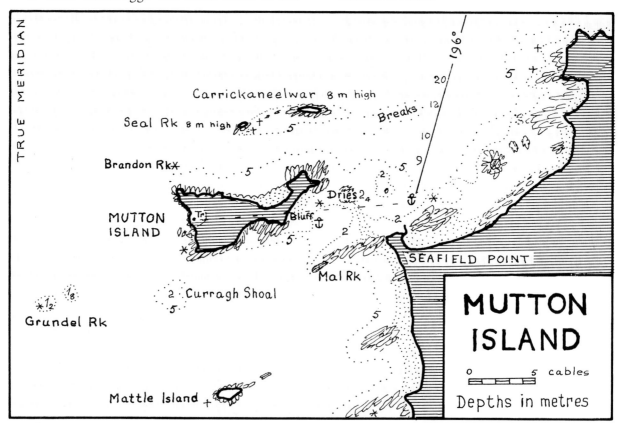

GALWAY BAY TO SLYNE HEAD

Galway Bay is a deep inlet sheltered from the ocean swell by the Aran Islands, but subject to the sea which can get up in the 20 mile fetch from Aran to Galway.

The S shore of the bay, E of Black Head, is fronted by rocks and shallows within which there are a number of creeks offering excellent shelter. Clearing marks are poor and it is not advisable to run for this part of the bay in strong W to NW winds with mist and rain. These creeks were formerly frequented by hookers bringing turf to Clare from Connemara but with the demise of this trade the quays have fallen into neglect.

Galway city near the head of the bay has a good harbour with wet dock and a basin at the entrance to the old canal in the R. Corrib to the westward. Railway to Dublin, airport and all facilities. A new marina is planned.

The N shore of the bay is exposed and there are no harbours for the 20 miles from Galway to Cashla Bay. From there to Roundstone 18 miles further W the coast is deeply indented with safe harbours but many dangers offshore. In reasonable visibility there is no difficulty in navigating along it and into the bays and among the islands which offer anchorages of all sorts.

The Aran Islands which provide shelter for much of the coast are well worth a visit and offer shelter in Killeany Bay on Inishmore – except in E to NE weather. The two smaller islands, Inisheer and Inishmaan, have only open roadsteads.

W of Roundstone the land is fronted by a maze of low and half-tide rocks which afford shelter only to those who know them. To a stranger the only safe refuge is Bunowen Bay immediately below the very prominent cone of Doon Hill (60 m). Finally, Slyne Head with its twin light towers stands out at the end of its long line of reefs.

Conspicuous Features

There are a number of prominent physical features which dominate this coast of which the following are the most important. On the Clare coast the Cliffs of Moher, 199 m with O'Brien's Tower and on Inishmore, Aran Islands, the old disused lighthouse on the summit of the island, 120 m. Further W on Inishmore is the great pile of Dun Aengus on the cliff edge, 82 m. On the Connemara shore Golam Tower, 24 m, at the entrance to Kilkieran Bay is the key to most of the inshore passages, while Knockmorden, 350 m, a long hill at the head of the bay is unmistakable. Above Mweenish and Ard Bays, Cuileen Hill stands out, 96 m.

Further W Cashel Hill, 307 m, at the head of Cashel Bay is a prominent conical hill which stands out from the higher Benna Beola (or Twelve Pins) behind it. Errisbeg Hill, 296 m, above Roundstone is easily identified. Nearer Slyne Head, Doon Hill, 61 m, with its tower is conspicuous. Offshore, Skerdmore, 18 m high, is the largest of the Skerd Rocks and quite unmistakable. Croaghnakeela (Deer Island), 60 m and St Macdara's Island to its E are both readily identifiable.

Approaches to the Connemara Shore

See under Passage Notes on page 119.

APPROACHES TO GALWAY BAY

South Sound is the passage between Inisheer and the mainland. Nearly 4 miles wide, it has no dangers except for Finnis Rock which dries 0·4 m and which lies $4^{1}/_{2}$ cables SE of the E point of Inisheer. It is marked by a E Card, Lt Buoy Q (3)10 s, moored ESE of it and is covered by the R sector of Inisheer light between 245° and 269°. The maximum tidal stream in the sound is 1 kn at springs, NE stream commences -0520 Galway and the SW stream at +0105 Galway.

Light

A light is shown from a W light tower with one black band on the SE corner of Inisheer. Iso WR 20 s, 34 m, 20-16 M; R from 269° to 245°; W thence to 231° and partially beyond 7 M to 225°; obsc from 231° to 115°; W thence to 269°. The R sector covers Finnis Rock.

Foul Sound

lies between Inishmaan and Inisheer and is free from danger except for Pipe Rock which dries at the end of a reef extending 3 cables from the NW side of Inisheer. The sound is about 1 mile wide with maximum tidal stream about $1^{1}/_{2}$ kn at springs. Tide times are as for South Sound. In a heavy swell the sea is said to be less turbulent than in Gregory Sound.

Gregory Sound

lies between Inishmore and Inishmaan, is free of danger and 1 mile wide. A berth of $2^{1}/_{2}$ cables should be given to both Straw Island and the NW corner of Inishmaan. Owing to the steep cliffs on both sides of the sound the sea can be very unpleasant in a high swell. Maximum tidal stream is $1^{1}/_{2}$ kn with times as for S sound.

Light

A light Fl (2) 5 s, 11 m, 17 M is shown from a W tower on the N side of Straw Island. This light is partially obscured from Gregory Sound. With caution, as mentioned earlier, it is possible to use this sound in the dark with a safe bearing on the light.

The S side of Inishmore is made up of fine cliffs, the highest 81 m being near Dun Aengus, towards the W end of the island. The valley which runs from Blind Sound to Portmurvy on the N sound makes the island look like two islands from a distance.

Light

Eeragh Island (Rock Island) off the NW point of Inishmore has a W tower with two B bands on its summit which shows Fl 15 s, 35 m, 23 M. When passing W of this light at night note that it must be given a berth of $^{1}/_{2}$ mile to clear the rocks off the islet.

North Sound

between Inishmore and the mainland, is the principal approach to Galway Bay. It is $4^{1}/_{2}$ miles wide. There are a number of dangers on the N side which will be dealt with when the directions for the Connemara coast are given. On the S side Brocklinmore and Brocklinbeg Banks break under gale conditions or a high swell, otherwise they can be ignored. The same applies to Murvy Shoal, 7 m, and Carrickadda Breaker and Priest's Shoal both NW of Killeany Bay. Cowrugh Shoal off Portmurvy with only 2·7 m might break near LW in much less rough conditions.

GALWAY BAY (chart 1984 new 1993)

Black Head, Light, Anchorage

The S headland of the bay is Black Head below the bare Doughbranneen (Black Head) Hill (312 m). There is a small lighthouse on the head showing Fl RW 5 s, 20 m, 8-11 M. The red sector from 268° to 293° covers the Illaunloo Rock in Ballyvaghan Bay. There is temporary shelter, subject to swell with S to SW winds inside the head.

Coast

Finavarra martello tower, Knockavorneen (Murlin Beg) Hill, 73 m high, and Aughinish Tower are all conspicuous. In addition a line of trees on the high ground W of the entrance to Kinvarra Bay stands out well. Deer Island, 2 m high, is joined to the mainland by a spit which nearly dries and is hard to pick up against the land, especially when approaching from the W.

Ballyvaghan Bay

In the centre of the bay Illaunloo is only 0·6 m high and difficult to identify against the land. It is foul for up to 1 cable all round.

At the S entrance to the bay the Farthing Rocks are an extensive patch, some of which dry 1·7 m, and lie up to 4 cables offshore. The inner part of the bay is shallow with extensive drying banks. Shannamuckish Castle (ruin) in line with St Patrick's church, 096°, leads between Illaunloo and Farthing Rocks.

At HW it is possible to go up to the old quay by the village and lie alongside its SE side, bottom shingle and small stones. It is also possible to go alongside the new quay on its SE side where the shelter is a little better. The end of this quay has been damaged and is foul. Both quays dry.

There is also a pool with about 3 m LWS off the end of the NE pier near the 3·4 m sounding on chart 1984. It is about 140 m long by 90 m wide, its long axis lying NE-SW in continuation of the line of the inner face of the end of the pier. Sound into it and preferably moor with two anchors to reduce swinging. It is very well sheltered at low tide and the NW-SE edges are clean sand.

At the NE end of the bay Shannamuckish Strait gives access to a long creek. It is shallow and not recommended. Carrickadda (Long Rock) dries 3·7 m and extends ³/₄ mile W from the shore NE of Finavarra Point. Gleninagh Castle in line with the N side of Illaunloo, 244°, leads just clear of Carrickadda. Note that Illaunloo is hard to pick up. This line also clears the 2·1 m patch NW of Aughinish Point.

Aughinish Bay

The entrance to this bay is straightforward. Anchor at or above New Quay. There is a strong tide in this anchorage. The anchorage off the pier is uncomfortable in NW winds as there are overfalls on the ebb and a yacht will be tide-rode. Under these circumstances go further up the bay, sounding continuously as the channel is unmarked.

Deer Island (2 m) lies 1 mile offshore N of the prominent martello tower NE of Aughinish Point. It is foul all round for 1 cable and a long, shallow spit which partially uncovers runs SE from it to the land. Again this island is hard to identify against the shore. Once identified it can be used to get a good fix in the entrance to South Bay.

Kinvara Quay and Bay.

South Bay

is divided by Eddy Island which can be identified when Deer Island comes abeam. The S part of this bay leads to Kinvarra Bay and the N part to the Kilcolgan River. There is a prominent line of trees just to the E of Newtown House, 1¾ mile W of Doorus Point at the entrance to Kinvarra Bay.

Kinvarra Bay

There are no marks for the deep water entrance between Madrallan Rock, with 0·5 m, and Goragh Rock, dries 1·8 m, and it is suspected that these rocks may be more extensive than charted. This passage should therefore be made with great care and frequent sounding. It is simpler with sufficient rise of tide to keep well N of Madrallan Rock, steering to pass 1 cable S of Fiddoun Island. When Fiddoun Island is abeam and Doorus Point bears about 205° it is safe to stand into Kinvarra Bay, giving Doorus Head a berth of 1½ cables and less than 2 cables to avoid Comb Rock which dries 2·9 m. There is good anchorage abreast the quay at Bush in 4 m.

To proceed further, first keep Bush pierhead 290° astern which leads N of both Madden's and Long Rocks. Tarrea pier will be seen ahead. It is at the end of the road leading W by N from Tarrea village; it must not be confused with the less conspicuous Poltagh quay NNW of it. When Poltagh quay bears N and Tarrea pier is about 1½ cables distant steer to pass W of Goormeen Rock which covers at half-tide and has a small perch which can be seen at HW. After this keep in mid-channel. At neaps there is anchorage ¼ mile from Kinvarra with 2 m at LW. Alternatively, berth at the S or W side in the small harbour; the bottom of shingle and small stones is suitable for drying out; it is the only spot in the inlet free of mud at LW.

Facilities

Kinvarra is an attractive village. Supermarket, butcher, chemist, garage, medieval banquets at Dunguaire Castle (book at Winkles Hotel). David FitzGerald is an excellent contact in this area if in difficulty. His house is close to the quay.

Kilcolgan River

Having entered through Mweenish Strait, which is fairly straightforward with regular shore lines of steep, shelving shingle, and favouring the Eddy Island side of the straight, alter to port to pass within 1 cable of Mweenish Point which is steep-to, thus avoiding Meelan Rock, a group of boulders which dries.

Anchorage

There is good, safe shelter NNE of the point in Ship Pool. No facilities. Alternatively, if proceeding further and awaiting sufficient rise, anchor in Tyrone Pool; Yellow Slate Rock, which dries 0·6 m, lies on the edge of the shallows on the N side of the pool opposite Bird Island.

After half-flood keep ½ cable off the S shore and enter the Kilcolgan River S of Corraun Point. Due to scour there is deeper water in the river than charted. Continue in mid-stream and anchor in 0·5 m LWS or 2 m LWN 150 m short of the quay wall on the N bank of the river at Weir village. The river shallows rapidly abreast the quay.

Facilities

Moran's Oyster Cottage at the far end of the quay specialises in sea-food meals, and is very well known. Phone, shops at Kilcolgan, 1 mile. Mr Moran might help with transport.

Kilcolgan Point

is deceptive and extends a long way into the bay. It is foul all round and must be given a wide berth. Mutton Island disused light in line with the white ice tower in Galway docks, 014°, or the large, dome-shaped silo in the docks just open W of the disused light tower, also 014° clears the point but lead **over** Kilcolgan Rocks in 3·4 m.

North Bay

is the approach to Galway docks, also to Oranmore Bay, New Harbour and Mweeloon Bay. Oranmore Bay is open to the W, holds no attraction for yachts and its head is choked with rocks. It is not recommended.

Mweeloon Bay is also open to the W and dries at its head. There is anchorage of sorts ¾ mile inside the entrance. It is important to keep close to Ardfry Point until the tower on it is passed to avoid the Creggaun Rocks (dry 1·5 m) in the middle of the entrance.

Approach to Galway and New Harbour

The main channel in from the W lies between Black Rock, dries 1·6 m, on the N and Margaretta Shoal on the S which has 2·9 m least water. Black Rock is marked by a red perch and by a R Can Lt Buoy Fl R 3 s moored 3½ cables SSW of the rock. Margaretta Shoal is marked by G Cone Lt buoy Fl G 3 s, whistle, moored to the W of the shoal.

Mutton Island gives protection to Galway roadstead in W and SW winds; it is foul 4½ cables on its W side and 2 cables on its S side. A mark to clear this is a conspicuous white tower on the skyline 2 miles E of Galway in line just open N of Hare Island. The E side of the island is shoal but may be approached cautiously if temporary anchorage is required. Tawin Shoals with 4 m least water lie 1 mile S of Mutton Island Tower.

Galway Docks and Harbour.

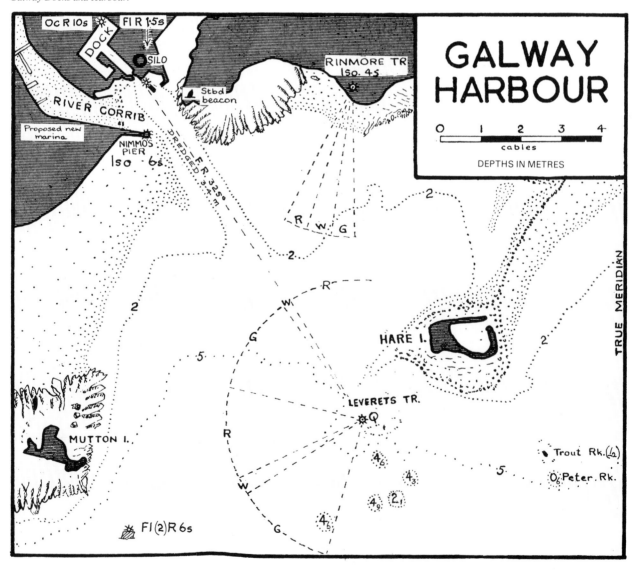

Lights — Buoys

Mutton Island, R Can Lt Buoy, Fl R (2) 6 s, is moored 2¹/₂ cables 136°, from Mutton Island Tower.

Tawin Shoals, G Cone Lt buoy, Fl G (3) 10 s, is moored 11¹/₂ cables 214° from Mutton Island Tower.

Leverets. A round tower with B and W bands, 2¹/₂ cables SW of Hare Island shows a light Q WRG 9 m, 10 M. The white sectors 058° to 065° and 143¹/₂° to 146¹/₂° leading in from seaward and out from Galway docks respectively, with R and G sectors port and starboard.

Rinmore. From a square W tower 7 m high and ¹/₂ mile E of Galway pier a light is shown Iso 4 s, 5 M. The W sector 008° to 018° leads from one Leveret W sector to the other. There are R and G sectors to port and starboard.

Leading Lights in line 325° lead up the dredged channel 3·45 m deep and 80 m wide. Front Fl R 1·5 s, 12 m, 7 M. B and Y beacon. Rear Oc R 10 s, 19 m, 7 M. B and Y beacon.

Nimmo's Pier. Iso Y 6 s, 7 m, 6 M.

Buoys – Unlit

S. cardinal pillar, Foudra Rock, 53°15'.05N., 9°04'.94W; N. cardinal pillar, Cockle Rock, 53°14'.35N., 9°01'.78W; S. cardinal pillar, Peter Rock, 53°15'.15N., 9°01'.07W.

Hare Island

is foul all round with isolated shoals, the Leverets up to 4 cables SW and Trout Rock and Peter Rock 3¹/₂ and 4 cables SE respectively. Leverets Tower stands 2¹/₂ cables SW of the island. St Nicholas Church spire kept 330° a little to port of the end of Nimmo's pier leads W of the 2·1 m rock, 2 cables SSE of the tower. Murroogh House, among trees, in line with the centre of Rabbit Island, 026°, leads close SE of Peter Rock.

GALWAY DOCKS *(see plan)*

Steer to pass 2 cables W of Leverets tower and the marks for the dredged channel will soon come in line bearing 325°, diamond shapes with RY diagonal stripes. The dredged channel is 6 cables long, 80 m wide and 3·45 m deep.

Mooring

The dock gates are opened 2 hours before HW and closed at HW. For a short stay or while waiting for the tide to enter the dock make fast alongside the E side of the pier extending from the dock gates in a narrow dredged cut with 3·4 m LWS known locally as the 'layby'. There is not room to round up in this cut. The berth is exposed in S or SE winds; in gales from these points it is dangerous as the pier is sometimes swept by the seas. A yacht should not be left unattended in the 'layby' for any period for the foregoing reason, and furthermore it is used by the fishing fleet and becomes crowded. When the dock gates open enter and pass through to the inner dock then turn to port and moor in the SW basin which is reserved for small craft. Note should also be taken if entering Galway under sail that, on the falling tide particularly at springs or after prolonged rain, there is a strong E set out of the River Corrib across the mouth of the harbour. A set of dock gates have been fitted to the canal basin at the Claddagh and the basin has been dredged. Depths of 2m can be maintained in the basin. Entry and departure is restricted to a short period before high water. A properly managed marina is proposed but not in operation in early 1993.

Facilities

All facilities. Railway, buses, shops, PO, petrol, diesel, water (chlorinated), boat repairs but no slipway. Some shops close all day Mon. HM, Captain F. W. Sheridan, Tel. (091) 62329.

Off the H.Q. of Galway Bay Sailing Club.

NEW HARBOUR (Rinville)

is the headquarters of the Galway Bay SC and yachts are moored at the head of the inlet. It is the nearest place to Galway where a yacht may lie safely to anchor. The shelter is better than would appear from the chart and some boats are moored here all winter.

The Clubhouse of the Galway Bay SC is situated close NW of the pier at the head of New Harbour - phone number (091) 84527. It is usually open at week ends and Wed night. There are two visitor moorings available off the Clubhouse with 2·1 m LWS and Capt Sheridan could most likely advise visitors if these are available. There are now a cluster of white bungalow's and houses at the head of the bay in the position where there was formally only a white bungalow with farm buildings.

The S side of the entrance is Ardfry Point foul along its N and NW side, W of which 1 mile long reef terminates in Cockle Rock which dries 2·3 m. Rinmore and Leverets Towers in line lead **onto** Cockle Rock. To clear it in more than 3 m Rinmore must be kept open at least 5° to port. There is a low tower (shown on the new chart 1984) about 2 cables from the end of Ardfry Point. The N side of the entrance is Rinville Point with a spit extending SW terminating in Dillisk Rock, dries 1 m. There is a tall radio mast about ½ mile from this point. The dome of Galway Cathedral in line with the W side of Hare Island, 312°, leads clear of Rinville Spit. Note that the other way it leads on to Trout Rock. The white bungalow shown on the chart at the head of the bay has fallen down but a cluster of white bungalows and houses have been built 100 m inland from it and serve as a mark instead.

Approach

If Mutton Island Tower is kept 289° astern the Cathedral dome - Hare Island transit will be reached at a point where the white buildings bear 090°. Proceed up the inlet on this line to clear Black Rock, dries 4·1 m, on the S shore. The N shore is clean and can be approached to within ½ cable.

Anchor with the quay bearing N and the white buildings E, 2 m, mud, or outside the moorings where available. It is safe to dry out between the central steps and the N corner of the quay where there is 2 m at HWN. S of the central steps a gravel bank has formed which dries 2½ hours after HW.

Facilities:

Pier to lie alongside at high water. Clubhouse open Wednesday and weekends during summer with showers, meals and bar. VHF watch on Ch.16. Water. No fuel. Nearest victualling in Oranmore 2M which also has a restaurant and pubs.

Coast

The N shore of Galway Bay for 20 miles to Cashla Bay is exposed and with no safe harbours. Black Rock, which has already been mentioned above lies 8 cables offshore opposite the prominent Blake's Hill (27 m). There is a channel between it and the shore obstructed by North Channel Rock which dries 0·6 m and is unmarked. The leading marks for this channel, only shown on old fathom chart 1984 are not easily identified.

Carrickanoge (Carigna Rock), 4 cables off Barna village, gives a little protection to a small, drying harbour. From Barna W the shore is bolder and an offing of 6 cables clears all outliers until Spiddal, 9 miles W of Mutton Island, is reached. Here there is a drying harbour with a clean, sandy bottom. The face of the quay is rough and it is subject to scend in winds from E through S to SW. There are small shops, a PO and bus to Galway from the village.

Light

There is a light Fl WRG 7·5 s, 11 m, 6-4 M on Spiddal pier head, G from shore to 282°, thence W to 024°, thence R to 066°. Vis officially 6 miles but it is difficult to see the white light at even 1 mile because of the brighter street lamps.

The dangerous Mantle Rocks, 3½ miles W of Spiddal Pier, dry and extend ½ mile offshore. They are hard to identify from seaward when covered as the coast has no outstanding features. Aille (Knock) Chapel is surrounded by trees and lies 1½ miles NE of the rocks. W of Mantle Rocks, there are no outlying dangers until Cloughmore Point at the entrance to Cashla Bay is reached.

The coast is continued after the Aran Island section.

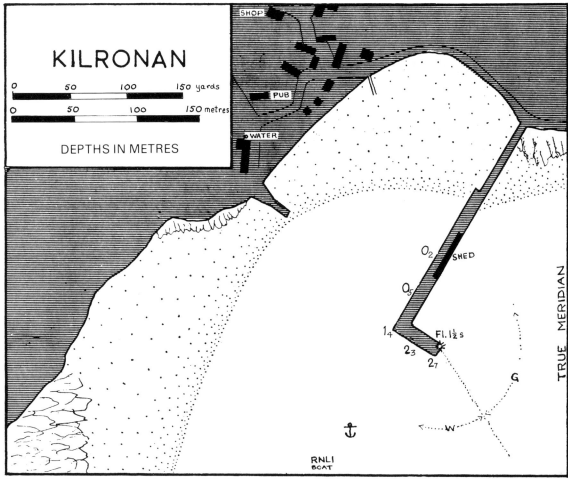

KILRONAN

| 0 | 50 | 100 | 150 yards |
| 0 | 50 | 100 | 150 metres |

DEPTHS IN METRES

Based on the Ordnance Survey by permission of the Government (Permit No. 2191)

ARAN ISLANDS (Chart 3339)

KILRONAN *(see plan)*
Killeany Bay on Inishmore is the only bay to give any reasonable shelter on the islands.

Lights
A light Fl (2) 5 s, 11 m, 17 M, is shown from a white tower on the N side of Straw Island, the E point of Killeany Bay. A light Fl WG 1·5 s is shown from a white column on Kironan pierhead. G from 240° through W to 326°, white elsewhere.

Dangers
The Bar of Aran with depths of 3·5 m extends nearly across the entrance of the bay, leaving a channel 1½ cables wide at its E end where a G Cone Lt buoy, Fl G 3 s is moored. Bar Rock which dries 0·4 m and the shoals around it extend to about ⅓ of the distance from Carrickadda Point to Bar buoy. The Bar of Aran breaks in a heavy NW swell. The W side of Straw Island is foul for 2 cables.

Approach
Leave Carrickadda Point a sufficient distance to starboard to clear Bar Rocks and shoals. About half way between point and buoy is adequate. If there is a swell running leave the Bar buoy to starboard.

Anchorage
S of Kilronan pier and either W or SW of the lifeboat. There are often wooden lobster boxes moored in this area and care should be taken to keep clear of these and of the lifeboat moorings and to allow room for the Galway packet to berth at the pierhead. Land at the steps of the pier or at the small W pier nearer the village.

In SE winds better shelter can be obtained by anchoring off Trawmore Strand, 1 mile SE in 5 m sand. An isolated situation without facilities.

Quays
The new L-shaped extension, which is unsuitable for berthing a yacht, has 2 to 3 m alongside and is used by the packet and fishing boats. The outermost berth inside this extension has 1·5 m with clean sand. The outer berths are usually occupied by fishing boats in the evening and night. Fisherman will advise whether an undisturbed berth alongside them is available. The old W pier has 2 m alongside after half-tide and a clean bottom and is often a less dusty berth than the main pier. The quays are now so crowded that a yacht could only dry out there in an emergency.

Kilronan - Inishmore.

Caution

The anchorage is untenable in strong E or NE winds and uncomfortable in strong N winds, becoming untenable. NW winds send in a considerable roll. If forced to leave, make across to Cashla Bay on the mainland or dry out alongside Kilronan pier or at Killeany pier *(see below)* where the local boats go in winter storms. In severe conditions it is unsafe to take the ground at Kilronan.

Facilities

Reasonable groceries available and daily milk. Butcher Wed. 1200-1700, Fri. and Sat. 0900-1800. Diesel is sometimes available from the fisherman's co-op on the quay. Water from tap half-way along the pier; the quality is excellent and yachts are advised to top up, particularly if bound N where there are few convenient sources of drinking water and sometimes a scarcity. Packet to Galway. Air service to Galway from a runway on the sand dunes on the E side of the bay. Dun Aengus, a most remarkable pre-historic fort, is well worth a visit. Engage a taxi or side-car. Like Skellig Michael it is one of the magic places in this world. The building itself is fascinating with its huge semi-circular walls right on the cliff edge and the chevaux de frise surrounding them. The view is superb with the Connemara mountains to the N and the Cliffs of Moher to the E. The cliffs are sheer, running down to deep water at their feet. The cliff walk from Dun Aengus to the E end of the island is marvellous, if somewhat strenuous with the many dry stone walls to be clambered over. Gas available. Doctor 099-61171. Garda 099-61102. Pubs, Restaurants, Coffee shops, Guest houses, Tourist Office, Heads, Bus tours, Cycle hire. HM Patrick McDonagh.

KILLEANY

is ¾ mile from Kilronan. There is a drying harbour formed by a pier projecting NE from the shore. A boat of 1·5 to 1·8 m draught can enter and berth alongside at 4 hours flood. Local boats take shelter here in winter. It is approached by a narrow channel which also dries. Two white 4 m high beacons in line 192° lead through. The channel is also marked by two haystack shaped beacons to starboard and two beacons to port. A ruined porthand haystack beacon covers at half tide and is inside the line joining the two concrete beacons. To enter, pass between the beacons and hold the line till 60 m from the quay, then swing to port after passing the second port hand concrete beacon and head for the end of the pier. There are lights on the beacons, Ldg Oc 5 s, which are not always operational. Visitors are very strongly recommended to take a pilot or get a local fisherman to guide one in.

PORTMURVY (chart 3339)

This bay offers reasonable shelter in fine weather and offshore winds. Approaching from Kilronan keep ½ mile offshore to avoid Carrickadda (Long Rock) and Carrickamonaghan. If coming from the W or N keep well clear of Scalraun Point on the W side of the bay to avoid Craghalmon Rock (Cragillaun) which dries 0·6 m and always appears to be surprisingly far offshore.

To pass between Murvy Shoal (7 m) and Cowrugh Shoal (2·7 m) bring a prominent white house on the shore in line with Dun Aengus bearing 224°. Usually if either of these shoals are dangerous the conditions are such that a yacht would not be going into the bay anyway. Anchor in 5 to 7 m sand off the strand and abreast the small pier on the E side. This pier is used by the local turf boats but the bottom alongside is foul. Land on the strand or at this pier. It is a convenient anchorage for a visit to Dun Aengus. Small shop ¼ mile from the pier.

Brannock East Sound

This sound is a possible short-cut for a yacht bound from Portmurvy to Kerry by daylight. The channel is less than 1 cable wide between covered rocks, a bearing on the S side of Middle Island being the best guide. Note that this sound would break right across in a heavy sea.

INISHMAAN

There is not a safe anchorage. There is a good boat-slip on the E side off which temporary anchorage may be had in fine weather and offshore winds. There is also a new slip at the NW point of the island which is sometimes used by local turf boats. A boat should not be left unattended at this anchorage. There is a very fine ring fort on the summit of the island.

INISHEER

The N strand is the best landing in fine weather only. Again, a boat should not be left unattended.

SOUTH CONNEMARA COAST

CASHLA BAY (Chart 2096) (see plan)

Cashla Bay is the easiest harbour on this part of the coast. There is a light at the entrance and given sufficient visibility it can be entered in any weather conditions and gives good shelter in the inner bay.

Cashla Bay

is entered between Killeen Point 53°14' N 9° 35' W and Cashla Point 1¼ miles East.

A light is shown from a white pillar NE of Killeen Point Fl(3) W.R. 10 s 6-3 M W 210°-000° R 000°-069° covering Narien Spit which extends ½ M Southward of Killeen Point.

Entrance Channel

The principal entrance channel is indicated by a directional light at Lion Point Iso W.R.G. 4 Secs 8 metres high 8-6 M. White Sector 008·5°-011·5° and a lighted starboard hand buoy Fl G 5 s South West of Cannon Rock, on which there is a black iron beacon with topmark.

The narrow entrance between Curraglass Point and Lion Point is marked with lighted green and red starboard and port hand buoys. Having passed the Northermost port hand buoy by ½ cable turn to port and steer WNW towards the anchorage off Shruthan Pier.

Leading lights 120° (T) lead into the busy fishing harbour of Rossaveel from where several ferry boats run to the Aran Islands. Yachts are unlikely to find a berth at Rossaveal due to the number of fishing vessels and ferries using the harbour.

Dangers

Coddu Rock which always shows and is steep-to on its N and W sides, lies near the E side of the entrance. Carrickadda (Laghan Rock) and Coastguard Rock, both of which dry 1·5 m, lie to the N of Coddu Rock and on the E side of the outer bay. A rock with 0·2 m at LW lies 2 cables W of Tonacrick Point on the E side of the outer bay. Cannon Rock, already mentioned, lies in the centre of the entrance. There is a clear channel between it and Coddu Rock. Carrickmarian, which dries 3·7 m, lies 2½ cables S of Killeen Point at the W entrance, and Narien Spit, a rock with 1·5 m on it, lies 2 cables S of Carrickmarian.

Approach

At the head of the bay two small round hills stand out clearly, Mt Ballagh and Round Hill. Quarrying for stone is taking place on Round Hill which may eventually cease to exist. Mt Ballagh and Curraglass Point, at the W side of the narrows, in one 355° lead in W of Cannon Rock. Round Hill and Curraglass Point in one 346° lead between Cannon and Coddu Rocks and also clears all dangers on the E side of the outer bay. Approaching from the W, the summit of Illaunnanownim (Live Island) just open S of Aillewore Point, astern, 265°, clears Narien Spit. The coastguard buildings on the E side of the bay, which are roofless and just above a pier, open

158

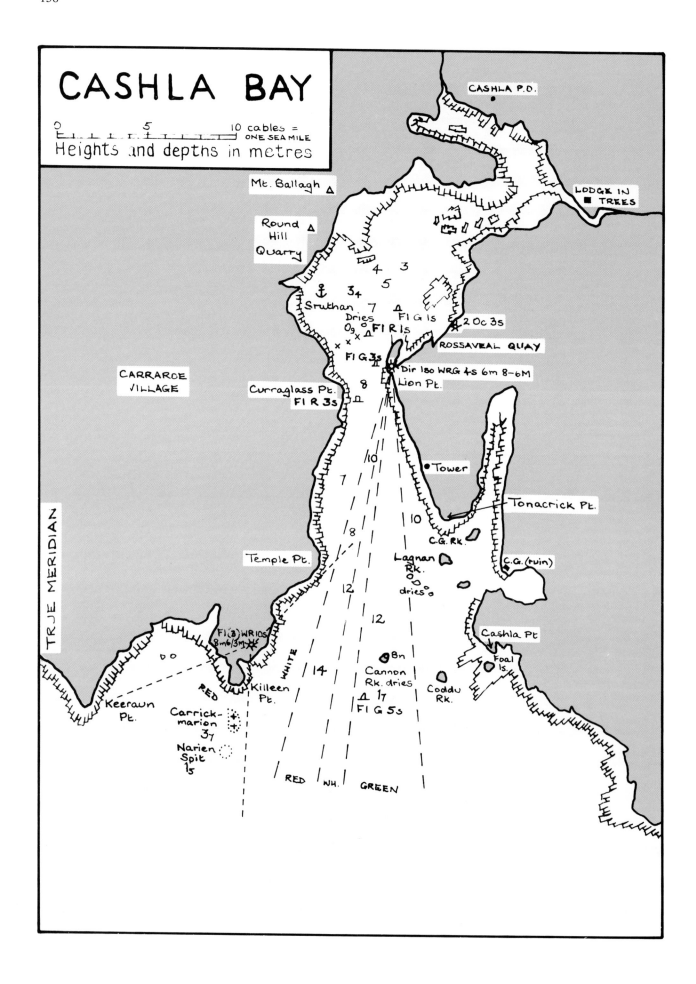

CASHLA BAY

0 ⸻ 5 ⸻ 10 cables = ONE SEA MILE

Heights and depths in metres

CASHLA P.O.

Mt. Ballagh △

LODGE IN TREES ■

Round Hill Quarry △

⚓ 3₄

4 3

5

Sruthan 7 △ FI G 1s
Dries △ FI R 1s 2 Oc 3s
O₉

ROSSAVEAL QUAY

FI G 3s

CARRAROE VILLAGE

Dir 180 WRG 4s 6m 8-6M
Lion Pt.

Curraglass Pt. 8
FI R 3s △

10

Tower

7

Tonacrick Pt.

10

C.G. Rk.

Temple Pt.

Lagnan Rk. dries

C.G. (ruin)

12

Cashla Pt.

12

TRUE MERIDIAN

FI(3)WR10s 8m6/3m ✴

WHITE

14

8n
Cannon Rk. dries

Foal Is.

RED

Killeen Pt.

Coddu Rk.

△ 1₇
FI G 5s

Keeraun Pt.

Carrick-marion 3₇

Narien Spit 1₅

RED WH. GREEN

Cashla Bay.

their own length N of Knockduff Hill, 150 m, bearing 054° also leads S of the spit. Knockduff Hill is shown on chart 2096 but not on the old fathom edition. It is shown on chart 3339 (fathom). Cruckdough Hill (Croghduff, just to the N of Knockduff, is a very noticeable pimple.

Just inside the narrows leading to the inner bay there is a rock which dries 0·9 m. Between this rock and the W shore there are a number of rocks with less than 2 m at LW. These rocks are in line with a grassy lane running down the W shore to the sea and form a broken ridge extending to the 0·9 m rock. There is deep water between the rocks. They are not marked on old chart 2096 but are shown on the metric chart.

Keep a mid-channel course through the narrows and if turning to windward do not close either shore as they are both foul for nearly 1 cable offshore. There are now red and green buoys to go between. Once through, and if the tide is above mean tide level, alter course for Sruthan (Glashnacally) pier on the W side. The course for Sruthan Quay from the port hand inner buoy N of Lion Point is 280° and if keeping to the E shore until well past the beacon off Rossaveal Quay, i.e., close to the strbd. hand inner buoy, the course to steer then is W by N. Anchor off the quay in 2 to 3 m, mud, good holding and safe in all weathers though it can be very rough in a S or SE gale and dinghy work would be impossible. Do not anchor near the line of a sewer indicated by two posts with triangular topmarks, one ashore near the pier and the other on the sewer off the pier, outer one reported missing. The new buoy on Cannon Rock Fl G 5 s must be left to starboard on the way in.

Sruthan Quay

is used by the local turf hookers to Aran which work in and out under canvas. It just dries at its outer end. The bottom is clean and it is safe to dry out alongside but care must be taken to avoid the little stone pillars built up to support the outer bilge at each hooker berth. It is about 100 m from anchorage to quay.

Facilities

Water and diesel close to quay. At Carraroe, 1 mile away, there are shops, hotel, PO, Bureau de change, RC Church, phone and bus to Galway. At Costelloe (Derrynea) 1½ miles E, there is an hotel, PO and garage.

Rossaveal Quay

on the E side of the bay is a busy fishing port with perfect shelter. The new harbour is dredged to 3·7 LAT. Leading lights Oc 3s, in line 116° lead into until the harbour opens up. There are a number of new buoys to be laid in 1993 as the harbour develops. These positions and characteristics will be promulgated as soon as known. Besides the large fishing flotilla, the ferry to the Aran islands uses the S pier. New temporary plan. Do not leave a yacht unattended.

Facilities

Bus to Galway. Spar shop ½ mile, will deliver. Pub 1 mile. Fuel and water on quays. Heads on shore. Garage at Costello (Derrynea) 2·5M. HM John Donnelly (Ch. 16, 14, 12), office 091-72109 and home 091-72190. New boatyard and slip being built. Tom Flaherty (091-95075); Hospital (091-24222); Garda (091-82202/82439); Maritime Rescue CG 061-471217; RNLI (099-61107/61132).

160

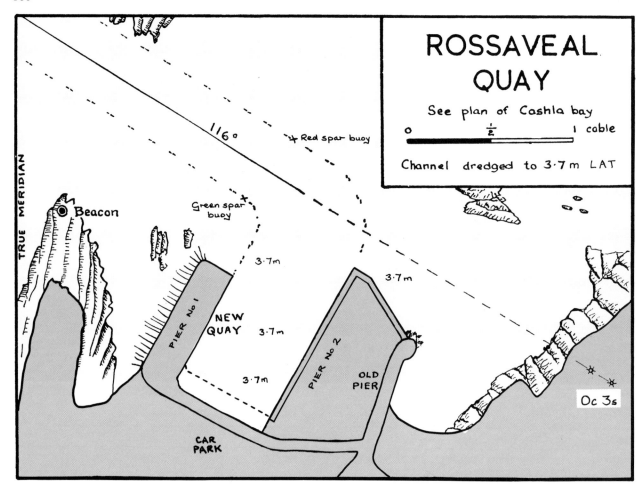

ROSSAVEAL QUAY

See plan of Cashla bay

0   ½   1 cable

Channel dredged to 3·7m LAT

TRUE MERIDIAN

116°

Red spar buoy

◉ Beacon

Green spar buoy

3·7m

3·7m

PIER No 1

NEW QUAY

3·7m

3·7m

PIER No 2

OLD PIER

3·7m

CAR PARK

Oc 3s

Rossaveal Quay.

GREATMAN'S BAY (Chart 2096) *(see plan)*

Greatman's Bay can be entered in any summer weather conditions but there are more dangers in the entrance than in Cashla Bay, and the shelter inside is not so good. The entrance is wide and easily identified from seaward.

Dangers. English Rock

which dries 1·2 m and is unmarked, lies 8½ cables SW of Trabaan Point, the W point of the entrance. This is the most dangerous rock along this stretch of coast from Cashla to Golam Head as when covered, it frequently does not break or show itself in any way. It lies in the red sector of Killeen light between 000° and 069°. Golam Tower, which is unmistakable, open S of Loughcarrick Island bearing 282° leads S of the rock. Golam Tower over the NE point of Live Island (Illaunnanownim) and bearing 277° leads N of the rock, and also S of Arkeena Rock and Keeraun Shoal. Dooleen beaches, which stand out well on the E side of the bay, open E of Trabaan Point (028°) leads clear E of the rock.

Keeraun Shoal

breaks in a heavy swell, but can generally be ignored by a yacht in summer conditions. The same applies to Arkeena Rock and Trabaan Rock, except near LW. Chart 2096 gives clearing marks for these rocks if required. Inchamakinna Building, which is two storied, slated, white and conspicuous, in line with Dooleen Point, 014°, clears both Trabaan and Arkeena Rocks and Rin Rocks as well. Lettermore Hill open W of Gorumna Chapel, which is roofless and does not stand out very well, bearing 344°, leads E of Trabaan Rock.

Rin Rocks

off the E side of the bay dry 1·8 m and are dangerous. The rocks are about 2½ cables SW of a prominent new bungalow S of Dooleen beaches. The shore abreast the bungalow is foul almost a cable offshore. Keeraun Point just open SW of Carrow Point 128°, leads SW of the rocks, as also Inchamakinna Building and Dooleen Point, 014°, as above. Temporary anchorage off the beaches in fine weather or in the bay to the N of Trabaan Point, but subject to roll.

Chapel Rocks

off Dooleen Point have 0·6 m. The old lighthouse on Inishmore (Aran) in line with Trabaan Point, 198°, leads E of them (chart 3339), The Lettermore Church, just NE of Carrickalegaun Pass bridge, is conspicuous from seaward.

Greatman Bay & Natawny Quay from SE.

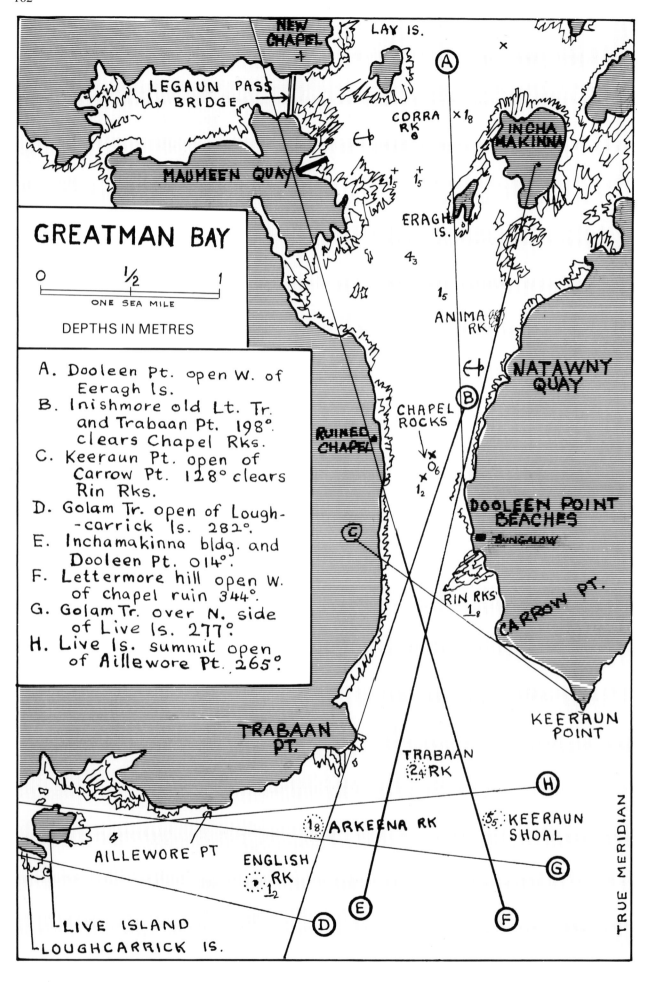

GREATMAN BAY

0   ½   1

ONE SEA MILE

DEPTHS IN METRES

A. Dooleen Pt. open W. of
    Eeragh Is.
B. Inishmore old Lt. Tr.
    and Trabaan Pt. 198°
    clears Chapel Rks.
C. Keeraun Pt. open of
    Carrow Pt. 128° clears
    Rin Rks.
D. Golam Tr. open of Lough-
    -carrick Is. 282°
E. Inchamakinna bldg. and
    Dooleen Pt. 014°
F. Lettermore hill open W.
    of chapel ruin 344°
G. Golam Tr. over N. side
    of Live Is. 277°
H. Live Is. summit open
    of Aillewore Pt. 265°

NEW CHAPEL

LEGAUN PASS BRIDGE

MAUMEEN QUAY

LAY IS.

CORRA RK

INCHA MAKINNA

ERAGH IS.

ANIMA RK

NATAWNY QUAY

CHAPEL ROCKS

RUINED CHAPEL

DOOLEEN POINT BEACHES

BUNGALOW

RIN RKS

CARROW PT.

KEERAUN POINT

TRABAAN PT.

TRABAAN RK

ARKEENA RK

AILLEWORE PT

ENGLISH RK

KEERAUN SHOAL

LIVE ISLAND

LOUGHCARRICK IS.

TRUE MERIDIAN

Anchorages

There is a quay at **Natawny** on the E side of the bay which encloses a small boat harbour. It is used by turf hookers and is not suitable for yachts. There is a broken-off concrete beacon off, and just to the N of, the entrance to this quay which is dangerous as it covers before HW. It should be left to starboard entering the boat harbour, not to port as would appear correct. There is indifferent anchorage off the quay with a 2 mile walk uphill to Carraroe.

The best anchorage, which is sheltered in all winds but is approached between unmarked rocks, is off **Maumeen Quay** on Gorumna Island. The beacon shown on the fathom chart E of the quay has gone. The reef on which it stood extends S and E ending in a big, square rock which dries about 1·8 m. If this rock is showing give it a good berth and steer for the W side of Inishlay. When the quay is well abeam alter course towards it and anchor in 2 to 3 m, mud. At half-tide and over, when the square rock is covered, approach close to Eragh Island as there is then no danger from the sunken rocks S of Eragh Spit and the two 1·5 m patches NW of Eragh Island. Corra Rock which dries 2 m is

a square pinnacle, bare of weed and with an outlier to the N of it. It is easily avoided approaching the anchorage either by keeping Lettermore Hill bearing 318° or the prominent church 313°. Land at the quay, 200 m from the anchorage. Carrickalegaun Pass bridge does not open and there is no navigation through this pass.

Maumeen Quay

is occasionally used by hookers. If going alongside leave a small beacon NE of the quay to port as it marks the end of a ridge of rocks which projects from the quay and covers at half-tide. The berthage is on the N side of the quay and the recommended berth, which dries 0·2 m, is between the end of the quay and the steps. The bottom is foul from the steps to the 16th stone on the edge of the quay beyond the knuckle.

Facilities

A few groceries in the village, a new and modern RC Church, bus to Galway. Phone. Petrol 1 mile beyond the pier beside a pub W of the church.

Bealadangan *(see plan)*

at the head of the bay has a suitable anchorage close to the bridge and is well worth visiting as it makes an attractive sail up into the heart of Connemara. This passage can be made at or after half-flood. To avoid Corra Rock keep Dooleen

Point 179° well open W of Eragh Island or Natawny pier closed behind the S point of the island 166°. Between Inishlay and Inchmakinna keep well over towards the latter. Thence steer to pass E of the small beacon off Nunra Point on Lettermore Island and continue N towards the beacons at the head of

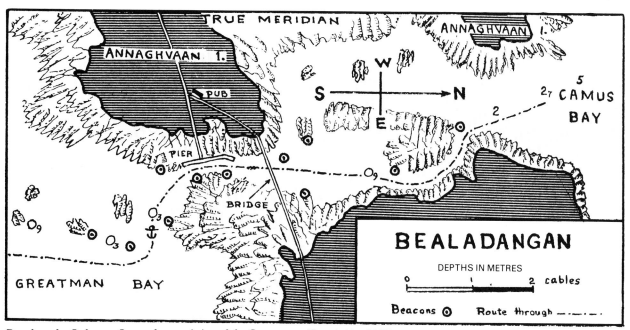

Based on the Ordnance Survey by permission of the Government (Permit No. 2191)

the bay. Leaving the first and second beacons to port, anchor between the latter and the third with the next beacon (close S of the quay) in line 289° with a low building with six small windows, depth 2 m.

The quay S of the bridge has a rough face and the bottom is foul, so it is unsuitable for drying out, but after half-tide it may be used for berthing. Facilities. Curragh Bar serves snacks and has a phone. Small supermarket at E side of bridge.

Bealadangan Pass
The bridge no longer opens so the pass to Camus Bay and Kilkieran Bay can only be used by boats without masts. It is best to make the passage near HW (+0010 Galway) as the flow reaches 4 to 5 kn at half-tide, the flood running N. The depth at half-tide is 1·8 m; the clearance under the bridge should be 2·4 m at HWS, 4 m at HWN and 4·9 m at half-tide. The beacons are large and the plan shows the way through them. The passage between the rocks is very narrow in places. Keep close to the mainland when abreast the rock with the two N beacons.

KIGGAUL BAY (Chart 2096) *(see plan)*
This bay is situated between Gorumna and Lettermullan Islands. It is easily identified from seaward by Illaunnanownim (Live Island) to the E and Golam Head 2 miles to the W. There is no difficulty in reaching the outer anchorage by day or by night.

Light
A light is shown from a rectangular white beacon in the centre of the bay. Fl WR 3 s, 5 m, 5-3 M. The red sector from 359° to 059° shows over the reefs to the W of the bay and the white sector from 329° to 359° leads in, but just touches Leacarrick on the W side. This light not sighted by a recent visitor. Be careful.

Kiggaul Bay.

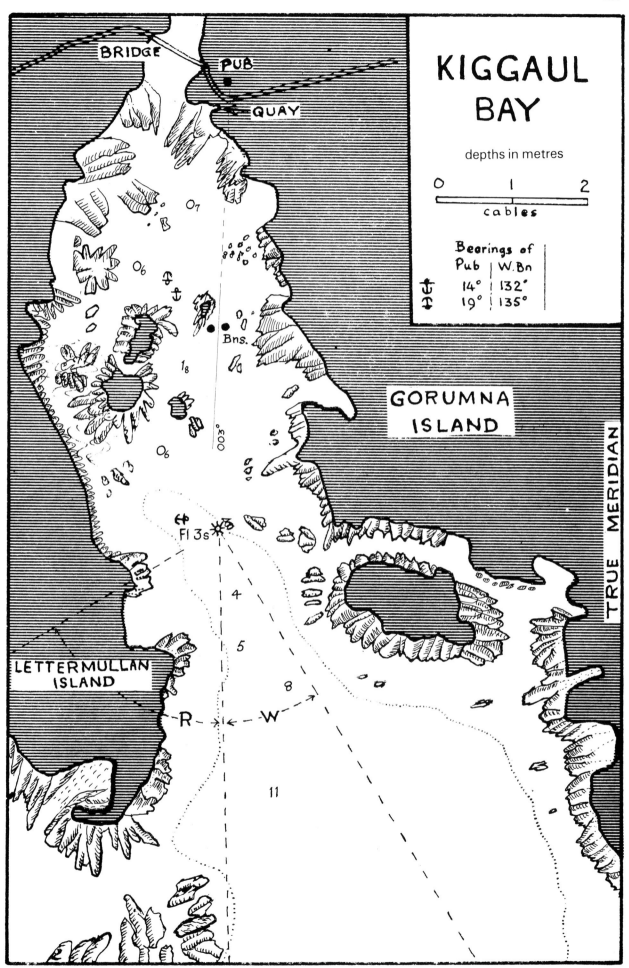

Anchorages

1. Close W or NW of the light in 3 to 4 m, mud with weed. There is not much room to spare. The anchorage is exposed to S and SE and would be untenable in fresh winds from this sector. Good shelter from W and N. Landing at a rough pier on the W side which is damaged and unsuitable for berthing a yacht. Nearest shop at Lettermullan village.

2. Two hours each side of HW with 2·4 m in the approach, a yacht could reach an inner anchorage with excellent shelter but very restricted space to lie afloat. Leave the light 25 m to starboard and immediately after passing it identify a prominent white building with two chimneys and an extension on its W side; it is a pub. Line up the centre of the main building midway between the two stone beacons, bearing 003°. Stick to this line, pass through the gap between the beacons and keep turning to port round the large, 1·2 m high rock N of the W beacon until heading SW towards a grass-topped islet. Anchor in 3 m, mud, with the W beacon bearing 132° and the pub 014°, which is very close to the rocks; or in 2 m a little NW of this, W beacon bearing 135° and pub 019°. Land at the small, rough pier below the pub. Facilities none, except the pub which has no phone. Shops at Lettermullan village, 1 mile.

GREATMAN'S BAY TO
KILKIERAN BAY (chart 2096)

Having observed the clearing marks for Arkeena Rock and English Rock (SW of Greatman's entrance) a reasonable berth should be given to Loughcarrick Island which is foul to the S for 1½ cables. The next danger is Dawsy's Rock which dries 2·4 m and lies about 5 cables S of Lettermullan Island. It is usually marked by a breaker when covered. Carricknamackan Rock open S of Eagle Island 290° leads S of it, and also of Griffin Spit. Eagle Island open of Golam Head 290° leads **over** it and also **over** Ullan Rock. This latter transit is of value when turning to windward. Griffin Spit with 3 m over it only breaks in a heavy swell.

If turning to windward give a good berth to the whole Lettermullan shore in particular at HW when the Dawsy's and Ullan Rocks may be covered and not showing. Redflag Island well open of Golam Head 305° leads just S of Ullan Rock. The whole area from Dawsy's Rock to Golam Head is usually a splendid taking place for mackerel from July onwards. There is more tide round Golam Head than elsewhere in N sound and often quite a tidal lop. No accurate information on directions and rates is available.

Eagle Rock, 8 m high, is nearly 1 mile WNW of Golam Head and the main entrance to Kilkieran Bay is through the channel between them. Eagle Rock is the largest of a group of rocks of which Seal Rock, which always shows, and Fairservice Rock with 0·9 m of water on it are those most S. Note Seal Breaker, awash at LW and which is 2 cables WNW of Seal Rock. Fairservice Rock is frequently not marked by a breaker even when Seal Breaker is showing. It is best avoided by keeping close to Golam Head which is steep-to.

There is a clear channel between the Carricknamackan group of rocks and the Eagle Island group. To the E, Fish Rock always shows and to the W Carricknamackan Little (Boat Rock), which is a very square shaped rock, dries 4·6 m and only covers at big tides.

KILKIERAN BAY (chart 2096)

Kilkieran Bay lies N of Golam Head and extends inland for 14 miles. It can be entered in any conditions and gives excellent shelter. It is easily identified from seaward by Golam Tower at the entrance which dominates all this stretch of coast. The tide runs at a maximum rate of 2 kn at the narrows by Kilkieran Point and at 1½ kn near the entrance to the bay and off Ardmore Point. The ingoing stream commences -0520 Galway and the outgoing at +0105 Galway.

GOLAM HARBOUR

Immediately N. of Golam Head, which is marked by a conspicuous Tower, is the entrance to Golam Harbour (chart 2096) which is obstructed by Binnock Rock. This Rock dries at about ½ ebb, it also has a further dangerous rock close S of it. The harbour can be entered with a fair wind or under power, the best water being about ⅔ S of the gap between Freaghillaunmore and Golam Island. Note that there are rocks with less than 2 m LAT in this fairway and that a close watch should be kept for lobster pots. As soon as the E side of Golam Island opens up turn sharp to port and keep ¾ cable off the HW shore of Freaghillaunmore till 2 cables from Crappagh when it is safe to turn E. Anchor anywhere inside. If going right up to the head of the harbour where shelter is best take care to avoid the sunken rock SW of the 2·4 m sounding. It is usually marked by long streamers of weed. The shelter is good under all conditions. There is no pier, but land near HW in the creek inside Crappagh Island and walk up to Lettermullan PO and shop just above. A few groceries and sometimes lobsters, telephone and bus to Galway. Fish farming takes place in this area.

There is another, unnamed, harbour E of Inisherk which affords complete shelter. The bay is, however, choked with rocks and local knowledge is necessary to find a safe berth. Bollegouh Creek has a number of drying rocks and should not be attempted without a pilot. The entrance to the S of Inisherk is clearer but also not to be attempted without a pilot or reconnaissance by dinghy.

Dangers

Dinish Shoals, with a least depth of 1·5 m lie W of Dinish Island and front the entrance from Golam Head. For a yacht they are of concern near low water or in a heavy swell. Lettercallow Hill and Dinish Point in one, 047°, leads between the two shoals. Inishmaan in line with Kilkieran Point, 033°, leads W of the shoals. The S extremity of Illauneeragh in line with Lettermore Hill, 066°, leads NW of the shoals. There are some ruined cottages and sand beaches at the S end of Illauneeragh.

Bruiser Rock

whose existence is doubtful, has less than 2 m on it and lies 1 cable W of Dinish Island. A yacht turning to windward might stand close to it and Lettercallow Hill and Dinish Point in line 047°, as above, clears it. E of Birmore Island there are rocks drying 1·8 m and 0·9 m so give the island a berth of at least 4 cables. Off Ardmore Point where there are sand beaches, there are another two rocks, the one furthest NE of the point dries 1·8 m and a yacht should keep 4 cables offshore.

Fork Rocks

to the N of Illauneeragh are extremely dangerous as the SW rocks cover first. The W summit of Green Island, W of Illauneeragh, in line with Lettermullan Islet Chapel, 168°, clears the rocks. Lettermullan Chapel is a grey, slated building. Birmore Island well open to the W of Illaunmaan, 230°, just clears Fork Rocks but leads **over** the end of Lettercallow (Callow) Spit with least water 1·2 m. Illaunmaan is a small island with grass and large boulders which never covers.

Anchorages

There are many anchorages in the bay to suit most weather conditions which can be picked from the chart. Beware of fish farms. The following are some of the more useful ones.

1. **E of Illauneeragh.** Approach S of the 0·6 m sounding on Eeragh Spit and keep well clear of the small spit SE of the island. Anchor in 2 m, shells, N of this spit with, to the N, the narrow cut in the island just closed in. It is exposed to winds from SE to SW. This lovely fine weather anchorage is off attractive sandy beaches and the island is now uninhabited. Despite the 2·1 m sounding on the chart it is impossible to get into or out of this anchorage at LW springs with 1·8 m draught. No stores.

2. **Inside Dinish Point** in 2 to 3 m sand off the beach between Dinish and Furnace Islands. Exposed from NE to NW. No stores. A lovely anchorage in fine weather with incredible views up the bay with the Connemara Mountains as a back-drop.

2A. **Knock Bay.** South of Innishbawa is 6 m halfway between the island and a reef to SE.

3. **Up Coonawilleen Bay.** There is a small bay just NW of Lettermullan Hill which gives excellent shelter, however there are local boats and fish farming gear in the bay. Unfortunately the channel in, with 2·4 m is very narrow and flanked by pinnacle rocks with 1 m LAT. It is on the E side. **Directions.** Keep to the Furnace side when entering and then anchor in 3 to 4 m, mud, off a prominent white cottage at the head of the bay. Landing on rock. Lettermullan PO and shop about ¹/₂ mile. **Caution.** A stranger would be well advised not to enter or leave below half-tide.

4. **Top of Coonawilleen Bay.** Anchor at the very head of the bay in 4 to 5 m with the high bluff of Knockfin to the SE. Landing over rocks, no stores, or row to Kiggaul bridge. Alternatively anchor N of the bridge in about 5 m. **Caution.** There are a number of concrete floating tanks for fish farming moored in the bay, but they present no obstacle in heading NW or SE or down the bay.

5. **Ardmore Bay.** Approach with a wide sweep to avoid the inner and outer Hard Rocks. Anchor off the pier at the head of the bay. Land at the pier, where there is a clean sand bottom, it is used by a number of lobster boats and dries out. Pub and small shop in about 1¹/₂ mile. Lobsters usually stored here. A delightful fine weather anchorage, but in S winds there is a roll. Fish farming reported.

6. **Kilkieran Cove.** Anchor 90 m off the pier with its head bearing 310° where the depth should be 2·4 m, mud, holding suspect. Good shelter except from SE to NE. A rather uneasy berth if there is much wind as the yacht will be tide-rode. Land at the pier. The pier is well built of cut stone and dries at LWOS but there is about 2 m at the head at LWN. Clean bottom and good shelter inside. Boats remain alongside all winter. It is occasionally visited by cargo vessels to remove the products of the alginate works. These, and the mud, make a smell in W winds.

Facilities

Pub sells petrol. Shop sells good meat. RC Church, telephone, bus to Galway.

NORTH KILKIERAN BAY

The bay to the N of Kilkieran Cove, while ideal for dinghy sailing, has so many isolated rocks that it is difficult to give directions to anyone unfamiliar with it.

CAMUS BAY

This is reached from Kilkieran by means of Gurraig Sound. The deep water channel through this sound is very narrow with patches of 1 m and 1·2 m very close to it. It is advisable to await sufficient rise of tide before passing through it. Once Bird Rock is reached there is no difficulty as there are three concrete beacons, one on Bird Rock and another N of Illaungurraig, which should be left to starboard going E and one on Yellow Rock to be left to port.

After passing Yellow Rock a house among trees will be seen on the N side of the bay. There is a good shop by this house. Anchor a cable SSE of the small quay in 2·1 m.

Beyond Leighon Island the entrance to Bealadangan Pass opens up, leading to Greatman's Bay, but available only to boats without masts, (see page 160). Above this the bay is straightforward though both shores are foul. There is anchorage off Rosmuck quay, 4 m, mud, at the entrance to the narrow channel W of Clynagh Island. RC Church at the top of the hill, shop and PO at Turloughbeg 1¼ miles away. Do not attempt to go beyond this as the tides begin to run very strong, forming rapids in places. Despite a number of beacons local knowledge is essential.

INNER PASSAGE (charts 2096, 2709).

Small craft making from Galway Bay to Roundstone can save both time and rough water by taking the inner passage from Golam Head to Croaghnakeela (Deer Island). It is wide enough to beat through and presents no difficulty in reasonable visibility. In bad visibility with a leading wind, or under power, rock hopping by compass course is quite feasible. The following description of the islands is added to help in the navigation of this passage. Further checking is requested from members.

(a) Birmore Island is long, low and green with greyish white shingle patches on south west face.

(b) Muskerry Island has gable walls showing on it, and a very obvious patch of sand on the south side.

(c) Mason Island has lots of house gables on it.

(d) S. Macdara's looks like a squashed edition of Deer Island, much lower and flatter with a fair bit of green grass showing, and a boulder looking rather like a house on top. The chapel which has a very sharply "V" shaped roof, is at the south end.

(e) Carricknamackan Little at about two third flood looks like an upturned boat from the north.

(f) Eagle Rock beside Red Flag Island has a top mark like a pork pie with a spike in the middle.

(g) Duck Island is a low flat rock with little feature.

(h) Erris Beg mountain is very distinctive and is well shown in the sketch at the bottom left hand corner of old chart 2096.

(i) Erris Beg, Doon Hill, Cashel (again shown on chart 2096) and Golam Tower are the main marks in this area.

The tidal stream

in the passage is not strong and can be ignored. The general stream in this vicinity runs NW and SE, and turns in and out of the various bays and sounds. Off the Skerd Rocks the NW stream begins -0320 Galway and the SE stream +0305 Galway.

Directions

Having rounded Golam Head and cleared NW of Redflag Island bring Golam Head astern, 125°, well N of Redflag Island and continue on this course which leads right through. An alternative transit is to bring the summit of Croaghnakeela (Deer) Island over the S point of St Macdara's Island, 308°. If turning to windward Feraun North Rock, dries 4·9 m, always shows except at highest springs when it would probably be marked by a breaker. Kenny Rock, dries 1·8 m, is a pinnacle W of the Ferauns and is usually marked by a breaker as is Carrickaview, dries 1·8 m, on the N side of the channel.

The shallowest parts of the Tonyeal Rocks usually break but these are very dangerous rocks which cover a wide area and are liable to break anywhere in a high swell. The channel between them and St Macdara's Island is only ½ mile wide. The S point of Inishmuskerry and Carrickaview Breaker in one, 114°, leads through. A white sector of Croaghnakeela light between the bearings of 311° and 325° also leads through.

Inishmuskerry Shoal

which has 0·9 m on it and rarely breaks in good weather must be avoided near LW. Namackan Rock open E of South Feraun, 210°, leads eastwards of Inishmuskerry Rock and Namackan Rock open W of West Feraun, 185°, leads W of it as also does Finish Island sandhill open W of Inishmuskerry, 018°. In between these bearings keep over to the North Feraun side of the channel. Carricknamackan Little (Boat Rock), dries 4·6 m, is the most E of the Namackan group and is a big, square rock, rarely covering.

As mentioned on page 166 there is a clear passage into the inner channel between the Namackan Rocks and the Eagle Rock group. Golam Tower open S of Eagle Rock 094° clears the breakers to the S of the Namackan Rocks. It is also possible to come in W of the Namackan Rocks. Carrickadoolagh, 2·1 m high, always shows and is steep-to on its W side. Watch out for Kenny Rock if it is not showing.

Skerdmore, 18 m high and Doonguddle, 12 m high the largest of the Skerd Rocks stand out unmistakably and there is no difficulty in passing S of them. Skerdmore and Doonguddle in line, 286°, clear all the shoals except for Wild Shoals with 16·2 m on them. There is a small bay on the S side between Skerdmore and Skerdbeg in which it is possible to land from a dinghy at any state of tide in very settled weather. It is a haunt of the Great Atlantic seal.

MWEENISH BAY

This bay opens to the N of the inner channel and can be entered either N or W of Inishmuskerry Island but there are so many isolated rocks that it is not recommended for strangers. It is however possible in fine weather and daylight to anchor off the NE side of Inishmuskerry Island and land on the beach of this very delightful island.

Straddle Pass

which leads E of Mason Island is not recommended to strangers.

MACDARA SOUND

This sound and also the passage between Whercom and Avery Islands are used regularly by the local boats and are quite possible in fine weather and smooth sea for those who like pilotage by eye. The rocks show vividly under the keel as the boat passes over the shallower patches. There is a steep sea on the ebb in Macdara Sound in fresh S winds or with any swell running outside.

ST MACDARA'S ISLAND

is 27 m high. Bring up in the little bay off the beach in the sound. Do not anchor too close in as there are isolated boulders near the beach. Keep to the island side during the approach to avoid Carrichaher which dries. This is a lovely island with wonderful views of the Connemara Mountains and the coast. The ruined church dates from the 6th century and is one of the oldest in the country. It has recently been restored. It is conspicuous from the S.

ARD BAY

affords shelter in all except NW winds and its continuation, Little Ard Bay, affords shelter in all winds.

Dangers

Lebros Rocks lie 5 cables SW of Mace Head with lattice tower and dry 0·6 m. They are frequently marked by extensive breakers but sometimes break intermittently and without warning. Inishnee light, a small, white column, in line with the SW point of Freaghillaun, 003°, leads E of the rocks. When the NE corner of St Macdara's Island bears 198° approximately it is safe to stand across towards the island. At this point the ruined church should be appearing clear of the shoulder of the island. Doonguddle, the southernmost of the Skerd Rocks, just touching Mac Point, 215°, leads E of the rocks. Golam Tower in line with the SW point of Mason Island leads S of them, 131°. The SW point of

Inishtreh (in the entrance to Traghboy Bay) just opening W of Freaghillaun, 018°, leads W of Lebros Rocks. Carrickhaher and Rourkes Slate lie on the S side of the bay and can be avoided by keeping over to the mainland shore which can be approached as close as 1 cable.

Anchorages

Anchor off the N shore of Mason Island or in mid-channel in the lower part of Little Ard Bay, sand bottom. In the latter anchorage a yacht will usually be tide-rode. If proceeding further up Little Ard Bay to get better shelter, the deep water is on the W side and there are half-tide rocks on the E side and in the centre as shown on old chart 2096 and larger on 2096 metric. Ard Castle ruins no longer exist but E of where they are marked on the old chart there is a small fish factory beside a small stone pier. The best anchorage is just off this and the pier is convenient for landing. No provisions. Take particular care not to anchor too close inshore here as near the shore the bottom shelves steeply. A shift of wind could swing a yacht over or onto the shelf thus formed so careful sounding is advised. In N winds there is good anchorage off the quay in the un-named bay NE of Rourke's Slate and lobsters can sometimes be obtained there. Mason Island is now uninhabited and has lovely beaches on the NE corner. Near its NW end there is a small harbour which is only suitable for boats. The island is well worth a visit.

ROUNDSTONE AND BERTRAGHBOY (BIRTERBUY OR CASHEL) BAYS

Chart 2709 m *(see plan of approaches)*

These bays offer safe shelter and can be approached and entered in any conditions except really bad visibility or storm. They are easily identified from seaward by Cashel Hill (307 m) and Errisbeg Mt (296 m) and Croaghnakeela (Deer) Island and the Skerd and Mile Rocks offshore. They should not be approached at night because of the danger from salmon drift nets which are numerous in the approaches.

Lights

Croaghnakeela. A light is shown from a white beacon on the SE side of the island. Fl (3) 7 s, 7 m, 5 M. It shows 218° to 286° covering Big Sound; from 311° to 325° between St Macdara's Island and the Tonyeal Rocks as already described; and from 034° to 045° between Mile and Skerd Rocks. Note that this sector is wider than shown on some old charts.

Inishnee. A light is shown from a white iron pillar on the W side of Inishnee. Fl (2) WRG 10 s, 9 m, 5-3 M. A green sector from 314° to 017° covers Small Breakers, Smith Rock, Freaghillaun, St

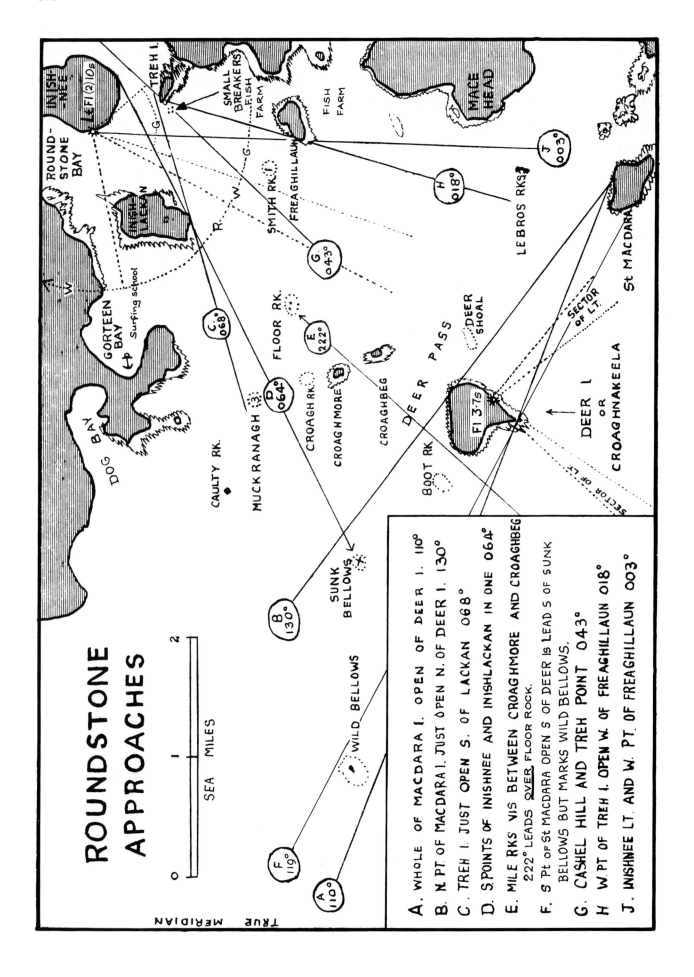

ROUNDSTONE
APPROACHES

SEA MILES

TRUE MERIDIAN

A. WHOLE OF MACDARA I. OPEN OF DEER I. 110°

B. N. PT. OF MACDARA I. JUST OPEN N. OF DEER I. 130°

C. TREH I. JUST OPEN S. OF LACKAN 068°

D. S. POINTS OF INISHNEE AND INISHLACKAN IN ONE 064°

E. MILE RKS VIS BETWEEN CROAGHMORE AND CROAGHBEG 222° LEADS OVER FLOOR ROCK.

F. S PT OF St MACDARA OPEN S OF DEER IS LEAD S OF SUNK BELLOWS BUT MARKS WILD BELLOWS.

G. CASHEL HILL AND TREH POINT 043°

H W. PT. OF TREH I. OPEN W. OF FREAGHILLAUN 018°

J. INISHNEE LT. AND W. PT. OF FREAGHILLAUN 003°

Macdara's Island and Lebros Rocks and Tonyeal Rocks. A white sector from 017° to 030° leads in through Big Sound; this sector is shown wider on some charts. A red sector from 030° to 080° covers all the islands and rocks to the W of Big Sound but is obscured by Inishlackan. Finally a white sector from 080° to 194° shows over Roundstone Bay.

Dangers

The approach from the S is obstructed by the Skerd and Mile Rocks, together forming a 4 mile wide belt of confused breakers with one deep-water passage leading through them. It is essential to identify Skerdmore (18·3 m) and from this pick up Doonmane (4 m) and Doolick (1 m) to the N and Mile Rock (5·2 m) 2½ miles to the NW. The limiting dangers in the 1½ mile wide channel between the Skerd and Mile Rocks will then be clear. Mweelmore with 0·3 m over it, to the NE of Mile Rocks must always be avoided and is usually marked by a breaker.

Pass E of Croahhnakeela into Big Sound and if turning to windward Doolick and Skerdmore in line, 222°, clears the Tonyeal Rocks. Clearing marks for Lebros Rocks have already been given (p169). Deer Shoal can be ignored in normal summer weather. Croaghnakeela, locally known as Deer Island, and Inishcroaghmore and Inishcroaghbeg, locally known as the Hard Islands, are steep-to on their E sides where landing can be made in fine weather.

Floor Rock

with a depth of 1·2 m, lies 6 cables NE of Inishcroaghmore. It is a very dangerous rock, sometimes marked by breakers or "blind" breakers and frequently breaking intermittently as the tide rises and falls. Mile Rocks in view between Croaghmore and Croaghbeg, 222°, **marks** the rock. The SW points of Inishnee and Inishlackan in one, 064°, lead W of the rock. Cashel Hill and Treh Point on Inishtreh in line 043°, lead E of Floor Rock and also W of Smith Rock. Treh Point is a boulder beach.

Smith Rock

with 3 m on it lies off Freaghillaun; it rarely breaks in normal summer weather. The Cashel Hill in line with Treh Point leads W of it and in line with E of Inishtreh leads E of it.

Small Breakers

which lie SW of Inishtreh are dangerous. St Macdara Island open W of Freaghillaun, 184°, leads W of them, while Croghnut, (28 m) a conspicuous, sharp pointed islet, well open N of Treh Point, 070°, leads NW of them. Note that the SE and SW points of Inishlacken are foul for 2 cables offshore.

Approach from the West

Having rounded Slyne Head and identified Split Rock (Carrickscoltia) course can be set to pass between Caulty Rock and Murvey Rock, both of which show.

Wild Bellows

which dries 3 m and is 2 miles SSW of Murvey Rock is always marked by a breaker.

Sunk Bellows

with 1·8 m of water is a most dangerous rock which often breaks intermittently. Being a considerable distance offshore the clearing marks for it are hard to identify. The N part of St Macdara's Island just open N of Croaghnakeela, 130°, leads N of the rock while the S points of both these islands just open 119°, lead S of the rock and **mark** Wild Bellows. The whole of St Macdara's well open S of Croaghnakeela, 110°, leads S of Sunk Bellows and Wild Bellows and all the dangers to Slyne Head except Toole Rocks which have 8·5 m over them. This is a most useful mark. Inishtreh just open S of Inishlacken, 075°, leads N of the rock and **marks** Wild Bellows. This line is not easy to identify; Inishtreh is low with a boulder beach. There is a fish farm 5 cables SSW of Inishtreh is marked by yellow buoys Fl (2) 10s, not to be confused with Inishnee.

The Boot with 8·8 m off Croaghnakeela and Toole Rocks further SW will rarely break in normal summer conditions. The same applies to Croagh Rock, N of Croaghmore. Deer Pass is free of danger but the sound between Croaghmore and Croaghbeg is very narrow and often lobster pots are set in it. It can break right across in bad weather. Muckranagh, with 6·4 m over it can break unexpectedly with an ebb tide.

A confused sea can be met N of Croaghmore in fresh W winds especially on the ebb. In storm force SW winds with a heavy sea the approach NW and N Croaghnakeela can be dangerous and this channel has been known to break right across in great winter gales.

In these conditions, standing on the road above Dog's Bay, and watching these huge, long seas rolling in from the SW is an awe-inspiring sight which will never be forgotten.

BIRTERBUY or TRAGHBOY BAY
locally known as CASHEL BAY *(see plan)*

This offers shelter against all winds and sea depending upon the choice of anchorage. It has lovely views of the Connemara Mountains. The tide runs about 2 kn in the narrows at the entrance, possibly a little more at springs, the ingoing stream starting at -0520 Galway and the outgoing at +0105 Galway. The lower part of the bay is free of shoals except for Oghly Shoal which can be ignored except

172

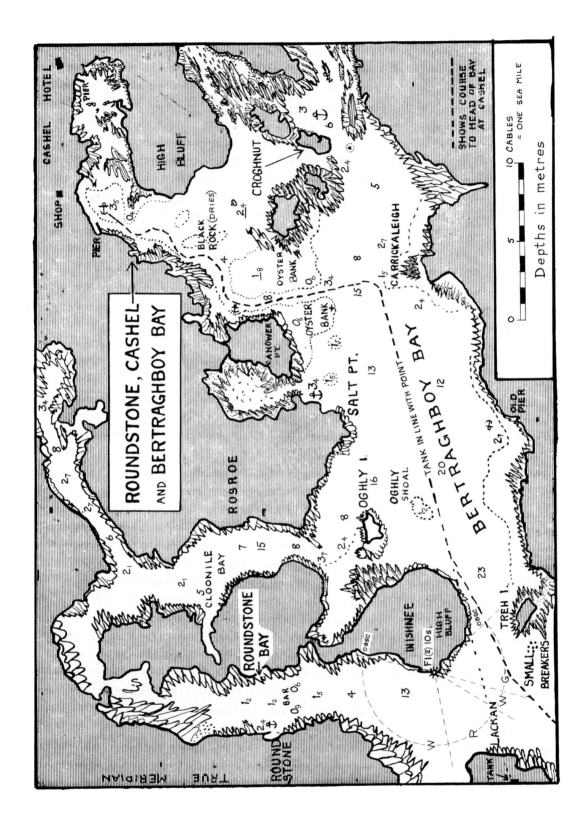

near LW. Keep the water tank on Inishlackan (which replaces Bodkin House on the old chart 2096) open S of Tawnrawer Point 254° to clear it to the S. There is now a Marine Farm just S of Salt Point. A good look out is required.

Anchorages

1. In S winds off a bold bluff half-way between the entrance and Carrickaleagh (Leagh Rock). No stores; land at the ruined pier.

2. **Inside Croghnut.** Beware of the half-tide rock on the starboard side of the entrance. No stores and rather poor landing over weed covered rocks, but good shelter.

3. **North of Salt Point.** Good shelter in W winds. No stores. Note that there are two 1·5 m patches in the approach. Anchor between the W patch and the shore, NE of Salt Point.

4. **NE of Canower.** After passing through the entrance make for Croghnut until Carrickaleagh is brought abeam when steer for the channel between the E and W oyster banks, course 350° with Carrickaleagh astern. If on the oyster banks the bottom can be seen very clearly. There is a small isolated rock, which never uncovers, near the tail of this bank. Oyster rock on the E bank is deeply covered with shell and the whole bank can be considered to be shell except for a few old stone pipes near the shallowest part, placed for breeding oysters. There are a couple of ruined cottages on the E of Canower. Keep close in to them and bring up just beyond them. No stores, but good shelter and holding. There is no buoy on the tail of the bank as shown on the old chart 2096.

5. Off the quay at the head of the bay. Do not attempt to come up to this anchorage before half-flood. Bring the roofless cottages at Canower abeam and then alter course for a prominent group of rocks above the "C" of CASHEL BAY on chart 2709. Leave these rocks well to port and make a wide sweep round them and identify a narrow iron pipe on Black Rock, the half-tide rock N of the "L" in CASHEL BAY. This will not be picked up till pretty close. Leave it well to starboard as there is a small, drying outlier which lies 10 m W of Black Rock. As soon as Black Rock is passed swing out to starboard to avoid a sunken rock on the W side, and then steer for the clump of trees on the W shore with the pier showing just beyond them. Pass very close to the shore here to avoid the 0·4 m sounding on the chart, S of the quay. Bring up in 3·5 m, mud, 150 m off the quay. Land at the quay. The bottom alongside is clean, but check before going alongside or drying out, especially the rocks in the entrance. The quay is pretty rough. A 10 m yacht has spent two winters alongside this quay.

Facilities

Water from a well just above the quay, shop ¼ mile up the road. Two good hotels, Cashel House and the Zetland, 1 mile. At HW it is possible to take a dinghy through a maze of rocks to the head of the bay and to land at a small quay below the Zetland.

6. In **Cloonile Bay.** There is a considerable tide here especially with a spring ebb and the Ballynahinch River in flood. Note that Rossroe Reef dries and extends almost right across. The holding is reputed to be bad near the "C" of CLOONILE.

East end of Bertraghboy Bay with High Bluff in the centre.

Salt Point to Canower Point.

Roundstone Bay and Quay from E.

ROUNDSTONE BAY AND QUAY

The entrance to this bay is between Inishlackan and Inishnee. Give Inishnee Point and lighthouse a berth of 1 cable. The W side of the entrance is fringed with half-tide rocks N of Inishlackan. There is a bar with least water 0·9 m on it, the best water being on the W side. A course of 347°, which keeps Inishnee Point Lighthouse bearing 167°, provides the best approach over the bar and avoids a sunk rock on the bar approximately 1 cable off the Inishnee shore. Bearings for anchorage, Harbour Lt 210° and Seal Rock Hotel 295°. It is possible to line up a white cottage with two white gables with a "V" notch in the trees in order to cross safely. In poor visibility it is rather difficult to pick up this transit. Anchor off the harbour a little to the S of the N quay as there is reputed to be foul ground off the N quay. Inside the harbour there is clear bottom alongside the N quay with two sets of steps and it is well built. Do not tie up against the E-W portion of the quay as the bottom is foul. There would be about 1·2 m at the pierhead at LWN. There is a tap on the South pier which is convenient to go alongside towards HW. Also water from a tap near the road and all provisions except diesel oil in the village. A useful place to stock up or to change crew. A small yacht might be left here unattended. Two hotels, PO and bus to Galway. This is one of the few harbours along this coast which is possible to enter at night. It is also a good shelter and victualling port before rounding Slyne Head. Fish farming reported

Gorteen Bay

A really delightful fine weather anchorage in crystal clear water off a magnificent sandy beach (popular with holiday-makers) and sheltered from most summer winds. Bring up according to wind, but usually in the SW corner of the bay. The bay is subject to roll if there is a swell running outside. Now has surfing school as shown on chart.

Inishlackan Sound

It is possible to sail between Lackan and the mainland. Coming from Roundstone, keep well out in the middle of the main channel to avoid the half-tide rocks on the W side. Bring the white light pillar on Inishnee in line 083° with the gap between the right-hand pair of three small humps on the skyline near the summit of the island. This line leads clear through the sound. The line also passes between two prominent rock outcrops as shown in the sketch. Coming from Gorteen Bay, keep well out from Inishlackan until the marks come in line so as to avoid Gun Rock and the breakers around it.

Coast

West of Roundstone the coast is fringed by a maze of rocks through which a number of channels lead into Ballyconneely Bay and which give it some protection. There is no safe anchorage in it which can be reached without local knowledge and the bay is not recommended. Local small boats take the ground inside the small islands in the N-E corner of the bay where the bottom is soft with 1 m at LWS. Murvey Rock, 6 m high, is easily identified W of the Gorteen Peninsula off which lies Caulty Rock which dries 4·3 m and always shows. Further W, Duke and Hen Rocks which are 1·1 m and 4·4 m high are next to be identified. Both are foul to the S for 2 cables. There is a passage 1¼ miles wide between Murvey Rock and Wild Bellows which has already been mentioned.

BUNOWEN BAY (Chart 2708 m)

Mullauncarrickscoltia (Split Rock) is 1·1 m high and is the key to the Bunowen Bay entrance and approach to Sylne Head from the E. The best entry to the bay is to the NE of Carrickscoltia. Cromwell Shoal is ½ mile N of Carrickscoltia and frequently breaks. When Bunowen House, a prominent, square and roofless building, bears due N and is over a small strand to the S of it, steer into the bay on this course. It should be possible to see right through the building by most of the windows on this course, which leads clear of both Carrickcummer and Fortune Rock which dries 0·6 m. Bring up N of the pier in 3 to 4 m, sand. Doon Hill is a steep, conical hill 61 m high and with a ruined tower on it. It cannot be mistaken. It is possible to lie alongside the N side of the outer pier, which dries, or alongside the outer, NE end, where a yacht might remain afloat in 1·8 m at LWN. There is usually a lot of long, green weed streamers off this pier which can foul up a yacht's propeller. The bay offers good shelter in winds from W through N to NE but would become untenable in a S gale. Shop at junction with main coast road about 2 miles, cafe 1 mile. Connemara Golf Club 2 miles.

Ballinaleama Bay to the W of Bunowen has long, sandy beaches but offers no shelter except in its E corner where there is a good quay which dries. It is NE of Horse Island. It might be useful in an emergency but the approach is intricate; it might be possible with chart 2708 early on the flood when all the rocks are showing. Smooth water and little swell would be essential and a pilot from Bunowen would be wiser.

SLYNE HEAD (Chart 2708 m)

A light is shown from the N tower of the two black stone ones on the NW corner of Illaunamid (Illaunimul) which is the outermost of a chain of rocks and islets extending SW from the mainland for over 2 miles. Light. Fl (2) 15 s, 35 m, 28 M. The island is 23 m high. With its strong tides, and long projection from the shore it is a formidable headland and should be given a berth of 2 miles or more in bad weather.

Joyce's Pass from the westward.

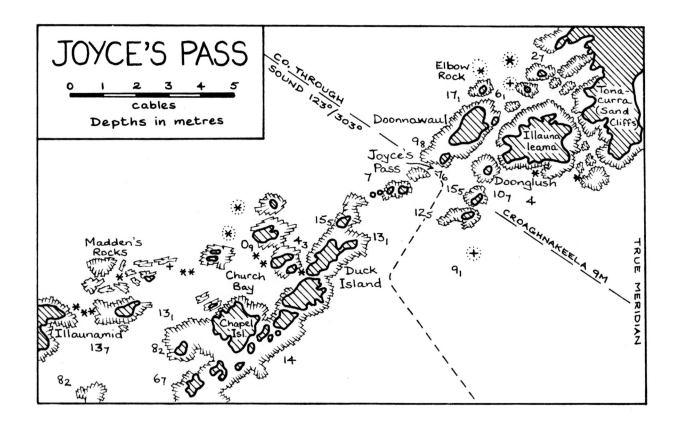

Tides

The N-going stream commences at -0320 Galway and the S-going at +0305 Galway. The rate is 3 to 4 kn at springs off the head and in the channels between the islets inside the head. 2 to 3 miles out, the streams become weak. The streams are considerably affected by the strength and direction of wind and sea. In any wind and sea these streams cause a dangerous race.

Direction – From the E

Having passed S of Carrickscoltia a course of 272° will lead to a position, with the lighthouse bearing 045°, 2 miles, from which position the head can be rounded with an offing of 2 miles. The sea will probably increase considerably as the point of the headland is approached. From 2 miles W of the lighthouse, a course of 011° will lead to High Island Sound between High Island and Friar Island. It will also lead W of Barret Shoals. A course of 005° with Inishark open W of High Island will lead W of High Island and one of 043° will lead to Carrickarone in the entrance to Clifden. This latter course will skirt the SE edge of Barret Shoals. There can be a very nasty sea on the Barret Shoals despite the least depth of 22 m.

From the North

Having rounded the headland, as above, and made the position with the lighthouse bearing 045°, 2 miles, pick up Croaghnakeela (Deer) Island which will be about 10 miles ESE and set course accordingly. If the visibility is poor set course 096° which will pass S of Carrickscoltia (Split Rock), 1·1 m high. This course will then lead S of Murvey Rock and Caulty Rock (dries 4·3 m) and so into the approaches to Roundstone.

Alternatively, set a course 130° which will lead S of Skerdmore (18 m high) which is steep-to on its S and W sides. Thence, it will lead just N of Eeragh Island (Rock Islet) light off Inishmore.

The Inner Channels

There are a number of channels inside the head formerly used by the sailing hookers when they carried most of the produce and provisions for Connemara. Now they are only used by the outboard-engined, wooden curraghs based on Bunowen and N of the headland. These boats fish lobsters and pollack among the islets, and are 5 or 6 m long.

JOYCE SOUND PASS

SW of Doomavaul is the only practical channel for a yacht. It is short and very narrow and in bad weather and wind against tide will frequently break right across. The tide sluices through, see above. Having once entered there is no room to turn round and go back. It should not be attempted except under really favourable conditions. The passage from the S is easiest in W and NW winds. Approach is made under the lee of Chapel and Duck Islands and conditions in the pass can be examined from to leeward and at close quarters before going through. Identification is also easy.

From the South

First identify the high ground of Keerhaunmore Hill, 36 m high, W of the beaches in Ballinaleama Bay and then Mweel Rock, dries 4 m, and Carrickmweelrough, 0·4 m high. Mweel breaker to the SW of Mweel Rock may not be showing if the sea is smooth. Illaunaleama which is 18 m high and Doomavaul, 15 m high, can then be recognised and from them the line of rocks terminating in Carrickclunamore with a breaker 1 cable S of it.

From Carrickscoltia shape course to pass close SW of Mweel Rock, then steer for Duck Island. When this is close aboard steer to pass NW of Carrickclunamore and Carrickclunabeg, avoiding the reefs extending W from the former. Note that there is a pronounced tidal set through Blind Sound. When the state of the sea can be seen through Blind Sound there is still plenty of room to turn back, or if necessary bear away between the two Carricks. As Carrickclunabeg comes abeam the pass will open looking extremely narrow. Turn hard to port and keep in the middle with plenty of way on. Even on a calm day the sea will be confused. As the stream fans out to the N there will be a few short, steep tidal seas so hold tight and use a safety harness even on a calm day.

Once through, Carrickarone West, 5 m high, will be seen bearing 338° with Clarke's Rock, dries 1 m, 1/4 mile NW of it and bearing 324°. Clarke's Rock may not show near HW with a smooth sea. Both of these rocks should be left to starboard.

From the North

Identification from the NW is not easy, especially in the hazy weather which may often be met with when the sea is smooth. Frequently a yacht will be running down on a lee shore, a long string of similar looking islets and fronted by breakers and half-tide rocks. **The conditions must be right.**

Doomavaul and Illaunaleama are 15 and 18 m high and considerably higher than the rocks immediately to the W by Blind Sound. However, Duck and Chapel Islands are nearly the same height and confusion can be caused. The only safe method is to approach on a course which will allow identification of Keerhaunmore Hill, 36 m high, and possibly the sand cliffs at Toonacurra, which will then allow Carrickarone to be picked up as the land comes closer. With a firm fix on Carrickarone there should be no difficulty in identifying Joyce Sound Pass. Knock Hill, 2½ miles to the N of Keerhaunmore Hill is isolated and distinctive. It is

38 m high. In good visibility as Carrickarone comes abeam Croaghnakeela (Deer) Island will be seen through the pass over Carrickclunabeg bearing 123° and this line leads clear through the sound.

The area is fascinating and tempting, but to repeat once more, it is only enjoyable and safe under ideal conditions. The headland itself, the tide race off it and the channels inside it must all be treated with the greatest respect.

In general the pass should not be attempted with the wind above force 4, though the state of the sea and the strength of the tide must be taken into account and may reduce the safe wind strength. It is advisable to transit at slack water and **never** at the full strength of a spring tide, especially against the sea or wind.

There must be little or no swell.

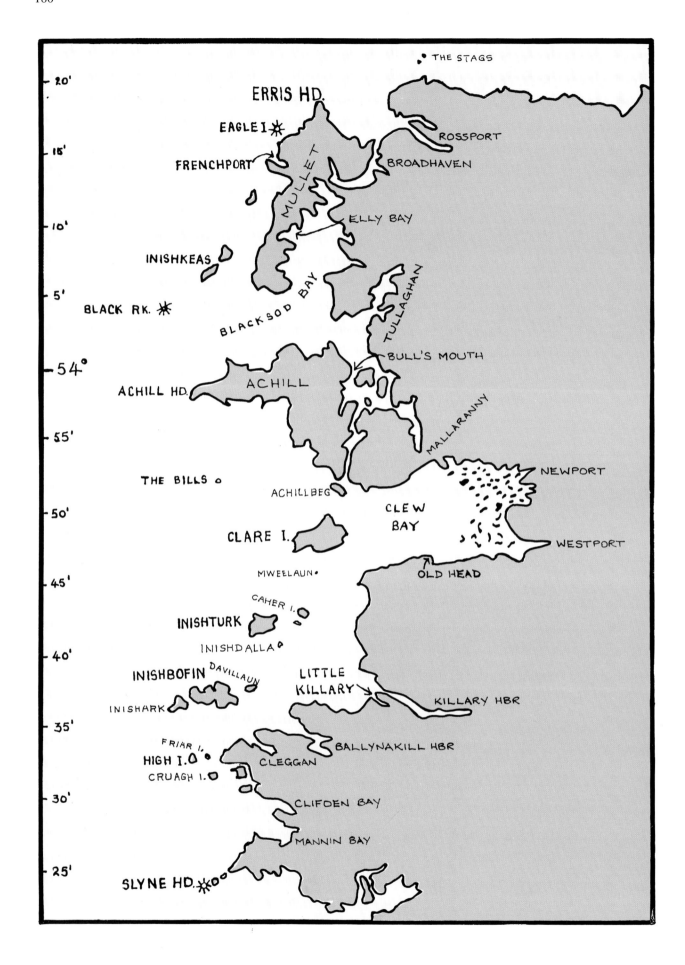

THE STAGS

ERRIS HD.

20'

EAGLE I.

15'

FRENCHPORT

MULLET

ROSSPORT

BROADHAVEN

10'

ELLY BAY

INISHKEAS

5'

BLACK RK.

BLACKSOD BAY

TULLAGHAN

54°

BULL'S MOUTH

ACHILL HD.

ACHILL

MALLARANNY

55'

THE BILLS

NEWPORT

ACHILLBEG

CLEW BAY

50'

CLARE I.

WESTPORT

MWEELAUN

OLD HEAD

45'

CAHER I.

INISHTURK

INISHDALLA

40'

INISHBOFIN

DAVILLAUN

LITTLE KILLARY

KILLARY HBR

INISHARK

35'

BALLYNAKILL HBR

FRIAR I.

HIGH I.

CLEGGAN

CRUAGH I.

30'

CLIFDEN BAY

MANNIN BAY

25'

SLYNE HD.

Chapter 7

SLYNE HEAD TO ERRIS HEAD

Charts *(for details see Appendix 1)*
From Slyne Head to Killary and Inishturk 3 large scale charts 2708, 2707 and 2706 are used. North of these two smaller scale charts 2667 and 2704 extend to Belmullet. Frenchport to Erris Head are on part of 2703. Chart 2057 is essential for going in to Westport and is good for anchoring as far in as to Collan More but it is possible to anchor there without the chart. This whole chapter is shown on 2420.

Tides *(for details see Appendix 2)*
HW occurs mostly about 15 mins. after Galway (5³/₄ hrs. before Dover), 45 mins. later at Bull's Mouth. Rise is from 3·6 m to 4·5 m, springs, 2·9 m to 3·4 m neaps.

Tidal streams
The streams offshore are weak, running S from 3 hours before to 3 hours after HW Dover and N for the other 6 hours. Near the coast they may attain 1¹/₂ kn. In the entrances of bays and e.g. N of Clare Island the flood starts running about 1 hour after HW Dover for 6 hours.

General
The coast from Slyne Head to Erris Head is deeply indented with many bays offering excellent shelter and magnificent scenery. Long stretches are fronted by islands and rocks which give some protection from the Atlantic swell to the channels and bays behind them. In good weather this is one of the finest day cruising areas imaginable but it is not well enough lit for sailing inshore by night.

The main features of the coast (with heights in metres) are as follows. The large offlying islands consist of Inishshark (96 m), Inishbofin (85 m), Inishturk (188 m), high and knobbly, and Clare Island (459 m), a beautiful island. On the mainland Diamond Mountain (441 m), and Tully Hill (353 m) dominate the coast by Ballynakill Bay.

The square massif of Mweelrea (815 m) rises N of Killary Bay and is the most imposing feature of the whole coast. The superb cone of Croaghpatrick (761 m) forms the S side of Clew Bay. N of Clew Bay, Achill, Ireland's largest island, rises to peaks of over 600 m and slopes W in a razorback to the cliffs of Achill Head. Its terrific cliffs, the highest in the British Isles forms the S side of the entrance to Blacksod Bay. To the W of the bay the low and sandy Mullet Peninsular extends with its offshore

islands to Erris Head. Between Slyne Head and Clifden Bay the coast is fronted by many rocks and breakers (see information page xi). Chart 2708 gives many clearing marks with the aid of which it is possible to approach the coast safely provided the weather is clear and the marks can be identified with certainty. It must be emphasised that some of these marks are not easy for a stranger to pick up and one in particular, Cleggan Tower, no longer exists.

Lahard Sound
The mainland running NE from Slyne Head is obstructed by a maze of rocks and breakers through which Lahard Sound leads to an area of sheltered water behind the outlying islands. The sound is open to the W and S and the approach is intricate so it is of little value to yachts and is not recommended. Chart 2708 would be essential.
Mannin and Clifden Bays. The best approach from the S is common to both these bays. The key is the prominent 11 m high white beacon on Carrickarana (Seal Rocks). Carrickarone on older charts is the right name.

From a position 2 miles W of Slyne Head a course of 043° leads to the beacon and unless it can be identified it would be imprudent to stand into the bays. It would not be advisable for a stranger to attempt to pass through any of the channels between the rocks and breakers which extend for 1¹/₂ miles NW of Knock Point. Young John's Rock which dries at LWS and Testy Breaker to the E of it with only 1·8 m are very dangerous being so far offshore and liable to break at any time and with no easily identified clearing marks. Mweem More has 6 m over it but in its very exposed position could break with any swell.

Clifden Castle on the N shore of Clifden Bay is a big, ruined, grey building with a few scrubby trees around it. It is not easy to identify from a distance and must not be confused with the ruined coastguard buildings W of it. Doolick Rock, 1 mile W of Errislannan Point always shows. It has deep water E and W of it but is foul for 2 cables to the N of the drying part.

MANNIN BAY (chart 2708)
is exposed to the prevailing swell and has indifferent shelter within. It is, however, a lovely bay with superb sandy beaches and well worth a visit on a fine day with time to spare. It is not recommended for an overnight stop and is not approachable in bad visibility or a heavy swell.

Having reached a position 5 cables S of Carrickarana alter course for the Doolick until the peak of Cruagh Island comes in one with Wavery More, 314°, and use this as a back bearing to stand into the bay. If approaching from Clifden pass close SE of Doolick, whence it is safe to stand into the

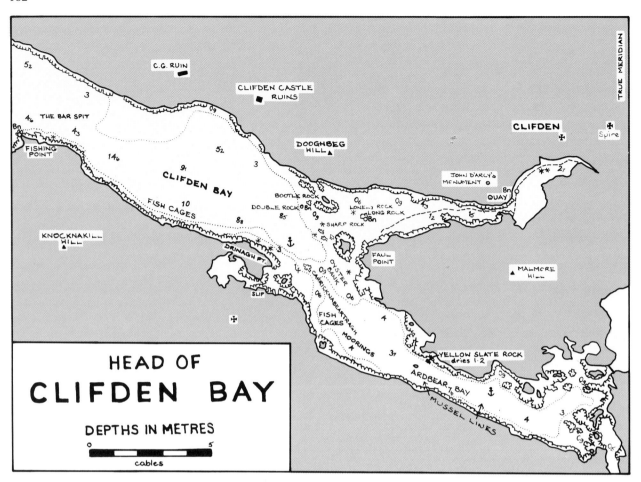

Clifden Bay from W.

bay. The easiest and best anchorage for a short stay is inside Knock Point in 3 to 4 m. This is a very beautiful spot. More secure anchorage can be found in Mannin Creek, crossing the bar at a suitable rise of tide and keeping towards the N shore. Anchor in 4 to 6 m in the middle of the creek.

CLIFDEN BAY

Having reached a position 3 cables S of Carrickarana beacon a course of 080° towards Fishing Point beacon, painted white, leads in between the rocks. There is room to tack if necessary but very careful pilotage is essential. Doolick Rock is always showing but it extends 2 cables N of the part which dries. Keep well clear of the neighbourhood of Coghan Rocks which dry at springs and lie 7 cables E of Carrigarana beacon. Having passed between these rocks the approach is fairly clear. Errislannon Point (7 cables SW of Fishing Point) is foul with rocks 1 cable N and 4 cables W of it. A number of fish farming cages are reported in this area, they are not particularly well marked; some have yellow flashing lights and there are sometimes red clearing marker buoys. A good look out should be kept.

Approach from the North

This is dealt with in the section on the coast N from Clifden to Aughrus Point and the channels between the offlying islands.

To cross the bar E of Fishing Point in the best depth keep Shindilla Islet just visible outside Fahy Point, 289°. Note that the sand bar has silted considerably on the north shore south of the C.G. Station and can break in heavy weather with ebb spring tides. An anchorage for fish cages close to the Errislannan shore due south of the Coastguard Station and within a line drawn from Fishing point east to Drinagh Point on Errislannan has been established. These cages will be marked by red clearance buoys and lit by yellow flashing lights (erratic). When not in place in Clifden Bay, these cages may be found within the Ardbear Bay just across the sand bar SW of the leading marks for entering Ardbear Bay, i.e., the outer beacon on the white concrete seat on the north shore west of the promenade.

Anchorages *(see plan)*

1. Off the promenade NW of the first Marker Beacon leading into Clifden Harbour, good holding in mud and sand. One yacht and a number of sea angling cruisers are moored off here during the Summer. Clifden Boat Club premises are situated on the promenade and have showers, heads, bar and snacks. VHF Ch. 37, Phone 095-21711. Diesel and water available by arrangement. Aster Boats Ltd., proprietor Adrian O'Connell, no longer operational, as the Boatyard has transferred to Kilrush Creek Marina. However mooring facilities are available in Ardbear Bay and visitors should contact John Brittain, on 095-32349 or contact Adrian O'Connell at Kilrush Boatyard, tel. 065-52072.

2. Between Larner Rock, 1·5 m high at the mouth of the river and Drinagh Point in about 5 m. This anchorage is reported to have poor holding ground with the ebb overfall from Ardbear Bay, particularly in NW winds. This is the most convenient for access to Clifden. The creek running up to the quay dries but is usually deep enough for a dinghy and a yacht can go up near HW. Leave the two beacons to port, keep rather towards the N side in the narrow entrance and as soon as inside of it turn almost N towards the quay. It is possible to dry out at the quay, water on pier. Look out for sewage outfall from house on pier.

3. Ardbear Bay, entered across a bar with 0·9 m provides complete shelter from swell and a yacht may anchor in any part of it. The outer beacon in line with an horizontal, white structure ashore about 034°, leads well clear of the rock on the bar, Carricknabertragh which dries 1·4 m. Yellow Slate Rock which dries 1·2 m must be avoided, also the rocks at the head of the bay. The NW end of the bay is rather deep and more convenient depths are found anywhere beyond Yellow Slate Rock. Care should be taken to keep clear of a number of fish-farming cages moored in this area. A more restricted and snug berth can be found at the head of the bay. Anchor in about 3 m with Flat Island bearing WNW. Here it is possible to land on the rocks near the road to Clifden, distant 1½ miles; beware, however, of the waterfall through the road bridge when the tide is up. Ardbear Bay is a good place to leave a yacht. There are now a number of yachts moored in this area and visitors might enquire from Luc Hallaire, Tel. 095-21136, nearest house to Salt Lake Bridge on the north shore, regarding possible vacant moorings.

Facilities

Clifden has good hotels, restaurants, guesthouses, shops, supermarkets, butchers, bakers, chemist, doctors, hospital, taxi service, bus to Galway, etc. Clifden boat club with showers, bar and meals, telephone, can be contacted on 095-21711, also through Sweeny Oil 095-21777. Clifden radio working channel 26. Electrical repairs at Wards in Market Street. Good fresh fish, launderette, showers in Youth Hostel which welcomes yachtsmen. RNLI Inshore Rescue Boat. John Ryan - boatman, good local contact. Six visitors moorings in Ardbea Bay. The bar at Crumpaun Bay entry has 3 m at MHWS and 5m in the bay. Tom Brittain keeps his MFV Lagosta in the bay and maybe persuaded to supply small amounts of diesel by can.

PASSAGES NORTHWARD FROM CLIFDEN
High Island Sound

The normal route in reasonable weather for a yacht making a N passage from Slyne Head or Clifden is through High Island Sound. In bad weather pass W of the island. A course of 011° from a position 2 miles W of Slyne Head leads to the sound and also W of Barret Shoals. High Island breaker with 8·2 m over it is very close to this line. Should there be a big sea running the breaker can be avoided by keeping to the clearing line shown on chart 2707 m, the E hill of Inishshark in line with the E side of High Island, 346° leading E of the breaker. This line also just clears Gur a Mweem breaker SW of Cruagh Island. Coming from the N the knobbly backbone of Errisbeg Hill is a good landmark.

From Clifden the safest course is to leave Carrickarana beacon to starboard and then shape course to leave Cruagh Island and Gur a Mween to starboard and so to the sound. If turning to windward, the N side of Turbot Island open S of Eeshal Island, 100°, leads S of Mweem Cruagh breaker with 3·4 m over it. Chart 2707 m gives clearing marks, which are easy to identify, to pass N, E and W of it.

If passing NW of Carrickarana, Carrickalahan, 0·8 m high, and Waverybeg, 1·6 m high, will always be seen. Do not attempt this channel in bad weather when the Middle Shoals with only 2·4 m would be dangerous.

If passing N of Cruagh Island note that Cruagh Rock, 1·4 m high, and Carrickaun, 2·2 m high, will always show but Glinsk Rock, dries 2·4 m, and Doolickcruagh must be avoided. They are usually marked by breakers. Keep close in to Cruagh Island to pass to the W of Doolickcruagh; bring the SW corner of Eeshal Island in line with Cruagh Rock, 135°, to pass W of Doolickcruagh coming from the N. This line also clears O'Malley breaker to the W. To clear Glinsk Rock to the W, bring the W point of Friar Island in one with Cruagh Rock, 315°; this line also leads W of Sharagmore which dries at LWS.

High Island Sound itself is clear but the sea can run high in it with formidable breakers on both shores. In really quiet sea anyone wanting to get onto High Island might anchor in about 20 m 1¾ cables SW of the S point of the E end of the island, and not less than ¾ cable ESE of the narrow point which leads S. Take the dinghy N up the W of this point and go ashore on the W side opposite Copper Mine.

COAST FROM TURBOT ISLAND TO AUGHRUS POINT

This stretch of coast with its many rocks and breakers and strong tides should be avoided in fresh onshore winds or a heavy swell. In fine weather it is a delightful area with good daytime anchorages and beautiful sandy beaches. The sound between Inishturk and Turbot Island is clear except for Careen Rock to the W of Turbot Island. This rock with the other shoals W of Turbot Island usually combine to form a truly massive breaker.

There is anchorage off the sandy beach on the N side of Turbot Island and in 1·5 m off the quay on Inishturk. The rocks SE of this quay extend further than charted so do not turn N until you are 1 cable SE past the point S of the quay, when the visible Middle Ship Rock is 2 cables E of you. There are other mostly invisible rocks more than 1 cable E and N of it so steer about 035° towards Ardroe Point till you see the NE side of Inishturk. Then head about NW and if Carricknageeragh rock is showing keep rather closer to it than to the island; it is a little less than 1 cable from the island, about 150 m, so if it is invisible aim to keep ½ cable from the island.

Kingstown Bay

is shoal and offers no good or safe anchorage for a yacht. The anchorage marked on chart 2707 NE of Inishturk is subject to a lot of roll. There is a pleasant, fine weather anchorage as marked SE of Omey Island. Again look out for a swell finding its way in.

Streamstown Bay

Caution. This bay is crossed by power lines 15 m above HW at the first narrows, 4 cables inside the entrance. There is an anchorage of sorts in 2·5 m, 2 cables inside the entrance and abreast a small bay on the N side. Sand bottom with patches of weed. The tide runs *very* hard and there is little room to swing, especially at low tide. It would be essential to moor if staying over a tide and to avoid spring tides. The strong ebb tide sluices out of the entrance to form a series of overfalls outside which would make entrance or exit dangerous in fresh onshore winds especially on the ebb. This bay cannot be recommended.

Omey Island

This island is joined to the mainland by a fine strand which dries up to 2 m. Its S shore is clear but there are rocks off its W and NW. A yacht making through the sound between Omey and Inishturk should keep up to the Omey side to avoid the drying shoals, Sharagmore and Sharagbeg and the rocks N of Inishturk. Continuing N, directions have already been given for avoiding Glinsk Rock see above. Chart 2707 m shows an anchorage NW of Omey Island. It is a very pleasant spot in fine weather only. There is a pier at Shindilla Point. Keeger Rock and Mween-navar, NW of Omey Island must be avoided.

Aughrus and Friar Island Passages

These are separated by Mwellauntragh Rocks, dry 1·8 m, Carrickaloo, 5 m high, and O'Malley breaker, which always show. They save considerable distance over the High Island Sound on the passage N or S from Clifden but the tides run fast through them, especially through Friar Island Sound, and set across the rocks. Coupled with the uneven bottom and their exposed position they can only be recommended in fine weather, moderate winds and little or no swell. A force 5 SW wind and spring ebb would be dangerous. In settled weather it is possible to anchor in 3m during the day in a little cove on E side of Friar Island. Land in dinghy on S side of cove. Wild life - seals and great black back gulls.

Aughrus Passage

This is obstructed on its E side by Mween Corakeen with about 1 m at LAT and by a 3·7 m patch 2½ cables W of Aughrus point. Drying rocks extend 2 cables W of the point and the channel between the 3·7 m patch and Carrickaloo is only 1¼ cables wide. The W side of Inishbofin in line with the W side of Carrickaphuill, 159°, leads through. Carrickaphuill only covers at high springs and would then usually be marked by a breaker. Once through bring the W end of Cruagh Island in line with the centre of Carrickaloo, 203°, and this line will lead between Feroonagh West and Cuddoo Rock.

Friar Island Sound is straightforward if course is set to keep close to the island shore. Watch out for the tide which sets across Mweelauntrough and races through the sound.

Tides

There is no reliable information about the strength or time of the tides in the channels between the islands. As a rough guess they might be taken as about the same as for Slyne Head, the N-going stream starting at -0320 Galway, (+0300 Dover) and the S-going stream at +0305 Galway (-0300 Dover).

Cleggan, approaches

When the S side of High Island comes in line with the N side of Friar Island, 236°, come onto this line as a back bearing and it will lead N of the rocks and shoals W of Cleggan Bay; Carrickamwellaun is the most NE of these. When it is aft of the beam alter course into the bay. Another line which clears all the rocks on the W approach is the summit of Tully Hill open N of Cleggan Point, 085°. The approach from the E is straightforward.

Cleggan Bay

This bay is open to the NW but offers tolerable shelter in summer and is easy of access. Anchor off the boat harbour which dries out. Local boats lie alongside but this is not recommended as scend is seldom absent and can be serious. In bad weather the harbour can be closed by timber baulks placed across the entrance by a crane. Water near the head of the quay. Good, small general stores, pub. Lobsters can sometimes be bought direct from fishermen. Ferry to Inishbofin. Tap at end of pier. Fuel from Sweeny Oil Co. (095-21777) delivered to pier. Walsh's fish shop, 1st turn right after PO is well worth a visit.

Light

A light is shown from a rectangular, white beacon, 3·5 m high, on the NE side of the entrance to the bay. Light Fl (3) WRG 15 s 20 m 6-3 M. W from shore to 091°; R thence to 124°; G thence to 221°. It is important to study these sectors on metric charts 2706, 2707. The G sector just barely clears NW of Mwellaunatrua and Illaunananima, 8 m high, but covers Lecky Rocks, 7 m high and Davillaun 24 m high. The G sector also covers the dangerous Carrickmahoy (Carrickmahoga), dries 1·9 m. The R sector leads clear of the rocks to the W of the entrance to the bay and the W sector shows over these rocks and up the bay. The light is reported to be very weak.

INISHBOFIN

Bofin Island is the centre of a large group of rocks, islands and breakers extending for 8 miles E and W. To the E of this group is Davillaun and to the W is Inishshark. The shore and sounds are all foul and any approach to the group from seaward in poor visibility or a high swell must be made with great caution. Bofin Island is a favourite port of call for yachts cruising in this area or on passage N or S. The harbour is secure and the islanders extend a welcome to visitors.

Lights

From Gun Rock at the E side of the harbour entrance a light is shown from a W beacon 3·7 m high. Light Fl (2) 6 s 8 m 4 M. Obsc N of 296°. From Lyon Head at the E end of Inishlyon, a light is shown Fl WR 7·5 s 13 m 7-4 M. R from shore to 184°; W thence to 325°; R thence to 036°, covering Carrickmahoy; W thence to 058° and R thence to shore. Both these lights are weak and cannot be seen from any distance. It would be most unwise for a stranger to get involved with this bit of coast in the dark.

Rusheen Bay

on the E side of Inishbofin offers sheltered anchorage with W winds off the sandy beach in delightful surroundings. It is a walk of about 1 mile across to the harbour. The local quay is dry at LW and unsuitable for visitors. There is a small restaurant close above the shore. Black Rocks will always show but New Anchor Shoal, with 1·5 m

186

Inishbofin from W.

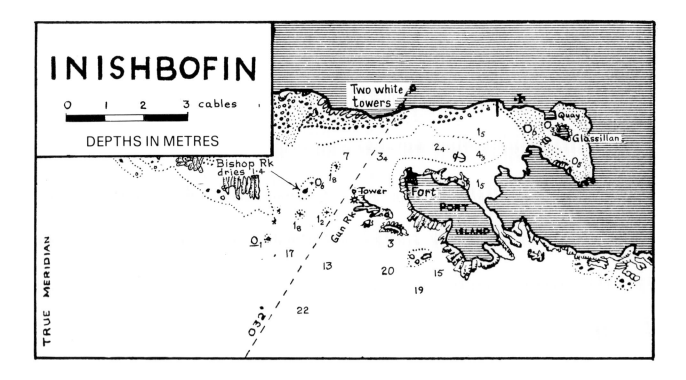

over it and on the S side of the bay, must always be avoided.

Bofin Harbour

From High Island Sound a course of 011° will lead up to the entrance to the harbour. If coming from the N beware of Carrickmahoy (see below). With strong SW winds or a heavy swell entrance and particularly exit, can be difficult if not impossible.

Two conspicuous W towers on the N side of the harbour in line, 032° lead in close E of a 0·2 m patch and then extremely close to Gun Island on which stands a W tower 12 m high. If beating it is permissible to borrow to the E of the line outside Gun Rock and to the W of it when abreast the rock. Near HW the 1·2 m patch might be ignored in smooth water but Bishop Rock, dries 1·4 m, must be avoided. Continue on the leading line until the ruins of Cromwell's Fort are well abeam, then alter to stand up the harbour. The best place to anchor is just N of the local boats. The next place is just W of them. If it is desired to go closer to the N shore do not go beyond the W end of the first of two buildings with 3 chimneys as it gets shallow beyond this.

Quay

dries 0·6 m alongside; a convenient place to dry out. It can be approached under power after half-flood by the narrow pass between Glassillan and the small rock SW of it; near HW the wider channel between Glassillan and the pier end can be used.

Facilities

The building nearest the quay is Micko Day's pub which also stocks some groceries. The nearby hotel welcomes yachtsmen. Paddy O'Halloran is a good local pilot. Ferry to Cleggan. Repairs to engines and electronics - Augustine Coyne, East End 095-45807. Tap at end of pier. Showers by arrangement in Miko's. Good local fish. Fishing boats work VHF Ch. 6 and Clifton Radio Ch. 26. Cycles for hire - Paddy Joe King in Lower Middle Quarter 095-45833.

Inishshark

This island, 95 m high, has no good anchorage or landing place. There are breakers and rocks off its NW, SW and SE corners. The Kimmeen Rocks extend 6 cables W of the island with a channel between them and the island through which the tide runs at 2¹/₂ kn. 1¹/₄ miles S of the island Mweemore with 7·5 m and Paddy Lenane's Rock with 7 m would break in heavy weather. Inishgort is S of Inishshark with foul ground all round and a rock strewn channel between the islands which is not recommended. Chart 2707 gives clearing marks to avoid these dangers.

Ship Sound between Inishshark and Inishbofin is straightforward but the strong 2·5 kn tide and uneven bottom with patches of 3 and 3·4 m confines its use to moderate winds and little sea. In bad weather it breaks right across. The N Stag Rock, 20 m high, in line with Colleen Rock, 12 m high, 055°, leads NW of all the dangers W of Inishshark. Boughill, 69 m high, is a very prominent rock 1 cable W of Inishshark. The Stags of Bofin, 26, 25 and 20 m high, extend 6 cables from the NW corner of Inishbofin. Gubatarraghna with foul ground all round it extends 3 cables from the N shore of the island.

Carrickmahoy (Carrickmahoga) is a very dangerous rock which dries 1·9 m and lies ³/₄ mile S of Lyon Head. It breaks heavily over an extensive area. Note that it is ¹/₃ of the way across the sound between Bofin and Cleggan Bay. Chart 2707 gives good clearing marks; however, if approaching from the N and intending to keep Ship Sound well open to pass S of the rock, note that the sound between Inishshark and Inishgort (which is very similar in profile but much smaller than Inishshark) opens first while still in the danger area. Check by compass bearing that it is the main Ship Sound which is open before turning W. In a swell always pass S of Carrickmahoy as there are breakers between it and Inishlyon.

Tides

In the channel between Inishbofin and the mainland and in Ship Sound the tidal streams run in the direction of the channels. The spring rate in Ship Sound is 2·5 kn and in the main sound 1·5 kn but more round Lyon Head. The ebb, running SW, sets more strongly across Carrickmahoy than the NE flood. The ebb starts 1¹/₂ hours before local HW and continues until 4, or occasionally 2 hours before the following HW. It is frequently rather rough in this strait due to the long duration of the SW ebb combined with its exposure to any sea from the SW.

Davillaun

local name Ox Island, 24 m high, lies E of Inishbofin. There are rocks 2 cables W of it of which the outermost, Mweeldyon, dries 1·8 m. Couraghy Rock, which dries, lies 2 cables E of Davillaun with a breaker, with 3 m over it, a further 2¹/₂ cables to the E. Landing can be made in fine weather from a dinghy in the little cove on the S side of the island.

Lecky (Leahy) Rocks which are extensive and consist of two groups with a narrow and shallow channel between them, lie 5¹/₂ cables SE of Davillaun. The N rock is 7 m high and the S rock 3·4 m. They are foul E and W for about 1¹/₂ cables.

There are deep channels between Black Rock, with Coramore breaker just E of Bofin, and Davillaun and also between Davillaun and Lecky Rocks.

188

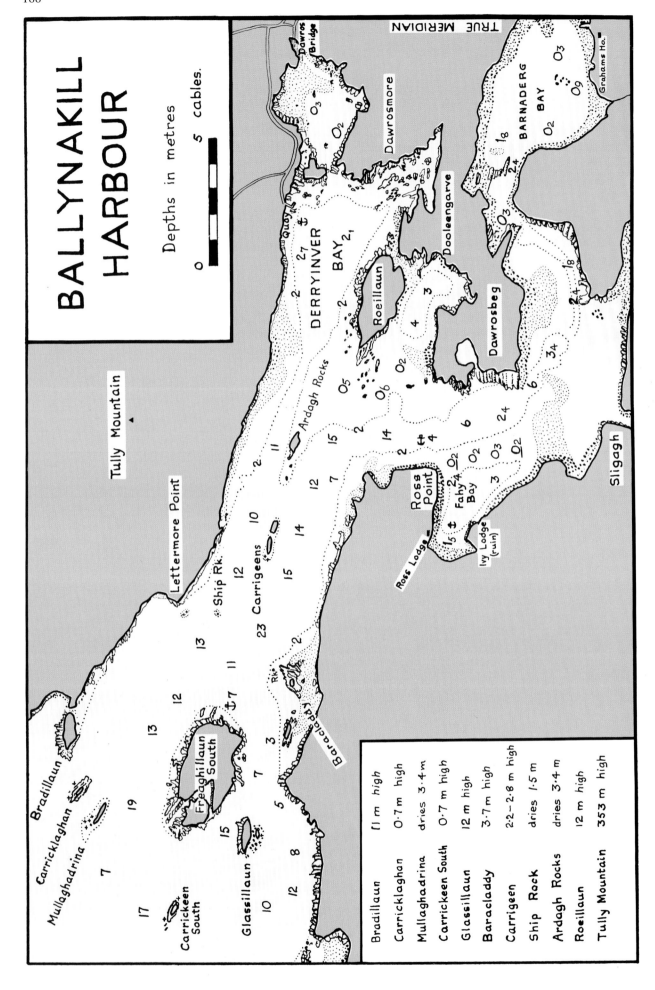

BALLYNAKILL HARBOUR

Depths in metres

5 cables.

Tully Mountain ▲

Lettermore Point

Carricklaghan

Bradillaun

Mullaghadrina

Carrickeen South

17

7

19

13

12

10

12

8

15

7

3

5

7

Freaghillaun South

Glassillaun

Baracladdy

Rk.

11

13

12

23 Carrigeens

Ship Rk.

10

14

15

2

Ardagh Rocks

11

2

15

12

7

2

14

2

Quay

2_7

2

2

O_5

O_6

O_2

2

2

14

4

2

O_2

O_2

O_3

O_2

3

6

2_4

3_4

6

2_4

1_8

O_2

O_3

DERRYINVER BAY

2_1

Roeillaun

Dawrosmore

Dawros Bridge

O_3

O_2

Dooleangarve

3

4

Dawrosbeg

Ross Point

Ross Lodge

Fahy Bay

2_4

1_8

Ivy Lodge (ruin)

1_5

Sligagh

O_2

O_9

O_3

BARNADERG BAY

O_2

O_2

1_8

Grahams Ho.

TRUE MERIDIAN

Bradillaun	11 m high
Carricklaghan	0·7 m high
Mullaghadrina	dries 3·4 m
Carrickeen South	0·7 m high
Glassillaun	12 m high
Baracladdy	3·7 m high
Carrigeen	2·2-2·8 m high
Ship Rock	dries 1·5 m
Ardagh Rocks	dries 3·4 m
Roeillaun	12 m high
Tully Mountain	353 m high

Passage from Inishbofin to Clew Bay

In fair weather with good visibility pass E of Couraghy Rock and Davillaun and head 040° which takes you just W of Pollack Shoal, E of Inishdalla and Cahir and W of Black Rock outside Roonagh Head.

Coast

Both sides of Cleggan Point and the coast W to Ballynakill consist of cliffs between 15 and 45 m high, backed by steep grass slopes with bare rock in places and with occasional guts known as 'ooeys', some with beaches at their heads. In thick weather it is worth noting that the 4 miles from the W side of Cleggan Bay to the S side of the entrance to Ballynakill is almost the only clean stretch for 20 miles N or S and from a local departure, say Davillaun or the Lecky Rocks, could be safely approached and either harbour made in visibility as low as 2¹/₂ cables.

BALLYNAKILL HARBOUR

(see plan) (chart 2706)

This fine bay is easily entered by day and is a good refuge with excellent shelter, as well as providing scope for day sailing inside in pretty surroundings. Tully Mountain on the N, much higher than any other hill so near the coast S of Killary, is easily identifiable. The clear approach from the S is mentioned above. The approach from the N is described under the Rinvyle paragraph below.

Entrance

A yacht may enter either side of Freaghillaun South, a most attractive island which was inhabited until about 1930; it has a good well only 0·5 m above the HW mark under the cliff on its S side. There is a good passage anchorage in 5 to 10 m on its E side. There is a line of mussel buoys starting about 3 cables SE of Freaghillaun and running towards the Carrigeen.

Entering S of Freaghillaun South you can go either side of Glassillaun, both channels being not less than 1 cable wide for berthing with a fair tide. Glassillaun (which with the small rock S of it is locally called the Cow and Calf), the two Carrigeens and the 3·7 m high rock off Barracladdy all have grass tops. There is a rock below water 70 m S of Cow and Calf. There is a dangerous drying rock 1 cable NE of the 3·7 m high rock off Barracladdy; holding a course directly between Glassillaun, or its S side, and the E Carrigeen Rocks, clears N of this rock by not less than ¹/₂ cable. To clear the shoals N of the point N of Ross Point keep the E Carrigeen Rock in line with the W end of Braadillaun 315°-135°. There are fish cages NE of Rosses Point which must be avoided when anchoring — see 2 below.

The normal entrance N of Freaghillaun is straightforward. Mullaghadrina dries and usually shows; at HWS its position must be established and if there is no break on it approaching from the W must be made towards the N shore of Freaghillaun keeping nearer to it than Carricklaghan. If Ship Rock is below water to the W end of Inishbroon showing open of Braadillaun 325° leaves you 1 cable SW of it. If heading to Derryinver Bay to pass between Ship Rock and Carrigeen Rocks keep Glassillaun just open S of Freaghillaun 273°. The jetty S of Letter More dries at LW and is not suitable for going alongside. No facilities.

Anchorages

1. Fahy Bay (locally known as Ross) approached over a bar with 0·3 at LWS is one of the best anchorages in the W with good holding, 2 to 3 m mud, and pretty agricultural surroundings. The only bad wind is SE, when it can become surprisingly rough; in these conditions choose a berth on the S side under the trees. The bar is of course quite sheltered and at neaps a yacht drawing 1·5 m could enter at LW. It is about the same depth across most of the entrance of the bay, a little deeper towards the S. side.

Facilities

Good spring water from a pump in the yard at Ross Lodge by arrangement with the owner. Provisions including frozen meat at excellent small shop with petrol and gas at Moyard, also PO and phone; Moyard is over 2 miles away by road but 1¹/₂ miles by dinghy, past Sligagh. Butcher at Rockfield, 2 miles.

2. Off Ross Point, always accessible, tide-rode but sheltered from the W.

3. Derryinver Bay. To pass N of Ardagh Rocks and between the banks bring the cliff on the N side of the 37 m hill on Dawrosmore in line with a roofless house behind it, 104°; keep on this transit until a conspicuous white house in trees disappears behind the 25 m hill E of Fahy Bay, about 210°, when a yacht will be through the narrows. Alternatively keep West Carrigeen on Glassillaun, 276°-096°, until Ardagh Rocks are abeam, then steer for Dawrosmore Hill with the N side of Freaghillaun dead astern, about 105°. Anchor off the two streams about 100 m SW of Derryinver quay, good holding but buoy the anchor as there are old mooring chains on the bottom. The quay has 1·5 m HWN for 7 m on the NE side, soft mud and a few stones. Nearest supplies at Tullycross 1¹/₂ miles or Letterfrack, 2¹/₂ miles; Rinvyle Hotel 3 miles. The 4·3 m pool through the narrows SE of the quay is not recommended as the tide runs strongly and the passage is difficult. With a bit of flood-water in the river it is worth rowing up to Dawros Bridge to see the salmon jumping the rapids during June and July.

Ballynakill Harbour from SE.

4. In strong SE winds the S side of Derryinver Bay or the pool W of Doleengarve, accessible at half-tide would be more comfortable than any of the above.

5. Barnaderg Bay. There is a good stone pier 50 m long with 3·2 m HWS at its head and 3 m at the W steps. The E steps are foul. It could be reached by careful sounding on a rising tide, but more easily by dinghy. Petrol and most supplies at Letterfrack, ½ mile.

KILLARY BAY AND APPROACHES
(chart 2706)

Between Ballynakill Harbour and Clew Bay there are only two natural harbours on the coast, Killary Bay and Little Killary, which lie side by side at the head of a large bay fronted by islands and rocks. Killary Bay is like a miniature fjord, though shallower than its Norwegian counterparts, and is well worth a visit for its magnificent scenery; it was formerly used as a naval anchorage. Little Killary is a first class yacht harbour in very picturesque surroundings. For a full description of the islands, rocks and breakers in the approach and entrance the yachtsman should refer to the chart and the Irish Coast Pilot which give many marks for clearing them. There is no simple line of approach

and the area should be avoided in poor visibility. Many of the transits shown on the chart are difficult to identify. The strands E and W of Culfin Point are conspicuous. The rear, white leading mark on the summit of Inishbarna shows up well.

Caution

The many submerged rocks in this area must be carefully avoided, not only because many of them break in bad weather, sometimes intermittently, but also because lobster pots are usually set on and around them.

Approach from the South — Rinvyle Point

The outermost danger off Rinvyle Point is Mweelaunatrua which dries 1·9 m. If it is neither showing or breaking it can only be avoided by giving Inishbroon a suitable berth of, say, ½ mile. Inishbroon has yellowish cliffs on its S side and grass sloping to the sea on the N. There is a small but conspicuous look-out hut on Caheradoona. When Rinvyle Point shows N of Inishbroon alter course for Illaunananima (Live Island) till you reach the transit N side of Freaghillaun in line with the S side of Shanvalleybeg, 089°; this leads between the very dangerous Puffin Rocks, dry 0·5 m, and the 2·7m patch 3 cables SE of Illaunananima; when Rinvyle Castle, a square ruin near the shore, bears SE, a yacht will be clear of these dangers and should steer for Corweelaun West, 1·9 m, to avoid the rocks extending NW from Freaghillaun North; Cleggan Point well open of Rinvyle Point, say over the E point of Inishbroon 233°, leads clear of these rocks. The above is the shortest route from Ballynakill but a simpler alternative and the best course if coming from Inishbofin, is to pass N and E of Illaunananima and then steer for Corweelaun West; note that in bad weather there will be breakers on the 5·8 m patch and the 7·9 m patch E of Illaunananima. The most E of these is half-way between Illaunananima and Corwellaun. Having identified Corweelaun there is no difficulty in closing the SW shore of Crump Island well N of Thos. (Tom's) Anchor; keep 1 cable off the island to avoid this rock, then give Shanvalleybeg a berth of 2 cables. When Blake's Point comes in line with Rinvyle Castle steer 073° with this transit astern which leads to the entrance to Killary. If bound for Little Killary this is also a safe course till Prahanmore (Mweelaun), 0·4 m high, has been identified when course may be altered to leave it to starboard.

Rinvyle Pier

3 miles E of Rinvyle Point and close E of Tully Point, might provide landing for stores in settled and absolutely swell free weather. The bottom off it is rock or gravel, poor holding, and the approach very foul. To go alongside steer in with the roofless boathouse just shut in behind the pier end to clear Aghty Rocks, dry 3 m, to port. Steps dry 0·3 to 0·6 m LWS at the outer end, sand bottom. Groceries, PO, petrol and telephone at Tully, ½ mile.

Approach from the West

Coming from the direction of Inishturk the Pollack shoal must be avoided as it has a 3·7 m patch and in a swell any part of it may break; the W side of Inishdalla under the summit of Inishturk, 320°, leads S of the shoal; the SW end of Inishturk opens S of Inishdalla by a width of the latter, 289°, leads N of it.

Once past the Pollack shoal course should be set to pass either N or S of the Carrickgaddy group of rocks of which Gaddymore is 6 m high and is not conspicuous against the land from any distance. It is 4½ miles from Inishdalla but only 1½ miles from Frehill Island, 20 m high and 2 miles from Crump Island, 23 m high. There should be little difficulty in getting a good fix.

To pass through the mile wide gap between Gaddy Beg, 0·4 m high, and O'Malley breaker, which dries at LWS, the view on metric chart 2706 (or view A on old chart) gives an excellent picture of the coast from this position. There are two distant transits for this gap both of which may be

obscured by low clouds or poor visibility. 1. Leenane Hill, 616 m high, (shown on chart 2420) in line with the N fall of Aillachoppal, 112°. 2. The stern transit Achill Head seen between Caher Island and Ballybeg, 334°, chart 2420. However, once Gaddymore is identified there is no difficulty, Gaddy Beg will be seen and course shaped to pass 2 cables W of it to avoid a rock which dries 0·9 m 1 cable to the W of Gaddy Beg.

The 6 m high white beacons in the entrance to the Killary can often be picked out clearly from a distance. In line 099° they lead Clear N of O'Malley Breaker and all the way in but between John Keneally's Rock and Conolly's Rock, with 11 and 10 m over them. In a bad sea or swell a yacht should keep well S of the leading line at this point. Having passed O'Malley breaker and being bound for Little Killary a direct course to the rocks S of its entrance will lead safely to the entrance.

If turning to windward on the S or W approaches, to avoid O'Malley breaker the following clearing lines will help. 1. The highest part of Illaunananima over Corweelaun Rock, 257°, leads SE of it. 2. Tully Mountain over the E point of Crump Island, 191°, leads E of it. 3. Tully Point touching the E side of Shanvalleybeg, 150°, leads SW of it.

If coming in N of Garrickgaddy Rocks course may be set for Inishdegil More 29 m high, passing about 3 cables N of Gaddymore. Keep the front beacon, on Doonee, in line with the S side of Inishdegil More to pass N of Thanybegnarusk, dries 0·6 m, and when about 3 cables from Inishdegil More, with Inishdegilbeg starting to close behind Cooneenfadda, (the islet NW of Inishdegil More) alter course S to clear the 1·8 m sounding before continuing towards the Killaries. When Roonagh Head, 8 miles to the N just opens E of Govern Island, 10 m high, 011°, a yacht will be E of Thanybegnarusk.

Approach from the North

From E of Clare Island, if the sea is slight and the visibility good a yacht may take the direct course for Killary. Having avoided Meemore Shoal (see p195), bring Mweelaun, 19 m high, under the centre of the sloping top of Clare Island 341° astern. This line leads well clear of Murder Rocks on the mainland and continues inside Frehill Island. However it passes over the 1·8 m patches E of Govern Island and W of Inishdegil More; keep more to the E and W respectively passing these two points.

KILLARY BAY

This spectacular inlet, 7 miles long, with mountains falling steeply to the water's edge on either hand, is one of the most remarkable pieces of scenery in the W and a visit to its head is well worth while for a

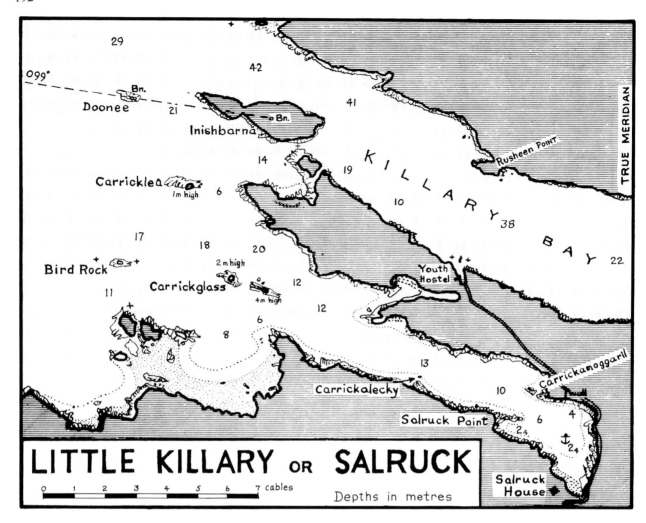

LITTLE KILLARY or SALRUCK

0 1 2 3 4 5 6 7 cables

Depths in metres

Little Killary or Salrock from W.

boat with an engine. In unsettled weather, however, any W wind funnels up the inlet and makes the usual anchorage at Leenaun an uncomfortable berth. The entrance is simple. There are some rocks on the N side which can easily be avoided by keeping over towards Doonee and Inishbarna Islands. Apart from occasional rocks close inshore there are no dangers in the length of the inlet but **Caution.** Salmon and mussel breeding is taking place in cages in the areas marked by pecked lines on the plan. The cages are visible and these areas should be avoided. There is yet another fish farm about a mile beyond Derrynasliggan on the starboard hand.

Anchorages
1. About half-way up on the S side off Dernasliggaun House, now known as Killary Lodge, hotel, surrounded by trees, there are four visitors moorings in 4/5m with good swinging room, designed for 40/45 ft. boats. There is a small pier to lie alongside at HW with tap. Meals, showers, etc., by arrangement. Proprietor, Jamie Young. Small fee for moorings after first night.

2. One mile further up on the N side off Bundorragha, outside the perch in 5 to 7 m. Landing at quay which dries and is approached along the W shore; the old chart shows another rock 70 m W of the rock with the perch but doubt about its existence has been expressed by local people and it is not shown on the new metric chart.

3. At the head in 2 to 3 m about 3 cables NW of Leenaun Quay which dries. Old fashioned pump across road from quay. Landing at slip beside quay. **Facilities.** Good hotel. Small shops. PO, RC Church. Petrol. Occasional bus.

At Gubbadanbo (Cooneenwaun) on the S side inside the entrance there is a small quay with a slip which dries out; the cottage on the quay is a Youth Hostel. Kitchen tap at Youth Hostel. Unfortunately, the approach to this quay is foul with submerged rocks.

LITTLE KILLARY BAY (Salrock) *(see plan)*
The head of this inlet is a first-class yacht anchorage which can be entered in any weather and provides good shelter; no swell reaches the anchorage, although it appears to be open to the NW. The bottom in the anchorage is softish mud and the holding somewhat suspect. In fresh winds a second anchor would be necessary. The shores of the inlet slope steeply, the S side being covered with trees right down to the water whilst the N side is barren, with Mweelrea (Muilrea) the highest mountain in Connaught, towering above it.

Caution
Salmon nets may be right across somewhere inside the entrance.

Directions
The sandy bays just W of the entrance are a good guide to its position. None of the rocks in the immediate approach covers completely and they may be passed on either side as convenient. Note, however, that at HW there are submerged ledges extending 1 cable both E, W and N of the visible parts of Carricklea. There are also covered rocks 1 cable E and W of Bird Rock (Mweelaun). If in doubt the safest is to pass between Inishbarna and Doonee (the islands with the beacons) and follow the shore to the entrance. Having passed Carricklass Rocks a mid-channel course leads safely to the anchorage. Should a yacht be beating in, Carrickalecky (dries 2·1 m) on the S side must be avoided and appears to be further N than charted. Care must be taken at the ½ cable wide passage between Carrickamoggaril and Ship Rock, the extension of Salrock Point. (Carrickamoggaril is not on the metric chart but it shows on the plan here.)

Anchor when the hall door of Salrock House appears to starboard through a gap in the trees; this will be in 4 m in the middle of the bay or in 2 m nearer the house. Good drinking water can be ladled from a well near the shore by permission of the owner of Salrock House. There are no public facilities or transport. An adventure School has dinghies and canoes in the bay.

Coast — Caution
The coast between Killary Bay and the entrance to Clew Bay consists of some 6 miles of sand beaches broken at intervals by rock outcrops. A number of groups of rocks, reefs and shoals extend up to 1½ miles out from the beaches and beyond these groups the depths are irregular up to 4 miles offshore. The beaches are exposed to the W and are subject to nearly continuous surf. No yacht working up or down the coast should approach it closer than

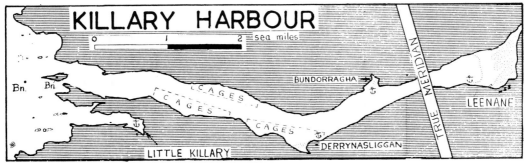

Killary Bay from W.

1½ miles in fine weather. In bad weather the whole coast E of a line joining Mweelaun to Caher Island becomes a mass of irregular breakers and should be avoided.

OFFSHORE ISLANDS

These islands and rocks form excellent marks to anyone working up or down the coast. The dangers are all visible, the distances between them short and the opportunities for frequent fixes continuous. The lights are not adequate for making through the inner passages by night.

Inishturk

is 188 m high and 2¼ miles long. It is the most isolated inhabited island on the W coast. It is, in general, steep-to except at the SE corner where Floor Shoals with 6·7 m least water extend for ¾ mile. There is anchorage, well sheltered from winds between SW and NNW, in the bay on its E side off the boat harbour in 3 to 6 m sand, good holding but somewhat exposed to swell. There is 2·4 m HWS alongside the wall beside the boat-slip in the harbour; a good place to land at HW, but the inner face is rough. There is 0·6 to 0·9 m LWS between

Innishturk anchorage looking S.

the slip and the outer wall, 2·4 m close to the end of the outer wall. Good well at the head of the harbour, small shop, PO, telephone, pub and restaurant. A new quay has been built which gives protection to the landing beach. There are fish boxes and fishing boat moorings in the bay.

Inishdalla

22 m high, lies 1 mile SSE of Inishturk and is foul for 3 cables to the SW with rocks drying up to 2·1 m. There is good pollack and mackerel fishing around this island.

Caher Island

57 m high, lies 1¹/₂ miles E of Inishturk. It has steep, high cliffs at its NW end. There are good boat landings at Port Temple on the E and Portnacloy on the W where local motorboats go alongside to land sheep and cattle.

Ballybeg

with foul ground and drying rocks to the N and E of it lies 2¹/₂ cables SW of Caher Island. There is deep water between them.

Mweelaun

an isolated rock 19 m high, lies 3 miles NNE of Caher Island and makes a useful transit with Clare Island, see above. It should be passed with a berth of 2 cables to the SE.

Meemore Shoal

1³/₄ miles E of Mweelaun dries at low springs and usually breaks. It is a dangerous rock owing to the ease with which it can be confused with **Black Rock** which dries 3·2 m and lies 1 mile off Roonagh Head. Note that the coast from Roonagh Head to Old Head is open from near Meemore and closed from near Black Rock. A useful clearing mark to keep N of Meemore is to keep the summit of Croagh Patrick (761 m) N of the summit of Carrowmore Hill (170 m) which lies 2 miles E of Roonagh Head.

CLARE ISLAND (chart 2667)

is a magnificent island 460 m high and with superb cliffs on its NW side beneath which there are a few isolated rocks close in. Two Fathom Rock with 3·4 m lies 1¹/₂ miles off the NW coast and breaks in bad weather. Calliaghcrom (Deace's) Rock which never covers lies 5 cables N of the island. Half way between it and the island there is a 7 m rock which breaks in gales. There is now a fish farm NE of Portlea.

Anchorage

There is a reasonable anchorage in winds between SW and NW in 3 to 6 m sand, N of Grania Waels Castle; in other winds it is uncomfortable or impossible. The small harbour dries with a sandy bottom but is subject to a heavy run in any sea. In 1982 a further pier was made leading out from the harbour but a visiting yacht should not consider going in alongside as it may not be safe.

There is a temporary anchorage on the NE side of the island in up to 6 m, sand, off the beach which has a small pier and slip used by curraghs at its W end. Beware of rock bottom further W than this.

Looking NE across the anchorage to Clare Island with Granuaile's Castle on right.

Facilities

Hotel, pub, general shop 1½M with variable opening hours and PO with telephone. Visiting doctor. Ferry to Roonagh Quay.

Clew Bay (chart 2667)

lies E of Clare Island and is about 6 miles wide and 12 miles deep. There is no shelter in the outer part of the bay but its head is filled with many small islands and there are several good anchorages behind them. There are also tidal channels to Westport Quay and to Newport. This inland part of the bay is fascinating for day sailing in a shoal yacht or a dinghy.

Roonagh Quay at the W end of the S side of the bay is used for Clare Island boats (with Iso 10s leading lights in line 144°) but is quite unsuitable for yachts and there are rocks off it.

Sound between Clare Island and Roonagh Head

In all normal summer weather this is the usual approach to Clew Bay from the S. Mweelaun is available for a fix which will ensure passing Meemore safely. In severe weather and with a big sea the N sound is preferable as the uneven bottom and patches down to 8 m and a SW going tide of 1·5 kn would make a dangerous combination.

Glenans Ireland base on Collanmore with Croaghpatrick beyond.

Passage between Roonagh Head and Meemore Shoal (chart 2667 essential)

This is a useful passage, but definitely only suitable in fair weather and good visibility, if bound from Inishbofin or the Killaries to Clew Bay, and vice versa, saving some distance, and possibly a beat, by comparison from the offshore course. It is easy to identify when leaving Clew Bay, less so when approaching from the SW. The passage lies between Black Rock, 6½ cables off the shore between Roonagh Head and Emlagh Point, and Meemore Shoal 7 cables WNW of Black Rock. The key to the passage is the identification of Black Rock, as there are no convenient leading marks in either direction. Black Rock which uncovers at ¼ ebb has a distinctive low appearance like a whale's back; covered at HW it will be invariably marked by a breaker, as absence of swell is rare. It may be

safely passed NW at a distance of 2 or 3 cables. It should not be kept further out as Meemore Shoal is often hard to see. It is of course most dangerous to go SE of Black Rock so be absolutely sure not to think it is Meemore. **Passage from South.** Do not approach the region of Roonagh Head unless you are sure of your position. Having identified Black Rock aim to leave it 2 or 3 cables to starboard and steer about 040° to avoid Emlagh Shoals, and when the rock is SE move into Clew Bay. **Passage from the North.** After passing Roonagh Point when N of Black Rock turn SW and pass 2 or 3 cables from the rock. A course of 220° leads E of Caher and Davillaun. If bound for Killary continue on this course for 2 miles to clear the dangers inshore, then make for the transit of Mweelaun and Clare Island's summit to Killary.

Lights. Achillbeg

light at the N extremity of the bay shows Fl WR 5s from a white tower 9 m high, 56 m, 18-15 M. Red from 262° to 281° covers the danger NW of Inishgort. White from 281° to 342°. Red from 342° to 060° over Clare Island and the dangers SE and W of it. White from 060° to 092° leads in clear S of the Bills Rocks. Red from 092° to 099° over Bills Rocks. White from 099° to 118° leads in clear from Achill Head. Obscure elsewhere and also obscure outside Clare Island and Bills Rocks. Clare Island has a light on its pier, Fl R 3 s, 3 M. There is a port hand beacon on NE Point Achillbeg showing Fl R 2s. **Inishgort** has a light at its SW end, L Fl 10 s from a white tower 8 m high, 11 m, 10 M; there is a large white wall back of it. **Dorinish Bar** G buoy, about 2 cables SW of Inishgort, shows Fl G 3 s.

The S side of the bay is dominated by Croagh Patrick with a chapel on its 756 m summit. The coast from Roonagh Head to Old Head is foul for 6 cables offshore. Old Head, 146 m, is conspicuous and surrounded by trees. There is a pier E of the head which dries, with clean sand bottom along its inner side; there are rocks not far E and S of the pier so if, at sufficient rise, going alongside approach it on a bearing of 190° and round the pierhead fairly close. There is a temporary anchorage NE of the pier, holding poor. Quiet, swell-free conditions are of course necessary.

APPROACHES TO WESTPORT

In rough weather head towards Inishgort Lighthouse bearing between 080° and 100°. Always keep N of bearing 080° when past Old Head as this is necessary to avoid (Creggan) Dillisk Rocks which extend N of a perch. It is always best to keep S of the W Card buoy. Enter fairly close N of Dorinish Bar buoy and then head in E from it. The entrance can be rough with tide against wind.

Warning

Yachtsmen are most strongly advised not to attempt to sail among the islands at night; it is impossible to see them after dark against the higher skyline of the land. Even if they are visible you might hit unlit racing marks. Do not arrange to go in after dark, but if for any reason you must, the only possible anchorage would be No. 1 leaving the Inishgort light between 315° and 325° and anchor when the depth is shallower. Wind of any strength coming across Croagh Patrick Hill from S or SE becomes so irregular that it is then impossible to sail between the islands or in the E part of Clew Bay, so an engine is essential.

Anchorages *(see plan)*

1. **Dorinish Harbour.** When Inishgort Lighthouse comes abeam steer for the SW point of Inishlyre, give it a berth of a bit more than 1 cable and when past it head towards Dorinish More. Anchor between 2 or 3 cables off it in about 2·3 m, good holding. Though the Dorinish Bar covers at HWS it still supplies shelter from the sea, but of course there would be no shelter from wind.

2. **Inishlyre Harbour.** This is a nice natural harbour giving good shelter from W and SW winds. Enter midway between the NE point of Inishlyre and the SW point of Collan More and when between them turn towards the SE point of Inishlyre and anchor a bit more than 1 cable from the point in 2 m. Further in halfway between the NE and SE points, or not less than 1/3 of the distance from either, there should be 1 m, i.e. 1·5 m LWS. If moving to Rosmoney Pier, beware of rock NW of Inishtaggart marked by a black conc buoy.

3. **Collan More Harbour,** N of the NW part of Rosmoney Hill, gives the best all-round shelter and is the most convenient for visiting the mainland. Mayo Sailing Club. Approach from between the NE of Inishlyre and the SW of Collan More with the S end of Inishgort in line with the N point of Inishlyre, but beyond the SW of Collan More keep N of Inishlyre in line with the wall N of the lighthouse. The entrance is 1 cable wide at HW but the shore on either side is foul and the navigable entrance is only 45 m wide. Enter halfway across in 1·7 m; the deepest part is NNE of the centre. A Glenans Sailing School is based on Collan More. It has a telephone and members bar. The new quay, which dries, is on the Rosmoney side of the harbour and the local Mayo YC yachts are moored N of it. Anchor just outside the moorings if it is deep enough. It is more sheltered than the part deeper than 2 m. Avoid the rock about 120 m off the Rosmoney shore, not on the chart but shown on the plan.

WESTPORT (chart 2057 necessary)

The course in to Westport quay has shallow places with 0·1 m near the quay. A pilot for Westport, Tom Gibbons, lives on Inishlyre, 098-26381. From Dorinish Harbour go between Inishlaghan and Inishimmel and then keep the summit of Pigeon Point above Finnaun Island, 099°, until past Inishraher. Then head 127° with the N lighthouse wall astern in line with the S cliff of Inishlyre. Carry on between 2 perches till the green box on top of a conical stone beacon near the entrance is in line with a hotel on Roman Island, 080°, and steer towards it until near Illanroe on the S side, then keep the beacon between a red buoy and a perch and go in leaving it fairly close to starboard. Carry on leaving the next perch and the pillar just off the NW end of Roman Island both to starboard, then head in with the line of the quay just visible and keep not more than 20 m off it. The quay mostly dries alongside at LWS, bottom clean mud. There

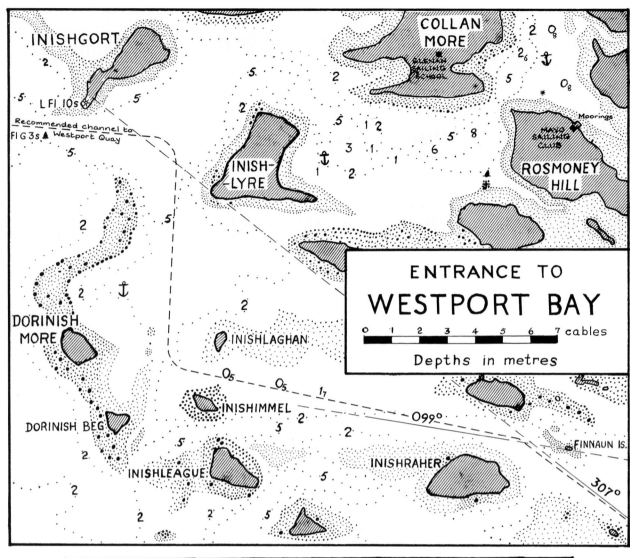

INISHGORT

2

5 L Fl 10s

Recommended channel to
Fl G 3s ▲ Westport Quay

5

2

2

5

DORINISH
MORE

DORINISH BEG

2

2

COLLAN
MORE

2 O₈

2₆ ⚓

5 O₈

*

Moorings

MAYO
SAILING
CLUB

ROSMONEY
HILL

5

INISH-
LYRE

2

5 1 2

3 1 6

⚓ 1

2

2

2

5 8

5

⚓

5

INISHLAGHAN

2

O₅

O₅ 1₇

INISHIMMEL

5 2

2

INISHLEAGUE

5

2

2 5

5

INISHRAHER

099°

FINNAUN IS.

307°

ENTRANCE TO
WESTPORT BAY

0 1 2 3 4 5 6 7 cables

Depths in metres

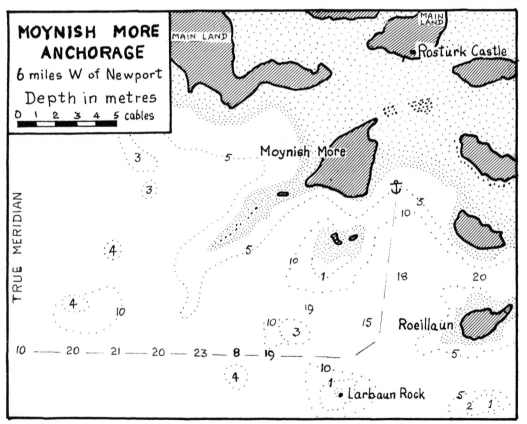

MOYNISH MORE
ANCHORAGE

6 miles W of Newport

Depth in metres

0 1 2 3 4 5 cables

MAIN
LAND

MAIN LAND

Rosturk Castle

Moynish More

⚓

TRUE MERIDIAN

3

5

3

5

10 5

5

4

10

18 20

10

4

10

1

19

15

Roeillaun

10

20

21

20

23 8 19

10 3

5

4

10

1

Larbaun Rock

5

2 1

should be 1·8 m of water 2 hours either side of HW. The bottom is clean sand if a yacht should touch coming up. The best place to berth is just beyond the tide gauge, reported missing, on the N side; this is opposite the Asgard Bar and there is another suitable berth opposite the Helm Bar. Good meals can be obtained in the former and adjoining the latter bar. Good supermarket near the Asgard Bar. Drinking water is very scarce. The town is 1 mile from the quays. EC Wed. This is an active sea angling centre. Sub aqua diver, motor repairs - William Quinn (098-41245), motor rewinds - T. P. Lynch (098-25389). Good rail connection to Dublin.

NEWPORT, APPROACHES and
OUTER ANCHORAGES (chart 2667).

Inner Passage from Westport entrance is about half as long as going out and then in the normal way, and of course is calmer but also more complicated and only possible above half tide; use chart 2057. Go NW between Inishgort and Collan Beg, then turn to go between Collan More and Clynish where the only small shallow drying part is. Having passed between the rocks SE of the E point of Clynish pass ½ cable off that point. Then follow the channel S of Moneybeg Island and finally pass either side of Carrigeennafrankagh which only covers near HWS. This leads to the anchorage E of Inishgowla which is just S of the main approach to Newport.

Moynish More (see plan)
is the first island you meet coming from the W along the N side. There is a suitable anchorage behind it in fine weather and with winds between NW and NE. It is completely exposed to the S. Do not go near this place in bad weather for, as already stated, there are several dangerous breakers well outside it.

There are different ways to approach. From the W, when past S of Mallaranny pier, (locally named Mulrany) head S of Roeillaun bearing E towards ½ the island's width S of it until the E side of Moynish More shows out, then head towards Rosturk Castle. Alternatively, going this direction, as soon as Rosturk Castle disappears behind the W side of Moynish More head NE towards its summit; when 1 cable off the island pass this far off between it and the shoal with two islets S of it; when the E side is well open turn to the anchorage. Coming from Westport go to the W Card buoy and from it go straight N towards Rosturk Castle passing ¼ mile E of Larbaun Rock. Alternatively head NW from W Card buoy until Rosturk Castle disappears inside the SE point of Moynish More and then head towards that point passing W of Larbaun Rock; when W of Roeillaun turn temporarily NE to avoid the shoal S of Moynish More. Anchor opposite the first pile of stones on the island, about 3 m, sand, a little more than 1 cable offshore.

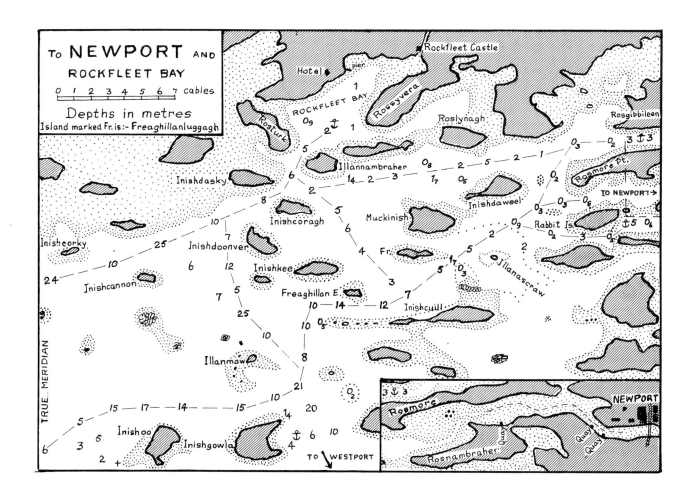

To NEWPORT AND ROCKFLEET BAY

0 1 2 3 4 5 6 7 cables

Depths in metres
Island marked Fr. is:- Freaghillanluggagh

Rockfleet Bay

is a good anchorage off the main shore but it is dangerous to approach towards the outer islands from the W in bad weather. In reasonable weather go in as above heading E towards S of Roeillaun and pass not less than 1 cable S of it. When past Roeillaun's S end head to between Inishcorky and Inishcannon and from there to between Inishdasky and Inishcoragh; when past their points head about 030° between the next islands ¼ mile away and when between them steer towards Rockfleet Castle, an old stone tower. Anchor in 2 m or in 1·5 m just W of Rossyvera Point. Pier being improved. **Other Approaches.** Going in the main channel to Newport (see below), or going up to it from Westport entrance (see above), after heading N and passing Illanmaw it is easy to head NW to join the above entrance. Or a little further towards Newport there is another safe way leaving Freaghillanluggagh to starboard and Inishcoragh to port, past the middle of which you head N to the entrance. The anchorage is sheltered in all winds but the bottom is very soft mud so a CQR or other self-burying anchor is best. The SW wind funnels strongly between the islands. No facilities.

Approach to Newport

The channel starts in N of Inishoo, about 2 miles NE of Cloghcormick W Card; this buoy should be left to starboard. Coming from the W you should start heading nearly E about 3 miles away with the N sides of Inishoo and Inishgowla in line. All the islands are surrounded by shoals which have large stones on them, so aim always to keep in the centre of the channel. It is important also to keep a careful tally of the islands, most of which are very similar in appearance. Illanascraw (Hat Is) is of distinctive shape rather like the bows of a ship when seen from seaward. Rosmore Point has a near vertical face, the only one in that vicinity. Beyond Muckinish it is shallow. A yacht 1·5 m deep might go in at half tide. Go in as shown on plan. Before heading N past Illanmaw keep the SE tip of Inishgowla well open of its N tip, about 190°. Go towards the middle of Inishkee till about 1½ cables past the line of rocks W of Inishcuill, then turn E and pass between these rocks and Freaghillan E. When past the latter head towards halfway between Fr. Island and Illanascraw (Hat Is) and pass just 1 cable SE of the E point of Fr. Then head towards Rosmore Point.

NEWPORT (see plan)

Head towards Rosmore Point till 2 cables from it, then turn E to go halfway between Rosmore and Rabbit Island. Continue to halfway between Rosnambraher Point and the point N of it, then continue as shown on the plan, or better chart 2667's plan. After passing the third small quay to starboard, head across to the main quay on the N side and berth between the end and the second pole on the quay. Alternatively, continue 18 m away from the quay and berth either side of the steps beyond the fourth pole. These berths have 2·4 m HWN, clay bottom covered with mud and small slaty stones. Between the second and fourth poles there is 0·6 m less water alongside. The face of the quay is rather uneven.

Facilities

Good shops. Butcher, chemist, garage (diesels repaired); bank open Tue. and Fri. Good hotel. Water.

Anchorages

For those who prefer to remain afloat there are two possible spots, each accessible only at sufficient rise of tide, see plan.

(1) S of the E tip of Rabbit Island in more than 3 m, fair shelter; a careful mid-channel course must be kept between Rabbit Island and the island and peninsula to the S of it; a dinghy can cut across to the Newport Channel halfway between Rosnambraher (Milcum) Point and the small islet just E of Rabbit Island, except at dead low water.

(2) N of Rossmore about 4 cables E of the point abreast the fence on Rosgibbileen, over 3 m in mid-channel, mud on sand; this is more exposed and further from Newport by dinghy than the S anchorage.

ACHILL SOUND

This sound, between the mainland and Achill, Ireland's largest island, is shoal for much of its length, with drying banks, but can be used by yachts of 1·5 m draught at HWN. It formerly provided a very useful short cut from Clew Bay to Blacksod Bay but now cables cross over the bridge so normal yachts cannot go through. Each end of the sound provides a useful natural haven. It is rather difficult to go down to the bridge from the N but is more complicated to do so from the S and simpler to go from there to the excellent shop beside the bridge by motor dinghy or easiest by car!

South Entrance (see plan)

The entrance is E of Achillbeg Island, easily identified by its lighthouse (see page ???). Conditions must be right for entering or leaving. About half way along the E side of the island, just S of the little bay on it, there is a bar with 1·5 m patches which breaks in SW gales. With W or NW wind or in calm weather it is possible to anchor temporarily just SW of the bar to await slack water for entering. Inside there is a covered rock, awash at LWS, in the middle of the entrance which now has a red beacon on it with Q R (2) 5 s. The leading lights (330°) are 0c 4s.

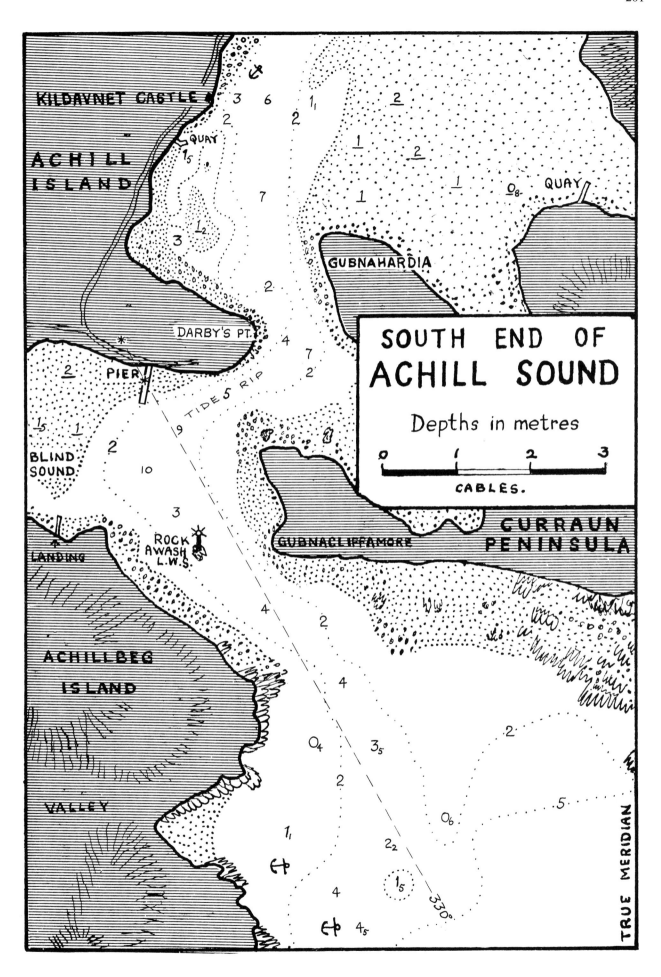

SOUTH END OF
ACHILL SOUND

Depths in metres

0   1   2   3

CABLES.

South End of Achill Sound.

The Tidal Stream

in the entrance runs 3 kn at springs, increasing to 4 or 5 kn in the narrows off Darby Point. Slack water lasts for about ½ hour at the turn of the tide, which occurs ½ hour after HW and LW by the shore. The flood stream sweeping round the S-bend forms eddies in the pool and sets strongly across the shallows NW of Gubnacliffamore, on which it breaks. The ebb sweeps to the S and sets strongly across the rock in the entrance.

Directions

Do not attempt to enter when the flood is running unless under power or with a good SE wind to give plenty of speed; anchor or heave to outside and await the slack. Enter with the pier bearing 330° when you should see two lights in line; there are a number of poles around the pier but the glasses of the lights on two of them can be distinguished. A yacht should not enter in the dark unless she particularly needs to and unless she has a reliable motor and is prepared to tie alongside a fishing boat on the E side of the pier which has strong flood and ebb running under it. The 330° line leads fairly close to the rocky NE point of Achillbeg and

then clear between Gubnacliffamore and the rock beacon; as soon as the latter is passed turn NW or a little further W to avoid being swept onto the shoals to starboard; when the pier is due N head for it if desired or turn sharp starboard and after passing fairly close to Darby Point head ENE towards the other side and when about 75 m from the Gubnahardia shore turn round and head straight for Kildavnet Castle, the square tower. When a shed appears to the right of the castle turn in towards it and anchor in 5 m. Land at stone slip SW of the castle. The tide runs strongly in this anchorage but the channel off the slip where fishing boats are moored is too narrow for visitors. However, Mr. John Kilbane at the PO across the road might advise whether a mooring were vacant for the night. To enter this channel (coming from Darby Point) do not turn in until all 3 chimneys of a cottage on the road are seen N of the castle. (If the central or S chimney is just open S of the castle you hit a rock.) There is also a pool S of this channel where there is room for one small yacht to swing. **Supplies.** None locally. Fishermen's diesel available at the pier. Phone at PO. Shop 2 miles N. Big shop and garage at Achill Bridge over 3 miles away.

Passage to the bridge (chart 2667)

Fishing boats drawing 2·2 m go up to the bridge at neaps, but local knowledge is needed for the narrow channel across the W side of the flats just S of the bridge. A yacht drawing 1·5 m should be able to make the passage at neaps without difficulty. The deepest channel is more or less straight, though it crosses and recrosses the winding sound. First it follows the island shore for 11 cables up from Kildavnet Castle to a church indicated on the chart which is in fact not obvious. Then head towards the E side, Gubrinnanoyster Point; keep the church on the mainland near the bridge just open of this point to pass E of Ship Rock, which dries, and clear of the rocks along the shore. From this point head for Straheen's Point on Achill, thence steer N and give the next points a reasonable berth, but keep 9 m away from the line of posts when approaching the bridge. There is a lot of seaweed on the shallow part between Straheen's Point and Achill Bridge.

Anchorage

When abreast the 3-storey house next to the bridge swing sharply to starboard and enter the small pool opposite the E opening of the bridge. The marks for anchoring are: middle chimney of 3-storey house in line with pole nearest the bridge; on the NE side the church should appear between the second and third poles from the bridge. This gives 3 or 4 m, just N of the sandbank and just S of a strong current which runs W towards the bridge on the ebb. (This pool is not shown on chart 2667.) Moor with two anchors. Landing at steps at the W end of bridge; the steps dry at LW but the ground is firm.
Facilities. All supplies at large store across the road. Petrol and diesel available at two garages at E side of bridge. Bus connects with train at Westport.

ACHILL SOUND BRIDGE

The positions of the channels near the bridge are not quite as shown on the chart. The bridge can be opened on request (it is hand operated) but 10,000 volt cables cross at 13 m and telephone wires at about 11 m above HWS. It can therefore only be used by motor cruisers or the smallest sailing yachts. For these it provides an interesting short cut, and a welcome one in windy weather when the sea can be very rough off Achill Head. The E passage through the bridge must be used, the depth in it being not less than 2 m at HWN. The opening on the island side is obstructed by rocks. There is a very strong tide through the opening with a visible difference of level, the ebb running N and the flood S, changing about 1½ hours after HW and LW at Bull's Mouth, or 2½ hours after Galway. Steer to pass fairly through the middle as there are footings on both sides, covered at HW. Entering from or leaving towards the S the approach to the opening is clear but on the N side a reef extends from the

island side quite close to and right across the direct approach. So going N, as soon as you are outside the bridge turn instantly to starboard towards the concrete beacon (QG) bearing about 002° which, on nearing it, must be left to starboard. Coming from the N approach the bridge opening with this beacon dead astern.

Anchorage North of Bridge

This is normally approached from Bull's Mouth, as described below. The pool for anchoring is W of the beacon. Keep the sixth pole (a short one) from the bridge opening just open of the big store at the Achill end of the bridge and anchor when the beacon comes in line with the end of the slip, or a bit further S. Mooring to two anchors is advised. Land at the quay or the slip near the E end of the bridge; the slip is surrounded by mud at LW. Facilities already listed.

ACHILL SOUND NORTH
(charts 2704 and 2667 and plan)

Bull's Mouth, the entrance to the sound, is ¾ cable wide and being deep, with no dangers in the middle, can be taken in any weather conditions going with the tide. The spring rate in both directions is 5 kn, and in some parts of the channel reaches 8 kn, so do not attempt to go through against the tide. There is no point in going in at night as you cannot go very far in the dark. If anyone particularly wishes to anchor beyond Carrigeenfushta in the dark instructions are given below.

By Day

The approach from seaward is as for Blacksod Bay (see page 207). Pass between ½ mile and 1 mile N of Ridge Point and then head about ESE, but keep Slievemore Point open of Ridge Point until Bull's Mouth entrance is S. Then head 182° towards Inishbiggle Point, which leads between the two deep tide rips, and when 4 cables away from this point, with Dooniver houses abeam, head towards the middle of the entrance, about 190°, and past Dooniver Point keep on 190° till the point just S of Portaghurra harbour is abeam; this avoids Inishbiggle 1 m drying rocks. Then steer to pass between ½ and 1 cable E of Carrigeenfushta beacon, 1¾ cables E of which are dangerous Shejoge Rocks. An anchorage if awaiting half tide, or if not wishing to proceed further, should be between 1 and 2 cables beyond the beacon keeping it just in line with Dooniver Point; just E of this position where it is deeper there are large stones on the bottom. This place has fairly strong tides and is exposed to a fetch of 1 mile or 2, so it is unsuitable in fresh wind.

A yacht drawing 1·5 m can start going up to Achill Bridge at half flood. The new metric chart has not been altered in here since 1850 and 1900 so

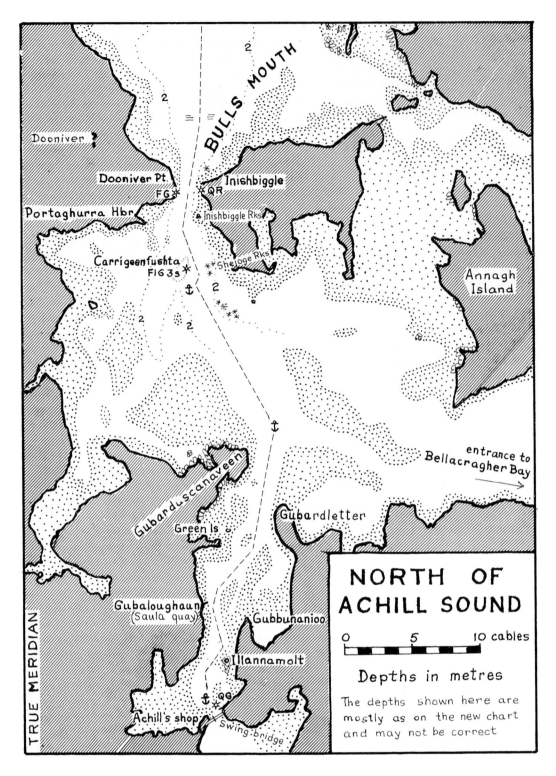

Dooniver

Dooniver Pt.
FG

Portaghurra Hbr

Carrigeenfushta
FIG 3s

BULLS MOUTH

Inishbiggle
QR

Inishbiggle Rks

Sheloge Rks

2

Annagh
Island

entrance to
Bellacragher Bay

Gubarduscanaveen

Green Is

Gubardletter

Gubaloughaun
(Saula quay)

Gubbunanioo

Illannamolt

Achill's shop

QG

Swing bridge

TRUE MERIDIAN

NORTH OF ACHILL SOUND

0   5   10 cables

Depths in metres

The depths shown here are
mostly as on the new chart
and may not be correct

several places may be different; the deep part W of Illannamolt is now where the chart shows it drying. Start going in by keeping Carrigeenfushta's beacon bearing 330° till the W side of Gubarnletter is just S, and when Doohooma Point (about 2 miles N of Ridge Point) shows in the middle of Bull's Mouth. This is a better place to anchor than near Carrigeenfushta. If going on to Achill Bridge turn round at this point and steer about 191° keeping two buildings just E of the Achill Bridge just open to the W of Gubbunanioo Point. When the small point about 1 cable SW of Green Island comes

abeam turn about 225° towards the Saula Quay, called Gubaloughaun, and when astern the E of Green Island is in line with Gubardascanaveen Point turn left to keep them in line until the inner end of Saula Quay is abeam, then head towards Illannamolt (grass-topped) until it is 1 cable away and then head about 215° until the point immediately SE of the E of the bridge is visible (about 155°), then steer towards the bridge opening (about 165°) until the anchorage is about SW. The anchorage has already been described.

North of Achill Sound with the Swing Bridge on the Right.

By Night

Keep near to Black Rock's W and R parts of the light until Ridge Point light, Fl 5s, is abeam, then head 120° till you see Inishbiggle Point QR, Carrigeenfushta Fl G 3s, and Dooniver Point FY. If these lights can be seen it is safe to enter the Bull's Mouth with Carrigeenfushta halfway between the other two or if anything slightly nearer Inishbiggle. In the narrows alter course to 190° until on the line between Dooniver and Carrigeenfushta lights, then steer to leave the latter ½ cable to starboard and anchor until daylight 1 cable or 2 beyond it with Dooniver FY in line with it. There is a light Fl G 3 s on the end of Saulia Pier.

Bellacragher Bay

can be seen on chart 2667. There is a long inlet to it extending about 4 miles of the entrance to Achill Bridge with some narrow entrances, fairly shallow in parts, until it runs S to Bellacragher Bay which ends ½ mile of Mallaranny at Clew Bay. There are now power lines only 10 m above HW at the first narrow entrance so it is not suitable for a normal yacht. It would be a splendid place to explore in a dinghy, but Bellacragher Bay might be full of salmon cages. The scenery is magnificent.

COAST OF ACHILL ISLAND

Between Achillbeg and Clare Island there is often rather a rough choppy sea with the ebb. Between Achillbeg and Achill Head 13 miles NW all dangers are above water except for the drying ledges ½ mile off Ashleam Point, and a breaking 10 m patch 1½ miles W of Dooega Head. Dysaghy Rocks, 1 mile SSE from Keem Bay are awash at HW so care must be taken to avoid them, especially in poor visibility; they are not far inside the direct course from Achillbeg to Achill Head.

The Bills

5½ miles S by W of Keem Bay, are steep-to and 38 m high; they are on the line from Inishbofin to Achill Head. The white sector of Achillbeg Light leads between these dangers; it is obscured over the Dysaghy Rocks and the Bills are in the red sector.

Gubalennaun Beg (Purteen)

a small artificial harbour N of Inishgalloon with light QR, is the centre for basking shark fishing. A further light has been established in position 53°57'.80N 10°05'.90W - 2 Oc 8s. The outer part, subject to swell, has about 1·3 m at LWS along the W quay. The entrance is sometimes obstructed by nets and their mooring wires. Keel village, 1 mile away, has shops and petrol. A member reports that he dried out alongside on the S side of the E extension of the harbour about in 0·6m LWS. It is possible to anchor to the E of Inishgalloon, but not to the N where it is rocky with a strong tide.

206

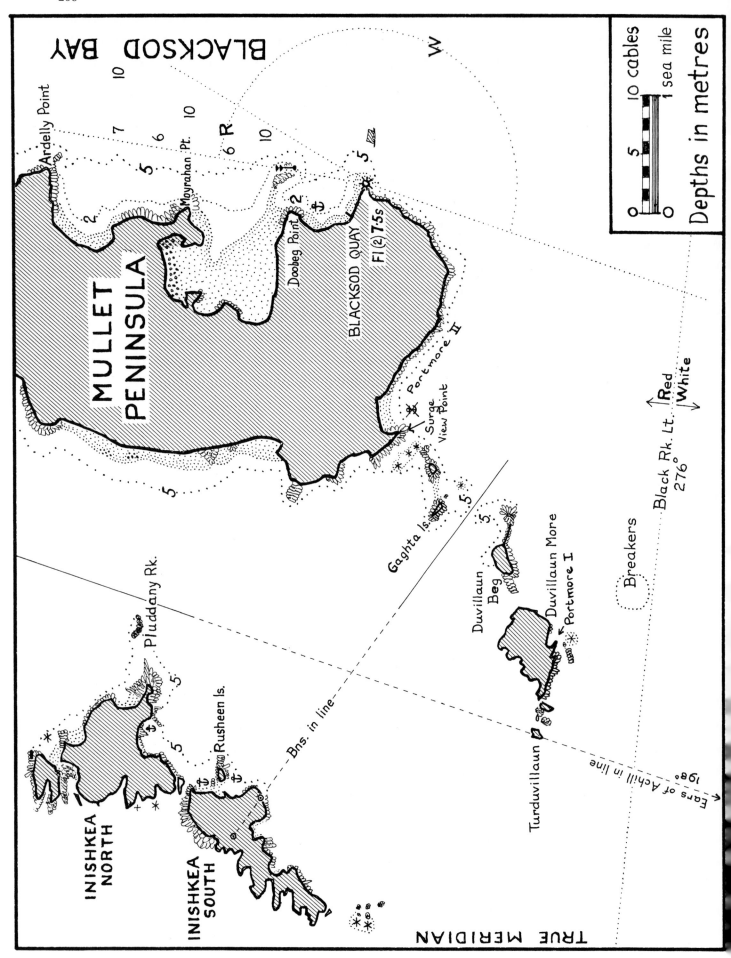

Keem Bay

in moderate W wind is a pleasant anchorage but in fresh NW wind big gusts come down from the hill and can cause the anchor to drag. The sand beach slopes gently and even in calm weather it is hard to land without getting wet. There is a spring of good water but no facilities for using it. Basking sharks are often killed of the S point of the bay.

Achill Head

is a most spectacular promontory, the cliffs on its N side being the highest in Ireland. The views enjoyed rounding it amply compensate for the rough sea to which a yacht is subjected in any but the lightest wind. The rock 2·9 m deep ENE of Carrickakin is a very bad breaker except in calm sea. Normally pass about 2 cables W of Carrickakin, but with calm sea it is pleasant to go either fairly close to the NE end of Carrickakin, or not more than ½ cable W of the Priest Rocks above the water close W of Achill Head. Keep not less than 2 cables S of Achill Head to avoid the rocks there, one of which shows below ½ tide.

Black Rock — Light — Danger

Black Rock, 82 m high is 6 miles NNW of Achill Head and has a lighthouse 15 m high showing Fl WR 12s, 16-22 M, R from 212° to 276° over the Mullet Peninsula and the islands off it, W elsewhere. There are small rocks above and below water close and up to 1¼ miles W and SW of Black Rock, other rocks close S of it and a clean 12 m

high rock ½ cable E of it. It is therefore wise to pass E of it at night or day. If in very calm weather you wish to climb up Black Rock it is possible to anchor close N of it in 20 m but there is always some swell so it is necessary to be able to pull the dinghy up the rocks immediately after landing on them. There are no lighthouse keepers now.

Valley Pier

E of Ridge Point (where there is now a light Fl 5s) is in ruins and is some distance, across a bog, from the road. There is however anchorage off it in 4 m sheltered from W and SW. It is the best place to anchor if awaiting the flood through the Bull's Mouth.

BLACKSOD BAY (chart 2704) *(see plan)*

is described in the Pilot as one of the finest bays on the W coast of Ireland. Though it has no yacht anchorage which is snugly sheltered from every wind it is a good place to make for in bad weather with safe anchorages from specific arcs which are easily accessible. There are no hidden dangers in the approach except that 1 mile SE of Duvillaun More there are breakers in W gales. In fresh S winds there are bad squalls off the Achill Hills. It is possible to enter by night. The bay is free of dangers except around the shores where many of the points are foul and the bays between them shoal; the only unmarked isolated danger is the rock which dries, 3½ cables SSE of Ardmore Point at the head of the bay.

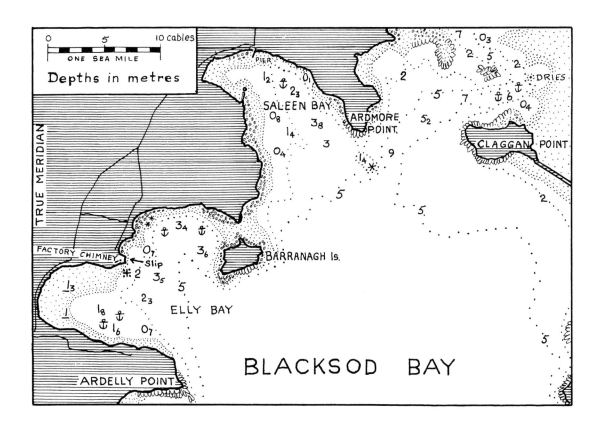

Elly Bay and Blacksod Bay from W.

From the North

a yacht coming inside the Inishkeas may take a short cut in swell-free, quiet conditions by passing halfway between Duvillaun Beg and Gaghta Island in 7 m with the beacons on Inishkea South in line; the rear beacon is on the skyline but the front beacon near the shore is not easily seen in certain conditions of light. There is a good anchorage on the S side of Davillaunmore known as Portmore I with about 4m with good holding. Landing difficult, exposed to E. Not marked on chart 2704 but on plan. Portmore II is just E of Surge View Point on the South end of Mullet, reported poor holding exposed to S. The tide sets across the points of the bay at 2 knots, starting 2 hours after HW Galway. Reported to be uncomfortable.

Light — Buoy

There is a light on Blacksod Point, Fl (2) WR 7 5s, 9 M. It first comes in sight bearing 018°, W thence to 210°, thence R to 189°, then obscured again, also 2FR 6m 3M on quay. There is an unlit red can buoy 3¹/₂ cables E of the quay.

By night

approach keeping near the edge of the white sector of Black Rock until Blacksod light appears. Then head about 030° into the mouth of the bay. It is better not to try to reach an inshore anchorage in the dark. When sure of being N of Carrigeenmore perch (³/₄ mile N of the light), head NW and anchor in the red sector in 7 m until daylight.

Anchorages

1. In the bay NW of Blacksod quay, about half-way between the quay and Doonbeg Point, outside or N of the local boats in 3 m sand. This is rather distant from the quay, but anywhere within 2 cables of the quay is only 1·4 to 1·8 m deep with poor holding, gravel and rocky patches. The quay dries and is foul alongside except between the two steps where a yacht may dry out if sufficient water for her. Vincent Sweeney, who attends the light, can give good advice. PO. Petrol, diesel and some food available 1¹/₂ miles away, possible to be driven. Mike Lavelle, garage owner in Aghlean, services engines of all types.

Saleen Bay and Blacksod from W.

2. Elly Bay is the most sheltered anchorage for small boats and is all right for most yachts as the LAT depths are 1·6 to 1·8 m. The SE half of the entrance is shallow so head in away from Ardelly Point towards the factory chimney and when halfway in head SW towards the moored boats and anchor outside them. There is now an activity centre in the old factory with showers and general support. Cafe, pub, slip with water. Garage and shop at Drum House 1¹/₂M. Tourist Office 097-82292. Bus to Ballina and connections onward. Visitors moorings in 1993. Good area for exploring on shore with heritage sites. Transport to Belmullet 10M can sometimes be arranged. Restaurant 4M. Repairs if required can be organised through Tourist office. Gold course 5M. There is a rock which dries at LW about 1 cable of slip and is not marked on chart.

3. Elly Harbour is more liable to swell than Elly Bay but is calmer in N to E winds and there is plenty of space for anchoring in 3 or 4 m, but keep 3 cables away from the W side and not too near the E either.

4. Saleen Bay may also have swell but it should be reasonable to anchor except in S to SE winds. It is the easiest place to land except near low tide and seems the best place for going shopping as the main road is just beside the quay so it should be easy to get a lift to Belmullet about 3 miles away.

5. North of Claggan Point is thought to be the best all round shelter in a gale, but no members are known to have anchored there. It appears safest to enter near LW so as to see the large drying rocks. Before entering the dangerous rock 30 c S by E of Ardmore Point must be avoided, then head in reasonably close to Claggan Point and when turning in to anchor N of it keep Barranagh Island a bit open of Claggan.

Belmullet

2¹/₂ miles N of Claggan Point, is a good town for supplies having butchers, garages, a hotel, a bank and bus service. It should be possible to get to it by car from Saleen quay or Blacksod quay and perhaps also from Frenchport or Broadhaven pier. EC is on Wed. or occasionally on Tue. **The Quay** at the Blacksod side of the town dries and at HWN might have 2 m in strong SW wind or only 1·3 m in N

wind. A yacht should not try to go there. It is reported that the canal to Broadhaven has 1·5m of water at half tide and about 2·5m clearance below the bridge at the same time. 400m long and 20m wide. VHF Ch. 16 and 83 to local HM.

Tullaghan Bay (chart 2704)

is mostly shallow and drying and is entered between Blacksod Bay and Bull's Mouth. The bars in the entrance are now shown 1·1 m, a bit shallower than on the previous chart. There is a strong tide in the entrance channel. The anchorage is a narrow channel just N inside between the E shore and a sandbank.

Directions

Assuming absence of swell it is best to enter at LW or soon after, if rise and draught permit, as the sandbanks will then be showing. There are two concrete beacons, the outer beacon near the end of a long rocky spit off the point 1¹/₂ miles E of Kinrovar Head and the other on a rock in the entrance channel; both must be left to port entering. Pass ¹/₂ cable SE of the first beacon, steer towards the second beacon and then leave it 20 m to port. Then steer 050° to give the point with a house on it a slight berth for there are rocky spits to the SW of it though the point itself is steep-to; when past it turn N.

Anchorage

The channel, ¹/₂ cable wide for anchoring at LW, runs 3 cables N of the point (and a further 2 cables NE). The deepest part (over 3 m) is close to the sandbank. It is best to anchor N of the local boats and just W of the deepest part, preferably with two anchors, N and S, to avoid the possibility of going aground at the start of the flood. The handiest place to land is just N of the house at the point. There is no slip.

Facilities

There is a shop and pub more than 1 mile away at Doohooma. The first house on the right of the road starting to Doohooma belongs to Mr Munnelly who can advise about the anchorage and has a coin-box phone.

Frenchport (Portnafrankagh) with Eagle Island in the background.

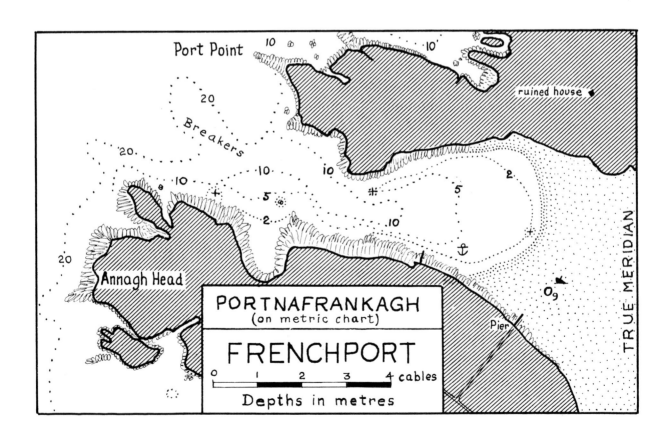

Islands off Mullet Peninsula (chart 2704)
There is a clear channel, partly sheltered from swell, inside the now uninhabited islands. It should not be used at night. Pluddany Rocks extend 6 cables E from the SE point of Inishkea North, beyond the 22 m sandhill; these rocks cover at half tide and should be avoided by keeping Turduvillaun 198° below the Ears of Achill (see chart). Indeed going N it is useful to keep this transit astern until the small N islands are sorted out. Duffur Rock with vertical cliffs is more prominent from a distance than the two rocks inshore of it. Inishkeeragh slopes gently to the sea. Inishglora has ruined cottages on its E end. Heading N, before Inishkeeragh comes abeam bring Leacarrick just open of Inishglora and then steer to pass close E of Leacarrick as the Mullet side is foul 5 cables offshore. In bad W weather the sea breaks right over Leacarrick and the passage E of it may be covered with foam. (continuing N see below).

INISHKEA ISLANDS (chart 2704).
It is fascinating to visit these deserted island on a fine summer day but overnight anchorage cannot be recommended unless the weather is very settled.

Anchorages (see plan)
1. The bay N of Rusheen Island between it and the N end of South Inishkea is the best anchorage. It is sheltered from all but winds with E in them but is subject to swell, a good deal of which can roll in through the narrow sound between the Inishkeas, so anchor as far clear of this as possible. There is a slip for landing.
2. Fishing boats also anchor at times SW of Rusheen Island off the old village quay which dries alongside but is still in good repair.
3. There is temporary anchorage, better sheltered in NE wind, off North Inishkea SW of the 22 m sandhill between the outer ends of two reefs which extend 1½ cables SW from the shore; the little bay thus formed has more reefs at its head.

Mullet Peninsula to Erris Head (chart 2703)
From Leacarrick steer for Annagh Head on which there is a hut; if beating keep clear of Edye Rock with 2·6 m on it. In fine weather you may pass inside Cross Rock, but there is always a bad sea in this channel and if at all rough it is better to go outside Eagle Island (see below for light). Do not pass close to Carrickhesk. Give Erris Head a berth of ½ mile. Heading S from Frenchport, if unable to identify Leacarrick, steer for Slievemore on Achill, which leads to the sound.

FRENCHPORT
This inlet, immediately N of Annagh Head, is a favourite port of call for yachts sailing round Ireland as it involves no deviation from the direct route. It provides safe shelter but often in discomfort due to the roll coming from the direction of the entrance irrespective of the wind direction. There is a rock awash at HW 1 cable off the S side just outside the entrance where there is an inlet. There is a dangerous covered rock ½ a cable off the N side just inside. There may be lobster pots in the entrance and the approaches. There is no light.

Directions
Only go in or out in daylight. In fair weather going in or out it is only necessary to avoid the rocks. In bad onshore wind it is necessary to avoid breakers outside the entrance in the middle and the S. It is necessary to pass reasonably close to Port Point and the point S of it. Coming from the S head N from Annagh Head until Port Point is E, then turn towards it and 2 cables away from its HW edge turn SE, keep more than ½ cable off the point a bit more than 1 cable S of Port Point, then head through the middle of the inner entrance. It is much more risky to have to go out this way against onshore wind, NW wind being the worst as its too narrow for tacking; if the engine is not reliable and not driving the yacht well it would be wise to turn back. In SW wind it might be possible to sail out successfully.

The best anchorage is on the S side close inshore in southerly winds to get sufficient shelter, either just short of moored boats in about 5 m or N of the boats in less depth; there is lots of room. The new pier on the S shore has a small slip on its SE side; a dinghy can go there at LWN but it is dry at LWS. No facilities. Nearest shop at Belmullet, 4 miles away, see page 209. John Lavelle may possibly be able to provide a taxi, is still working there and might still help. His house is close to the left after walking up from the slip. If you have reason to get to the telephone, pub or shop at Corclogh, it is much better to land on the Cats Tail, a shingle reef at the head of the bay, and walk past the graveyard, than to land at the pier.

Scotchport
just S of its named rock on the new chart, is a clean narrow inlet with rocky sides and a steep beach at its head where curraghs may still be pulled up. It's a pleasant place to visit in quiet weather but not suitable for a yacht to spend a night.

Eagle Island Light — Radiobeacon
The light, elevation 67 m from a 11 m white tower, shows Fl (3)10 s, 19 M. The Main Light will be exhibited during periods of poor visibility. Radiobeacon, see Appendix 6.

212

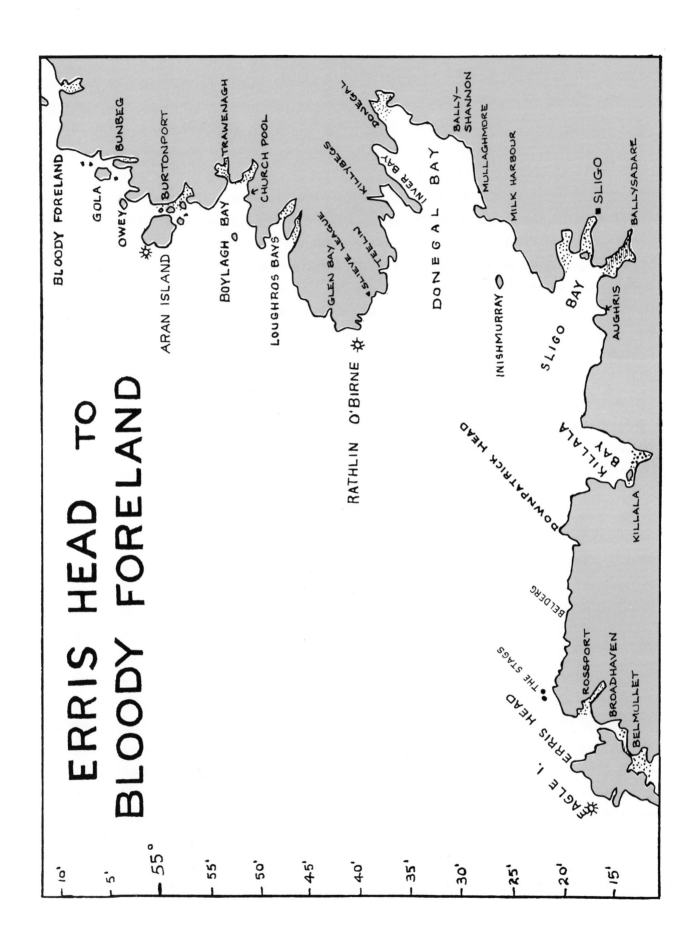

ERRIS HEAD TO BLOODY FORELAND

BLOODY FORELAND
GOLA
OWEY
BUNBEG
BURTONPORT
ARAN ISLAND
STRAWENAGH
BOYLAGH BAY
CHURCH POOL
LOUGHROS BAYS
KILLYBEGS
GLEN BAY
SLIEVE LEAGUE
TEELIN
INVER BAY
DONEGAL
DONEGAL BAY
BALLY-SHANNON
MULLAGHMORE
MILK HARBOUR
SLIGO
BALLYSADARE
INISHMURRAY
SLIGO BAY
AUGHRIS
RATHLIN O'BIRNE
DOWNPATRICK HEAD
KILLALA BAY
KILLALA
BELDERG
ROSSPORT
BROADHAVEN
THE STAGS
ERRIS HEAD
BELMULLET
EAGLE I.

10'
5'
55°
55'
50'
45'
40'
35'
30'
25'
20'
15'

Chapter 8

ERRIS HEAD TO
BLOODY FORELAND

Charts *(for details see Appendix 1)*
The new small-scale chart 2725 from Blacksod Bay to Tory Island is essential for sailing from Erris Head to the W of Donegal. The medium scale charts 2703, 2767, 2702 and 1879 and the larger scale 1883 deal with the whole coast in this chapter and are essential except that 2702 need not be taken if you are sure you will not go to the shore E of Rathlin O'Birne or to Donegal Bay. Chart 2792 with large scales of Aran Sound, Killybegs, Teelin and Church Pool is rather desirable. Chart 2715 is desirable but not essential for entering Killala and Donegal Harbours. Chart 2852 is essential for Sligo but it is possible to go just to Rosses Point without it.

Tides *(for details see Appendices 2 & 3)*
On this part of the coast the time of HW is between 35 and 70 minutes after Galway (or between 4 hrs 40 and 5 hrs 40 before Dover). Spring tides rise between 3·7 and 4 m and neaps rise between 2·7 and 3 m above LAT.

Tidal Streams
Between Erris Head and Rathlin O'Birne the tidal set is negligible except when close to the land at either end. From Rathlin O'Birne to Bloody Foreland the tide outside the islands turns S at about 3 hours before and N at 3 hours after Dover, rate 0·8 to 1 kn. Inshore it turns 1 to 2 hours earlier and so is in effect running S during the ebb by the shore and N during the flood. Near salient points the rate reaches 1½ to 2 kn springs. The stream in Tory Sound changes at about the same times so a fair tide can be carried round the Bloody Foreland in either direction.

BROAD HAVEN (chart 2703) *(see plan)*
Broad Haven is the large inlet, some 5 miles long and up to 1 mile wide in parts, which leads from the head of Broad Haven Bay to Belmullet. It is the best overnight anchorage for a yacht crossing to or from Co. Donegal. It is also a safe harbour of refuge in most summer gales, but a bad NW or N gale can cause the entrance to break right across. The approach across Broad Haven Bay is clear of all danger except for Slugga Rock, 1 m high, on the E side, with a drying rock 1 cable NW of it, 0·3 m high at LAT, and Monastery Rock on the S side, also 0·3 m high at LAT. The first 1½ miles of the inlet is clean except near the shores but further in

the navigable channel lies between extensive shallows. There is no attraction in visiting Belmullet at HW; the canal to Blacksod Bay is open for boats of shallow draft. See page 207. The tide flows at up to 1½ kn past the anchorages.

Lights
From a 15 m tower on Gubacashel Point Iso 4s, WR 12, 9 M, W from outside and to 355° inside the inlet. R from 355° to the W shore inside. From a beacon on a rock ½ cable SE of Gubaknockan Point Fl G 3s.

Anchorages
1. In 3·5 m about 2 cables N of Gubaknockan Point with Gubacashel Point just in line with the W side of Kid Island, or perhaps just a little further in. This is the most convenient anchorage, out of the main stream, good shelter in winds from SW to NW and it can be found in the dark.

2. Just beyond Gubaknockan Point there is the modern Ballyglass Pier so for landing it is handy to anchor not far beyond the pier in 3 m with its outer end bearing 035°, however this is sometimes subject to swell. Pass outside the beacon on the rock which has a Fl G 3 s. There is a cable 2 m high between the beacon and the shore. It is somewhat more exposed to SW wind than in anchorage 1, but should be calmer in N wind. The pier has many tyres as fenders, however if there is a trawler alongside it is handy to tie up to it having found out how long it will be there. The depth alongside the pier is not less than 2 m. Water. The PO is just up the road from the pier. Lifeboat. Belmullet town is 6 miles away. If necessary it is possible to get a taxi by phone at pier. Fuel by tanker if quantities are sufficient.

3. In strong E wind the best shelter is in 3·7 m not far off the shore about 1 cable S of Inver Point. But if you want to go ashore anchor a bit further S in 3 m about 2 cables off the inside of Inver Hamlet Bay, which is shallow further in. There is a very small shop there; 3 miles S at Barnatra crossroads there is a slightly larger shop with a phone.

Broad Haven Bay Anchorage
In reasonable weather or with wind N of W there is a convenient anchorage on the NE side of the bay NE of Rinroe Point. If going round this point keep 1½ cables away from it, then head up to the E of the new pier and anchor E of it in 3 or 4 m. This is also a suitable place to anchor if waiting for the tide to rise on the bar to Ross Port. If going ashore it is best to land on the slip just N of the pier and pull the dinghy up. The pier is 25 m long and near the outer end it is 1 m deep at MLWS, but a further extension of 13 m is going to be made and then it may be suitable for a small yacht to lie alongside. There is a small shop, PO and phone in Carrowteige a bit more than 1 mile NE up the hill.

Broadhaven from N/W.

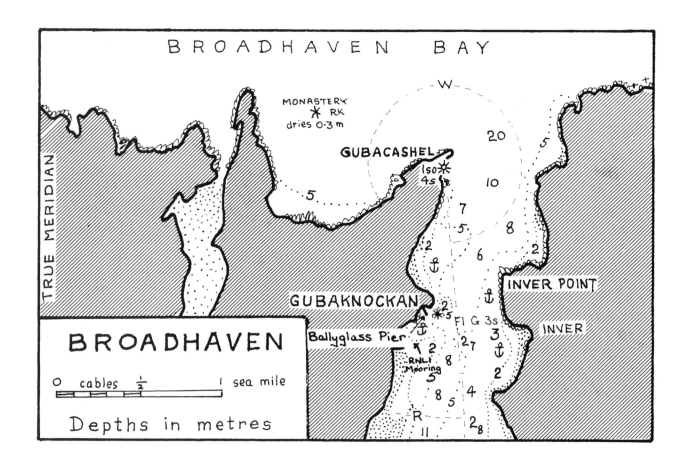

BROADHAVEN BAY

TRUE MERIDIAN

MONASTERY
✳ RK
dries 0·3 m

W

20

GUBACASHEL

Iso
4s

5

10

5

7

5.

8

2

6

2

⚓

INVER POINT

GUBAKNOCKAN

2

⚓

⚓

2.5

Fl G 3s

Ballyglass Pier

⚓

2.7

3

INVER

⚓

2

RNLI
Mooring

2

8

5

2

8

5

4

R

2

11

8

BROADHAVEN

0   cables   ½   1 sea mile

Depths in metres

Channel from the West into Ross Port.

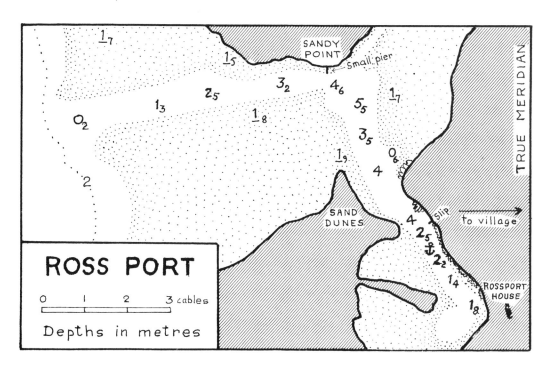

SANDY POINT

Small pier

1_7

1_5

3_2

4_6

5_5

1_7

2_5

1_3

1_8

3_5

O_2

0_6

1_9

4

2

SAND DUNES

Slip

to village

4

4

2_5

2_2

1_4

ROSSPORT HOUSE

1_8

TRUE MERIDIAN

ROSS PORT

0   1   2   3 cables

Depths in metres

ROSS PORT *(see plan)*

The narrow creek inside the sand hills offers anchorage in completely sheltered water, but it has rather strong tides. The outer entrance across a rather shallow bar is exposed to ocean swell. A reasonable calm sea and the prospect of its continuance until the yacht departs are necessary for a successful visit. It definitely can only be entered and left in daylight. A yacht 1·6 m deep might go in at ½ tide and one 1·8 m might go in ½ hour later.

Directions

The bar at the entrance is not very wide so to go in keep in line two white leading marks which are on the ground N of Ross Port houses. As soon as it gets a little deeper turn slightly port and head towards the Sandy Point, about 078°. When off the N shore keep about 25 m from it. Except near HW the small track leading down to the pier just W of Sandy Point can be seen. When this point is abeam turn round and head about 147° towards the middle of the narrows between the shore and some knobbly sandhills. Beyond the narrows and past the slip keep the same distance from the shore to port.

Anchorage

It was best to anchor not far S of the slip but this is probably impossible now because of the local fishing boat's mooring. The best depth extends 1 cable beyond the slip but if necessary most yachts could anchor within another ½ cable where it is 1·4 m at LAT. Beyond that it is a bit deeper but long drying sand banks lead E from the point so the place to anchor is somewhat narrow; it would be best to have two anchors NW and SE. Better not go as far as opposite the old Ross Port House. Further in it becomes shallower and there is an overhead HT cable.

Facilities

About ¼ mile up the road there is a small shop, PO and phone. Ross Port is a most remote place with a vast area of bog E of it.

The Stags of Broad Haven

is a superb group of four steep-to rocky islets all over 70 m, the highest 92 m, with deep water all round, but keep 1 cable away from them. There is a clear passage 1 mile wide between them and the curiously-shaped rocks under the cliffs inshore; yet in strong onshore weather it would be better to sail right outside.

Coast

The 24 miles stretch from Broad Haven Bay to Killala is most inhospitable and should be given a good berth; there is no safe anchorage, no shelter from the usual swell and fierce gusts off the cliffs.

The coast is very sparsely inhabited and there is little attraction in attempting a landing. In really quiet weather, however, or in a S breeze the cliffs, 150 m high in many places, with numerous lofty offlying pinnacles, are an unforgettable spectacle and there are five coves or bays, each with a small slip on its W side, where landing might be effected. Portacloy and Belderg are the best of these and a yacht with an engine might find either a useful **Passage Anchorage,** e.g. Yachts bound SW from Donegal and unable to fetch Broad Haven might find Belderg a good alternative to Kilcummin - it is better sheltered in S winds and should the wind veer NW the latter is at hand to run for shelter.

Portacloy (chart 2703)

Best identified by being close E of the Buddagh, 78 m high, a straight-sided tower-like column of rock which presents a steeply sloping grass top to the N; and from close in, by a small lookout hut on the head at its W side. The inlet is about 1½ cables wide and clean rock shores and a beach at its head; sand bottom, good holding. Fishing boats often use it as a base for a week or two in the summer and ride out NW blows, but it is extremely uneasy in these conditions, and only recommended in moderate winds with S in them. Fresh S winds funnel down the inlet with great violence. Some curraghs and small lobster boats work out here. There is a pier beside the slip with 0·4 m near the outer end.

Porturlin (charts 2703 and 2767)

is 2½ miles E of Portacloy. Pig Island ½ mile W of the entrance has a cave right through and appears as part of the mainland though only about half as high. Glassilaun is capped with grass and from NE appears as part of the shore of the W entrance until you are very close. Carrickduff off the NE of the entrance is a bare rock. The sky-line behind the port is low and the white houses show up well when you are abreast. Chart 2703 shows the rock S of Glassilaun which covers near HW, so keep nearer the SE side of the bay which is all quite clean. There are a number of open boats moored in Porturlin. The holding is reported poor.

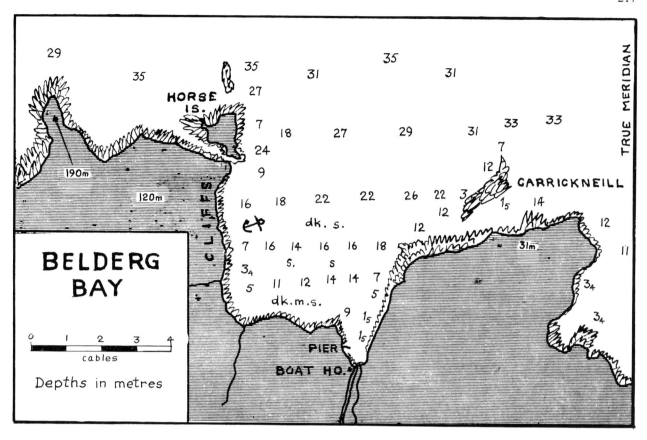

Belderg (chart 2767) *(see plan)*
is just E of the last of the high cliffs all the way from
Broad Haven. E of Belderg it is comparatively low
though still impressive, 30 m cliffs backed by gentle
grass slopes which run E to Killala. Illanmaster,
103 m high with immense domed grassy top, is a
good mark 3 miles W of it. Horse Island, the W of
the entrance, is comparatively low with 15 m cliffs
on its W side and grassy slopes on its E. Carrickneill
E of the entrance covers at HW except for one or
two small tops. The disused boathouse shows up
well from due N but is obscured from NE and NW;
the rocky gut on which it stands is too narrow for
anchoring, but has a breakwater and a slip for
dinghy landing. Anchor in less than 10 m off the
inner half of the W shore of the bay, good holding
on sand.

Bunatrahir Bay (chart 2767)
has less formidable surroundings but the bottom is
rock. Ballycastle village, 1¹/₂ miles from the slip,
offers petrol, shops and 'phone, but the poor
holding and ground swell make this bay potentially
very dangerous.

Lackan Bay (chart 2767, also on large scale 2715)
is so near Kilcummin and so more exposed that
probably no yacht has ever anchored there. But if
by any chance there was no swell it might be a
better place than Kilcummin in S or SE wind. The
SE corner in 4 m would then be the best but
another possible anchorage is off the pier on the W
side in 5 m, presumably sandy bottom everywhere.

Killala from SW.

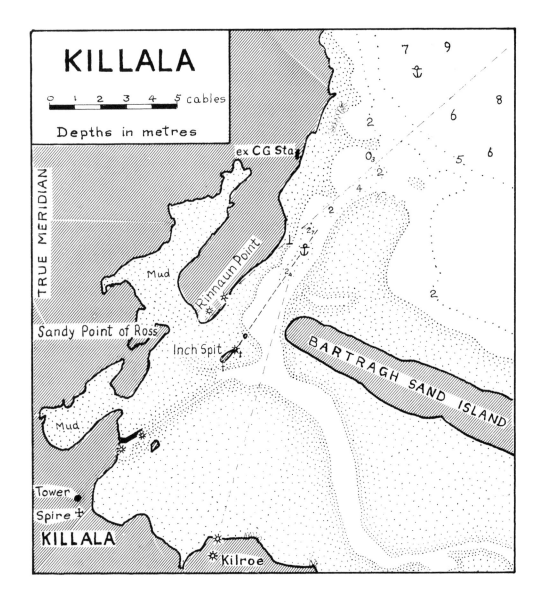

KILLALA BAY

(with chart 2767 and our plan it is possible to enter Killala Pier. Chart 2715 is necessary for other places in Killala Bay, Kilcummin, Ballina, Inishcrone and Pollacheeny.)

Warning

A yacht should not go into the bay in the dark. There are no lights on either corner and Lenadoon Point on the E has dangers ³/₄ mile outside. The Inishcrone light range is stated to be 2 miles so it might not be visible at all 4¹/₂ miles away where, coming from the W, the outer St Patrick Rock might be hit. The lights for entering Killala Harbour are only of use when you have gone well inside the bay when it is still daylight. For instance Rinnaun Point lights in line if seen as far out as Lenadoon Point would be leading over the rocks there. **St Patrick Rocks.** Kilcummin and Creevagh Heads in line, 308°, lead NE of the rocks. Killala's round tower bearing 221° just open SE of Ross Sandhills leads SE of the rocks.

There is a light on the beacon at Bone Rock with characteristics N. Card Q Position 54°15'. 80N 9°11'. 20W.

Kilcummin Roads

(Landing place of the French in 1798)

This passage anchorage, conveniently situated on the W of Killala Bay 1 mile within Kilcummin Head, gives a surprising amount of shelter in winds between N and SW but is completely open to onshore winds and somewhat exposed to S winds. Small fishing craft lie on moorings there all summer. Approaching from the NE the position may be identified by a large square slab of concrete on the cliff 1 cable S of the pier. Unfortunately the approach is very heavily netted for salmon (which goes on from May to 25 July) which is yet another reason for not coming in when it is getting dark; it is sometimes very difficult to avoid the nets and of course a look-out from the pulpit and motoring slowly are essential. The best berth is with a two-storey house (red door) bearing 285° and as far in as draught permits. Small pub. House beside the pier has a phone. The pier gives a little shelter from E but open to S. 0·6m at LAT.

KILLALA (Chart 2715) *(see plan)*

in the SW corner of the bay, can be recognised by its Cathedral spire and Round Tower. In front of the town is a large inlet which mostly dries and is sheltered by Bartragh sandhills. The approach is across a bar with 0·3 m. Within, a natural channel leads to a dredged channel up to the pier near the town. Due to its position the bar is reasonably sheltered but it should not be attempted with fresh NE wind. It is a safe but not ideal harbour for yachts.

Directions

Enter with the flood or not too long after HW. Most yachts should not go in before half flood when the reported depth on the bar is 2·4 m; an hour earlier it should be 1·5 m, unsuitable for keel yachts. There is no Carrickpatrick perch now; but a buoy named Carrickpatrick Q(3) 10 s is in a position approx. 9 cables NW of the rock. Also Killala buoy 4·5 cables from the rock (Fl G 6 s) has been moved out from where it was, so leave it to starboard. Then identify the white beacons on Rinnaun Point and head in with the after higher beacon left of the front one with the width of a beacon open between them. When the Inch Island beacons come in line turn 215° towards them.

Lights

Rinnaun Point, Oc 10s. Only the near beacon on Inch Split shows FlRWG2s; it shows 4°W in line with the front beacon and 8°G to starboard and 8°R to port. Kilroe, Oc 4 s. Pier, Iso 2 s.

Anchorage

The only suitable anchorage is very soon after turning 215°. There is plenty of space with 2 m to 2·7 m but do not anchor near any mooring. Shelter is good at LW and not too bad at HW except with E or NE winds. It is 1 mile by dinghy to the pier near the town.

Harbour

From the anchorage near the Inch Island line it is again wrong to follow the next leading beacons as the Inch Spit has extended a bit E and the directions are as follows. Head in with the perch near the shore in line astern with the end of the old coastguard station on the cliff until a little E of the line of the Kilroe Beacons and head towards them with a gap the width of a beacon between them, the front one to the right. Carry on until the second perch of the straight line of perches on the NW side of the channel leading to the pier is in line between the two little hills SSW of Sandy Point of Ross and then turn round and go straight for that second perch until close to it when you turn up the channel. Note that the tide is flooding E there and you might soon be aground if you delayed turning W towards the perch as instructed. The straight channel is only 15 m wide and nearer half tide than HW the banks show on both sides. There are two red beacons to keep in line, the front one on the end of the pier. The width alongside the pier is 45 m. Moor alongside or outside a fishing boat. Most yachts would remain afloat except at LWS when the depth may be 1·4 m or less. There is a good deal of traffic on the pier so it is better not to leave the yacht unattended. The tide runs in past the pier and through the gap between the mudbank and the old pier; the ebb sets onto the new pier near the SW end.

Facilities

Water taps on the quay. It is less than ¹/₂ mile to walk into the small town of Killala with shops and a garage, EC Thurs.

River Moy — Ballina

The bar is dangerous due to its exposed position and shifting sandbanks and is not recommended. It would be essential to engage a pilot (at Inishcrone) to ascend the river to Ballina quay, 5 miles up, which is still over 1 mile short of Ballina. This prosperous town is therefore rather inaccessible to yachtsmen.

Inishcrone

This village is a seaside resort and is fairly conspicuous on the SE corner of Killala Bay. The breakwater runs out 280° and its S side is a quay 130 m long but a yacht can only go alongside at or above ¹/₂ tide when the depth near the outer end just beyond the steps is 2 m. There is also a slip. Two concrete pillars in line mark the S end of the channel to the slip. The quay is subject to swell after N to W winds. The place might be useful for a yacht to get petrol in calm weather.

The E coast of Killala Bay

is bordered by layers of flat rocks and you should keep at least 3 cables away for 3 miles N of Inishcrone and at least ³/₄ miles away for 2 further miles past Lenadoon Point. Pollacheeny "Harbour" is shown on chart 2715 and does not look much use for yachts being just a gap between large flat rocks. If anyone wishes to try anchoring there in E wind the slip must first be identified from at least 3 cables out and then approached between 085° and 090° to avoid rocks on either side. Anchor about 1¹/₂ cables from the shore or outside local boats if they are moored there.

Coast

From Lenadoon Point to Aughris Head 11 miles further E the coast is fringed by rocky ledges and should be given a berth of at least ¹/₂ mile. Pollnadivva Pier harbour in Dromore Bay is not recommended even in calm weather; it dries and has a rocky bottom and there are no facilities ashore. Aughris Head ends in a slightly overhanging cliff; rocks awash at HW extend 1¹/₂ cables seaward from it.

A member (Walace Clark) has reported anchoring in Coanmore. It lies 1M E of conspicuous tower at the mouth of the Easker River inside the Temple Rock. In 2m it provides a temporary anchorage from winds from SW through S to SE. Mr. Michael Munnelly keeps a boat in the bay there at a private slip, and he is very helpful. Easker village is about 1M away with limited supplies. Further information required.

SLIGO BAY (chart 2852)

The entrance is 4 miles wide between Aughris Head on the SW and Seal Rocks, 1 m high, on the NE. Midway between these points is The Ledge, 8 m deep, which breaks with a high swell when it is simplest to pass S of it. Within the points of the bay are off-shore anchorages in Aughris Hole and Brown Bay. The best anchorages are in Ballysadare Bay but the normal place to visit is Rosses Point in the entrance to Sligo.

Aughris Hole

provides shelter in winds from SE to SW. At LW a ridge of stone and rock protects the anchorage from the E. It is important to realise that submerged rocks extend half-way from this ridge towards the W shore. Having given Aughris Head a suitable berth the shore is clean to the quay, off which there is anchorage in 2·7 m sand and stones. In W wind a sea or swell rolls in, particularly with the flood. The quay gives no protection from this and no yacht should attempt to go alongside. It is suitable for dinghy landing and has a recently improved slip.

Facilities

Small pub ¹/₄ mile, guesthouse ¹/₂ mile, shop 1 mile away.

Brown Bay

between Seal Rocks and Raghly Point, provides reasonably good anchorage and shelter from swell in winds from NW to E, anywhere a bit more than 2 cables off the beach in 5 m, sand. No facilities ashore.

221

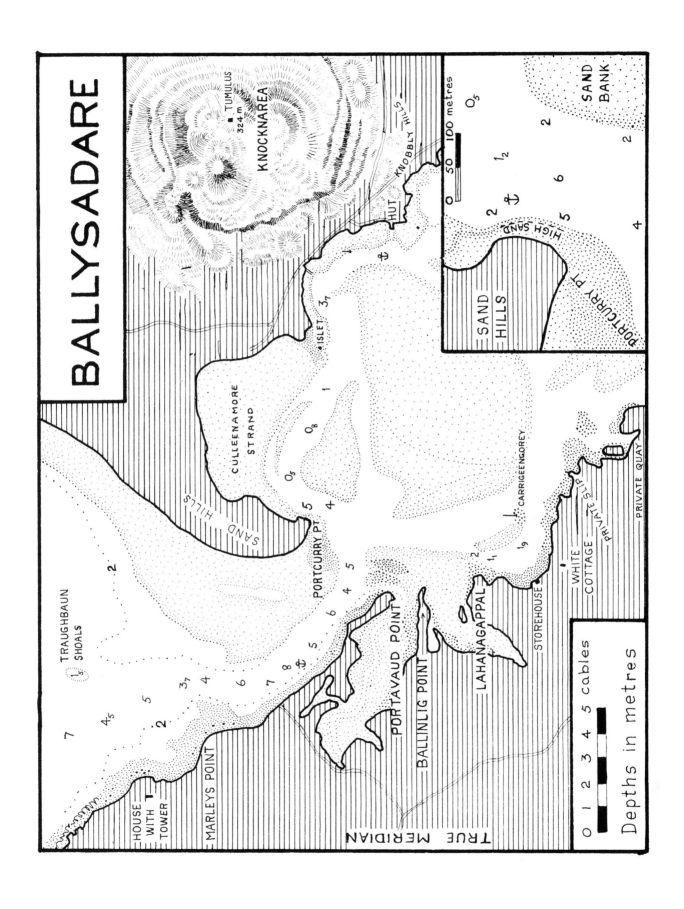

BALLYSADARE

BALLYSADARE BAY

(chart 2767, surveyed in 1852) *(see plan)*

This large enclosed bay, the N of which lies close W of Knocknarea Mountain, is mostly occupied by drying sandbanks now somewhat different from on the chart, though the banks in the approach and entrance do not appear to have changed at all. There is a safe anchorage close within the entrance and in W winds the shelter there is very good. There are no other places inside safe to go in to anchor except off Hut which is possible to reach. There is no village anywhere near the shore; do not think of going to Ballysadare town which is 6 miles from the bar beyond long narrow unmarked channels. The entrance, which is 3 miles S of Raghly Point and about 4 miles E of Aughris Head, can be approached in any reasonable weather but should not be attempted by a stranger in heavy sea from NW. The passage over the bar in 3·7 m is narrow, so a leading wind or an engine and good visibility are necessary. It is definitely best to go in at, or soon after, LW as then the banks and some rocks inside are showing which makes it much easier to be sure where you are going. However it was reckoned you might go over 1·2m S of Portcurry Point, though it may not be there now, so at very LWS enter 1½ hours later.

Tides

The stream in the entrance turns at about local HW and LW. The flood has a spring rate of 1 kn on the bar, 3 kn N and NE of Portavaud Point and mostly 1 kn in the inner channels; but the corresponding spring rates for the ebb are 2½ kn, 5 kn, and mostly 1½ to 2 kn inside.

Directions

If coming from Sligo be sure to avoid Traughbaun shoals; the house on the W side between Derkmore and Marley's Points with a small tower on its N end should not bear more than 210°. When about 2 cables from the shore steer exactly 153° for the E extremity of Portavaud Point, not very easy to see being low and flat with bent grass, but on this bearing it should be exactly below Carricknasheeogue, an isolated rock like a tooth on the skyline 5 miles away which is very conspicuous unless of course it is hidden by cloud. This 153° clears spits of stones extending more than 1 cable from Marley's Point. When just past this point, before it bears W, alter course to 180° until within 1 cable of the HW mark of the shore and then continue in at that distance off. When Portcurry Point comes in line with the N slope of Knocknarea bearing 062° steer 096° towards the knobbly hills just S of Knocknarea. When Black Rock

Lighthouse (at the entrance to Sligo) closes behind the W side of the sandhills N of Portcurry Point steer 073° towards the middle of Knocknarea; it is here that it may be 1·2 m deep at LAT. Very soon you will see the Golf Club building N of Culleenamore Strand and away beyond it Benbulben Mountain with a 45° slope beneath its vertical brow. When the building comes under the centre of this slope turn towards them which leads up between Portcurry Point and the sandbank E of it.

Anchorage

may be made anywhere E of Portcurry Point but the best place, out of the strongest tide, is to go reasonably close to the W shore and as far up as there is suitable depth. It is about 3 m opposite the high sandhill behind the NE corner of the point. It is deep quite near the beach which goes down about 45°. There is good shelter in W and NW winds. It is easy to go ashore and there are some facilities at Strandhill 2 miles away; walk across Culleenamore and not very far from its E side is a road running N to Strandhill.

It is suitable to anchor near the boats moored SE of Marley's Point which of course is the easiest place to get to and quite safe. It is rather deep outside the moorings and perhaps more suitable to anchor just SE of them closer in. There is a road down to the beach but it does not lead to anywhere of interest to visitors. There is of course a fairly strong tide. There is nowhere suitable to anchor in the channel S of Portcurry Point. The entry towards the Storehouse on the plan is very unsuitable and down there the sand banks are continually changing and the channel is getting steadily shallower. The N channel E of Portcurry Point is now the main outflow of the Ballysadare River, so it may be getting a bit deeper. The Hut SW of Knocknarea is an old two-storey house on a point just above the only public slip in the bay; a public car lane runs up from it. Anchoring a bit NW of it is presumably nice in E wind and is suitable to go ashore. It would be best to start from Portcurry Point 2 hours after LWS or at LWN when the channel should be deep enough and the banks still visible. Steer 114° in the N channel towards Hut until the grass islet is abeam, then run E until the point is abeam and then head NE to avoid the rocky N end of the sandbank. When past it run SE and when the perch (see plan) is abeam head S and anchor NW of Hut. The perch is covered around HW and if you don't see it steer 327° towards the house on Hut and turn S opposite the little point about 2 cables N of Hut. Chart 2767 shows an anchor further N, perhaps because it shows a pier there, however it is a private one.

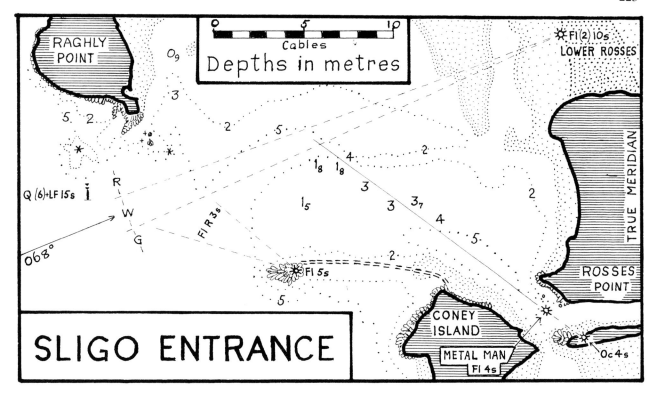

SLIGO ENTRANCE (chart 2852) *(see plan)*
It is normal to go in with a flood tide but with a
fresh W wind or a good engine it is usually possible
to get in against the ebb. In strong W wind it is
essential to use the marked channel which visitors
should use anyway. To go in at night you must of
course be able to see all the leading lights, which
are marked on the plan. The chart warns that there
are continual changes on the entrance banks. It was
quite different early this century, but the present
marked entrance channel had not had to be
changed for the last 30 years.

Directions
Coming from the N keep 2 cables W of Seal Rocks
and leave Wheat Rock S Card buoy to port.
Coming from the W in fine conditions it is simplest
to head towards Black Rock lighthouse until Wheat
Rock buoy is visible and then head for it. If there is
swell avoid The Ledge by keeping 1 mile off
Aughris Head and continuing E for 2 miles before
heading for Wheat Rock buoy; to go N of the
Ledge the N end of Coney Island should be just N
of Black Rock lighthouse bearing 098°. From 2
cables S of Wheat Rock buoy head for Lower
Rosses beacon or if you can't spot it steer 068°. This

heads port of Bell buoy, but before you are near
that buoy you turn to starboard and steer with
Metal Man and Oyster Island lighthouse in line
until about ½ cable from Metal Man then head
close NE of it leaving the two perches to port,
which brings you to Rosses Point.

N.B: During 1993 it is planned to move the Bell
buoy to position indicated on plan. Vessels may
check with Harbour Office or pilots for information
before entering.

224

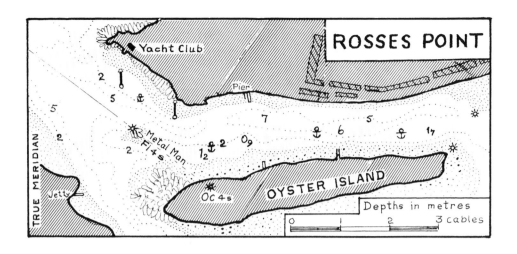

Coney Island in the foreground leading to Rosses Point with a backdrop of Ben Bulben.

Rosses Point *(see plan)*

This is unfortunately not a good anchorage as the holding is poor, the tide strong, up to 5 kn at springs, and with any wind short waves get up. It's handiest to anchor about the same distance from Oyster Island as the local moored yachts, or just outside them, but not too close ahead of one as the anchor often draws a bit before it holds, in fact if there is any wind it is wise to have a second anchor ready to drop. It is safer to anchor further E away from the mooring but this has the disadvantage of being further from the landing pier. The slip for landing is on the W side of the pier. It is convenient to berth temporarily at the head of the pier, where

the tide is not too strong, but a local trawler usually berths there in the evening. In quiet weather a temporary anchorage on sand is possible off the Yacht Club, not more than 1/2 cable from the NW perch with the other perch in line at LWS or a bit nearer the shore at high tide. Shower and bar at Y.C. Westport town with all facilities is 5M. Rosses Point village is convenient for some shopping and it is possible to go to Sligo by bus. There are two local pilots who can give yachts good advice. The Irish Coast Pilot says that the Pool, 7 cables E of Oyster Island and NE of the unlit post mentioned below, is where local small vessels anchor in less tide and on sandy bottom.

Sligo.

Rosses Point to Sligo (chart 2852 essential)

Off the E end of Oyster Island there is a perch which must be left to starboard and course altered to 120°, leaving the next beacon marking Blennick rocks to port; these rocks lie beyond the beacon and care must be taken not to be set onto them. This 120° course leads towards a perch, approaching which alter course to 090° to leave it to starboard and leave the next unlit post, 2 cables further on, ½ cable to starboard. The next perch, another 2 cables on, marks the end of a training wall and must be left to starboard. The wall is marked by perches and should be followed at 30 m off for over 1 mile. Then there is a perch on the end of the other training wall which must be left to port. Proceed thence between the parallel walls, keeping to port side of channel marked by stakes, up to the deepwater quay with 1·3m. If going to the inner quays keep close to the deepwater quays until clear of the berths, then keep about the centre of the fairway until abreast of

Campbell's Mill, a five-storey concrete building. Then steer across towards the NE side, leave a post with lamp to starboard, and head in for the quays. There is 2 m alongside, soft mud; there is mooring space off the quays; consult the HM. There are steps between the two transit sheds with water and electricity on jetty. This is now a fenced in area with key to gate available from Harbour Foreman who visits the jetty each morning or on request. Sligo has excellent shops and every facility short of a boatbuilder and sailmaker. Railway to Dublin. EC Wed.

Coast (chart 2702)

From Sligo Bay to Mullaghmore Head the coast should be given a good berth in any height of sea from the W, a course halfway between the shore and Inishmurray is a safe one. Apart from the coastal bank, beware in any weather the Black Bull Rock 3 miles up from Ardboline Island and the rocks 1 mile offshore at Milk Harbour (see below). Along this coast a good lookout should be kept for lobster pots which are often set very far out.

INISHMURRAY

has been uninhabited since 1950 and is well worth a visit, weather permitting, to see the remarkable collection of unusually well preserved 6th century monastic buildings. Clashymore Harbour on the S side is a rocky gut, off which, in perfectly calm weather only, a yacht may be anchored in 7 m weed over rock; on the E side of the gut there are natural quays and mooring rings where local boats go alongside near HW when it provides good dinghy landing; this is more difficult at LW. **Caution.** With any sea, or at LW, the shoal patches close E and NE of the island must be avoided. Bomore Rock and its outliers, 1½ miles N of the island, must be given a proper berth. Have a trip line on your anchor.

MILK HARBOUR (chart 2702)

This little creek at the front of Benbulbin Mountain has a secure anchorage, but in strong tide, and across a bar with 0·2 m LAT completely exposed to the W and encumbered with rocks. It is really only suitable for one or two local boats. As there used to be an owner of a yacht who lived there, and who told the ICC the way to go in, it is still stated below. It would be dangerous for a stranger to enter and yachtsmen are definitely recommended not to try going in, particularly as at half tide when the least depth would be 2 m the rocks on either side are probably covered. A motor boat might try going in at LWN or between 1 and 2 hours above LWS, only of course in calm weather. If anyone has a particular reason to wish to take a yacht in it is suggested to get in touch, before going there with Christy Heraughty who has a fishing boat there and might agree to drive his boat in ahead of the yacht.

Directions

If Bulligbeg, a rock 3 m deep, is breaking do not attempt entrance. Do not approach S of Carrrick-na-Spania. Approach the tower on Dernish Island bearing 145° which leads just SW of Bulligbeg and in towards Carrigeen. Carrigeen is a stone bank, dry at LW, which extends NW from the N tip of Dernish and is not shown on the chart. At half tide small bits of it are visible above water. Keep it fairly close to starboard following its line in to the entrance, taking care to avoid the two spits of rock sticking out a little from Dernish and the larger rock at the edge of the sand on the other NE side. Once past the inner spit rock there is plenty of water but swing wide of the sand spit at the corner of Dernish when rounding the bend. Tidal stream runs strongly at 3 or 4 kn round Dernish except just at HW and LW. The flood frequently sets towards the sand spit E of the entrance.

Anchorage

The only place is in mid-stream opposite the disused quarry beside a lane running up to the main road; there is ample depth and room to swing. The quay dries out and has 2·4 m alongside at MHWS, 1·5 m at MHWN.

Facilities

Small shop, PO and bus route ½ mile from quay. Grange, 2 miles away, has more supplies. John and Tom McCann, phone (071-63217), smith and boatbuilders, can do repairs and could give a message to Christy Heraughty.

MULLAGHMORE APPROACH

From the W the headland should be given a 2c berth to avoid rocks to N.

MULLAGHMORE (chart 2702)

The best anchorage is off the harbour mouth in 2 m, but there is plenty of room S or SE of this in 3 m. There is fair shelter here in settled weather except in winds from between NE and E. A yacht should not remain there if bad weather threatens. A dangerous sea comes in to this anchorage in a W gale.

Local twin-keel yachts are moored inside the harbour which is safe in any weather. Yachts up to say 10 m long can conveniently berth in there and dry out against the N pier or on the S pier which is even more sheltered. The depth in the harbour two hours before and after high tide is more than 2 m. At LWN it is about 1·2 m deep and at LWS it just dries out except for a small pool with 0·6 m between and immediately inside the pier-heads. There is a rock which dries about 1 m right in the harbour entrance, one third of its width from the S pier; therefore when entering or leaving keep fairly near to the N pier.

Facilities

Shop, pub, improved hotel, seafood restaurant, phone, water, also boatbuilder Rodney Lomax, who can supply diesel. No petrol available. Visitors mooring just off the pier. VHF Ch. 16 and 18 in use in this area.

BUNDORAN

There is a boat pier at the SW end of the town with about 0·6 m LAT where the inshore RNLI lifeboat is stationed. The approach with rocky shoals extending a cable to seaward is shallow, tortuous and not recommended.

BALLYSHANNON (chart 2702)

was a commercial port long ago but has not been used since 1940. Cruising yachts are definitely recommended not to try to go in. The shallow exposed bar is very dangerous and from it to the town a partially marked narrow channel meanders across a wide expanse of drying sand. It was never accessible except in calm sea conditions and definitely inaccessible if waves are breaking on the bar.

Immediately above the town there is a Hydro-electric dam, and on either side, at the end of its tail race, are deep pools completely sheltered from all winds and currents where vessels up to 18 m can moor safely within 1 cable length of the town quay. Anyone wishing to take a vessel in should have a prior consultation with Jim Slevin (072-51177), or local yachtsmen who would have up-to-date information on conditions on the bar and estuary. There are no professional pilots. The old pier at Kildoney ³/₄ mile N of Kildoney Point which lies on the north side of Ballyshannon Harbour has recently been improved to provide alternative access. There is a concrete slip and approach road.

DONEGAL HARBOUR (chart 2715 necessary for above Green Island) (see plan)

The estuary provides fair access and sheltered anchorages beyond Green Island are in very pretty surroundings. Strangers should approach on a rising tide. The entrance is usually sheltered from swell and is only dangerous in very bad conditions. On the other hand under apparently safe conditions the swell can sometimes start to break far out off Murvagh Spit. Therefore, if in any doubt, approach Rock Point about 2 cables off the shore, but not within 1 mile of Doorin Point where reefs extend a quarter of a mile.

Marks

Doorin Rock, 70 m, flat-topped hill surrounded by trees, stands above a low cliff NW of Rock Point. Ball Hill, 63 m, is limpet-shaped with fields and hedges and shows up very well. Bell's Island (S of Murvagh Point) and St Ernan's are wooded. Barnesmore Gap on the skyline 11 miles to the NE is unmistakable if visible. Note that Doorin Rock, Rock Point, Black Rock and Blind Rock are all in one line. Barry's House is large, white and 3-storied just SE of the plantation on Mountcharles Hill and at the NW end of the village. Furey's Shed is W of a terrace of white cottages and its asbestos-sheeted roof is conspicuous. Tigan Bay is a very conspicuous white bungalow with slate roof on the shore 3¹/₂ cables W of Salt Hill quay. Salt Hill house above the quay is visible from seaward but not conspicuous, being covered with creepers.

Directions

Entrance to Salt Hill. Keep not more than 2 miles SE of Doorin Point to avoid Carrickfad Rocks (chart 2702). A reasonable approach is with Barry's House - or Mountcharles - in line beyond Rock Point until within ¹/₂ mile of the latter. Or as stated above keep close to the shore from not more than 1¹/₄ miles W of Rock Point. When Doorin Rock is still well left of Rock Point bring the NW cable of Furey's Shed just open to the right of Tigan Bay and on this line go in past Blind Rock (visible before ¹/₂ tide). When not quite 1 cable in from Blind or Black Rock steer 057°, towards Barnesmore Gap is visible. When Tigan Bay is N of you steer to pass 70 m off Salt Hill quay, which should bring you well off the stones which reach 1¹/₂ cables out from Salt Hill Point. (Starting 057° leads over 1·5 m which at LW should be all right for most yachts; the chart shows lines to enter in deeper water.)

Anchorages

1. It is possible to anchor in the lee of Black Rock. Buoy the anchor, for as well as any visible moorings there are the remains of old ones around the bottom. This place is exposed to S to E winds.

2. SE or E of the end of Salt Hill quay outside moorings in 2 to 5 m on sand, good holding, but exposed above half tides to waves from wind from SW to E. The quay is in good repair, except for broken-off wooden fenders. It dries about 0·5 m at the outer steps on the E side where between 2 hours before and after high tide a yacht would be calmer alongside in SW wind.

Inner anchorages

From off Salt Hill quay steer straight for the gap between Green Island and Murvagh Point, Salt Hill Point dead astern. Pass about 80 m S of Green Island Point after which turn a little N of E. Tide here runs up to 5 kn in springs and in the ebb it runs over towards Green Island from the Mullanasole exit. The banks off Murvagh Point are steep-to and if visible one can sail very close to them if necessary. Head up E of Green Island exactly 353° when this direction heads just off the E side of Loughaun. The deep channel just W of St Ernan's spit is only 40 m wide. Beyond this with the N end of Green Island abeam you either head NE towards the Youth Hostel or the slip, or anchor as soon as Donegal Hill (2 miles beyond the town) is open of the steep N side of Ballyboyle Island. This anchorage is on sand in 2·5 m, well sheltered but in

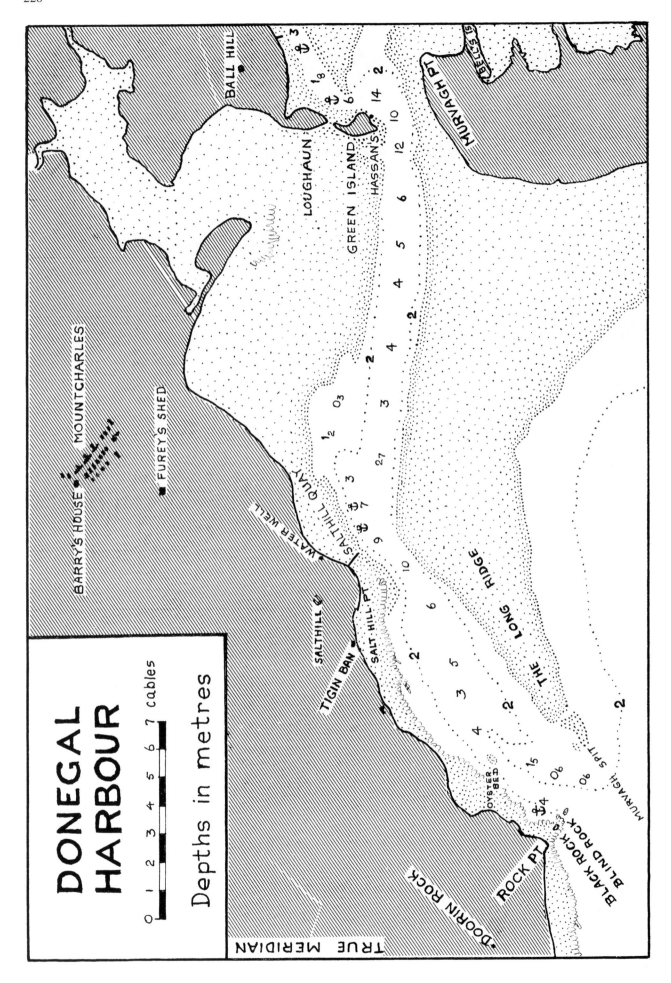

228

strong tide. A yacht can only go in a further ¹/₂ mile, beyond which the channel to the town is very shallow and dries here and there. On the N shore of the ¹/₂ mile deep channel the building just NW of the slip, unnamed on the metric chart and called Stn on the old chart, is now the Youth Hostel. If desired anchor S of it not less than ¹/₂ cable from the shore in about 3·5 m. The furthest E anchorage is better sheltered in E or SE wind. It is about 1 cable SE of the point 1¹/₂ cables beyond the slip where on the metric chart the road alters from lines to dots. Inside this point the first two storied house has two chimneys. The marks for the anchorage are: the line of a hedge running up beyond that house: and the top of Drumcliff Hill central in the gap between Ballyboyle Island and the fir-covered shore beyond it S of Rossylongan House. Drumcliff Hill is just W of Donegal town, is named on the old chart but just marked 50 m on the metric chart. This position is probably about 4 m deep, just a little SW of the anchor on the metric chart.

Donegal

The channel to the town can only be entered in a dinghy, preferably before half flood. To pass between Lug Rock and Ballyboyle keep the Youth Hostel in line with the two storied house with two chimneys. There are two quays on the S side, the old one close to the town.

Facilities

All supplies, hotels, banks, garages. EC Wed.

South Channel to Mullanasole

Pretty at HW but not recommended for keel boats. Tide runs very strongly W of Rooney's Island so unsuitable for anchoring.

Coast

between Donegal and Inver. Doorin Point and the coast for 1 mile each side of it should be given a good berth as reefs project up to 4 cables seaward from the bottom of the cliffs.

INVER BAY

is exposed to the SW but provides sheltered anchorage in offshore winds. The shores of the bay are mostly foul and care must be taken, especially if beating. The chart shows a line to clear Menamny Rock which dries at springs and lies 3 cables off the NW shore with foul ground inside it. It is about halfway between Ballyederlan Point and the ruined CG Sta. The Whillins SW of Inver Port is a dangerous rocky area parts of which dry. Inver church in line with the left hand sandhill of Drumbeg, 046°, clears both Whillins and Rock of the Port (both dry 2 m), as also does Ballyederlan Point in line with St John's Point. The chart also shows a line to clear the rocks on the E side of the bay N of Doorin Point.

Inver Port

1 mile SW of Inver, has a drying pier and an anchorage S of it. A stranger must not go near it in the dark as the lights on the pier are confusing. There is now a fish farm in the bay. The port must be approached on a N course keeping the pierhead in line with the left hand end of a prominent short sandstone wall above the road and just to the left of a green roofed bungalow. This leads inside Rock of the Port where there is a mooring and room for a visitor to anchor near the line. N of this the water shoals. Local boats take the ground in the lee of the pier. A keel boat should not berth to dry alongside the pier because the sand is irregular with soft spots. A small twin-keel yacht could lie aground and afloat in absolute security in any weather well up in the bight towards the wall where there are trees to which lines may be made fast.

Inver Roads

at the head of the bay NE of Inver Port, provides safe anchorage in 3 to 5 m well sheltered in offshore winds, but without convenient landing nearby. However, it is now reported blocked by fish farms to E.

Eany Water

runs out across drying flats at the head of the bay. It would provide absolute security for a twin-keel or CB yacht and a shallow draught yacht might lie afloat at the Old Church corner. There is also a small pool with 1·8 m LWS right up at the bridge but with many drying patches on the way up to it. However, after heavy rain with the river in spate neither of these anchorages would be tenable.

CASSAN SOUND

(chart 2702, also 2792, Killybegs plan)

This open anchorage is 1¹/₂ miles NE of St John's Point and just N of another bay off which is the dangerous Black Rock which is covered 2 hours either side of HW. The S bay has rocky bottom inside and a bright yellow beach. Cassan Sound has a small stony beach beneath a 3-chimney cottage and should be approached bearing NW or W to avoid Black Rock. Anchor in 3·5 m close inshore between the end of the little breakwater and the shore N of it. It is nicely sheltered in winds between W and N and has a handy slip for landing. **Caution.** If swell comes in it can be dangerous so if ashore keep an eye on the yacht.

Bruckless Harbour.

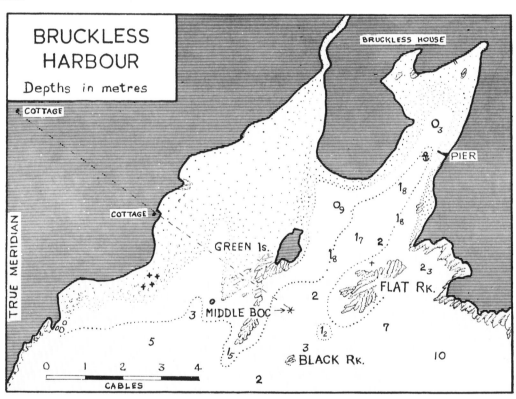

BRUCKLESS (chart 2702) *(see plan)*

This pretty creek, with trees down to the water's edge, lies at the head of McSwyne Bay close E of Killybegs. It is well sheltered except from due SW and local people state that gales from this exact point are rare. It is unsuitable for a visiting yacht without a working engine as it is too narrow for any stranger to try beating. It is just deep enough for most yachts being hardly anywhere deeper than 1·8 m LAT between the lines on the plan marked 1·8 m. Green Island, 10 m high, is prominent, especially at LW when the extensive reefs on which it stands are uncovered. Black Rock (locally known

as the round rock) stands out well and never covers. Coming in, Flat Rock is not easy to see; it covers completely only at big springs but the small reefs projecting about 20 m from its W side cover at half flood. Middle Boc is a small isolated rock which dries 1 m and lies between Green Island and Black Rock. The marks for it are two white thatched cottages on the W side, one low down near the shore, the other near the top of the first ridge inland from the shore. Middle Boc lies on the transit of the SW gable of the upper cottage with the NE gable of the lower one.

Directions

Leave Black Rock 18 m to starboard and steer 038° for the head of the pier. On this course Pound Point (Ellamore on the old chart) will be dead astern and so, coming out, should be kept just open to the right of Black Rock. (Going in near HW this mark astern is useful if the pier should be covered.) The above line passes less than 45 m SE of Middle Boc. Anchor in mid-channel just short of the pier, bottom soft mud. The pier dries out to the head at LWS and sometimes is covered at HW. A large square roofless shed near the root of the pier indicates its position if covered. A twin-keel boat could take the ground in safety in the W bight of the harbour which dries out.

Facilities

Small shop, PO and petrol at Bruckless village ³/₄ mile to NW. Shops and garages at Dunkineely 1¹/₄ miles to E. There is also a small shop near Bruckless House (but the boat slip there is in ruins). Restaurant - Castlemurray (073-37022) - ¹/₂ mile S of pier – book.

KILLYBEGS

(chart 2702 adequate. Plan here and on 2792)
This is now a major fishing port and still increasing. It is not such a charming place for a yacht as it was 50 years ago, but it is one of the best natural harbours in the country, accessible in all weathers by day or night and a safe place to make for in bad weather. It is good for supplies and facilities.

Outer lights

St John's Point: Fl 6s on a 14 m white tower, 40 m, 14 M. Rotten Island: Fl WR 4s on a 14 m white tower, 20 m, 15-11 M. R from 008° to 039°, W elsewhere.

Approach by day. From West

In bad conditions pass 2 miles S of Muckros Head and head E till the E side of Drumanoo Head bears NE when turn in to pass a bit E of it, thus passing midway between Ellamore Shoal and the 14·3 m shoal 1¹/₂ miles W of it, both of which can break in a gale. For inshore passage from Teelin keep fairly close to Muckros Head and then steer into Fintragh Bay well N of Manister Rock which is always covered. When Black Rock is seen (it only covers at spring tides) head to leave it close to starboard and then pass 2 cables from Drumanoo Head to clear Horse Head Rock. Alternatively to pass well SW of Manister Rock keep Slieve League summit or Dundawoona Point bearing 309° and when Rotten Island lighthouse appears turn in to leave it to starboard after leaving Drumanoo to port.

From South

Leave Bullockmore W Card buoy Q Fl (9) 15s (1¹/₂ miles W of St John's Point) 1¹/₂ cables to starboard and then steer for Rotten Island. The buoy is small and if not seen, or if coming from the E, the NE peak of Crownarad should be well W of Drumanoo Head bearing 349° which leads clear of St John's Point shoal and E of Bullockmore (2·1 m deep). Keep on this bearing till St John's Point is SE, then head for Rotten Island.

Approach by night. From West

Steer for St John's Point light keeping it bearing not more than 108° until Rotten Island light bears 039° (W edge of red sector), then steer in on this bearing and leave light to starboard.

From South

Steer to pass 1¹/₂ miles W of St John's Point and keep it bearing less than 073° until you pass through red sector of Rotten Island light. Then steer in with Rotten Island light bearing 039°, not less.

Caution

The switchback nature of the roads ashore makes car tail lights appear remarkably like the Fl R sector of Rotten Island at times, particularly in bad visibility, so time the flashes carefully.

Entrance. By day

Keep mid-channel until abreast Rough Point which has a pillar buoy on it Fl R 3 s, and then head towards the S Card buoy VQ(6) + LFl 10 s and when near it head towards the W area or the W pier or if heading to anchor N leave both Card buoys to port. **By night.** There are now leading lights Oc R 8 s on the N shore 338°. Above Rotten Island keep nearer the E side as it is cleaner. Half-way across Walkers Bay, where the shoreline is seen to fall away, steer for the N Card buoy and after leaving it to port head N to anchor, watching with a torch if necessary to avoid a possible mooring.

Anchorage

The best place to anchor overnight is E of the town in 2·5 m to 3 5 m, mud. This is not the snuggest part in S winds, nor is it very convenient for landing, but the important thing is that it is clear of the very heavy fishing-boat traffic in W part of the harbour. Much of the area SW of the W town pier was dredged to 4 m or 7 m and until a new quay or pier is made there it should temporarily be a nice place to anchor, possibly also at night. As things will keep changing it is wise to consult the HM (Mr. Hodgman) call on VHF 14 or 16 about staying there and also about berthing on the pier.

A good berth is off the blue shed marked "Gallagher Brothers". This is clear of traffic, and Jack Gallagher who lives in Teelin may be able to help with arrangements to leave a boat for a period. Look out for fish farm rafts to the SE of this berth.

Killybegs.

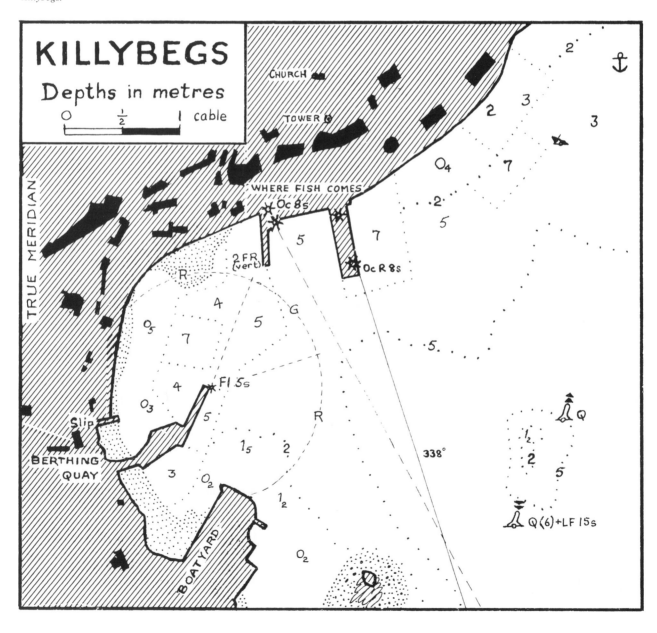

Facilities

All stores and amenities, new hotel, banks, garages (mobile cranes) in the town. Hydrant on W town pier with a £10.00 charge! During working hours only. Ship's chandler and hospital on S side near boatyard now taken over by Mooney Bros. with some assistance for repairs. Kosangas from Gallaghers Bros. shop..

Walkers Bay

on the E of the entrance is a pleasant overnight anchorage. It is well sheltered in SW or W winds and should it go round to NW the shelter E of the town is close at hand. The area with suitable depths is narrow and it shoals quickly inside it. Anchor in 5 to 8 m NW of the slip but keep clear of local moorings.

Port Roshin, opposite Rotten Island (300° from RI) has min. depth 2m, the entrance is only 20m wide at LAT and is not difficult, however, care should be taken to avoid rocks to S which cover shortly after MLWS. Possibly scout with dinghy to enter this quiet and beautiful anchorage.

Teelin Harbour.

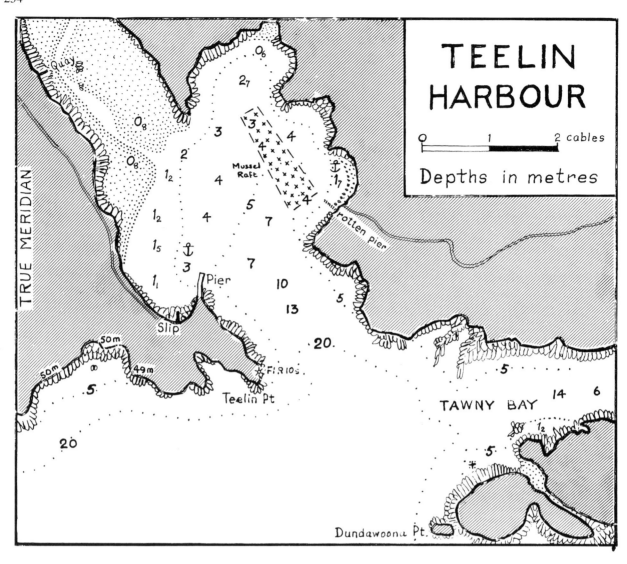

TEELIN HARBOUR
(chart 2702. Plan here and on 2792)

Teelin is a picturesque natural harbour suitable for a night at anchor in reasonable weather. It is exposed to S and SW swell. In NW winds very severe squalls can come down off the mountain. It is used by a good many fishing boats. It has the attraction of being only half as far as Killybegs from Rathlin O'Birne for a yacht heading S, but in unsettled weather it would be wiser for the yacht to go the further 8 miles to Killybegs.

Approach
The entrance cannot be seen until fairly close. Coming from the E you don't see it until you pass Dundawoona Point beyond which the entrance is only 3 cables away. Coming from the W keep fairly near the shore E of Carrigan Head when Tawny Bay will be visible which is just E of Teelin

entrance. **Light,** on top of the W point of the entrance, shows Fl R 10 s so if it is seen it is safe to go in at night. There is no beacon so it is not visible by day from any distance to the S.

Anchorage
The normal place is off the moorings on the W side, depth 3 or 4 m, not too far N of the pier as there is more swell further N. The pier has a 3 m depth for 15 m, but often several local boats are tied there outside each other. The small area N of the rotten wooden pier on the E side is also slightly sheltered and not so bad on NW squalls, but there are also moorings there.

Facilities
Water on pier and diesel probably obtainable. Carrick village with shops is 2½ miles inland.

COAST WESTWARD OF TEELIN
Caution — Uncharted rocks

The cliffs of Slieve League present a fine spectacle. The pebble beaches at their base, inaccessible from the shore, are attractive landing places in very fine weather, but yachts should approach with great caution as there are known to be a number of uncharted rocks close off Carrigan Head and between it and White Strand. The point called Gubbaunna Bullig on the old chart has no name on the metric chart. It is exactly S of the Slieve League summit and on the metric chart has a shallow rock off it, SW of 11·9 m. Immediately E of this is a bay marked 10 m which has a beach and can be safely approached heading in N. On the metric chart the beach E of this one has a rock shown SE of its W point, but we believe that a reef of five rocky heads, locally known as "The Boys" extends ESE of this point. Therefore to approach this beach the cliffs should be closely approached about 1 cable E of the E of the beach and then skirt NW along the cliffs (in 8·8 m on the chart) and anchor between "The Boys" and the shingle in about 14 m (which is shown white on the metric chart).

A different navigators assessment of this part of the coast - The Cliffs of Bunglass (Slieve League) are a stupendous sight, falling almost sheer 1973 feet to the water. There are two sandy beaches at the W end, both of which may be landed upon in favourable conditions. A clearing line, 190° from the eastern beach leads clear of the numerous off-lying rocks between Carrigan Head and this beach. Between the clearing line and Thorlea Bullig there are no dangers and yachts may enjoy a three mile passage along one of the most exciting cliff faces in Europe.

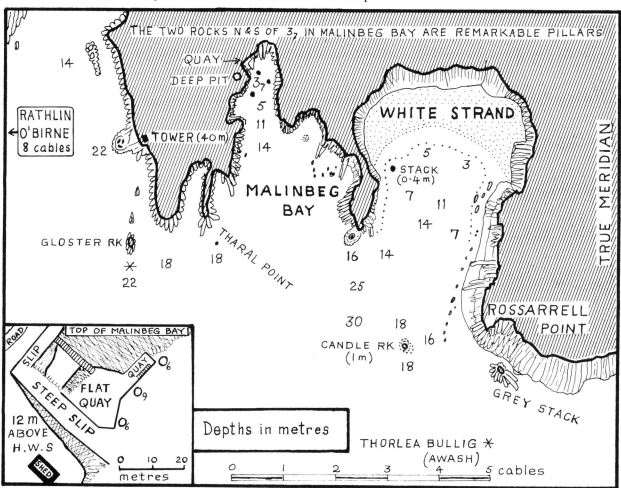

White Strand Bay (see plan)

offers temporary anchorage in N winds in about 5 m, sand, in pretty surroundings. Coming from the E, to avoid Thor-Lea Bullig keep ½ mile offshore till Candle Rock is to the right side of the W side of the bay, then head in to leave Candle Rock to starboard. Anchor in the middle of the bay E of the Stack which might be covered at high tide.

Malin Beg Bay (see plan)

has a slip for hauling up local boats and a small quay with about 1 m alongside at LWS. A yacht should only enter in really fine weather as the top of the bay is less than ½ cable wide with three rocks, the two left ones being remarkable pillars. A yacht might temporarily anchor just beyond the first rock, but the simplest would be to go in above half tide and berth at the quay. Malin Beg, ¼ mile away, has some shops and a PO.

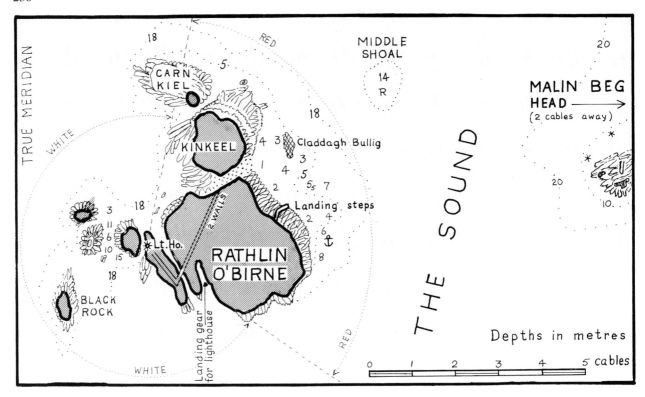

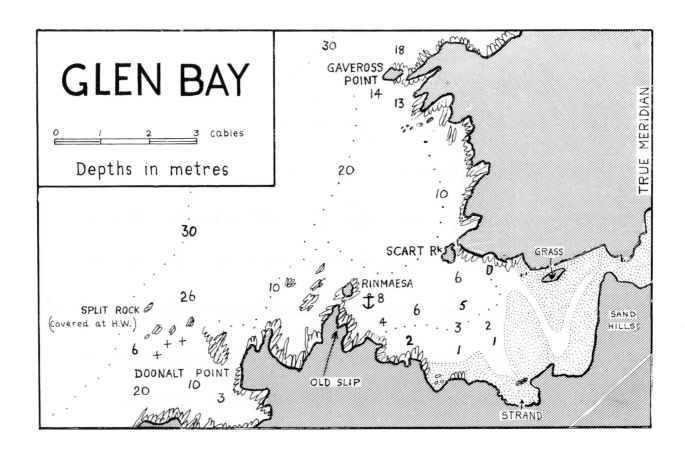

Rathlin O'Birne Sound *(see plan)*

is the normal entrance from the N to Donegal Bay. The island is 1 mile from the shore and the clear passage ½ mile wide is nearer the island as the rocks extend 4 cables from Malin Beg Head, so sail somewhat nearer to Rathlin O'Birne. The tide runs N at 1½ kn in spring for 9¼ hours, starting 4 hours after HW Dover. The S going tide is very weak. The streams may be strongly affected by N or S winds.

Rathlin O'Birne Island

is worth a visit on a quiet day. The Pilot states that landing is possible in calm sea SW of the lighthouse but it is too deep to anchor there. It is much better to land on the white-washed steps on the E side. Beware of White Claddagh Bullig which extends further S than would appear. It is best to anchor NE of the SE corner where the holding is better than off the landing steps. There is no anchorage or landing off the S shore where the material for the lighthouse is lifted by a crane. **Light** on the W of the island is on a 20 m tower, Fl WR 20s, 35 m, 22-18 M. It shows W from 307° to 195°, seen from N, W and S, and R elsewhere to the land.

GLEN BAY (chart 1879) *(see plan)*

provides temporary anchorage if there is no swell with winds from NE through SE to SW. Anchor close E of Rinmaesa Point in about 7 m, sand. Do not chance getting caught here in W or NW winds as the anchorage is then untenable and there would be no shelter closer than Teelin. There are some stores in Glencolumbkille village 1 mile to the E and Malinmore Hotel 1 mile SW. The E of the bay is very shoal.

Coast

N from Glen Head there are spectacular cliffs and tors. The coast is foul up to ½ mile offshore so sail at least 1 mile away. Close S of Toralaydan there is a small pier, but its approach is strewn with rocks and there is nothing ashore so do not go near it even in the calmest weather. Heading N in bad weather the normal anchorage is Aran Road, entered from the N after going round the island, 28 miles from Rathlin O'Birne. The only possible nearer place is Church Pool, entering in daylight, keeping not more than ½ mile off the clean shore E of Dunmore Head. The rest of Boylagh Bay, full of rocks and uneven depths on which the swell breaks with violence at times, should be avoided in bad weather when entering through Aran's S entrance should not be considered. In rising tide there is a strong set into the bay.

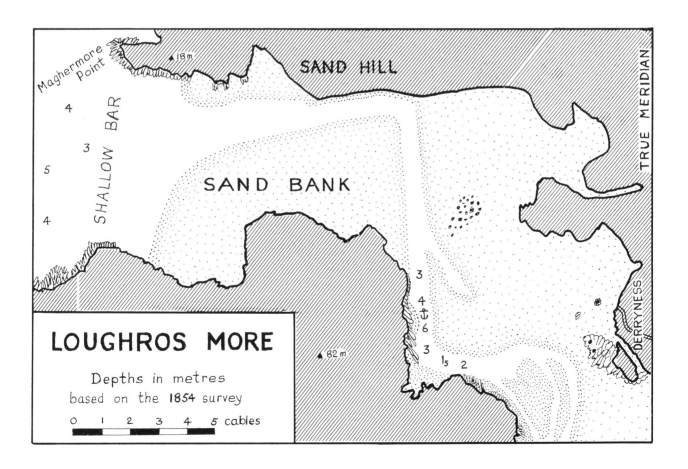

LOUGHROS MORE and BEG BAYS

are not normally accessible and have little to attract yachts. The inner parts are more or less as shown on the chart but the entrance channels in both bays are at present nearer the N side, quite different from the chart. The bars outside must be pretty shallow as, especially at LW, they are nearly always covered with breaking waves. If anyone wants to try entering in fine weather the best would be to sail near the bar and look at the entrance at LW and come back to go in 3 hours later. In light W wind you can anchor while waiting off the E side of Inishbarnog, S of Dawros Bay.

Loughros Beg

has not been known ever to have been entered by a yacht. The present entrance is quite near the N side so it is not necessary to go anywhere near Meadal Rock, shown on the chart. The only suggested anchorage is round the corner SE of Cloghboy where some local boats are moored. It is not known if the depth there is about 4 m, as on the chart.

Loughros More *(see plan)*

had an ICC yacht anchored there in 1959. In 1974 another yacht tried but could not find an entrance on the S side as shown on the chart and then on our plan. At present a sailing yacht is kept in the bay at Derryness where she is on the dry sand at LW but goes to sea and returns near HW in suitable weather. The present entrance is between a sandbank off the N shore and the large sandbank extending from the S shore. The channel goes just S of the corner of the sand hill and then continues fairly close to it until the S coast leading down S to the more distant S shore appears; then the channel turns round towards it, very nearly S. When past the point close to the channel - you keep about 130 m off the shore which is rocky, and the 1959 anchorage is about 1½ cables S of this point. It seems suitable to go 1 cable further S where the depth should be less. The depths on the plan were surveyed more than 100 years ago.

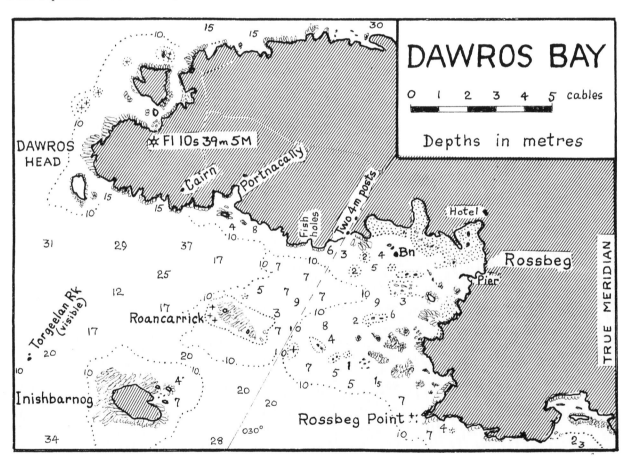

DAWROS BAY *(see plan)*

Dawros Head Light shows Fl 10 s 39 m 5 M. This only has a temporary anchorage in calm sea conditions with N or E wind. It is a popular place ashore for holiday people. There is a hotel as shown, a PO just E of the pier and a small shop about ½ mile SE on the road. The bay may be entered from the W, or from the S with the two 4 m posts in line 030°. The easiest anchorage is on this line near the shore; another possible anchorage is just W of the beacon reported missing 1989 but avoiding the rock SW of it. The pier is dry at LW and too difficult for a stranger to approach at HW. A shallow yacht might visit Portnacally just W of the bay, a delightful little inlet, the entrance being W of the island with rocks outside it.

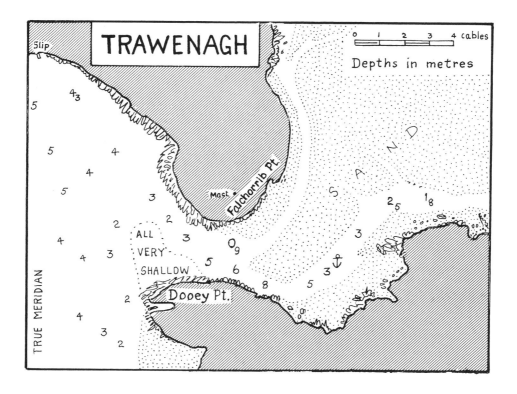

BOYLAGH BAY

There is a string of shoals and rocks stretching into the bay from Bullig More 3 miles outside it. There are also some shoals in the N of the bay SW of Aran and of the Sounds SE of it. These should all be avoided though some of them are only dangerous in a big sea or swell. Roaninish, 4·6 m high, is clean on its S side but has reefs extending up to 7 cables N and W. (Anyone wishing to try landing on Roaninish should row into the gut N of the W of the island; the bottom all along the N side is foul.) The innermost danger is Bullig Connell, 0·3 m deep, which lies less than 1 mile N of Inishkeel, the island W of Church Pool.

Approach

There is no problem approaching Church Pool from Dawros Head, which is rocky and now has a small beacon 2 cables inside the head with Fl 10s; there is a clear passage S of the dangers mentioned and keep not more than ½ mile off Dunmore Head, 127 m and Inishkeel. Coming from the N is more difficult and always needs careful pilotage. Without good visibility it would be unwise to approach from outside Aran. Coming from Aran S Sound past Crohy Head in poor visibility it is best to head about 160° for the rocks E of Church Pool with Illancrone's Beacon astern so as to pass well inside Bullig Connell; the chart shows clearance marks to pass E or W of this rock.

Anchorages

1. **Church Pool** (chart 2792). This is a pretty bay and safe to anchor but the best place S of Church Point is occupied by a few local moored boats, however, there is plenty of room. Outside there is still excellent shelter in winds between WNW and SE and good holding in about 3 m, sand. It is best to moor with one anchor just E of the moorings and the other well out to NE in case of a shift of wind. It is safe but of course uncomfortable in any strength of N or NE wind. No facilities on the island. There does not seem to be any reduction of depth now as mentioned on the chart. Easy access to Portnoo beach by dinghy.

The Gweebarra River E of Church Pool has a dangerous very shallow bar and should never be approached.

2. **Portnoo.** This inlet S of Inishkeel is much more exposed to swell than Church Pool and swell might make it dangerous. However in absence of swell it provides better shelter in NE wind and in really calm conditions it is a pleasant place to stay overnight. Anchor just ¾ cable opposite the end of the pier in more than 2 m or there is plenty of room to anchor further out in less than 5 m. **Facilities.** Hotel, shops, PO. Fuel 1M.

3. **Trawenagh Bay** *(see plan)* is at the NE corner of Boylagh Bay. It has a narrow entrance marked by a tall thin mast on Falchorrib Point and most of the bay is dry at LW but there is a suitable area for anchoring. Its shores are sparsely populated and without facilities. It is not much used by boats, partly because the entrance is shallow, and for yachts sailing along the coast it is abviously normal to anchor further out in the better places behind Aran or in Church Pool. But Trawenagh has a safe anchorage and anyone who wants to go in can do so

in reasonable weather without serious swell. The shallowest middle of the entrance is now 2 m, but as it might become less it is best to go in at half tide and check the depth so that if desired it may be all right to leave at LW. Approach almost 1 mile from the entrance along the NE shore and when near Falchorrib Point keep a little less than 1 cable away from it to be halfway between it and the shallow area which heads N from Dooey Point and which does not now dry as on the chart. Continue on the same SE direction till close to the S shore just S of the mast and then keep alongside it in deep water till the shore turns slightly SE when you must turn away. At this point you may see a small square rock up on the shore painted pink which is handy to head for going out. Head up about 060° and anchor fairly soon in about 3 m, not more than 2 cables up. There is no point in going up further between the sands; if you particularly wish to, it would be easier near LW.

ARAN ISLAND TO BLOODY FORELAND
(chart 1883)

See page 255 for Southbound passage. The coast from Illancrone, 2 miles S of Aran, to the Bloody Foreland is sheltered by a string of islands, a few still inhabited. It contains a number of good anchorages in varied scenery and is an attractive compact cruising ground. The islands give a useful amount of shelter for coastwise passages and the pilotage while interesting is not unduly difficult.

OFFLYING DANGERS. Leenon More

2 miles W of Inishkeeragh, is 8 m deep but breaks with heavy swell. **Stag Rocks**, 1¼ miles NW of Owey Island, consist of three 9 m high and one SW of them which only dries 1·2 m. **Bullogconnell Shoals** (locally called The Blowers) are 1 mile NW of Gola Island and are the most dangerous. A small bit of the N shoal dries 1·4 m and the middle and S shoals both have depths of 2 and 3 m. In a swell they break at irregular and at times infrequent intervals. They should be given a good berth. To sail between them and Gola keep Bloody Foreland just behind Inishsirrer the end of which should bear 045°, which also leads safely NW of Rinogy Rock, N of Gola. To sail outside the shoals keep Cluidaniller, the top of Aran, just W of Owey Island, but in bad weather keep it further out from Owey. At night of course you must sail outside the quick flashing Aran red light which covers these shoals and Stag Rocks.

ARAN ISLAND AND SOUND

The W side of Aran consists of high rocks, some of the finest cliff scenery in Ireland. In the sound and between the islands within it there is a choice of anchorages. The N entrance to the sound has good depth and is what is normally used. A yacht can go in or out through the S entrance in reasonable weather and at high enough tide, the depth near the SE of Aran being only 0·3 m. There are many beacons and leading marks inside Aran, most of them with lights, but as they are not absolutely reliable visiting yachts should not attempt to use the channels after dark. The principal beacons are listed below the Aran lighthouse for convenience of reference, starting with the S approaches.

Aran Island
main light. On the NW point, Rinrawros, a white tower 23 m high shows Fl (2) 20s, 71 m, 29 M. Lower on the same tower Fl R 3s shows from 203° to 234° over the dangers mentioned above, 13 M.

Illancrone
The square 3 m high beacon on the rocks SE of the island shows Fl 5 s, 6 M. A small stone hut on the island is an easier mark than the light, particularly from the N.

Wyon Point
The white tower shows Fl(2) WRG 10 s, 8 m, 6-3 M. G from shore to 021°, W thence to 042°, R thence to 121°, W thence to 150°, R thence to shore. This tower is on the mainland abreast Ilancrone at Termon.

The Clutch. South of Aileen Reef has beacon on SE Point.

Turk Rock has a green square 6 m tower showing Fl G 5s.

Aileen Reef off the SE point of Aran has a square 6 m beacon, painted red, QR shows.

Carrickbealatroha Upper (Stream Rock) has a wide square 5 m tower with white tiles and shows Fl 5s.

Correen's Rock off the SE of Rutland Island is a red square 6 m tower showing Fl R 3s.

S Rutland unlit conical beacon is about 100 m N of Correen's Rock.

Yellow Rock unlit beacon is on the E side of the channel E of Rutland Island.

Teige's Rock, N of Yellow Rock and also on the E side, has a 5 m tower and shows Fl 3s.

Above are for S approaches.

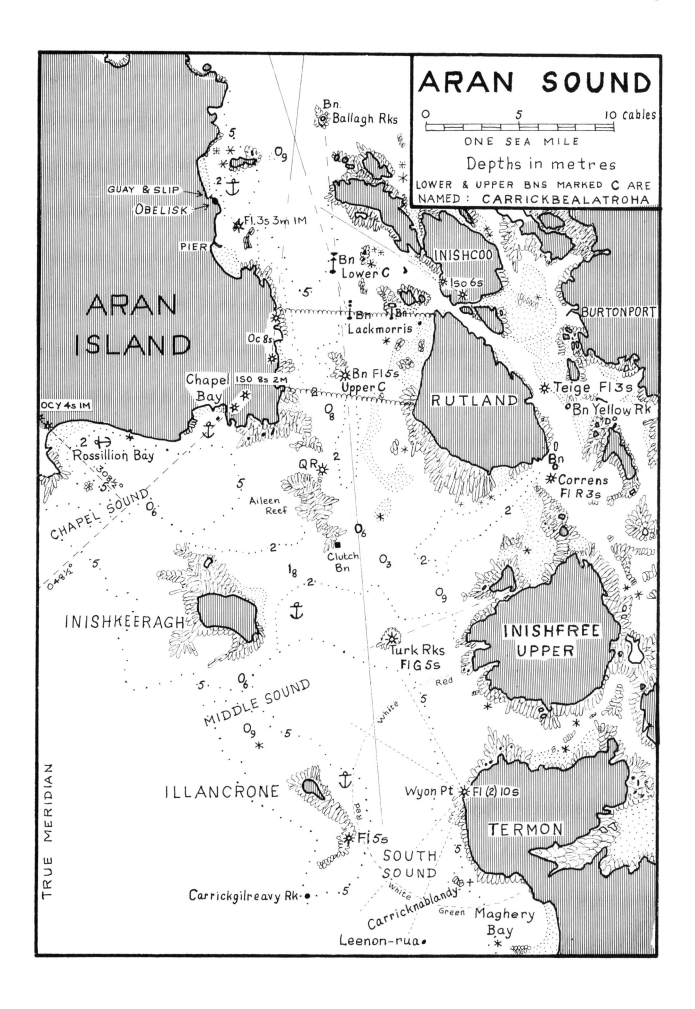

ARAN SOUND

0   5   10 cables

ONE SEA MILE

Depths in metres

LOWER & UPPER BNS MARKED C ARE
NAMED : CARRICKBEALATROHA

Bn.
Ballagh Rks

5

O 9

GUAY & SLIP
OBELISK

2

Fl. 3s 3m 1M

PIER

Bn
Lower C

ARAN
ISLAND

5

Bn
Lackmorris

INISHCOO

Iso 6s

BURTONPORT

Oc 8s

Chapel ISO 8s 2M
Bay

Bn Fl 5s
Upper C

RUTLAND

Teige Fl 3s

Bn Yellow Rk

OC Y 4s 1M

O 8

Bn

Correns
Fl R 3s

2

Rossillion Bay

308½

5

CHAPEL SOUND

O 6

QR

2

048½

5

5

Aileen
Reef

2

2

O 6

O 3

2

O 9

INISHKEERAGH

1 8

2

Clutch
Bn

Turk Rks
Fl G 5s

Red

INISHFREE
UPPER

O 6

5

MIDDLE SOUND

White

5

O 9

5

ILLANCRONE

Red

Wyon Pt Fl (2) 10s

TERMON

Fl 5s

SOUTH
SOUND

5

Carrickgilreavy Rk

5

White

Carricknablandy

Green Maghery
Bay

Leenon-rua

TRUE MERIDIAN

These below are listed from N.

Ballagh Rocks (previously Black Rocks) 9 m high conical beacon, white with black band, showing Fl 2·5s.

Black Rocks. Port hand light beacon, Fl R 3 s 1 M.

Carrickbealatroha Lower (North Perch) a thin pipe with triangular stays, is an unlit old perch, now coloured yellow-black-yellow with W Card cones.

Lackmorris perch, a thin pipe with triangular stays, is now an Isolated Danger, black and red with two black balls on top, no light.

South Channel perch, nearly 2 cables E of Lackmorris, is red with a can topmark, no light.

Aran leading lights are near the shore S of Charley's Point. The front 3 m beacon is black with a white band; the rear 5 m beacon is black. They are in line 186° and lead in close E of Blind Rocks. Lights Oc 8s.

Carrickatine, off S end of Eighter Island, is No. 2 beacon, red, 2 m high, light QR.

Inishcoo leading lights, both beacons 5 m high, front one white with black band, rear one black with yellow band. In line 119°. Lights Iso 6s.

Inishcoo beacon No. 4, on SW corner of Inishcoo, is painted red, 4 m high, light QR.

Rutland leading lights. Front beacon 4 m high, white with black band; rear beacon 8 m high, black with yellow band. In line 137°. Lights Oc 6s.

Nancy's Rock, beacon No. 1, painted green, 7 m high, light QG.

Edernish Rock, beacon No. 6, painted red, 4 m high, light QR.

Burtonport leading lights. Front FG 17 m, 1 M. Rear FG 23 m, 1 M.

Approach from the South

A local sailor who knows the outside marks can, with visibility, reach a safe anchorage in any weather. A stranger heading N in nice weather can safely go in through the S Sound to an Aran anchorage or would enjoy passing inside Aran on the way to an anchorage further N. But in rough sea and especially with strong winds from S to W a visitor would be well advised to sail outside Aran Island and use the main entrance from the N.

Marks

Inishkeeragh which is low-lying and flat is best identified by its single row of roofless houses. Illancrone, also low-lying, has a single stone shelter about the middle of the ridge and the light beacon on the rocks to the SE. The rounded height of Crohy Head (tower not conspicuous from seaward) and Croaghegly (243 m) with low-lying ground for some miles N and S of it are very distinctive.

SOUTH SOUND

nearly ½ mile between Illancrone and Termon, has the deepest water of the three S entrances and is by far the best approach and the only one which can be recommended.

Directions — By Day

Approach from the W towards half-way between Crohy Head and Termon to avoid Bullig-na-naght, a rock with 3 m over it which is more than 1 mile SW of Illancrone's Beacon. Meadalmore, the S extremity of Illancrone, covers only at very high springs. Give it a berth of 3 cables to clear Carrickgilreavy (Mulravy) rock which dries 2·7 m and when covered is often marked by breakers. After passing it turn slowly round to the N keeping 3 cables off the rocks as they are foul on their S and SE sides. Having passed the beacon you can head for a local anchorage or for the S Sound of Aran.

By night

it is only possible to enter in good conditions and at the beginning of the night, finally approaching in the SW white sector of Wyon Point. But this can only be recommended if, before it gets dark you can see the coast to be sure to enter Boylagh Bay more than 1 mile N of Roaninish and to arrive safely into the white sector passing S of Bullig-na-naght which is immediately W of the white sector. When E of Illancrone Light proceed roughly NW and anchor in 3 m when Illancrone Light bears exactly S and Wyon Light bears 100°. A stranger should proceed no further until daylight.

Middle Sound

is scarcely more than 3 m deep and 1 cable wide between rocks extending from both islands. It could only be safe to use in settled swell-free conditions and preferably not at LW so it cannot be recommended. If the sea is suitable and a yacht going to head S coming from Aran Road over half tide it would be attractive, especially if the wind was W, to go out this way. The direction out is to have the Turk Beacon in line between Inishfree Upper and Inishinny. The beacon 069° in line with the S end of Inishinny gives the deepest exit but rather close to the N of the 0·6 m rock, so it might be safer to have the beacon bearing between this and 066°, a little nearer to Inishinny's W point.

Chapel Sound

has a 1½ cable gap between rocks and a 2·4 m area outside. It is definitely not recommended. There is

South side of Aran Island with Aranmore Lifeboat heading N of Aileen Reef to Chapel Sound.

normally no reason to wish to use it but someone leaving or heading for Rossillion Bay or Chapel Bay anchorage might like to go through in calm sea and towards HW. There are now leading lights through Chapel Sound Iso 8s 2M 048$\frac{1}{2}$° from seaward, which lead into Chapel Bay. If going for Rossillion Bay turn onto the leading lights Oc Y4s on a bearing of 308$\frac{1}{4}$° when through Chapel Sound.

Anchorages S of Aran

(All somewhat exposed to the swell).

1. 1$\frac{1}{2}$ cables NE of Illancrone in 3 m, sand.

2. Between 1$\frac{1}{2}$ and 2$\frac{1}{2}$ cables E of Inishkeeragh in 2·5 m or 3·5 m sand. Both the above are sheltered in W or SW winds. The following may be reached by crossing the shoal between Inishkeeragh and the Clutch Beacon in a least depth of 1·8 m by keeping Turk Rocks Beacon between 120° and 125°.

3. Rossillion Bay is sheltered from winds between W and NE. Plenty of room to anchor in a bit more than 2 m, or less further in, sand. Small pier which dries alongside, leading lights.

4. Chapel Bay is well sheltered between NW and NE. Anchor $\frac{1}{3}$ cable S of the 2 m high rock in 4·3 m or SW of this position in 2·7 m. It is shallow further in. Small boat pier, leading lights.

SOUTHERN APPROACH TO ARAN ROAD

The least depth is 0·3 m so most yachts should not pass below $\frac{1}{2}$ tide. Turk Rocks Beacon must be left not less than 1 cable to starboard and beyond it keep Carrickbealatroha Upper (Stream Rock) Beacon in line with Ballagh (Black) Rocks Beacon, about 354°, which leaves Clutch Beacon 1$\frac{1}{4}$ cables to port; keep on this line till Cloghcor Point, the SE corner of Aran, comes abeam, then steer about 325° for the N concrete beacon on Aran shore. When the S beacon on the shore comes abeam head N where the whole middle of the area is deep and clear of dangers. The South Sound has power cables between Rutland Island and Aran Island, see Chart 1883 and plan.

If you happen to want to go S of Duck Island into Rutland Harbour (which is more difficult than the normal entrance round through the N channel) instead of turning port off Cloghcor Point turn a little starboard towards halfway between Lackmorris perch and S Channel perch (Duck Sound explained further on).

The sound W of Aileen Beacon is not recommended for yachts. Boats going through to Chapel Bay leave Aileen Beacon to port and then head towards one or other of the two inner beacons, leaving either of them fairly close to starboard.

244

North entrance to Aran Sound viewed from S with Calf Island in lower middle and Ballagh Rock to its NE.

Looking NE across the pier at Aran Island.

NORTH ENTRANCE TO ARAN SOUND

This is the normal approach to Aran Road and Burtonport. It is safe in almost any weather the exception being NW gales; a prolonged NW winter gale is said to cause the entrance to break right across. A NW summer gale might produce breakers on the 5 and 6 m patches W of Ballagh Rock.

Directions for Aran Road

The entrance is marked by the 9 m high Ballagh Rocks Beacon a dominating feature of the sound now has a light and which should be approached from NNW so as to leave Rinnagy and Bullignamirra Rocks well to port. Before the beacon comes abeam get onto one of the leading lines or approach between them. The old line is Lackmorris perch a little to the left of Carrickbealatroha Lower. **Caution.** These perches in line lead onto Blind Rocks, so keep them well open passing Calf Island. They lead in line well W of Dirty Rock off Eighter Island. The new line, with lights, is from pillars on the E shore of Aran; in a big sea keep a little W of this line abeam of Ballagh Rock Beacon. This line leads fairly close E of Blind Rocks. Just past it when the Obelisk on Aran shore comes in line with Moylecorragh (Ballintra) peak 241° this line may be followed, passing N of Calf Island shoal which has a 3·4 m rock. If in doubt carry on until the Obelisk bears W and steer in S of the shoal.

Anchorage

The best area is NE of the Obelisk and S of Calf Island. There are a good many moorings there but room to anchor outside them. This is a safe anchorage, usually comfortable in settled or W weather, but sometimes subject to swell. There is also plenty of room to anchor E of the Obelisk but it is probably more exposed to swell there. Stackamore quay is just W of the Obelisk with a slip and FY light. There is 0·7 m alongside at the steps and a little less along the inner half. This is the best place to land on the island. There is a drying pier at Leabgarrow ¼ mile further S but it is not good to anchor near it as there are so many rocks to avoid there. If intending to go to Leabgarrow, there is a perch on the end of Black Rocks which must be left to Port when approaching from N, the only recommended way in.

Facilities

Good general store, two small hotels, PO, phone, doctor, well water at Leabgarrow, ferry to Burtonport from Stackmore quay. No petrol.

APPROACHES TO RUTLAND HARBOUR AND BURTONPORT *(see plan)*

North Channel is the main approach, well lit and beaconed. With winds between SW and N it is easy and pleasant to sail all the way in, but the yacht must be under complete control as the rocks are very close in places. A yacht without a good engine should however stay in Aran Road as it is very often impossible to sail out.

Having cleared Dirty Rock by keeping Carrickbealatroha Lower and Lackmorris perches in line, pick up the Inishcoo leading beacons, 119°, which leads in and very close S of Carrickatine Beacon, immediately beyond which the leading line of the Rutland Beacons, 137°, must be followed exactly until Duck Island is abeam to starboard when you will be in the N part of Rutland Harbour. Beware of mistaking a ruined gable for a Rutland Beacon. If bound for Burtonport steer next for Nancy's Rock Beacon, leave it close to starboard and then leave Edernish Beacon to port.

South Channel or Duck Sound

This is a difficult entrance and it is simpler to use N Channel. The narrow and shallow part is just SE of S Channel red perch where it is 0·9 m. At adequate rise pass 40 m S of S Channel perch and head E towards a small rock W of Rutland. When the Inishcoo aft leading beacon is in line with the N point of Rutland steer towards it and pass close to the point after which you are soon in the main channel. If turning N wait until Nancy's Rock Beacon is visible, this avoids a rock extending ESE from Duck Island. Going out use the same line until the NW corner of Duck Island bears N when turn to pass 40 m S of the red perch.

Rutland South Channel

This is a difficult entrance firstly because there are many unmarked rocks to be avoided and secondly because of the extremely strong tide which sluices through the narrow and shallow gap between Rutland and Inishfree Islands. This limits its use to

Burtonport looking NW with Burtonport Pier on the mainland. N end of Rutland Island to left and Inishkoo over Edernish borders the N. Channel.

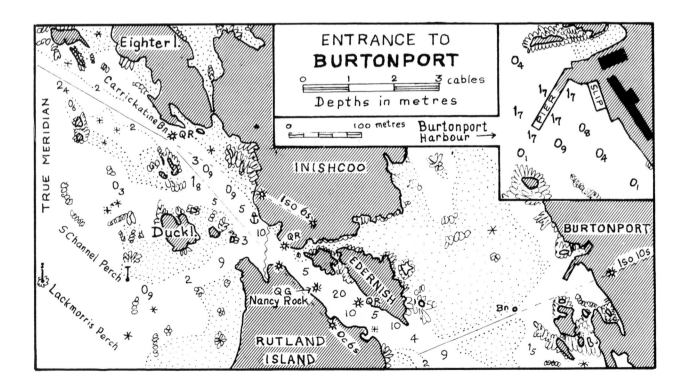

around HW as the passage is 0·3 m in the gap and in other places. Start the approach from near Illancrone at HW Galway or 15 minutes later. (The same time is about right for leaving Burtonport.) Leave Turk Rock Beacon to starboard and head for the middle of Rutland Island; if more convenient to leave Turk to port, head N until on the first transit. This involves identifying Corren's Rock Beacon and S Rutland conical beacon to the left of it, both off the SE point of Rutland. Bring S Rutland Beacon in line with a church on the skyline 057°; the church has a slate roof and is towards the right of a group of buildings. When nearly half-way along the S shore of Rutland if Errigal Mountain is visible bring it in line with S Rutland Beacon 071°. When the beacons are equidistant steer midway between them. If Errigal cannot be seen and if there is difficulty in getting the exact bearing on the beacon, it is better to steer for the tip of Rutland Island and turn to pass between the beacons when Corren's comes abeam. After passing between the beacons continue E for ³/₄ cable (140 m) before heading due N for Yellow Rock Beacon. Approaching Yellow Rock alter course to leave it 65 m to starboard, then steer to leave Teague's Rock Beacon 20 m to starboard and from it steer W to the Rutland shore where there is a slightly prominent boulder. When the shore is just 40 m away turn towards the S point of Edernish Island, which means continuing close to Rutland at the start of the passage.

Going out, a good mark to steer for from Yellow Rock Beacon is a group of houses on Inishfree. When passing between the pair of beacons steer well over towards Rutland to get the conical beacon bearing 071° as soon as possible.

RUTLAND HARBOUR

is the part of the channel between Inishcoo and Duck Island. It is a good base for exploring the area as it is accessible at all states of the tide by N Channel and at suitable rise by the other two entrances just described. It is an anchorage completely sheltered from sea and swell, but the tide runs in and out at 2 or 3 kns. Anchor anywhere E of the W half of Duck Island in 5 or 7 m in mid-channel. Avoid anchoring near the electric cable which runs S from the ruined quay on Inishcoo. The best berth is perhaps to drop anchor in 4 or 5 m a little nearer Inishcoo and abreast one third of the distance from the corner of the ruined quay to the front leading light, and then run a warp ashore. It is rare to find another craft anchored here but there is a lot of fishing-boat and ferry traffic so a riding light is essential and possibly a duty watch on deck as the traffic in and out of Burtonport is heavy night and day. No facilities. **Quay.** It is possible to berth at the old quays on the small W Edernish Island opposite Nancy's Rock. There is 3·5 m alongside. Beware of a couple of iron projections about 1·5 m above

LWS. Large fenders would be needed because of the wash from fishing boats.

Black Hole

is the local name for the little bay just E of the rear leading light beacon on Rutland Island. It is 55 m wide and 35 m deep inside with the depth mostly about 4 m, definitely not drying as shown on the metric chart. It is an excellent berth in gales between S and NW for a yacht awaiting an improvement in weather conditions. A yacht well provided with warps may moor all fours here out of the strength of the tide and so sheltered that in a gale it is possible to row ashore to the island, where drinking water is available. Communication with Burtonport by hailing the ferry. **Instructions.** Drop anchor 18 m ENE of the W point of the Black Hole, no further out as the bottom is foul; take a stern warp ashore to the ruined kelp store on the SE side, smartly if during the ebb when an eddy swings the yacht towards the W shore. A bow warp should then be led to a ring on the W point, a breast warp to an iron bar in the direction of the white bungalow and a starboard quarter warp to a ring on the E point (but at HW this is submerged). It is best to have everything prepared and try to complete this mooring operation during slack tide at LW.

RUTLAND HARBOUR TO BURTONPORT
(see plan)

There is no room now to anchor in Burtonport but it is possible to berth outside the local vessels on the pier, preferably with someone remaining on board unless it can be found that nothing inside will be leaving. It is normally best to go out to Rutland or Aran before 3 hours after high tide but it might be convenient to stay a night at the berth after consulting the locals. The depth around the pier is believed to be 2 m. It is preferable to go in with the rising tide as in the narrows it can sometimes reach 5 kn, and it is believed that the depth in the dredged entrance is good enough for most yachts at half tide. Leaving Rutland harbour keep nearer to Rutland as there is a rock which rarely dries about 40 m outside the entrance of the passage between Inishcoo and Edernish. Leave Nancy's Beacon to starboard and Edernish Beacon to port, then keep rather nearer Edernish Island and from its S end head towards Teige's beacon until the Burtonport leading lights come in line 068°. Turn in on this line along the dredged channel and, after passing close S of the conical beacon, head towards the NW side of the pier and wait till fairly near the end before turning in to its SE side. It is normally best to tie alongside the vessels nearest the slip.

Facilities

Two good general stores, butcher, small hotel and bar, PO, phone. Water tap N side of building nearest pier. Petrol pump ¹/₂ mile inland, just right

Cruit Bay looking towards Gola Is.

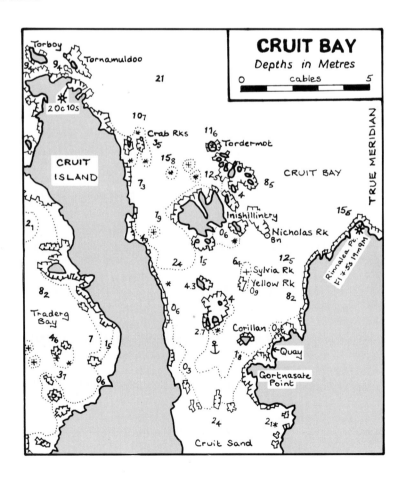

on the main road. Diesel available just inside the pier. Harbour Master Stephen McGonagle (075-43170). VHF Ch. 16 - 14. Fishermans Co-op for stores (075-42046). Local help with engine and hull repairs. Electronics (075-21082). Gas, taxi, public transport to Donegal town.

OWEY ISLAND AND SOUND (chart 1883)

The island is free of of flying dangers except on the SW side where a number of rocks terminate in Tornagaravan (Bream) 9 m high, and on the SE where a spit extends part of the way across the sound. Red granite cliffs with many caves on the W and N sides make impressive scenery. There is no secure anchorage but in settled sea conditions there can be good shelter in W wind on the SE side of the island off the village in 5 m. There is a good boat landing at a small quay in the deep, narrow gut just N of the E point. The island is inhabited but offers no facilities except a phone. There is a boat slip for them on Cruit Island just inside Horse Rock.

Owey Sound

presents no difficulty except in high swell or strong SW or N winds, but definitely cannot be used at night. It is possible to go through in a W gale when it would be particularly unpleasant W of the island. Heading straight from Aran Sound leave Tornamullane Rock 1 cable to starboard and then head N until in line with the beacons near the N of Cruit Island and head in to them, 070°, which leaves some covered rocks to starboard and the 3 m spit to port. (The Oc 10s lights are only for local boats arriving.) When the middle of the N exit is just N turn round and go out. In the N exit nearly 1/2 cable in the middle is deep but close to both sides is foul. It is sometimes possible to beat through and if desired you can go on the beacons line till the middle of Toratrave (Swim) Island is N. It is normally safe to cross the spit with the NW ends of Toratrave and Torboy (Torbwee) in line.

CRUIT BAY (chart 1883)

(Cruit is pronounced Critch)
This is a good anchorage easy of access and secure in all summer winds. Swell or N wind makes it uncomfortable at times. It used to be very suitable for visiting yachts but now the best part is filled with local moored fishing boats.

Light

On Rinnalea Point, the N extremity of Mullaghderg, there is a light Fl 7·5s, showing only between 132° to 167°, 5 M. It is at a height of 19 m on a 2·5 m tower which scarcely shows at all by day as it is exactly the same colour as the rocks behind it. On Gortnasate Quay there is a FY light. Visiting yachts should not try to go in if it is really dark and Corillan (Odd) Island cannot be easily seen.

The tower in ruins standing at a height of 48 m on the level ridge of Mullaghderg is conspicuous from all angles and an unmistakable mark, being the only stone tower between Horn Head and Crohy Head S of Aran.

Approach

From Owey Sound or the W there are no of flying dangers apart from Stag Rocks (see p240) and there is a rock 1½ cables NE of the N point of Cruit Island. All rocks E of the N part of Cruit and of Inishillintry remain above water. The sound W of Tordermot (Darby) and Inishillintry, though it may appear clean, is foul and should not be mistaken for Cruit Bay. From the N see channels under S approach to Gola (below). The entrance is W of Mullaghderg. Leave Nicholas Rock Beacon to starboard and steer straight for Corillan (Odd Is) 10 m high and rocky. To avoid unmarked Sylvia and Yellow Rocks the E side of Corillan in line with Gortnasate Point leads well E of them. The ebb tide runs out strongly.

Anchorages all on sand.

1. The snuggest position is S of Corillan in 2 m.
2. The good area a bit more than 2 c SW of Corillan has also a lot of local moorings so it is best to anchor just N of them. Do not go more than 1/2 cable N by W of Corillan as there is a dangerous rock further out (150 m) in this direction.
3. A previous anchorage which was not often used after the Yellow Beacon disappeared a good while ago might be nicer now than W of Corillan. Enter fairly close SE of Nicholas Beacon and keep the beacon bearing between 045° and 055°. This brings you safely between two rocks and beyond them there is an area about 3 m deep and good room to anchor. The best sheltered part is probably NW away from the rocks say Nicholas Beacon bearing 065° and Gortnasate Quay bearing between 150° and 156°. There is also an entrance from Corillan keeping Gortnasate Quay bearing 151° and heading towards the right hand of two rocks just S of Inishillintry's S point, passing through a 1/2 cable gap between Yellow Rock and the rocky area SW of it.

Gortnasate Quay

just inside Corillan, running NW, 45 m long, has at least 3 m LWS alongside. Water from fish factory; PO and some stores at Kincaslough 1/2 mile away. Nearest petrol 2 miles. Kincasla Pier, just SE of Gortnasate Point, dries 0·5 m alongside but is completely sheltered and would be a good place for a yacht to dry out. The road shown on chart 1883 stopping at Kincasla Pier runs to Gortnasate Quay, where there are concrete slips (2) to haul out quite large MFV's.

Gola E anchorage looking SE.

GOLA ISLAND AND SOUND (chart 1883)

There are many dangers N and S of Gola and several ways of going inside. Gola Roads is a good anchorage for small coasters but may be a bit exposed for yachts which can use small sheltered places or go right into Gweedore. None of the approaches are simple for a stranger and in bad weather and especially poor visibility a yacht coming from the S would be safer to make for Cruit Bay or Aran Road. Coming from the N if there is visibility it should be safe to go in through the N Sound. There are now leading lights on Gubnadough with day marks Oc 3 s 171°. Any entrance is of course only possible with a fair wind or a good engine. No facilities in Gola. It is no longer inhabited but there are visitors in summer.

From the South. Carnboy Channel

It is simple to go in fairly close S of Rabbit Rock which always shows. The main difficulty is passing through the cable wide gap between the rocks extending 2 cables out from Carnboy Point and on the W side Bullignagappul which dries 0·3 m and Bullignamort which is 0·3 m deep. A stranger may find it very difficult to identify the E point of Gubnadough (Table) just open of which

Innishmeane's summit is the entry line 012°. At HW of course a yacht is less liable to hit the rocks if it goes over them by mistaking the leading marks. For locals to go through at night there are leading lights, Iso 8s, 184°, above Mullaghdoo Point, but in daytime it is impossible to see where they are (even if you sail close to the S shore). Having passed the gap, head for the red buoy and leave it, and the next one, close to port. Going S from Gola it is of course easy to identify Gubnadough before you are far S from it so you can recognise it going through the gap.

Gola South Sound

is NE of Inishfree and you must keep away from all the rocks up to 7 cables S of Allagh Island. Local fisherman coming from the S usually go in this way. Approach well N of Inishfree to avoid the breaking rock 3 cables NW of it and turn 147° towards Annagary Hill (103 m) when it is seen just left of Inishfree. Go in on this until about 2 cables N of Inishfree and then steer 120° until Owey Island is just shut in behind the height of Inishfree, then steer about 085° with this part of Inishfree astern until Gubnadough is below the top of Inishmeane and then head up leaving the buoys to port.

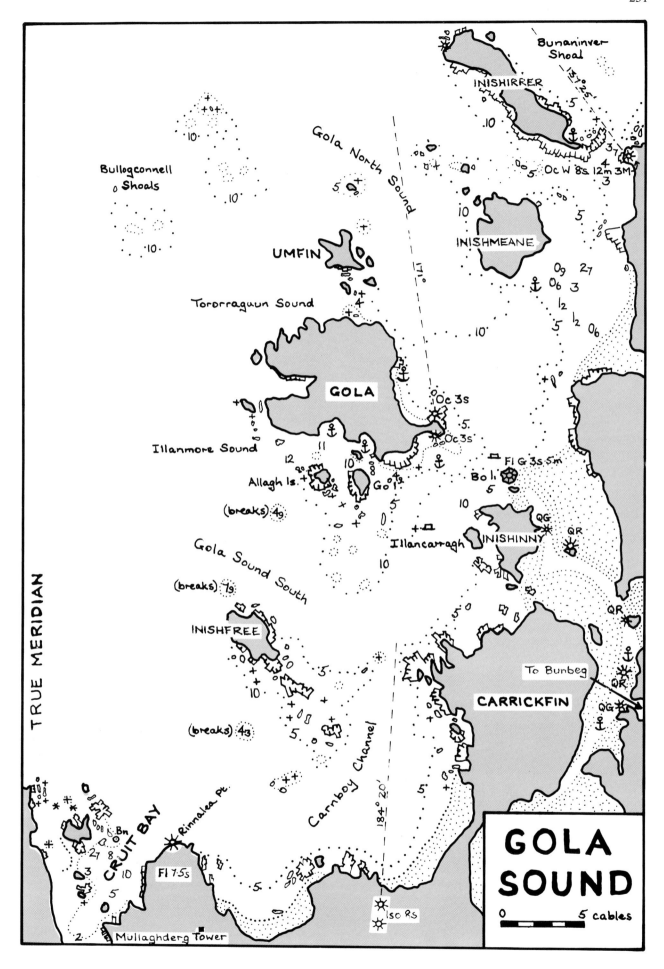

Bunaninver Shoal

INISHIRRER

Gola North Sound

Bulloqconnell Shoals

UMFIN

INISHMEANE

Oc W 8s 12m 3M

Tororraguun Sound

GOLA

Oc 3s

Oc 3s

Illanmore Sound

Fl G 3s 5m

Allagh Is

Go I.

Bo I.

Illancarragh

INISHINNY

QG

QR

Gola Sound South

(breaks) 7₉

INISHFREE

QR

To Bunbeg

CARRICKFIN

QR

QG

(breaks) 4₃

Carnboy Channel

TRUE MERIDIAN

CRUIT BAY

Rinnalea Pt.

Bn

Fl 7.5s

Iso 8s

Mullaghderg Tower

GOLA SOUND

0   5 cables

Illanmore Sound

is the most direct passage from seaward but has rocks to be avoided. Passage Rock 1·2 m deep in the middle N of Allagh Island would not be dangerous to most yachts near HW but to avoid it identify Torroe (Carrua) off Gola and enter ½ cable off it and when SE of it turn to port towards the large bay in Gola. When off the middle of the bay turn to starboard and head towards the NW end of Go Island. Keep 50 or 80 m away going along the N side of Go Island and continue keeping the NW point of Allagh Island only just outside or inside the N of Go so as to pass N of Leonancoyle Rock and carry on through Gola Roads in this direction until Gubnadough is in line with the top of Inishmeane.

Tororragaun Sound

is the gap between the N side of Gola and Tororragaun Rock, 19 m high. It is easy to identify and in fine weather is the shortest and simplest route from Owey to Gola Pier. It is probably dangerous in any swell as there is a ridge of rocks right across it, with less than 1 m and two drying rocks in the S half but with 4·6 m least charted depth on the N half. Enter just 50 m off the SW of Tororragaun which is steep-to and thence steer for the NE point of Gola, Carrickacuskeame on the chart.

From the North. Inishsirrer Strait

is fully explained near the end of this chapter. It is the shortest and often the most sheltered route to Gweedore Bay for a yacht after rounding the Bloody Foreland. It is necessary to have enough water to pass over the 1·2 m area SE of Inishmeane. Keep halfway between Inishmeane and the shore to find the deepest water. Then give Maghera Point a berth of 3 cables to clear Emlin (Emlaghmore) Rock.

Gola North Sound

From Bloody Foreland leave Inishsirrer's NW point 1 cable to port and keep on SW for another cable to avoid a possible breaker. Next you must pass between Keiltagh Rocks which only show at LWS and Rinogy Rock which dries 3 m, but if you see waves breaking on both it is simple. There are now leading lights on Gubnadough with day marks, Oc 3 s 171° from seaward. Otherwise steer towards the N point of Umfin Island until Gubnadough bears 168° and then turn towards it with Illancarragh just to port of it. When Tororragaun Sound is abeam head towards Bo Island, or if you want to anchor near Gola's pier turn in when you see it.

Anchorages

1. On E side of Gola there is plenty of room SSE of the pier. Local boats used to be moored here all winter, so it is tenable in all weather, but plenty of swell may roll in. The bottom is sand, mostly 3 m, but anywhere near the pier, buoy the anchor as the ground is foul with old moorings. There are still two moorings as people sometimes stay there in summer.

    2. In E wind it might be more pleasant to anchor 1 cable ESE of the S point of the E side of Inishmeane between 2 and 5 m.

    3. In winds between NW, and E the bay on the S of Gola and N of Allagh is a very suitable anchorage and easy to enter approaching as explained in Illanmore Sound above, depth 5 m; do not go within ½ cable of the W side or too close to the NE.

    4. The anchorage off Gola's S pier is smaller and not so easy to enter, but more convenient for going ashore. Approach from the N of the E of Go Island and head 355° towards the pier with a long one storied house above it. The entrance between the rocks is very narrow so it is simpler to go in near LW. Anchor in 4·5 m with the pier in line and opposite the other possible entrance from the W.

South cove on Gola looking SW.

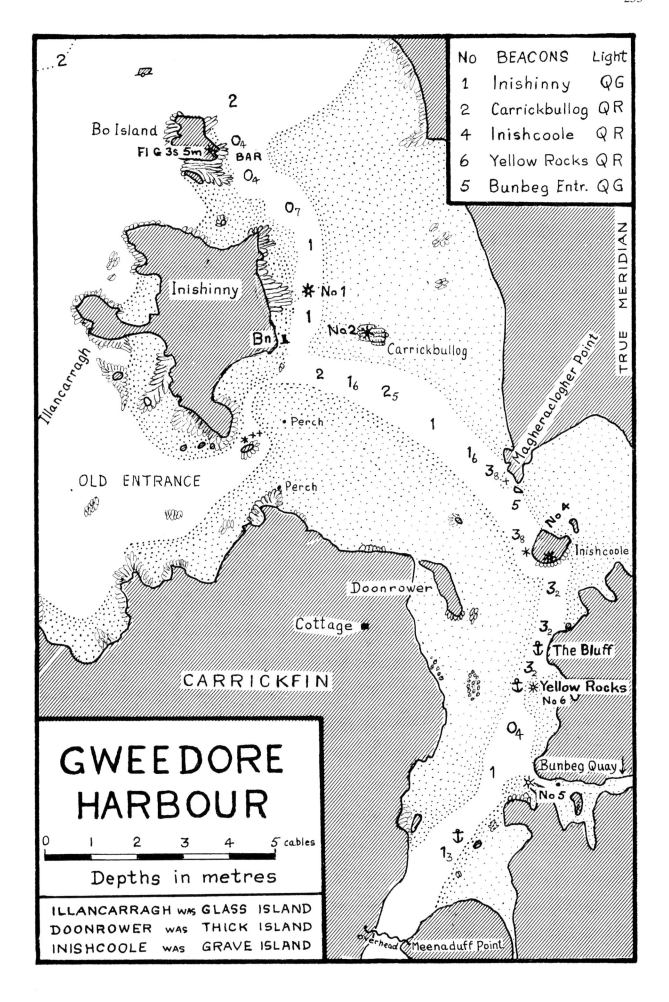

GWEEDORE
HARBOUR

0 1 2 3 4 5 cables

Depths in metres

ILLANCARRAGH was GLASS ISLAND
DOONROWER was THICK ISLAND
INISHCOOLE was GRAVE ISLAND

No	BEACONS	Light
1	Inishinny	QG
2	Carrickbullog	QR
4	Inishcoole	QR
6	Yellow Rocks	QR
5	Bunbeg Entr.	QG

GWEEDORE HARBOUR AND BUNBEG
(chart 1883). *(see plan)*
The entrance through Gweedore is quite complicated. It is well sheltered and a pretty place. The inner part is a possible place to leave a yacht. **Lights** mark the channel for local fishing boats which usually stay on Bunbeg Quay. The lights are shown on the plan, but a visitor should definitely not attempt to enter in the dark. A light, Fl G 3 s 5 m is on the E side of Bo Island. There is a QR 12 m 1 M now on S side on Inishcoole.

Directions
The bar E of Bo Island has increased in depth and now has about 0·4 m at LAT, so some yachts might go in at LWN on about 1·9 m. The best depth is close to the rocks extending E of Bo which can usually be seen below water, so it is not too difficult to keep fairly near them. As soon as the S end of Bo is abeam steer towards Carrickbullog and when E of the NE point of Inishinny turn S to pass just 12 m E of No. 1 beacon. From No. 1 beacon steer SSW and when abeam of the beacon near the S of Inishinny (which now has no light) turn briefly SE about 60 m and then turn to pass between 120 and 150 m S of Carrickbullog's Beacon No. 2. When the E of Carrickbullog is abeam turn 140°. Before passing Magheraclogher Point get No. 4 beacon on Inishcoole (Grave Is) in line with the left end of a new bungalow built where the old CG Station was situated. Do not go E of this line as it just clears the below water rock about 50 m off Magheraclogher Point. Next keep 70 m SW of Inishcoole to clear the rock which is only above water near LAT and is just SW of the beacon; the running tide might show it up. When past the rock keep a little nearer to the island and go round to its S end; this is necessary to avoid a spit which extends E just S of the island. Then head past The Bluff where the water is deep alongside and from it head W of No. 6 beacon which is on a rock and all the ground E of it dries at LWS. Beyond this beacon there is an area which is now 0·4 m deep, not as shallow as on the chart; it is all right for a yacht which has come in with the flood but the beacon should be kept in line with the edge of The Bluff until past the Bunbeg entrance.

Anchorages
1. Off The Bluff drop the anchor about 35 m from it and then bring a warp ashore round the iron stake near the S end and keep the yacht reasonably close to avoid passing boats. Good holding in 3 m right up to the rocks. But it might be unsuitable in June and July when salmon netting might be going on there.

2. Close W of Yellow Rocks (No. 6 beacon) with an anchor 5·5 m off it with a warp to the ring on the rock. E of this there is an old slip convenient for landing except near LW.

3. The nicest anchorage is SW of the Bunbeg entrance where there is lots of space and no traffic, but it is unsuitable for a deep yacht as it is mostly 1·8 m at LWS, though it may be getting deeper. Further down there are electric wires 6 m above HW across the narrower part which anyway is not nice for anchoring as the current there is stronger. A convenient place to anchor is a bit W of the islet about 2 cables beyond the Bunbeg entrance. Even there the ebb is fairly strong so it might be worth mooring with two anchors. The distance from there to the Bunbeg slip is about 4 cables so a dinghy with a motor is really necessary because the tides make it difficult to row either direction.

Bunbeg Quay
is fairly new and the channel in to it has been deepened to about 0·8 m, so at LWN it is about 2·3 m, but the N side is shallower. The stream may run out at 3 kn and may even be running out, not so fast, when the tide is rising. The quay is used by so many fishing vessels that it is not really suitable for a yacht to stay there. Beyond the quay there is an area for turning round, which is often impossible off the quay when many vessels are moored outside it. The slip is in the inner area. If a yacht wants to go in keep No. 6 beacon in line with The Bluff until W of No. 5 beacon, then go in fairly close to No. 5, leave the small perch to port and head towards the N end of the rocky point just S of the far end of the quay. Only when the W end of the quay comes abeam is it safe to turn in towards it.

Facilities
Water and diesel available at the quay. The village is ½ mile up the road and has a general store, butcher, chemist, two banks, hotel, garage and PO. Expert local advice can be had from Jim Boyd whose house is on the right side where the road goes up steeply from the slip.

INISHMEANE
There is a small pier on the E side a bit N of the normal anchorage ESE of the S point. It would be possible to anchor fairly close just N of the middle E point, but this of course is N of the bar running from the island to Magheragallan Creek. Sailing E of the island was described earlier for going to Gola.

Inishsirrer
A light Fl 3·7s, 4 M, shows to the N between 083° and 263° from a 4 m beacon on the NW of the island. The island has a few houses but is only inhabited in summer.

Anchorage

At the SE of the island there is a good little anchorage sheltered from WNW through S to ENE, sand bottom. It should be approached with the Kelp store just inside the W of the quay in line with the W side of Inishmeane. When Damph More Rock comes abeam to port steer for the summit of Inishmeane. This leads to an anchorage in 3·5 m E of Kelp store. If desiring to go further in steer S from here to anchor in 2 m.

Inishsirrer Strait

A safe and simple passage except in strong onshore wind or high swell when it should not be attempted. The important fact is that Damph More Rock always shows, but all the other rocks SW of it and E of the anchorages cover. From the S enter the strait with E side of Damph More bearing 000° to pass between the spit E of Damph Beg and the reefs SW of Glashagh Point. Then steer 030° to leave Damph More ½ cable to port. Two beacons Oc W 8s 12 m and Oc W 8s 17 m 3M on the shore N of Glashagh Point, in line 137¼° leads NE of the small rocks N of Damph More and SW of Bunaninver Shoal, so in bad weather keep a bit nearer to Inishsirrer. This is the best way in or out but in calm sea after heading 030° to the line you could head N until near Bloody Foreland.

Bunaninver Port

is a pleasant temporary anchorage in good weather. The entrance breaks right across in any rough sea. Keep well outside until you can head in exactly 134° to the inner end so as to avoid the outer rocks on either side. Anchor outside the narrower part. There is a slip on the N side.

Bloody Foreland Hill

315 m high, slopes down gradually to the low point of the headland from which reefs extend for 1 cable. Swell is apt to run high off the point, so it should be passed at a respectful distance. **Light**. There is a 4 m high beacon near the end of the point showing Fl 7·5s, WG 6-4 M to seaward between 062° and 232°, G between these bearings and the land on either side of the headland. The W light is stated to have a nominal range of 6 miles, but the G light only 4 miles and the two places which it is supposed to warn against, Bulligconnel Shoals to the SW and Inishbeg to the NE, are both 5 miles away. However, if sailing round this coast at night it is simplest and safest to pass outside Tory Island and anyway Aran has a good lower R light to ward against Bulligconnel shoals.

Yachts Bound South

See page 239 for North bound passage.

This is a simple description of the passage S from Bloody Foreland

Pass inside Inishsirrer; then if on the top half of the tide pass east of Inishmeane. If water on the bar inside Inishmeane is not sufficient, pass west of the island, i.e. between Inishmeane and Keiltagh Rocks.

From here pass inside Gola using the two channel buoys and between Carnboy Point and reefs east of Inishfree. (That is Bullignamort and Bullignagappaul) using the leading marks and lights shown on the chart for the Carnboy Channel. From about two cables north of Mullaghadoo Point, alter course west to pass south of Rabbit Rock and round Tornamuldoo and Torboy to pass through Owey Sound. From here the large striped beacon on Ballagh Rock at the north end of the Sound of Aran can usually be readily made out, leave it to port and follow the detailed directions on pages ??? et seq. for passing through the Sound of Aran.

The simple route through, from a point about half a cable west of Ballagh Rocks is to pass close west of Eighter Island and west of Carrickbealatroha Lower (North Perch) (an old pipe perch with triangular stays and top mark coloured yellow, black, yellow). West of Lack Morris beacon (a thin pipe with triangular stays, top mark black and red with two black balls on top). West of Carrickbealatroha Upper which has a very conspicuous wide square tower faced with white glazed tiles.

Pass east of Aileen Reef provided there is sufficient water; west of Turk Rock Beacon and out through South Sound, east of Illancrone.

The coast N beyond Bloody Foreland is described in a companion volume "Sailing Directions for the East and North Coasts of Ireland", published by Irish Cruising Club Publications Ltd. and obtainable from all good chandlers in England and on the Continent of Europe. Members and local Irish yachtsmen may obtain it from Mrs. Barbara Fox-Mills, The Tansey, Baily, Co. Dublin or through their local chandlery. In case of difficulty contact Imray Laurie, Norie and Wilson Ltd., Broadway, St. Ives, Huntington, Cambridge, who act as the companys distribution agents on the mainland UK and Europe.

Appendix 1

ADMIRALTY CHARTS AND PUBLICATIONS

Chart No.	Title of Charts (most plans larger scale)	Scale 1:	Publication Date
1123	Western approaches to St. George's Channel and Bristol Channel	500,000	12-84
1121	Irish Sea with St. George's Channell and North Channel	500,000	11-92
2049	Old Head of Kinsale to Tuskar Rock	150,000	7-83
2740	Saltee Islands	25,000	8-76
2046	Waterford Harbour (plans: Dunmore E, New Ross)	25,000	4-84
2017	Dungarvan Harbour	15,000	4-78
2071	Youghal Harbour	12,500	10-91
1765	Old Head of Kinsale to Power Head	50,000	6-79
1777	Port of Cork. Lower harbour and approaches	12,500	1-93
1773	Port of Cork. Upper harbours, east and west	12,500	1-93
2424	Kenmare River to Cork Harbour	150,000	12-81
2053	Kinsale Harbour and Oyster Haven	12,500	11-76
2081	Courtmacsherry Bay	25,000	11-77
2092	Toe Head to Old Head of Kinsale	50,000	2-79
3725	Baltimore Harbour	6,250	11-91
2129	Long Island Bay to Castlehaven	30,000	1-79
2184	Mizen Head to Gascanane Sound	30,000	3-79
2423	Mizen Head to Dingle Bay	150,000	12-81
2552	Dunmanus Bay. (three harbour plans)	30,000	5-80
1840	Bantry Bay – Black Ball Head to Shot Head (plan)	30,000	10-79
1838	Bantry Bay – Shot Head to Bantry (plan)	30,000	10-81
2495	Kenmare River (5 plans)	60,000	11-81
2125	Valentia Island. (large plan of Valentia Harbour)	30,000	11-78
2789	Dingle Bay and Smerwick Harbour. (Smerwick 40,000)	60,000	11-79
2790	Ventry and Dingle Harbours. (Blaskets 37,500)	15,000	11-79
2739	Brandon and Tralee Bays. (plan, Fenit Harbour)	37,500	5-80
2254	Valentia Island to River Shannon	150,000	11-81
1819	Approaches to River Shannon	50,000	12-79
1547	Shannon – Kilcredaun Point to Ardmore Point	20,000	1-87
1548	Shannon – Ardmore Point to Rinealon Point	20,000	12-86
1549	Shannon – Rinealon Point to Airport (plan: Foynes)	20,000	12-86
1540	Shannon Airport to Limerick	12,500	6-81
1125	Western approaches to Ireland	500,000	1-85
3338	Kilkee to Inisheer	50,000	4-80
2173	Loop Head to Slyne Head	150,000	7-84
3339	Approaches to Galway Bay and Aran Islands	50,000	12-81
1820	Aran Islands to Roonagh Head	75,000	3-84
1984	Galway Bay	30,000	2-93
1903	Galway Harbour	10,000	2-79
2096	Cashla Bay to Kilkieran Bay	30,000	10-81
2709	Roundstone and approaches	30,000	11-83
2420	Aran Islands to Broad Heaven Bay	150,000	7-84
2708	Ballyconneely Bay to Clifden Bay and Slyne Head	25,000	11-83

Chart No.	Title of Charts (most plans larger scale)	Scale 1:	Publication Date
2707	Kingstown to Cleggan Bays and Inishbofin to Inisturk	25,000	11-83
2706	Ballynakill and Killary Harbours and approaches	25,000	5-82
2667	Clew Bay and approaches	50,000	2-83
2057	Westport Bay	15,000	3-81
2725	Blacksod Bay to Tory island	200,000	7-82
2704	Blacksod Bay and approaches	50,000	11-81
2703	Broad Haven bay and approaches (plan: French port)	50,000	2-80
2767	Porturlin to Sligo Bay and Rathlin O'Birne Island	75,000	12-79
2715	Killala Bay (also Donegal Harbour 15,000)	25,000	7-77
2852	Approaches to Sligo (Sligo Harbour 12,500)	20,000	5-87
2702	Donegal Bay	60,000	10-79
2792	Plans on the NW coast: Teelin Harbour, Church Pool	10,000	10-81
	Killybegs 12,500. Sound of Aran and Burtonport	16,000	
2723	Western approaches to the North Channel	200,000	2-90
1879	Rathlin O'Birne Island to Aran Island	75,000	10-79
1883	Crohy Head to Bloody Foreland including Aran Island	30,000	9-81

Irish Coast Pliot (12th edition, 1986).
Admiralty Tide Tables, volume 1 current edition.
Admiralty List of Lights, volume A, 1993.
Admiralty List of Radio Signals, volume 1, 1992.

Agents for Admiralty charts:
Union Chandlery Ltd., Anderson's Quay, Cork (021) 21643. Telex 24914.
Galway Maritime Services, New Docks, Galway. (091) 66568.
Windmill Leisure and Marine Ltd., 3 Windmill Lane, Dublin 2. (01) 772008. Telex 24511.
Tedford's the Chandlers, Carrickfergus Marina, Rodgers Quay, Carrickfergus, BT38 8BE, (09603) 69600.
    Fax: (09603) 51164.
Todd Chart Agency, 76 Hopefield Avenue, Portrush, Co. Antrim BT56 8HE. (0265) 824176.
    Fax: (0265) 823077

New charts 2092, 1547, 2053, 2790

Appendix 2

TIDAL CONSTANTS

To find time of HW at	Apply to HW at		Rise (in meters) above chart datum at		
	Dover h.m.	**Cobh** h.m.	HW Springs	HW Neaps	Half Tide
Carnsore Point	-5.25	+0.24	3.0	2.3	1.3*
Saltee Islands	-5.35	+0.14	3.8	2.9	1.7*
Dunmore East	-5.35	+0.13	4.1	3.3	2.2
Waterford Town	-4.55	+0.57	4.5	3.6	2.4
New Ross	-5.05	+0.45	4.5	3.8	2.6
Dungarvan	-5.40	+0.08	4.1	3.4	2.3
Youghal	-5.45	+0.06	4.1	3.3	2.3
Ballycotton	-5.55	-0.05	4.1	3.3	2.3
Cobh	-5.50	—	4.1	3.3	2.3
Kinsale	-6.00	-0.12	4.0	3.2	2.3
Courtmacsherry	-6.10	-0.18	3.7	3.0	2.1
Castlehaven	+6.05	-0.28	3.7	2.9	2.0
Baltimore	-6.05	-0.15	3.6	3.0	2.1
Schull	+6.10	-0.27	3.2	2.7	1.8
Crookhaven	+5.50	-0.45	3.3	2.7	1.8
Dunmanus Harbour	+5.45	-0.50	3.4	2.7	1.9
Dunbeacon Harbour	+5.55	-0.40	3.3	2.6	1.8
Bantry	+6.00	-0.35	3.4	2.6	1.9
Castletownbere	+6.05	-0.30	3.5	2.7	2.0
Ballycrovane	+5.40	-0.55	3.5	2.8	2.0
West Cove	+5.40	-0.53	3.5	2.8	2.0
Dunkerron	+5.45	-0.52	3.9	3.0	2.2
Knightstown	+5.35	-0.58	3.8	3.0	2.1
Castlemaine Harbour	-6.05	-0.16	4.5	3.5	2.6
Dingle	+5.40	-0.56	3.8	2.9	2.1
Smerwick	+5.50	-0.47	3.8	2.9	2.1*
Fenit	+6.00	-0.37	4.6	3.5	2.6
Kilbaha	+6.05	-0.15	4.3	3.3	2.4
Carrigaholt	+6.05	-0.15	4.9	3.7	2.8
Kilrush	-5.55	+0.10	5.0	3.7	2.7
Tarbet	-5.30	+0.35	5.0	3.8	2.7
Foynes	-5.15	+0.50	5.2	4.0	2.8
Limerick	-4.35	+1.30	5.9	4.5	2.9
Mutton Island (Clare)	+6.10	-0.10	4.6	3.5	2.6*
Galway	-6.05	—	5.1	3.9	2.9
Kilronan	+6.10	-0.08	4.7	3.6	2.6
Kilkiernan Cove	-6.00	+0.05	4.8	3.7	2.7
Roundstone Bay	-6.00	+0.03	4.4	3.4	2.5
Clifden Bay	-6.00	+0.05	4.4	3.4	2.5*

*Estimate

To find time of HW at	Apply to HW at		Rise (in meters) above chart datum at		
	Dover h.m.	**Cobh** h.m.	HW Springs	HW Neaps	Half Tide
Inishbofin	-5.55	+0.10	4.1	3.1	2.3
Killary Harbour	-5.45	+0.18	4.1	3.1	2.3
Westport Bay	-5.45	+0.20	4.5	3.4	2.5
Clare Island	-5.50	+0.15	4.1	3.2	2.3
Bull's Mouth	-5.05	+1.00	3.6	2.9	2.1
Blacksod	-5.35	+0.30	3.9	2.9	2.2
Broadhaven	-5.20	+0.45	3.7	2.8	2.1
Killala Bay	-5.20	+0.45	3.8	2.7	2.1
Ballysadare Bay	-5.00	+1.05	3.9	3.0	2.2*
Sligo Harbour	-5.15	+0.50	4.1	3.0	2.3
Mullaghmore	-5.25	+0.40	3.7	2.9	2.1
Killybegs	-5.20	+0.45	4.1	3.0	2.3
Burtonport	-5.15	+0.50	3.9	2.9	2.2
Bunbeg	-5.10	+0.55	3.8	2.9	2.2

*Estimate

Appendix 3

TIDAL STREAMS — CARNSORE POINT TO LOOP HEAD

Ref: HW Cobh	HW	Hours after						Hours before				
		1	2	3	4	5	6	5	4	3	2	1
Carnsore Point	ENE	ENE	ENE	ENE	ENE	WSW	WSW	WSW	WSW	WSW	WSW	ENE
Saltees	E	E	E	E	E	W	W	W	W	W	W	E
Conningbeg	E	E	E	E	E	W	W	W	W	W	W	E
Hook Point	E	E	E	E	W	W	W	W	W	W	E	E
Ram Head	E	E	E	W	W	W	W	W	W	W	E	E
Youghal	NNE	SSE	SSE	SSE	SSE	SSE	SSW	SW	SW	W	W	N
Cork Hbr entr	S	S	S	S	S	S	N	N	N	N	N	N
Old Head	E	E	W	W	W	W	W	W	E	E	E	E
Seven Heads	E	E	W	W	W	W	W	W	E	E	E	E
Galley Head	E	E	W	W	W	W	W	W	E	E	E	E
Gascanane Sound	NW	NW	NW	NW	NW	SE	SE	SE	SE	SE	SE	NW
Cape Clear	E	E	W	W	W	W	W	W	E	E	E	E
Mizen Head	S	NW	NW	NW	NW	NW	NW	S	S	S	S	S
Dursey Sound	S	N	N	N	N	N	N	S	S	S	S	S
Bull Rock	SE	SE	SE	NW	NW	NW	NW	NW	SE	SE	SE	SE

Information for places below is referred to HW **Galway**

Skelligs	N	N	S	S	S	S	S	S	N	N	N	N
Bray Head	S	S	S	S	S	N	N	N	N	N	N	S
Blasket Sound	S	S	S	S	S	N	N	N	N	N	N	S
Inishtearaght	S	S	S	S	S	N	N	N	N	N	N	S
Brandon Point	SW	SW	SW	SW	SW	NE	NE	NE	NE	NE	NE	SW
Magharee Island	SW	SW	SW	SW	SW	NE	NE	NE	NE	NE	NE	SW
Loop Head	NE	NE	NE	SW	SW	SW	SW	SW	SW	NE	NE	NE

TIDAL STREAMS - WEST COAST OF IRELAND

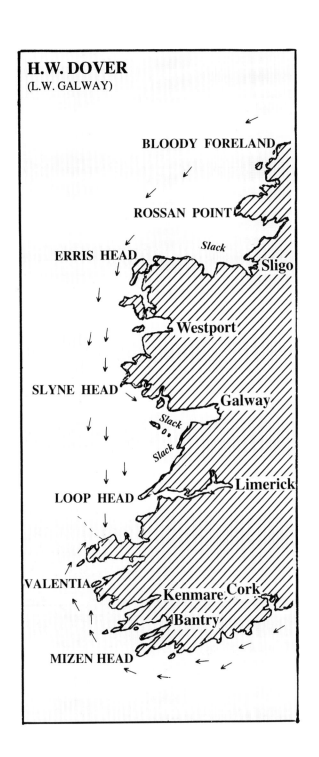

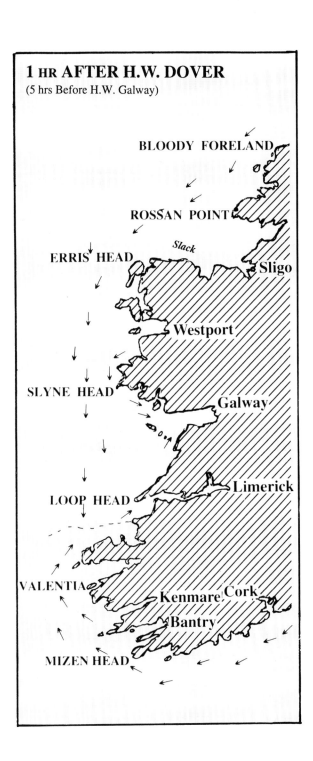

Note by the Honorary Compiler: Tidal stream information for the whole of the West coast of Ireland is extremely sparse. This tidal stream atlas is based on research work done by Wallace Clark (ICC) using very old Admiralty Pilots, also from his personal observations. It is our constant endeavour to improve all our information, so any mariner who can help with further information should send it to the Honorary Compiler, 11 Old Holywood Road, Belfast, BT4 2HJ. Essential are: Dates, Times, Tide Direction and if possible, an estimate of Rate.

TIDAL STREAMS - WEST COAST OF IRELAND

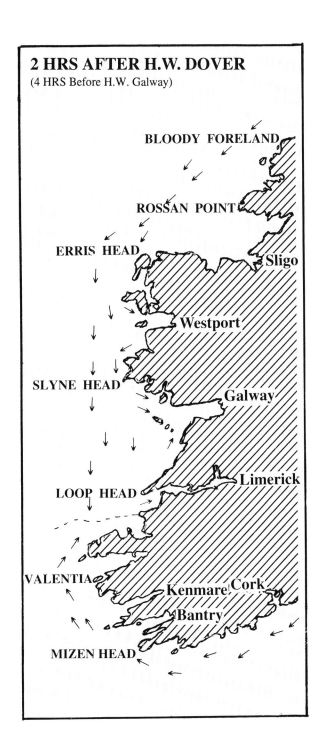

2 HRS AFTER H.W. DOVER
(4 HRS Before H.W. Galway)

BLOODY FORELAND

ROSSAN POINT

ERRIS HEAD

Sligo

Westport

SLYNE HEAD

Galway

LOOP HEAD

Limerick

VALENTIA

Kenmare Cork

Bantry

MIZEN HEAD

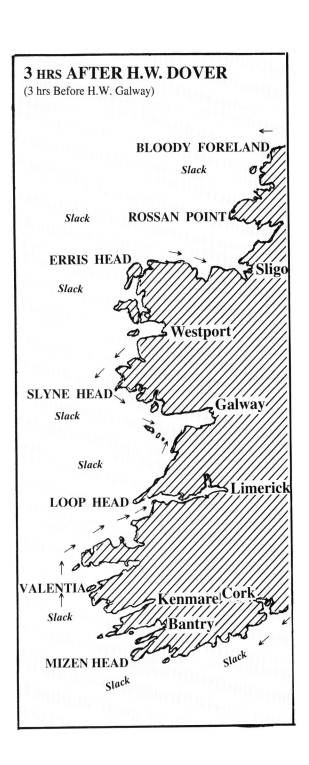

3 HRS AFTER H.W. DOVER
(3 hrs Before H.W. Galway)

BLOODY FORELAND
Slack

Slack   ROSSAN POINT

ERRIS HEAD
Slack   Sligo

Westport

SLYNE HEAD
Slack   Galway

Slack

LOOP HEAD   Limerick

VALENTIA
Slack   Kenmare Cork

                  Bantry

MIZEN HEAD   *Slack*

Slack

Note by the Honorary Compiler: Tidal stream information for the whole of the West coast of Ireland is extremely sparse. This tidal stream atlas is based on research work done by Wallace Clark (ICC) using very old Admiralty Pilots, also from his personal observations. It is our constant endeavour to improve all our information, so any mariner who can help with further information should send it to the Honorary Compiler, 11 Old Holywood Road, Belfast, BT4 2HJ. Essential are: Dates, Times, Tide Direction and if possible, an estimate of Rate.

TIDAL STREAMS - WEST COAST OF IRELAND

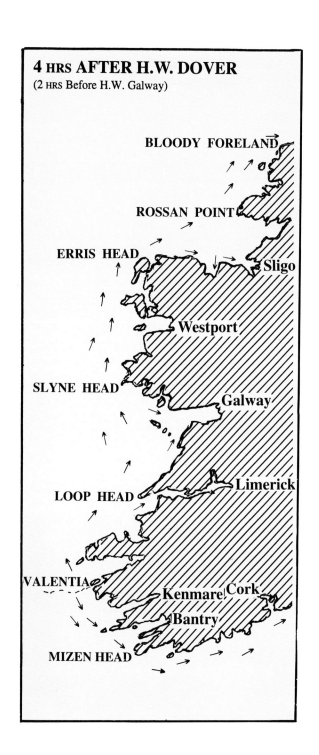

4 HRS AFTER H.W. DOVER
(2 HRS Before H.W. Galway)

BLOODY FORELAND
ROSSAN POINT
ERRIS HEAD
Sligo
Westport
SLYNE HEAD
Galway
LOOP HEAD
Limerick
VALENTIA
Kenmare Cork
Bantry
MIZEN HEAD

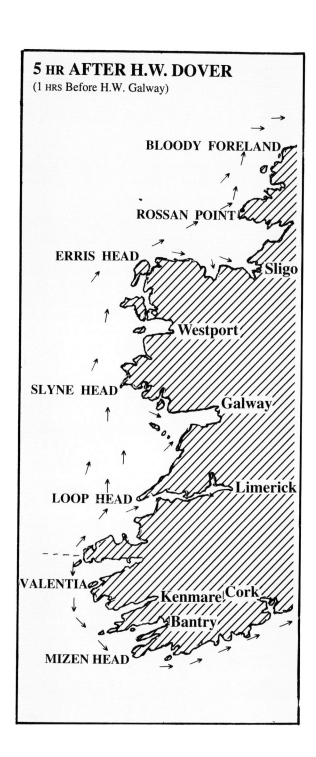

5 HR AFTER H.W. DOVER
(1 HRS Before H.W. Galway)

BLOODY FORELAND
ROSSAN POINT
ERRIS HEAD
Sligo
Westport
SLYNE HEAD
Galway
LOOP HEAD
Limerick
VALENTIA
Kenmare Cork
Bantry
MIZEN HEAD

Note by the Honorary Compiler: Tidal stream information for the whole of the West coast of Ireland is extremely sparse. This tidal stream atlas is based on research work done by Wallace Clark (ICC) using very old Admiralty Pilots, also from his personal observations. It is our constant endeavour to improve all our information, so any mariner who can help with further information should send it to the Honorary Compiler, 11 Old Holywood Road, Belfast, BT4 2HJ. Essential are: Dates, Times, Tide Direction and if possible, an estimate of Rate.

TIDAL STREAMS - WEST COAST OF IRELAND

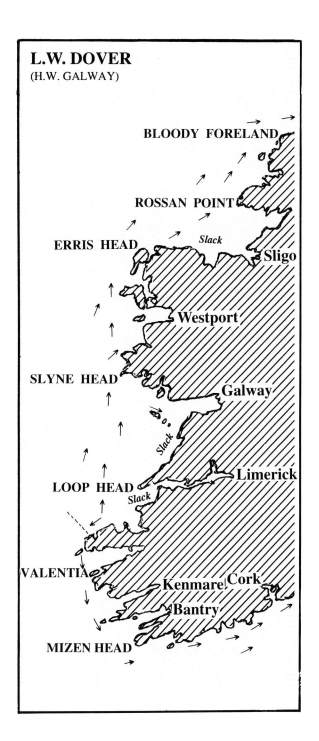

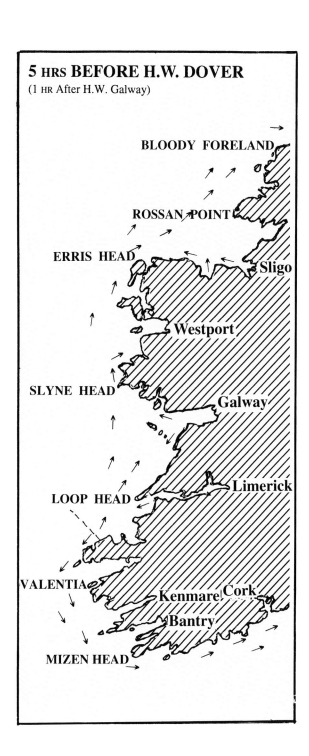

Note by the Honorary Compiler: Tidal stream information for the whole of the West coast of Ireland is extremely sparse. This tidal stream atlas is based on research work done by Wallace Clark (ICC) using very old Admiralty Pilots, also from his personal observations. It is our constant endeavour to improve all our information, so any mariner who can help with further information should send it to the Honorary Compiler, 11 Old Holywood Road, Belfast, BT4 2HJ. Essential are: Dates, Times, Tide Direction and if possible, an estimate of Rate.

TIDAL STREAMS - WEST COAST OF IRELAND

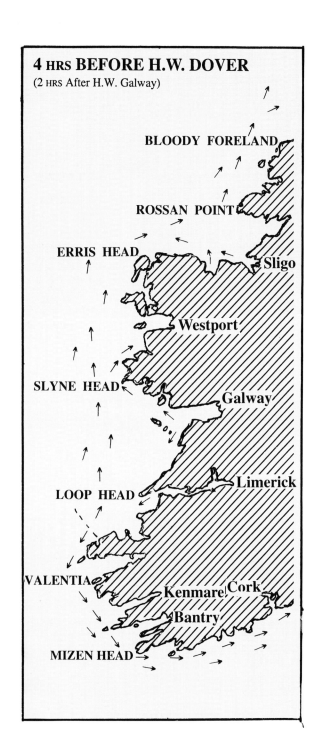

4 HRS BEFORE H.W. DOVER
(2 HRS After H.W. Galway)

BLOODY FORELAND

ROSSAN POINT

ERRIS HEAD

Sligo

Westport

SLYNE HEAD

Galway

LOOP HEAD

Limerick

VALENTIA

Kenmare Cork

Bantry

MIZEN HEAD

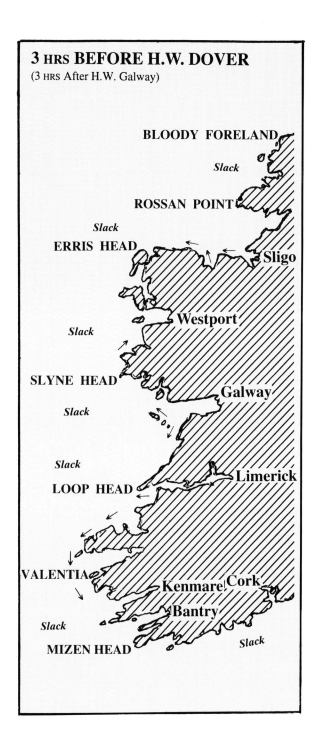

3 HRS BEFORE H.W. DOVER
(3 HRS After H.W. Galway)

BLOODY FORELAND

Slack

ROSSAN POINT

Slack

ERRIS HEAD

Sligo

Westport

Slack

SLYNE HEAD

Galway

Slack

Slack

LOOP HEAD

Limerick

VALENTIA

Kenmare Cork

Slack

Bantry

MIZEN HEAD

Slack

Note by the Honorary Compiler: Tidal stream information for the whole of the West coast of Ireland is extremely sparse. This tidal stream atlas is based on research work done by Wallace Clark (ICC) using very old Admiralty Pilots, also from his personal observations. It is our constant endeavour to improve all our information, so any mariner who can help with further information should send it to the Honorary Compiler, 11 Old Holywood Road, Belfast, BT4 2HJ. Essential are: Dates, Times, Tide Direction and if possible, an estimate of Rate.

TIDAL STREAMS - WEST COAST OF IRELAND

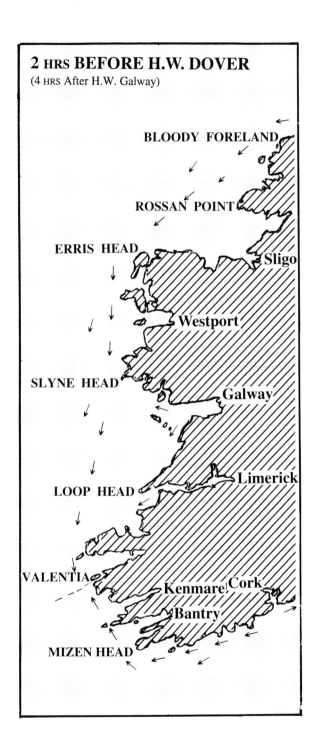

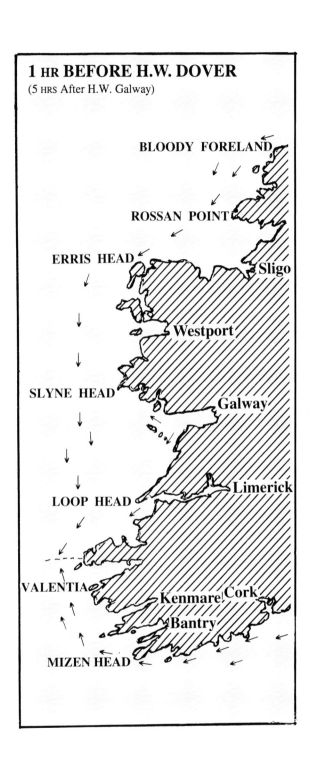

Note by the Honorary Compiler: Tidal stream information for the whole of the West coast of Ireland is extremely sparse. This tidal stream atlas is based on research work done by Wallace Clark (ICC) using very old Admiralty Pilots, also from his personal observations. It is our constant endeavour to improve all our information, so any mariner who can help with further information should send it to the Honorary Compiler, 11 Old Holywood Road, Belfast, BT4 2HJ. Essential are: Dates, Times, Tide Direction and if possible, an estimate of Rate.

Appendix 4

TABLES OF DISTANCES, SOUTH COAST

Upper table (rows beginning at each headland, reading across):

CARNSORE POINT	25	45	58	65	78	84	88	98	114	116	125	128
DUNMORE EAST		22	35	43	55	61	65	75	91	93	102	105
HELVICK			18	25	38	44	47	57	73	75	83	87
YOUGHAL				11	24	30	34	43	59	61	70	73
BALLYCOTTON					15	21	25	34	50	52	61	64
CROSSHAVEN						14	17	27	43	45	54	57
OYSTERHAVEN							5	15	32	34	42	46
KINSALE								15	32	34	42	46
COURTMAC-SHERRY									23	25	34	38
GLANDORE										6	16	20
CASTLEHAVEN											12	16
BALTIMORE												8
C. CLEAR												

Lower-left table:

BALTIMORE	SKULL	CROOKHAVEN	KITCHEN COVE	DUNBEACON	BEREHAVEN	GLENGARRIFF	BANTRY	SNEEM	KILMAK-ILLOGUE	DARRYNANE	BALLINSKELLIGS BAY	PORT MAGEE
9												
14	8											
32	27	21										
36	31	25	4									
32	27	21	19	21								
43	38	33	29	32	18							
42	37	32	28	31	17	6						
51	46	41	40	43	30	45	45					
52	47	42	41	44	31	46	46	4				
44	39	34	33	36	23	38	38	14	15			
48	43	38	37	40	27	42	42	18	19	6		
56	51	46	45	48	35	50	50	28	29	16	13	
63	58	53	52	55	42	57	57	35	36	23	20	4

KNIGHTSTOWN

Distances are through Saltee, Gascanane and Dursey Sounds
To Knightstown W of Valencia I. (except P. Magee)

TABLES OF DISTANCES, WEST COAST

VALENTIA — 13, 12, 22, 34, 46, 48, 58, 85, 103, 94, 93, 94, 97

DINGLE — 10, 20, 32, 44, 46, 56, 83, 101, 92, 91, 93, 95

BLASKET SOUND — 10, 22, 34, 36, 46, 73, 91, 82, 81, 82, 85

SMERWICK HARBOUR — 15, 25, 28, 38, 66, 84, 74, 75, 77, 75

BRANDON BAY — 15, 19, 27, 58, 75, 66, 67, 70, 70

FENIT — 20, 26, 58, 77, 66, 70, 72, 72

LOOP HEAD — 11, 38, 57, 48, 48, 52, 54

CARRIGAHOLT — 53, 68, 58, 62, 65, 67

KILRONAN (ARAN) — 25, 10, 14, 22, 30

GALWAY — 24, 35, 40, 50

CASHLA BAY — 15, 23, 32

KILKIERAN — 15, 24

ROUNDSTONE — 15

SLYNE HEAD

SLYNE HEAD — 13

INISHBOFIN — 28, 16

CLARE IS. — 44, 29, 15

WESTPORT — 36, 25, 16, 28

ACHILL HEAD — 53, 38, 32, 44, 16

ELLY BAY (BLACKSOD) — 55, 46, 37, 50, 20, 19

FRENCHPORT — 67, 58, 48, 61, 31, 30, 13

BROADHAVEN — 92, 81, 72, 84, 56, 56, 40, 37

KILLALA — 108, 97, 88, 100, 72, 72, 55, 53, 23

SLIGO — 116, 105, 96, 108, 80, 80, 63, 62, 38, 26

KILLYBEGS — 110, 99, 90, 102, 74, 74, 57, 54, 33, 23, 9

TEELIN — 103, 92, 83, 95, 67, 67, 50, 48, 29, 26, 18, 10

RATHLIN O'BIRNE — 128, 117, 108, 120, 92, 90, 75, 69, 54, 51, 43, 35, 25

BURTONPORT — 139, 128, 119, 131, 103, 101, 86, 80, 64, 61, 53, 45, 35, 12

BLOODY FORELAND

Appendix 5

WAY POINTS

These positions have been prepared to give approximately 1M clearance of prominent headlands, buoys, etc. or approximately ½M off the entrance to harbours, when visual fixing should be possible in average visability. The South and West coasts of Ireland have many deep indentations of the coast line, also numbers of offlying islands, rocks and areas of breaking water in heavy weather. **Positions should be very carefully checked before entry into an electronic means of assistance to the navigator.**

Place	Way Point Positions	Way Point	
Carnsore Rock	3M S	52 07 40 N	06 22 00 W
Connigbeg Lt.	1M S	52 01 40 N	06 39 30 W
Hook Head Lt.	1M S	52 06 20 N	06 55 80 W
Helvick Head Lt.	1M E	52 03 20 N	07 30 50 W
Mine Head	1M E	51 59 55 N	07 33 00 W
Ballycotton Is.	1M E	51 48 40 N	07 59 00 W
Cork Whistle Buoy	1M N	51 43 90 N	08 15 30 W
Old Head of Kinsale	1M S	51 35 20 N	08 31 80 W
Seven Heads Tower	1M S	51 33 10 N	08 42 90 W
Galley Head	2M S	51 29 78 N	08 57 00 W
Toe Head	2M S	51 26 80 N	09 13 70 W
Cape Clear	1M S	51 24 20 N	09 30 80 W
Mizzen Head Lt.	1M S	51 25 98 N	09 49 10 W
Three Castle Head	1M W	51 28 87 N	09 51 85 W
Dursey Head	2M S	51 32 60 N	10 13 90 W
The Bull	1M SW	51 34 60 N	10 19 40 W
Great Skellig Lt.	2M W	51 46 15 N	10 35 70 W
Great Foze Rock	2M W	51 01 40 N	10 44 50 W
Tearaght Is. Lt.	2M NW	52 06 00 N	10 42 00 W
Loop Head Lt.	2M W	52 33 60 N	09 59 20 W
Black Head Lt.	2M W	53 09 20 N	09 19 00 W
Rock Is. Lt.	2M N	53 11 00 N	09 51 30 W
Slyne Head Lt.	2M W	53 24 00 N	10 17 30 W
Innishshark	3M W	53 36 60 N	10 22 50 W
Achill Head	2M W	53 58 50 N	10 18 80 W
Black Rock Lt.	1M E	54 04 00 N	10 17 45 W
Eagle Is. Lt.	2M NW	54 18 45 N	10 08 00 W
The Stags	1M N	54 23 00 N	10 47 22 W
Downpatrick Head	1M N	54 20 70 N	09 20 70 W
Lenadoon Pt.	1M NW	54 18 30 N	09 04 50 W
Ardboline Is.	1M W	54 20 79 N	09 42 30 W
Rathlin O'Birne	1M W	54 39 80 N	08 51 75 W
Arranmore Lt.	1M W	55 00 90 N	08 35 32 W
White Rock (Owey)	½M NW	55 03 96 N	08 28 00 W
Togglass Is. (Gola)	1M W	55 05 21 N	08 24 70 W
Innishsirrer Lt.	½M W	55 07 41 N	08 21 72 W
Bloody Foreland	1M W	55 09 52 N	08 18 74 W

Appendix 6

WEATHER FORECASTS AND MARINE RADIO SERVICES

RTE gives forecasts for all coastal waters at 0633, 1253, 1823, 2355 civil time. These are broadcast on RTE Radio 1 566 kHz Tullamore and 1188 kHz Cork. (529m and 412 m). Also on FM, 90.0 MHz for chapters 1, 2, 3, 4; 88.8 MHz for chapters 5, 6 and 88.2 MHz for chapters 7, 8. Gale warnings are broadcast at the first programme junction after receipt.

Central Forecast Office gives forecasts on request. Tel. (01) 424655.

COAST RADIO STATION SERVICE – VHF/MF BROADCAST SERVICE

Traffic Lists, Navigational Warnings including Decca Warnings, Gale Warnings and Weather Forecasts are broadcast on the Coast Stations Working Channel/Frequency at scheduled times GMT following a preliminary announcement on Channel 16 VHF and 2182 kHz MF.

DUBLIN CONTROL. Tel.01 6620922/23. Telex 01-93039

DUBLIN RADIO	WICKLOW HEAD RADIO
VHF Ch 83 C	VHF Ch 87 C
ROSSLARE RADIO	MINE HEAD RADIO
VHF Ch 23 C	VHF Ch 83 C

MALIN HEAD CONTROL. Tel. 077-70103. Telex. 42072 MALR EI

MALIN HEAD RADIO	GLEN HEAD RADIO
VHF Ch 23 C	VHF Ch 24 C
MF 1667 kHz A	
BELMULLET RADIO	CLIFDEN RADIO
VHF Ch 83 C	VHF Ch 26 C

VALENTIA CONTROL. Tel. 066-76109. Telex. 73968 VALR EI

VALENTIA RADIO	SHANNON RADIO
VHF Ch 24 D	VHF Ch 28 D
MF 1752 kHz B	
BANTRY RADIO	CORK RADIO
VHF Ch 23 D	VHF Ch 26 D

For calling and answering use Channel 16 VHF and 2182 kHz MF to call the nearest station to your own position. The control centre will answer on the same channel or frequency. Working channels VHF, frequencies MF and broadcast group schedules are shown under each station.

Broadcast Group	Traffic Lists	Navigational Warning	Weather Bulletin	Gale Warning
A	0103 1503 0503 1703 0903 1903 1103 2103 1303 2303	0033 0433 0833 1233 1633 2033 Note 1	No Service	No Service
B	0333 1533 0733 1733 0933 1933 1133 2133 1333 2333	0233 0633 1033 1433 1833 2233 Note 1	0833 2033 Note 4	0303 0903 1503 2103 Note 2
C	0103 1503 0503 1703 0903 1903 1103 2303	0033 0433 0833 1233 1633 2033 Note 1	0103 1303 0403 1603 0703 1903 1003 2203 Note 5	0033 0633 1233 1833 Note 3
D	0333 1533 0733 1733 0933 1933 1133 2133 1333 2333	0233 0633 1033 1433 1833 2233 Note 1	0103 1303 0403 1603 0703 1903 1003 2203 Note 5	0033 0633 1233 1833 Note 3

NOTES:

1. Navigational Warnings including Decca Warnings are broadcast at scheduled Navigational Warning times and may also be broadcast on receipt and at other times following an announcement on 2182 kHz and Channel 16.

2. Gale Warnings are broadcast on (MF) at the end of the first silence period after receipt and repeated at the next one of the following times 0303 0903 1503 2103 or, if the first broadcast is at a scheduled time, the message is repeated at the end of the next silence period.

3. Gale Warnings are broadcast on (VHF) on receipt and repeated again at the next one of the following times 0033 0633 1233 1833 or, if the first broadcast is at a scheduled time, the message is repeated one hour later. (The above times will be one hour earlier when DST is in force).

4. Gale Warnings, if in force, general synopsis and are forecasts are broadcast on (MF) at 0833 and 2033 for Shannon and Fastnet Areas valid for 24 hours from time of issue. (Issued by the UK Met. Service).

5. Gale Warnings, if in force, general synopsis and detailed weather forecasts are broadcast on (VHF) at 0103 and every three hours for Irish coastal waters and for the Irish Sea, valid for 24 hours from the time of issue. (The above times will be one hour earlier when DST is in force). (Issued by the Irish Met. Service).

6. MF Range 200 NM. VHF Range 45-50 NM.

7. In addition to the listed VHF channels, the Coastguard Channel 67 and emergency 16 are also guarded.

NOTE: Schedule times are one hour earlier when DST is in force from last Sunday in March to 4th Saturday in October.

Other Forecasts:

(1) A forecast is given after RTE 1 television evening news at about 2115. This time may differ with special programmes. It includes weather maps, satellite photo and forecast. It is very good value and can usually be obtained ashore in a hotel or pub.

(2) Shannon Airport Met. office (061) 61333 (Aviation only).

(3) Cork Airport Met. office (021) 965974.

(4) South Munster Weather (021) 964600.

(5) North Munster and South Connaught Weather (061) 62677.

(6) Leinster Weather (01) 425555.

(7) North Connaught/Co. Donegal (071) 69111.

MARINE RADIO BEACONS

Name	Range	Freq kHz	Signal	
Tuskar Rock	50M	286.0	TR − .−.	3 times 13 secs long dash 47 secs
Old Head of Kinsale	50M	288.0	OH − − −	3 times 13 secs long dash 47 secs
Mizzen Head	100M	300.0	MZ − − − − ..	3 times 13 secs long dash 47 secs
Eagle Island	100M	307.0	GL − −. .−..	3 times 13 secs long dash 47 secs
Tory Island	100/70M	308	TY − −.− −	3 times 13 secs long dash 47 secs
Loop Head	50M	311.5	LP .−.. .− −.	3 times 13 secs long dash 47 secs

Now all continuous transmissions.

Old Head of Kinsale provides a calibration beacon on request, see Admiralty List of Radio Signals.

RADIO BEACONS FOR AIRCRAFT

Name	Signal	Freq kHz	Last	Long
Ennis..........................	ENS . −. ...	371	52 54 16 N	08 55 37 W
Bunratty.....................	BNY −... −. −.−−	352	52 41 47 N	08 49 20 W
Foynes........................	FOY ..−. −−−−.−−	395	52 33 58 N	09 11 40 W
Cork..........................	OC −−− −.−.	343	51 54 18 N	08 31 47 W
Carnmore	CRN −.−. .−. −.	321	53 18 00 N	08 57 00 W
Waterford...................	WTD .−− − −..	368	52 11 17 N	07 05 13 W

All beacons A0A2 transmission. During recognition BFO Off. During DF transmission BFO On. Beacons operate continiously.

Appendix 7

PORT VHF RADIO STATIONS

Dunmore East (Waterford). Ch. 16-14. 24 hours.

Waterford Harbour Sailing Club 16-39. Summer daylight sailing times.

New Ross. Ch. 16-12-14. 0900-1700.

Cork Harbour. Ch. 16-14-12. 24 hours.

Kinsale. Ch. 16-12. 24 hours.

Valentia Ch. 16-15-23-26-85. 24 hours.
   (With repeater, covers area from Aran Islands to Baltimore with certain blank areas).
   Best to use Ch. 23 as far as Seven Heads and Ch. 26 from thence when going W.

Kilrush (Shannon). Ch. 16-12-13. 24 hours.

Galway. Ch. 16-12. 0900-1700 (also 2 hours before HW until HW).

Sligo. Ch. 16-12. On request.

Killybegs. Ch. 16-14. 0900-1700.

Appendix 8

PRINCIPAL LIGHTS

Light On in Fog, marked "On," as exhibited during daylight when the fog signals are sounded, or in the case of lights without fog signals then in periods of poor visibility.

RANGE.—Luminous range is the maximum distance at which a light can be seen at a given time, as determined by the intensity of the light and the meteorological visibility prevailing at that time; it takes no account of elevation, observer's height of eye or the curvature of the earth.

Nominal range is the luminous range when the meteorological visibility is 10 sea miles.

The ranges included in the List of Lights are those published by the competent authority.

Geographical range is the maximum distance at which light from a light can theoretically reach an observer, as limited only by the curvature of the earth and the refraction of the atmosphere, and by the elevation of the light and the height of eye of the observer of two metres in this table.

Name	Lights In fog	Character and colour	Period secs	Elev m	Range miles		Fog signal	Type and height of lighthouse
					Nom	Geo		
Tuskar	On	Q (2) W	7·5	33	28	14	Horn (4) 45 secs	Wh Tr 34 m
Coningbeg Light Float	On	Fl (3) W	30	12	24	10	Horn (3) 60 secs	Red hull and tower lantern amidships Racon
Hook Head	On	Fl W	3	46	24	16	Horn (2) 45 secs	Wh Tr 35 m 2 black bands Racon
Dunmore East		L Fl WR	8	13	R9 W12	10		Stone Tr 16 m on pier
Duncannon Fort		Oc WRG	4	13	W9 RG7	8		8 m Both Wh Tr with red stripe 11 m
Duncannon North		Oc WR	4	13	W9 R7	8		
Ballinacourty Point		Fl (2) WRG	10	16	RG9 W 12	11		Wh Tr 13 m
Mine Head		Fl (4) W	20	87	28	22		Wh Tr 21 black band
Youghal		Fl WR	2·5	24	R9 Wl2			Wh Tr 15 m
Ballycotton	On	Fl WR	10	59	W22 R18	18	Horn (4) 90 secs	Bl Tr 15 m (wh. walls)
Roches Point	On	Oc WR	20	30	R16 W20	14	Dia (1) 30 secs	Wh Tr 15 m
Charles Fort (Kinsale)	On 24 hrs	Fl WRG	5	18	RG6 W9			Lantern on SW rampart of fort
Old Head of Kinsale	On	Fl (2) W	10	72	25	20	Horn (3) 45 secs	Bl Tr 30 m 2 Wh bands
Galley Head		Fl (5) W	20	53	28	17		Wh Tr 21 m
Fastnet	On	Fl W	5	49	28	17	Horn (4) 60 secs	Gray granite Tr 54 m
Crookhaven		L Fl RW	8	20	R11 W13	12		Wh Tr 14 m
Mizen Head		Iso W	4	52	16	14		Concrete platfrom Racon

APPENDIX 8 — PRINCIPAL LIGHTS — *continued*

Name	Lights In fog	Character and colour	Period secs	Elev m	Range miles		Fog signal	Type and height of lighthouse
					Nom	Geo		
Sheep Head		Fl (3) WR	15	83	R15 W18	16		Wh hut 7 m
Ardnakinna		Fl (2) WR	10	62	R14 W17	15		Wh Tr 20 m
Roancarrigmore		Fl WR	3	18	R14 W18	11		Wh Tr 19 m black band
Dinish Castletown Dir Lt		Dir OcWRG	5	4	RG11 W14	7		Wh hut, red stripe 6 m
Bull Rock	On	Fl W	15	83	23	21		Wh Tr 15 m
Skelligs		Fl (3) W	10	53	27	17		Wh Tr 12 m
Cromwell Point (Valentia)		Fl WR	2	16	R15 W17	11		Wh Tr 15 m
Inishtearaght	On	Fl (2) W	20	84	27	21		Wh Tr 17 m
Little Samphire Island		Fl WRG	5	17	RG13 W16	13		Blue Stone Tr 18 m
Kilcredaun		Fl W	6	41	13			Wh Tr 13 m
Loop Head		Fl (4) W	20	84	28	21		Wh Tr 23 m
Black Head		Fl WR	5	20	R8 W11			Wh square Tr 8 m
Inisheer		Iso WR	20	34	R16 W20	15		Wh Tr 34 m black band
Straw Island (Inishmore)		Fl (2) W	5	11	17	9		Wh Tr 11 m
Eeragh (Inishmore)		Fl W	15	35	23	15		Wh Tr 31 m 2 black bands
Slyna Head		Fl (2) W	15	35	28	15		Black Tr 24 m
Achillbeg		Fl WR	5	56	R15 W18			Wh Tr on 9 m square building
Inishgort		L Fl W	10	11	10			Wh Tr 8 m
Blackrock (Mayo)		Fl WR	12	86	R16 W22	21		Wh Tr 15 m
Blacksod		Fl (2) WR	7·5	13	R9 W12	10		Wh Tr 12 m
Eagle Island	On	Fl (3) W	10	67	26	19		Wh Tr 11 m
Broadhaven		Iso WR	4	27	R9 W12			Wh Tr 15 m
Blackrock (Sligo)		Fl W Fl R	5 3	24 12	13 5			Wh Tr 25 m black band — vis. over Wheat and Seal rocks
St. John's Point		Fl W	6	30	14			Wh Tr 14 m
Rotten Island		Fl WR	4	20	R11 W15	12		Wh Tr 14 m
Rathlin O'Birne		Fl WR	20	35	R18 W22	15		Wh Tr 20 m
Rinrawras Point (Aran Island)		Fl (2) W Fl R	20 3	71 61	29 17	20		Wh Tr 23 m
Tory Island	On	Fl (4) W	30	40	30	15	Dia (1) 60 secs	Black Tr 27 m Wh band

Appendix 9

A yacht could be left unattended at the following places where it should be possible to get someone reliable to keep an eye on her. Those whose names are mentioned would either do so or could give good advice on the subject.

Cheek Point (Waterford Harbour)	Jim Doherty (051) 74499
Crosshaven	Crosshaven Boatyard (021) 831161
	RCYC (021) 831440
Kinsale	Harbour Master, Kinsale YC (021) 772186
Courtmacsherry..	M. L. Hurly at Lifeboat Bar (023) 46218
Union Hall (Glandore)	
Castlehaven	R. Slater-Townshend (028) 26100
	(Essential to moor with 2 anchors)
Rossbrin Cove, Nr. Schull	Andy Stott (028) 37165
Baltimore..	Vincent O'Driscoll (028) 20125
Derrynane (Kenmare River)	John O'Shea
Cahirciveen	Harbour Master
	(Essential to moor with 2 anchors)
Galway Dock	Harbour Master-Capt. F. W. Sheridan (091) 62329
Galway Bay Sailing Club	Contact Galway HM
Roundstone	
Ardbear Bay, Clifden	Adrian O'Connell
	Note: Adrian O'Connell can be contacted at
	the yard at Kilrush marina on the Shannon
Ballynakill, Fahy Bay	Fishermen
Westport Quay	Harbour Master
Achill Bridge	John Corrigan (098) 45192
Sligo	Harbour Master(071) 6119
Mullaghmore.	
Only twin-keel yachts not longer than 10 m	Rodney Lomax Boatbuilder (071) 66124
Bunbeg	Jim Boyd (075) 31014

Also the following Marinas: Crosshaven
Kinsale
Dingle
Kilrush

Appendix 10

SAILING ROUND IRELAND

Ireland is ideal for sailing round. Doing so is difficult enough to be interesting and yet the distance of 681 miles fits well into a cruising holiday of two or three weeks. It would be impossible to explore all the many anchorages in any one year, however one rapidly becomes fascinated by the wonderful scenery and the excellence of the sailing. The numbers circumnavigating increase year by year, and more yachts are now to be found using the west coast anchorages as their base. An increasing number of members of the Irish Cruising Club come from the more remote areas and are always ready to give assistance in every possible way to visiting yachtsmen. A list of port members, giving their addresses and telephone numbers, is available from Mrs Barbara Fox-Mills, The Tansey, Baily, Co. Dublin.

Time

Yachts cruising normally, anchoring for the night with only occasional longer passages, seldom take less than 21 days from an Irish port or a couple of days more from the west of England. It can be done in less time, but this means by-passing a very high proportion of the attractive parts. Anyone who can afford the time could easily spend two months circumnavigating without seeing everything.

Which way round?

The majority of Irish-based boats have gone anti-clock and the English ones clockwise. Analyses of wind records coast by coast for June and July show a variation of only 3% for clockwise and anti-clockwise passages; so in an average year it does not matter from a wind point of view which way you go in these the two most popular months. Allowing for the fact that it is easier to beat on the east coast where there is less swell than on the west, a clockwise passage in July offers the best statistical chance.

The chief consideration is your home port or starting point. The west coast is the least known and most interesting and it is a sound principle to begin by heading for whichever end of it is nearest. Some people may prefer to get half way round as quickly as possible and leave the part they want to visit individually, in which it is all too easy to stay longer than intended, until the second half of the cruise.

Boats from the south of England or the Bristol channel should find clockwise best, but may leave the decision until they see what winds blow as they make the passage up and head for the Tuskar or Fastnet accordingly. For Clyde, Liverpool and Welsh boats the same consideration as for Irish ones would apply.

The Kenmare-Bantry area has always been popular with yachts from Cork and the south of England. Roundstone-Kilkieran, and also in good weather Achill-Slyne are both magnificent cruising grounds, but unfortunately not places to dally in, unless you have plenty of time, say four weeks at least for an Irish-based boat. Aranmore area, also Lough Swilly, are other little known but most attractive places, and if keen to see a bit of these parts, go clockwise.

General

Some yachts have been round under sail alone, but this is not recommended, for a good engine is of much greater value on the exposed coasts than say in the Irish Sea. On the west coast particularly, a large swell and awful sea can persist long after the gale which caused it has ceased, shaking any wind there is out of the sails and making for miserable conditions aboard a pure sailing vessel.

Much time can be absorbed in the west getting stores; the nearest town is often a couple of miles or more from the anchorage; water and fuel likewise, so ship as much as you can before starting, and top up when opportunity offers.

Have two good anchors plus a spare, and plenty of chain, warps and fenders. On the west you will be relying almost entirely on natural anchorages, as opposed to largely man-made ones on the east coast. But if you have good enough gear to lie alongside a rough pier in a bit of swell without damaging the boat, it may save lot of dinghy work and wettings.

Unless you have time to spare keep to the islands as much as possible. You will almost invariably be in a much better position to take advantage of the next day's winds if you bring up in the roads at, for example, Gola, Inishkea or Turk, than in the corresponding bays or anchorages of the mainland. These and several others similar are safe and comfortable anchorages more often than not in summer.

Gales

Irish Coast Pilot gives tables for their incidence and June and July both average two force 7 gale days apiece. This ties up with experiences of yachts—in a three week cruise you will almost certainly be held up once, perhaps twice, by gales lasting one or two days, but there is generally warning and nearly everyone has managed to get shelter before the blow really developed. VHF coverage is virtually complete for the whole coast. Lighthouse keepers in the remaining manned lights guard Ch 16 at 0850 GMT, and may be listening out at other times particularly in bad weather. It is also very important to watch the sky and the barometer for it is a fact that the forecast warning is often received subsequent to the gale. R.T.E. shipping forecasts apply to Irish coastal waters and so are more likely to be accurate for the coastal cruiser than the B.B.C. shipping forecasts which refer to much wider areas of open sea.

Fog

Ireland as a whole is lucky in this respect and complete days of persistent fog occur on average less than once in ten years. Fog generally only occurs with winds between SE and SW and is much less common on the west coast than elsewhere.

Crew changes

On the West coast it is not always necessary to go a long way to leeward to pick up relief crew. Shannon area, there are trains to Limerick and planes to Shannon, with bus connections to Kilrush marina. At Galway there is an airport and trains from Dublin. A bus service runs along the N shore of Galway Bay as far as Roundstone and Clifden. In Clew Bay the train goes to Westport and it is possible to get a bus to Achill Sound. Further N the trains from Dublin go to Sligo and buses run along the S side of the bay towards Belmullet. Donegal town is also a good centre for transport. Buses run along the N shore to Killybegs and Teelin. Telephone connections on the coast are very much improved and many of the inhabitants helpful with lifts and information on the bus times.

Appendix 11

GENERAL SUPPLIES

Cork is of course the largest centre. It is most easily reached by road from Crosshaven. The western cities, Limerick, Galway, Westport, Sligo and Donegal involve rather a long detour to leeward. Waterford is also rather far from the sea. The larger convenient shopping centres are: Dunmore East, Dungarvan, Youghal, Ballycotton, Crosshaven, Kinsale, Baltimore, Skull, Bantry, Castletown, Cahirciveen, Dingle, Clifden, Killala and Killybegs. Food supplies are usually easy to find. There are few villages where basic groceries are not available and many small shops sell deep-freeze meat. In some places the choice may be a bit limited.

There is a general shop, pub and petrol pump at most places, but often a long walk from the anchorage. Throughout the book an indication is given after the directions for each place. Wherever diesel is available at the quayside the opportunity should be taken to top up the tank. A yacht sailing west from Cork should keep topped up with stores and fuel and water. In the west, especially after a dry spell, water may be hard to get near some anchorages; excellent places to fill the tank are Baltimore, Castletownbere, Kilronan, and Killybegs. The quality of water in Ireland is usually very good indeed and seldom requires any adulteration.

Kosangas is stocked at most places but the smaller cylinders are very scarce and it is better to carry enough for the whole cruise. Calor gas cylinders are not obtainable in the Republic, so it is essential to carry sufficient. Camping gaz cylinders can be found in most shopping centres. Paraffin is not available everywhere but can generally be found in the better shopping centres. Diesel fuel may be obtained in the following ports and anchorages: Dunmore East, Dungarvan, Crosshaven, Kinsale, Courtmacskerry, Baltimore, Castletown, Dingle, Foynes, Galway Docks, Kilronan (Aran Is), Newport, Pier N of Achill Bridge, Blacksod Bay ($1^{1}/_{2}$ miles away), Mullaghmore, Killybegs, Teelin, Rutland, Bunbeg Quay (Gweedore).The fishing community are usually quite helpful regarding the times when they top-up with fuel themselves.

Alcohol is very expensive in the Republic of Ireland, so visiting yachtsmen would be well advised to bring their full allowances of Duty Free

Ice is rather difficult to obtain, friendly hoteliers may be willing to provide. Some of the fishing ports have ice plants, but beware of the quality.

Appendix 12

REPAIR FACILITIES

Undernoted are a selection of companies which are capable of doing repairs. It is be no means complete; so reference to the Golden Pages of the local telephone book is advised. Most businesses listed will be able to put you in touch with a company that can do your particular repair, if they are unable to undertake it themselves.

Boat Builders and Repairers:

Youghal: Ferrypoint Boat Co Ltd (024) 94232.
Crosshaven: Crosshaven Boatyard Co Ltd (021) 831161.
            Salve Engineering (021) 831145.
            Castlepoint Boat Yard (021) 831587.
Bandon: Kilmacsimon Boatyard Ltd (021) 775134.
Skibbereen: Donal O'Donovan Ltd (028) 21249.
Baltimore: Skinners Boatyard Ltd (028) 20114.
Ballinaskellings: Teoranta Muntic Ltd (0667) 9285.
Valentia: Valentia Marine Ltd (066) 76184.
Limerick: Paddy Horan (061) 310363.
Kilrush: Marina Boatyard (Adrian O'Connell) (065) 52072
Killaloe: Kevin O'Farrell (061) 76565.
Galway: Frank Kavanagh & Co Ltd (091) 63330.
Mullaghmore: R N Lomax Ltd (071) 66124.
Killybegs: Killybegs Shipyard Ltd (073) 31061.
Killybegs: Mooney Board (073) 31152.

Engine Repairs:

Youghal: Ferrypoint Boat Co Ltd (024) 94232.
Carrigaline: Hanson Engineering Ltd (021) 372648.
Courtmacsherry: Aqua-fix marine (023) 41070.
Union Hall: O'Donovan and William Fry.
Carrigtwohill (Co. Cork): Perkins Marine Engines (021) 883310.
Baltimore: Wm. Nolan marine Engineering (028) 20297.
Castletown/Berehaven: John O'Sullivan (027) 70129. Richard Powes (027) 70298.
Cahirciveen: J. Kelly (066) 72502.
Knightstown: Nolan's Garage (066) 76200.
Dingle: Griffins or Harrans Garage, R & S Engineering, Harris Engineering.
Tralee: O'Sullivans Marine Ltd (066) 24524.
Aghleam: Blacksod Bay: Mike Lavelle.

Electrical :

Youghal: Ferrypoint Boat Co Ltd (024) 94232.
Cork: Rider Services, Passage West (021) 841176.
Cork: Micro Marine Systems Ltd (021) 965409.
Cork: DDE Ltd (021) 542253.

Cork: O'Connell Bros. (021) 277790.
Courtmacsherry: Gerard Hilland (023) 40302.
Skibbereen: Belcoo Marine Electronics (028) 22233.
Baltimore: Wm. Nolan (028) 20297.
Castletown: Millcove Engineering (027) 70129 also (027) 70016.
Knightstown: Nolan's Garage (066) 76200.
Dingle: Tom Hand Electronics (066) 51640.
Killybegs: Atlantic Marine Supplies Ltd (073) 31440.

Outboard Engines:

Dublin: Allweather Marine Ltd (01) 713655.
Cork: Marine motors (021) 503753.
Cork: Union Chandlery Ltd (021) 271643.
Kinsale: Atlantic Yacht Co Ltd (021) 772167.
Middleton: Middleton Marine Ltd (021) 613157.
Tralee: O'Sullivans Marine Ltd (066) 24524.
Galway: Michael Flaherty Eng. Ltd (091) 95032.
Galway: Ivors Ltd (091) 64408.

Sailmakers:

Dublin: Watson & Jameson (01) 326466.
Dun Laoghaire: Downer International Sails Ltd (01) 804286.
Bray: Sterling Sails (01) 862257.
Crosshaven: McWilliam Sailmakers Ltd (021) 831505.
Ennis: Ocean Sails (065) 20888.
Sligo: Sunset Sails (071) 62792.

Electronics/Hydraulics:

Dublin: Irish Marine (01) 766400.
Dublin: Marconi International Ltd (01) 749157.
Dublin: Western Marine Ltd (01) 800321.
Cork: Rider Services (021) 841176.
Tralee: GK Hydraulics Ltd (066) 22768.
(after hours (066) 34320).

Chandlery:

Cork: Union Chandlery Ltd (021) 271643.

Appendix 13

MARINE RESCUE AND
CO-ORDINATION CENTRE

Rescue at Sea

Rescue at sea and round the shores of the Irish Republic is the responsibility of the Irish Marine Emergency Service, (IMES).

In emergency, the Service can best be contacted on vhf radio through the nearest VHF Radio Station on channel 16 or 67, or, by dialling 999 and requesting "Marine Rescue".

The IMES maintains a medium range Search and Rescue helicopter at Shannon Airport and a network of Coast and Cliff Rescue (CCRS) teams around the coast of the Republic.

The Service, through the Marine Rescue Coordination Centre, avails of the services of The Irish Air Corp SAR helicopter crews, the RNLI, the Irish Naval Service, The Gardai, Coast Radio Stations and other organisations engaged in SAR activities.

Close liaison is maintained with the rescue services in adjacent countries and yacht safety information is exchanged on a routine basis.

A passage surveillance scheme is operated, free of charge, for yachts bound to or from Ireland or round the coast.

For routine information, the IMES can be contacted at IMES HQ, Leeson Lane, Dublin 2, Tel (01) 785444, or, the Marine Rescue Coordination Centre, Shannon Airport, Tel (061) 471219 or 9061) 471969.

The Coast and Cliff Rescue Service (CCRS)

The CCRS is maintained by the IMES and staffed by part time volunteers.

Personnel are trained in cliff rescue and local search techniques.

Inshore rescue craft are maintained at several of the stations.

Watch is not kept except when required during an emergency.

Stations are best contacted through the Marine Rescue Coordination Centre, or, through the CCRS Regional Officers

Capt. Peter Brown, Tel (01) 785444

Capt. David Sheil, Tel (021) 968935

Helicopter Operations

There is an increasing use of helicopters at sea for the rescue of mariners where vessels are in danger of sinking, also for the transfer ashore of sick and injured crew members, also from time to time it is necessary to transfer ashore an important person – surgeon, politician, or for a family bereavement. The following notes are published to assist skippers to operate with helicopters to the best of their ability under the circumstances prevailing: The helicopter used by Shannon SAR is supplied and maintained by Irish Helicopters Ltd (061) 47233, and is on call 24-hrs a day, 7 days a week.

Irish Helicopters Shannon Search and Rescue – Hi-Line Transfers

Winching to high masted vessels creates a degree of difficulty for the standard vertical lift, particularly in heavy seas. In most cases, the Hi-Line technique is used, both by military and Civilian SAR units.

Initially, the helicopter will contact you on Channel 16, and may request you to change to a working channel, although he may ask you to stay on Channel 16 for the casualty working.

Normally you will be requested to keep steerageway with the wind approximately 30° on the Port bow but wind speed and direction, sea state, the position of transfer area and manoeuvreability of the vessel may necessitate variation to the above. In any case the helicopter should hover into the relative wind and care should be taken that variations in the vessels course do not prejudice this during transfers.

The transfer area should be selected to give as clear an area as possible with unobstructed access to the deck edge. Normally, the vessels port quarter would be used. however, circumstances may dictate otherwise. The helicopter crew will advise you where the transfer is to take place.

The "Hi-Line", itself, is a 120' length of ¼" braided nylon line. A screw gate Karabiner is attached to either end. The top end, which includes a weak link, is attached to the helicopter winch hook and the bottom end has weights attached to it.

The weighted end of the line is lowered on to the deck of the vessel. Two deck crew on the vessel should receive this end and take in the slack, coiling loose line on the deck, clear of deck obstructions. THE LINE MUST NEVER BE ATTACHED TO THE VESSEL. Tension on the line should be maintained to keep the line taut. Do not heave in the hi-line at this time. Deck crew are advised to wear gloves whilst handling the hi-line.

Once the line has been accepted by the vessel's deck crew, the helicopter will move away from the vessel to prepare the winchman for lowering to the deck. At this time, the vessel's deck crew must pay out the Hi-Line. The helicopter will then climb to a safe height over the masts and any obstructions whilst lowering the winchman to keep him level with the transfer area.

The helicopter will then move across towards the transfer area. At this stage, the deck crew handling the Hi-Line continue to take up the slack and on instructions from the winchman haul him on board. When the winchman is on the deck, he will disconnect himself from the winch wire and the helicopter will move away from the vessel. The deck crew should now pay out the Hi-Line. The winchman will now brief the deck crew on any requirements.

For recovery, the winch hook is pulled inboard to allow the winchman and casualty to be attached. They will then be lifted off the deck. The deck crew should retain tension on the Hi-Line to prevent excessive swinging.

Once the winchman and casualty are onboard the helicopter, the hi-line will be recovered by taking up the Hi-line until just the weighted end is left on the vessel. The deck crew should clear the weighted end from all obstructions and the Hi-line will be fully recovered by the helicopter.

Hi-Line Techniques

1. Wind 30° on port bow.
2. Maintain heading unless instructed otherwise by helicopter.
3. Accept hi-line in clear area on port quarter.
4. Deck crew should wear gloves.
5. Take in slack as hi-line is lowered.
6. Do not attach hi-line to any part of the vessel.
7. Pull in winchman when he indicates.
8. Maintain tension on hi-line at all times.
9. On recovery of hi-line, maintain tension until weights are in hand and then release them clear of obstructions.
10. Static electricity can build up in any hovering helicopter. A static discharge wire is attached to the end of the winch cable. Deck crew should ensure that the static electricity discharges through the discharge wire or the winchman (who is used to the shocks) and not through them.

Royal National Lifeboat Institution

Lifeboat Station:	Launching Authorities Telephone Numbers	
	Honorary Secretary	*Deputy*
Kilmore Quay	(053) 29636	(053) 35149
Dunmore East	(051) 83359	(051) 83249
Tramore (inshore rescue boat)	(051) 81438 Office: (051) 73581	(051) 81390
Youghal	(024) 93119 Office: (024) 93315	(024) 92636
Ballycotton	(021) 646759	(021) 646715
Courtmacsherry	(023) 46199	(023) 46189
Baltimore	(028) 20125 Office: (028) 20119	(028) 20101
Valentia	(0667) 6126	(0667) 6109
Galway Bay, Kilronan, Aran	(099) 61131 Office: (099) 61109	(099) 61280
Clifden (inshore rescue boat)	(095) 21437	
Ballyglass	(097) 81039	(097) 81076
Bundoran (inshore rescue boat)	(072) 51620	
Arranmore	(075) 21533	(075) 21508

Appendix 14

LIST OF PLACES TO VISIT

From time to time yachts get held up by bad weather, have to wait at anchor or in port for crew changes, or just want to stop sailing for a day or two. The list below, by no means exhaustive, gives some ideas for places to see and visit ashore, it is primarily directed towards overseas visitors to our shores. All the places can be easily reached from the anchorages mentioned either by walking, public transport, or short taxi journeys.

Dunmore East –	Park; Wood; Beaches
Waterford –	Waterford Glass, with guided tours. Reginald's Tower.
New Ross –	Historic Town.
Youghal –	Historic Town - from 5th century onwards - good local booklet.
Ballycotton –	Blue Flag Strand 3M with Garryrow hotel
East Ferry –	Fota Wildlife Park (7M).
Kinsale –	Charles Fort; James' Fort; French Prison; Old Courthouse; Church of St. Multore.
Glandore –	Drombeg Stone circle 1½ M.
Castletownshend –	Historic village.
Derryane –	Daniel O'Connell's House.
Baltimore –	Lough Ine.
Schull –	Tourist Office for information
Castlebeare –	Beare Peninsular; Ring of Beare; Beare Island.
Glengariff –	Famous garden - Tourist resort.
Bantry –	Bantry house - Armada Display & Gardens; Historical Society Museum; Abbey Ruins; Kill na Ruane (Standing stones).
Killmakillogue Harbour –	Dereen Gardens.
Valentia –	"Skellig Experience" - tourist info. 066-76306.
Dingle –	Good centre for tours. Many ancient sites. Tourist Office 066-51188.
Tralee –	"Kerry the Kingdom" in three parts in Ashe Memorial Hall 066-27777. Siamsa Tire - National Folk Theatre. The Blennerville Windmill - working. Tralee and Blennerville Steam Railway.
Fenit –	Good walks; Golf course 3M; Sea angling; Fenit Island Castle; Barrow Castle.
Kilrush –	Slattery Island - Monastic settlement in 540 A.D.; Sea angling.
Foynes –	Foynes Aviation Museum; Golf Course; Forest walks; monuments; Franciscan Abbey 6M.
Kinvara –	Medieval banquets at Dunguaire Castle.
Galway – New Harbour –	Rinville Park - Golf Club - Country Club.
Kilronan –	Dun Aengus - pre historic fort. Cliff walks.
Skerdmore –	Haunt of the Great Atlantic Seal.
Friar Island –	Seals and Great black backed gulls.
Clare Island –	The O'Malley Castle.
Westport –	Westport House; Croagh Patrick mountain.
Blacksod Bay –	Erris Tourist Centre 097 - 82292. Golf Course 5M.
Mullaghmore –	Blue Flag Beach; Walks.

Appendix 15

PLACES TO EAT AND DRINK

This is a new innovation and is therefore on trial for this edition. It must be appreciated that all those who go to sea in small ships do not have the same tastes or standards. Furthermore, hostelries open and close; their chefs move on; the proprietors change, so this list is based on pubs and eating houses that have been mentioned in member's logs, by correspondents or from local knowledge. It is primarily intended to help visitors to our shores.

Dunmore East –	Hotels: "The Candlelight"; "Strand"; "Ship".
	Pubs: "Powers", "Ocean".
Ballyhack –	Restaurant; Pub.
Cheek Point –	Restaurants; Pubs.
Waterford –	Hotels; Restaurants; Cafes; Pubs.
New Ross –	Hotels; Restaurants; Cafes; Pubs.
Dungarvan –	Hotels and Pubs.
Youghal –	Hotels; Restaurants; Cafes; Pubs.
Ballycotton –	"Ballymaloe House" - book $3\frac{3}{4}$ M 021-654531.
	Pub - "O'Sullivan's Bar". 021-646736.
	"Bay View Hotel" 021-646746;
	"Spanish Point" Restaurant 021-646177.
Crosshaven –	RCYC; Small restaurants and pubs in village -
	"Cronins"; "Ancient Mariner"; Kelly's"; "Webb's"; "The Anchor".
Carrigaline –	About 3 M by car /taxi: "Pews Bistro" 021-371512;
	"Uncle Tom's" 021-371481; "Rosies Pub".
Myrtleville –	About $2\frac{1}{2}$ miles by car/taxi: "Bunnyconnellen Hotel" 021-831213.
Tracton –	About 7M by car/taxi: "Overdraught Bar" 021-887177.
Nohoval –	About 11 M by car/taxi: "Finder's Inn" 021-770737.
East Ferry –	Good restaurant and bar just above the marina.
Kinsale –	The "gourmet capital of Ireland".
	The famous restaurants are too many to mention by name (15).
	Also hotels and pubs (30). Literature at tourist office. 021-774026.
	"Max's Wine Bar". "The Vineyard".
Courtmacsherry –	Hotel; Pubs.
Clonakilty –	Hotel on Inchydoney Island.
Glandore –	"Glandore Inn"; "Haye's Bar"; "Marine Hotel"; "Casey's Bar".
Leap –	"Leap Inn".
Union Hall –	"Dinty's".
Castletownshend –	"Mary Annes"; "The Castle".
Rineen –	Restaurant 2 M.
Baltimore –	Hotel; Restaurants; Pubs. "Chez Youen".
Ballydehob –	Restaurant.
Schull –	Hotel and 2 Restaurants. Pubs.
Crookhaven –	3 Restaurants. 2 Pubs. Cafe "Matthews".
E. of Port Kilcronane –	Restaurant. 2 Pubs.
Kitchen Cove –	"Shiro's" – Japanese!!
Dunbeacon Harbour –	2 Restaurants. 4 Pubs.
Castletown –	Hotels and Pubs.
Lawrence Cove –	Restaurant; Pub at Rerrin – opening unreliable.
Glengariff –	Hotels - best known "Eccles".

Bantry –	Many Restaurants & Pubs.
Kilmakilloge –	"Bunow". "O'Sullivans".
Sneem –	"Parkinsilla Hotel" - well known. Other hotels in town 2 M.
	"The Stone House".
West Cove –	Beach Bar and restaurant.
Derrynane –	"Keatings Hotel".
Valentia –	"Galley Kitchen" 066-76105; "Island Grill" 066-76171; "Boston's" 066-76140;
	"The Royal" 066-76144; "Lavelles" 066-76124; at Rinard Pier – "O'Neills".
Dingle –	Large number of Restaurants; Cafes (22) Pubs (52). Two grand hotels.
	"Doyle's Sea Food" 066-51174.
Brandon Quay –	Two restaurants
Fenit –	"Lighthouse Inn", "Tankard" $2^{1}/_{2}$ M. "Oyster Tavern" 4 M.
	Pubs: "West End"; "O'Sullivans"; "Godley's Hotel".
Kilrush –	Hotels; Pubs ; Restaurants; Cafes.
Foynes –	"Shannon House Hotel"; "Burgerbite"; "Kerry Bar"; "Foynes Inn";
	"O'Connor's Bar".
Kinvara –	Restaurant, Pubs and Cafe.
Kilcolgan River –	"Moran's Oyster Cottage".
Galway –	Major city with all facilities.
Galway New Harbour –	Oranmore 2M "The Moorings"; 4 pubs.
	Clarenbridge 6 M "Paddy Burke's Restaurant".
Kilronan –	4 Restaurants & 4 Pubs. Outside village "Dirrans".
Rossaveal –	"Terry's Bar" 1 M 72123
	"Peader Dicks Thatch Bar" 2 M
	"O'Flaherty's (Kitts) Bar" 72233 $2^{1}/_{2}$ M.
Bealadangan –	"Curragh Bar" – Snacks and 2 hotels.
Roundstone –	"Beola" – seafood.
Clifden -	Hotels; Restaurants; lots of pubs. "O'Grady's" seafood.
Inishbofin –	"The Lobster Pot".
Rinvyle –	Hotel.
Killary Harbour –	"Killary Lodge Hotel" 095-43411.
Innishlush --	Pub and restaurant
Clare Island –	"An Fulacht Fiadh" 098-25048.
Westport –	Town with most facilities.
Blacksod Bay –	Elly Bay – "Curragh" Cafe & Pub.
Sligo –	Major town with all facilities.
Mullaghmore –	Restaurants: "Eithnes"; "Pier Head"; "The Schooners".
	Pubs: "Boatman's"; "Pier Bar".
Bruckless –	"Castlemurray" $^{1}/_{2}$ M 073-37002 - booking advisable.
Killybegs –	Major fishing/tourist port with hotels, restaurants, cafes and pubs.
Burtonport –	Major fishing/tourist port with hotels, restaurants, cafes and pubs.

Appendix 16

LIST OF YACHT CLUBS ALONG THE COAST

This is by no means an exhaustive list, however it includes those yacht clubs who replied to a recent circular. It gives their proper name, the name of the hon. secretary and his/her telephone number together with a brief outline of the facilities available. The names of the Commodores have been omitted as the holders of high office change more frequently than the hon. secs.

VM = visitor's moorings; AB = alongside berths; S = showers; M = meals; B = bar; F = fuel; W = water (some amenities have limited opening times).

Dunmore East –	Waterford Harbour S.C. – Neil Breheny. 051-83230/83389. S; M; B; F; W.
Youghal –	Youghal S.C. – Michael Haig; Assistance from Bruce Bell 94232; Tadgh Killeher 93119; David Kelly 92412; Albert Muckley 92636 and Dick O'Reilly 92088.
Crosshaven –	Royal Cork Yacht Club with permanent Secretary. Oldest Y.C. in the world.
Kinsale –	Kinsale Y.C. Olaf Maxwell. AB; S; M; B; F; W.
Glandore –	Harbour Y.C. Donal Lynch 021-545333/Fax 342457; W. (The Glandore Inn is used as a Club House!)
Castletownshend –	South Cork S.C. Robert Salter 028-36100 S; M; B; F; W – all in local pubs.
Baltimore –	Baltimore S.C. VM; S; F; W.
Bantry –	Bantry Bay S.C. 027-50081 Gordon Hardwick; VM; S; F; W.
Fenit –	Tralee Sailing Club, Jack Galvin VM; AB; S; M (in local pubs/cafes); B; W.
Foynes –	Foynes Y.C. Pat Moran 069-65641 VM; AB; S; M; B; F; W.
Galway – New Harbour –	Galway Bay S.C. Beverly Moran; VM; AB (Tidal) S; M; B; W.
Clifden –	Clifden Boat Club – M/s Emer Joyce, VM; S; M; B; F; W.
Westport –	Mayo Sailing Club – Jim Finan 094-2375 VM; S; B; W.
Blacksod Bay –	Elly Bay Watersports Centre – John McNamara; VM; S; M; B; F; W.
Mullaghmore –	Mullaghmore Y.C., T. Lomax; VM; F; W.

Appendix 17

CUSTOMS REQUIREMENTS

Yachts should preferably make their first call at one of the following places where Custom staff are available: Waterford, New Ross, Cork, Ringaskiddy, Bantry, Foynes, Limerick, Galway, Sligo and Killybegs. On arrival, yachts should fly the Q flag by day or show a red light over a white light by night.

Where the first place of call is one of the above listed ports and the yacht is not visited by Customs within a reasonable period of time, the owner/skipper should go ashore and report the yacht's arrival to Customs. When the first place of call is not one of the above listed ports and the yacht is not visited by Customs within a reasonable period of time, the owner/skipper should go ashore and notify the yacht's arrival to the nearest Garda (Police) Station.

Persons whose normal residence is outside the European community may temporarily import for a period not exceeding twelve months a pleasure boat which they use for their private or business use, without payment of import charges. Information regarding temporary importation may be obtained from Division 1, Office of the Revenue Commissioners, Government Buildings, Nenagh, Co. Tipperary.

Customs requirements in the case of yachts are framed with a view to causing the minimum of inconvenience to owners. The Commissioners rely on owners and masters to take such measures as may be necessary to prevent the irregular landing from, or shipment on, their vessels of any dutiable, prohibited or restricted articles. A yacht used in connection with traffic in prohibited or uncustomed goods is liable to forfeiture, and the owner and master to heavy penalties.

Compiler's Note: Since the arrival of the EC Single Market (1993) Yacht owners are strongly advised to obtain a "Single Administrative Document" from their local customs, to show that V.A.T. has been paid on their vessel. This document can be obtained from Dublin Castle for boats registered in the Republic of Ireland, and from H.M. C&E, Dover Customs, Yacht Team, PO Box 1993, Dover Kent CT16. IAQ for British registered boats. This document is very important and should be kept with the ships papers, and transferred to the new owner on sale.

The R.Y.A. have published a series of leaflets regarding the payment of V.A.T. under the new E.C. Regulations. They can be obtained from Royal Yachting Association, RYA House, Romsey Road, Eastleigh Road, Hampshire, SO5 4YA. Phone 0703 - 629962 or Fax 0703-629924.

APPENDIX 18

IRISH WORDS OCCURRING IN PLACE NAMES

A knowledge of the commonest of the following, colours in particular, often helps with identification, eg, Carrickglass - Green Rock (generally one with grass on top). Carrickbwee - Yellow Rock, Freaghillaun - Heather isle.

Ail, alt—Cliff, height.
Aird, ard—Height, high
Ane—Birds (Illaunnane)
Anna, annagh—Marsh
Ath—a ford (Athlone)

Bal, bally—Town
Ban (gen plur)—Woman
Barnog, barnagh—Barnacle (Inishbarnog)
Barra—Sandbank, or head
Ban, bawn—Fair, whitish
Bel, beal—Mouth: hence strait (Bealadangan, Belmullet)
Beg—Little
Ben, bin, binna—Hill
Bo—Cow: hence sunken rock
Boy, bwee—Yellow
Brack, breaga—Speckled
Brad, bradan—Salmon
Breole, breel—Cormorant
Bullig—Belly: hence shoal or rounded rock, hence breaker
Bun—End. River mouth

Caher—Fort
Camus—Bay or River Bend (Cambridge)
Carrick, carrig, cloy, clough—Rock (Portacloy, rocky port)
Cladach, Chaddy, Choch—shore (Cloghane)
Cloon, lon—Meadow
Coor, cuar, cour—Foam (Couraghy)
Cor, car—Small Hill
Corraun, corran—Reaping hook, hence curved point
Cuan, coon—Harbour, particularly a winding bay
Cul, cool—Recess
Cowan (cf gamhain)—Seal (Co Donegal)

Derg, dearg—Red
Derry—Oakgrove
Dillisk, dulk dulse—Edible seaweed
Drum—Hill, ridge (Drumbo)
Duff, duv, dhu, dubh—black
Dun, doon—Fort
-een—Small
Ennis—Island

Fad, fadda—Long (Carrickfad)
Fan—Slope
Fin —White
Freagh, free—Heather (Inishfree, Freaghillaun)

Gall—Stranger
Glas, glass—Green (Glassilaun)
Glinsk—Clear water
Gola, gowla—Fork (Inishgowla)
Gore, gobhar, gower—Goat
Gorm—Blue
Gub—Point of land

Hassans—Swift current, waterfall or stoats

Inish, innis, inis, illaun—Island
Inver—River mouth

Keel, keal—Narrow place, sound
Keragh, keeragh—Sheep (Inishkeeragh)
Kill—church or cell (Killybegs)
Km, ken—Head, promontory
Knock—Hill

Lag, log—Hollow
Lahan—Broad
Lea—Grey
League, legaun—Pillar stones (Slieve League)
Lenan, leenan—A weed covered rock
Lis—Ancient fort
Long, luing—A ship (Annalong)

Maan—Middle (Inishmaan)
Maghera, magher—Plain
Maol, mwee—Bare (Mweelaun, bare islet)
Mara—Of the sea
More, mor—Big (Dunmore)
Muck—Pig
Murren, murrisk—Place of sea grass or low lying seashore

Og—Young
Ooey, owey—Cave

Partan, portaun—Crab (Carrickaportaun)
Pool—Hole or pool

Rannagh, ranny, rin run, rue, rush, ros—Point
Roe, ruadh—Red
Ron, roan, rone—Seal (Roancarrick, Roaninish)

Sal, salia—of the sea, hence salty
Scolt—Split, rocky gut
Scrow, scrah, scraw—Boggy, grassy sward
Slieve—Mountain
Slig—Shells (Sligo)
Stag, stac, steuc, stook—High rock

Tawney—Low hill
Thangy—Rock or bank (Usually underwater)
Tigh, Ti—House (Tinabinna)
Tir—Land (of)
Tober—Well
Togher—Causeway
Tor—Tower, pointed rock
Trusk—Codfish
Tra, traw—Strand (Tramore)
Turk—Boar
Turlin —Boulder beach

Vaddy, maddy—Dog
Vad, bad—Boat
Vore—Great ("more" changed by aspiration)

Will, whill, wheelaun—Seagull

Appendix 19

ABBREVIATIONS

Aero	*(light)* for aircraft	kHz	kilohertz
Alt	*(light)* alternating	kn	knot or knots
B	black	Lanby	large automatic nagivational buoy
Bn	beacon	LAT	lowest astronomical tide
BST	British Summer Time	LFl	*(light)* long flash (2s)
		LOA	overall length (of vessels)
Can	can red buoy	LV	light vessel
CB	centre board	LW	low water
CG	Coast Guard	LWN	low water neaps
CO	Commanding Officer	LWS	low water springs
Cone	conical green buoy	LWOST	low water ordinary spring tides
Card	cardinal (mark)		
CQR	type of anchor	max	maximum
		m	metre or metres
derv	diesel oil for road vehicles	M	miles
Dia	*(foghorn)* diaphone	MFV	motor fishing vessel
		MHWS	mean high water springs
E	east *(see opposite page)*	MHWN	mean high water neaps
EC	early closing	MLWN	mean low water neaps
elev	elevation	MLWS	mean low water springs
ESB	Electricity Supply Board	MTL	mean tidal level
		Mo	morse code
F	*(wind)* force		
F	*(light)* continuous	N	north *(see opposite page)*
Fl	*(light)* flashing	NB	note well
F Fl	fixed and flashing		
		Obsc	obscured
G	*(light)* green	Oc	*(light)* occulting
GMT	Greenwich Mean Time		
		PO	post office
Hbr	harbour		
Hon Sec	Honorary Secretary	Qk	*(light)* quick (ls)
HM	Harbour Master		
hrs	hours	R	Royal, *(lights)* red
HQ	headquarters	Rly	railway
HT	high tension cable	RNLI	Royal National Lifeboat Institution
HW	high water		
HWN	high water neaps	S	south *(see opposite page)*
HWS	high water springs	s	second, seconds
HWOST	high water ordinary spring tides	SC	sailing club
		SS Co	steam ship company
IALA	International Association of	St	Saint
	Lighthouse Authorities	st	starboard
ICC	Irish Cruising Club		
ICP	Irish Coast Pilot	T	T-shaped road junction
Iso	*(light)* isophase	Thur	Thursday

UK	United Kingdom		
		W	west (*see opposite page*)
vert	vertical	W	(*light*) white
vis	visible, visibility	Wed	Wednesday
VHF	very high frequency		
VQ	(*light*) very quick ($^1/_2$ s)	Y	yellow

Cardinal points N = north, S = south, E = east, W = west

The old 32 compass card points, H 11$^1/_4$° apart; directions shown below to the nearest or lesser degree.

N	360°	E	090°	S	180°	W	270°
N by E	011°	E by S	101°	S by W	191°	W by N	281°
NNE	022°	ESE	112°	SSW	202°	WNW	292°
NE by N	034°	SE by E	124°	SW by S	214°	NW by W	304°
Ne	045°	SE	135°	SW	225°	NW	315°
NE by E	056°	SE by S	146°	SW by W	236°	NW by N	326°
ENE	067°	SSE	157°	WSW	247°	NNW	337°
E by N	079°	S by E	169°	W by S	259°	N by W	349°

N quarter means directions between NW and NE.

N as well as north may mean northern, northward, or northerly, and other abbreviations are similarly used. The full cardinal point words are only used in names, eg South Rock, North Channel.

Lights and foghorns. The abbreviations are included in the above list. Some specimens of their combinations are explained below.

2 FG (vert)	two fixed (continuous) green lights one above the other.
Q	continuous quick white flashes, about every second.
Fl 30s	a white flash every half minute.
Fl (2) WRG 20s	two flashes repeated every 20 seconds, white red and green in different sectors which would be described afterwards.
Iso 4s	white light for two seconds and eclipse for two seconds.
Oc R 10s	red light for 8 seconds followed by eclipse for 2 seconds.
Aero Alt Fl WG 7$^1/_2$s	light for aircraft, alternative white and green flashes, 71/2 seconds from one white lash to the next white flash.
V Q (6) + LFl 10s	six very quick white flashes (3 seconds) followed immediately by a long white flash (2 seconds), then a 5 second eclipse (S Cardinal buoy light).
Dia (4) 60s	Four low-pitched sounds from a diaphone at one minute intervals.

Appendix 20

CONVERSION TABLES

In the first three tables metres are converted to the nearest inch, $^1/_4$ fathom or yard; in the right-hand table feet are converted to the nearest 0.1 metre. Exact equivalents are as follows: 1 metre = 3.28084 feet. 1 foot = 0.3048 metres. For readers unfamiliar with local units: 12 inches = 1 foot. 3 feet = 1 yard. 2 yards = 1 fathom. The Nautical mile ("mile" in the text) is 6,080 feet, about 1,853 metres; it is the average local Sea Mile which is a minute of latitude and therefore variable. The cable is one tenth of a Nautical Mile, approximately 203 yards or 185 metres, usually thought of as 200 yards, $^3/_4$ cable = 139 m. $^1/_2$ cable = 93 m. $^1/_4$ cable = 46 m.

Metres	Ft. inches	Metres	Fathoms	Metres	Yards	Feet	Metres	Feet	Metres
0.1	4"	2	1	10	11	1	0.3	30	9.1
0.2	8"	3	$1^3/_4$	15	16	2	0.6	31	9.4
0.3	1'	4	$2^1/_4$	20	22	3	0.9	32	9.7
0.4	1' 4"	5	$2^3/_4$	25	27	4	1.2	33	10.1
0.5	1' 8"	6	$3^1/_4$	30	33	5	1.5	34	10.4
0.6	2'	7	$3^3/_4$	35	38	6	1.8	35	10.7
0.7	2' 4"	8	$4^1/_4$	40	44	7	2.1	36	11.0
0.8	2' 7"	9	5	45	49	8	2.4	37	11.3
0.9	2' 11"	10	$5^1/_2$	50	55	9	2.7	38	11.6
1.0	3' 3"	11	6	55	60	10	3.0	39	11.9
1.1	3' 7"	12	$6^1/_2$	60	66	11	3.3	40	12.2
1.2	3' 11"	13	7	65	71	12	3.7	41	12.5
1.3	4' 3"	14	$7^3/_4$	70	77	13	4.0	42	12.8
1.4	4' 7"	15	$8^1/_4$	75	82	14	4.3	43	13.1
1.5	4' 11"	16	$8^3/_4$	80	87	15	4.6	44	13.4
1.6	5' 3"	17	$9^1/_4$	85	93	16	4.9	45	13.7
1.7	5' 7"	18	$9^3/_4$	90	98	17	5.2	46	14.0
1.8	5' 11"	19	$10^1/_2$	95	104	18	5.5	47	14.3
1.9	6' 3"	20	11	100	109	19	5.8	48	14.6
2	6' 7"	21	$11^1/_2$	110	120	20	6.1	49	14.9
3	9' 10"	22	12	120	131	21	6.4	50	15.2
4	13' 1"	23	$12^1/_2$	130	142	22	6.7	51	15.5
5	16' 5"	24	13	140	153	23	7.0	52	15.8
6	19' 8"	25	$13^3/_4$	150	164	24	7.3	53	16.1
7	23'	26	$14^1/_4$	160	175	25	7.6	54	16.5
8	26' 3"	27	$14^3/_4$	170	186	26	7.9	55	16.8
9	29' 6"	28	$15^1/_4$	180	197	27	8.2	56	17.1
10	32' 10"	29	$15^3/_4$	190	208	28	8.5	57	17.4
		30	$16^1/_2$	200	219	29	8.8	58	17.7

GENERAL INDEX

NOTES